BOUND BY WAR

Also by Christopher Capozzola

Uncle Sam Wants You: World War I and the Making of the Modern American Citizen

BOUND BY WAR

How the United States and the Philippines Built America's First Pacific Century

Christopher Capozzola

BASIC BOOKS
NEW YORK

Basic Books
Hachette Book Group
1290 Avenue of the Americas, New York, NY 10104
www.basicbooks.com

Printed in the United States of America
First Edition: May 2020

Published by Basic Books, an imprint of Perseus Books, LLC, a subsidiary of Hachette Book Group, Inc. The Basic Books name and logo is a trademark of the Hachette Book Group.

Portions of Chapters Four and Five previously appeared in "The Philippines and the Politics of Anticipation," in *Beyond Pearl Harbor: A Pacific History*, edited by Beth Bailey and David Farber, published by the University Press of Kansas, © 2019. www.kansaspress.ku.edu.

Print book interior design by Linda Mark.

Library of Congress Cataloging-in-Publication Data

Names: Capozzola, Christopher, author.

Title: Bound by war : how the United States and the Philippines built America's first Pacific century / Christopher Capozzola.

Other titles: How the United States and the Philippines built America's first pacific century

Identifiers: LCCN 2019057160 | ISBN 9781541618275 (hardcover) | ISBN 9781541618268 (ebook)

Subjects: LCSH: United States—Military relations—Philippines. | Philippines—Military relations—United States. | Americans—Philippines—History—20th century. | Filipinos—United States—History—20th century. | Philippines—History—20th century.

Classification: LCC E183.8.P6 C36 2020 | DDC 355/.031095990973—dc23

LC record available at https://lccn.loc.gov/2019057160

ISBNs: 978-1-5416-1827-5 (hardcover), 978-1-5416-1826-8 (ebook)

LSC-C

10 9 8 7 6 5 4 3 2 1

For Keith O'Brien

Contents

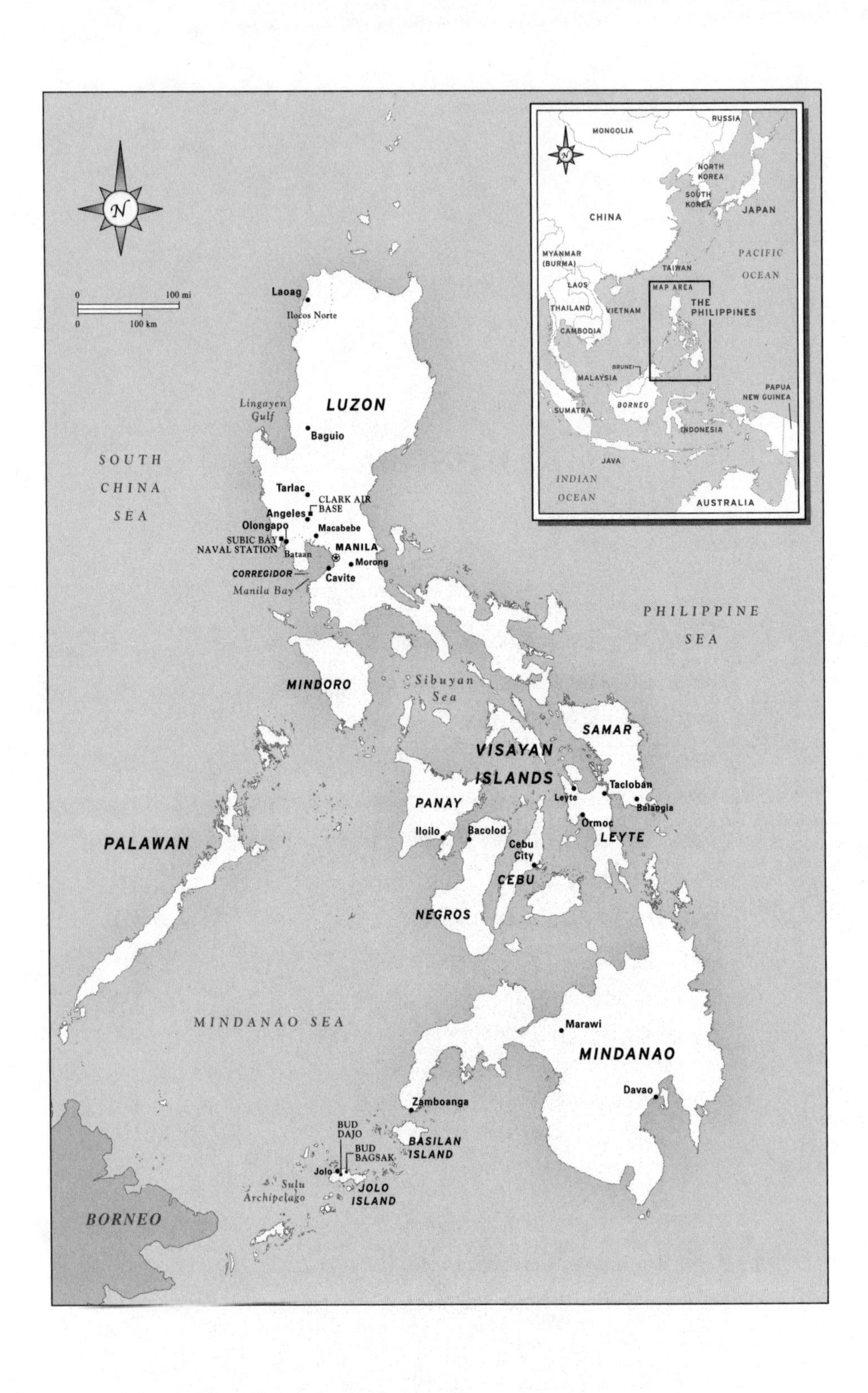

N
0
100 mi
0
100 km
Laoag
Ilocos Norte
Lingayen Gulf
LUZON
Baguio
SOUTH CHINA SEA
Tarlac
CLARK AIR BASE
Angeles
Olongapo
Macabebe
SUBIC BAY NAVAL STATION
Bataan
MANILA
Morong
CORREGIDOR
Cavite
Manila Bay
PHILIPPINE SEA
MINDORO
Sibuyan Sea
SAMAR
VISAYAN ISLANDS
Tacloban
Leyte
Balangiga
PANAY
Ormoc
Iloilo
Bacolod
LEYTE
PALAWAN
Cebu City
CEBU
NEGROS
MINDANAO SEA
Marawi
MINDANAO
Davao
Zamboanga
BUD DAJO
BASILAN ISLAND
BUD BAGSAK
Jolo
Sulu Archipelago
JOLO ISLAND
BORNEO
RUSSIA
MONGOLIA
NORTH KOREA
SOUTH KOREA
JAPAN
CHINA
PACIFIC OCEAN
MYANMAR (BURMA)
TAIWAN
LAOS
MAP AREA
THAILAND
VIETNAM
THE PHILIPPINES
CAMBODIA
BRUNEI
MALAYSIA
PAPUA NEW GUINEA
SUMATRA
BORNEO
INDONESIA
JAVA
INDIAN OCEAN
AUSTRALIA

INTRODUCTION

The Manila American Cemetery, located on 152 acres just a few miles outside the Philippine capital, memorializes 36,285 soldiers and sailors who fought and died under the American flag somewhere in the Pacific during the Second World War. To enter here is somehow to leave the noise and pace of twenty-first-century Manila. The spacious grounds, maintained more carefully than a golf course, offer the city's freshest air and its greenest grass. From a hilltop near the former site of the US Army's Fort McKinley, the cemetery and its central memorial command remarkable views of the skyscrapers and apartment buildings of a booming Asian metropolis, rolling hills to the east, and the hazy sunsets over Manila Bay that cast shadows over the white marble gravestones. As a memorial to the sacrifices of war, the cemetery is altogether fitting and proper.

It is also, on most days, remarkably empty. The first time I visited, I was one of the only Americans there. The guestbook listed Australians, Indians, Japanese, several local residents enjoying the breezy Sunday afternoon, and just one other American: a woman from Burbank, California, with a typical Filipino surname. Perhaps she was a *balikbayan*—a returning migrant—home for a visit and there to pay respects. Even in Manila, it is easy to overlook this place. Neighboring Fort McKinley is gone, turned over in 1949 to the Armed Forces of the Philippines, and more recently replaced in part by an upscale shopping center known simply as The Fort.

In the quiet moments that predominate on that Manila hilltop, the names of the dead tell a shared history of two nations bound by a century of war. As the stones attest, the US military has been in the Philippines for a long time, beginning in 1898 when America conquered the Spanish colony and annexed it to the United States, then in the years from 1898 to 1946 when the Philippines was a US colony, and in the decades since independence, when the Philippines has been an American ally in Asia.

Filipinos have been in the US armed forces for just as long. Beginning in 1899 and continuing to this day, hundreds of thousands of Filipinos and Filipino Americans have served under the American flag. The first were the Philippine Scouts, recruited into Uncle Sam's service by US Army officers eager to defeat the Filipino independence struggle they referred to as the "Philippine Insurrection." Over time, the Army's temporary tool of counterinsurgency became America's permanent mode of colonial rule, and by the 1920s Philippine Scouts outnumbered US soldiers in the territory. In the years between the two world wars, thousands of Filipinos joined the US Navy, some enlisting in the Philippines, others in the United States, nearly all of them restricted to bottom-rung positions as cooks and stewards. The Second World War called up hundreds of thousands more. About 7,000 Filipino migrants in the United States joined the US Army's First and Second Filipino Regiments; more than 120,000 served in the ranks of the doomed Philippine Army that met the invading Japanese force in 1942; at least 70,000 men and women fought in the guerrilla movements that battled Japanese occupation. The walls of the Manila American Cemetery include some of these names.

The memorial does a better job of recording Filipinos' wartime service than most history books do. Walking down the east colonnade devoted to the US Army, it is hard to miss the overwhelming number of Philippine Scouts recorded there—whole columns filled with names such as Gonzales or Torres or Velasco. Across the way, on the colonnade that honors the US Navy, the names and ratings of the missing and dead tell the same story of service and sacrifice: Steward's Mate Second Class, Mess Attendant, Water Tender, Cook. These men, too, went down with the ship, from the morning of December 7, 1941, to the summer of 1945. Some 64,000 of the 76,000 prisoners on the Bataan Death March were Filipinos who served under the American flag. Yet most of those men waited until 2009 to receive equitable veterans benefits from the US government. But what were they doing in the US armed forces in the first place? And why did they wait so long?

We know the story of one of them, a man by the name of Pastor Amarillento. In December 1991, newly arrived in San Francisco from the Philippines, he walked proudly out of the city's federal courthouse with his US naturalization certificate in hand. The seventy-four-year-old Amarillento had become a US citizen under the provisions of a 1990 law extending citizenship to veterans of the Philippine Army who, like him, had fought for the United States during World War II. He bought a bus ticket to Los Angeles, where he planned to stay with his cousin. On the way to Los Angeles, a pickpocket stole Amarillento's last two hundred dollars. He tried to find his cousin, only to be told by a cab driver that her address was fifty miles away in Orange County. The sun was setting, and then it was gone, and Pastor Amarillento spent the night in a park in the City of Angels. And the next. And the next. Only then did he find his way to the Filipino-American Service Group, a shelter in Filipinotown just west of downtown, where a Christmas party was under way. Amarillento was a veteran, a sergeant in the army of the Greatest Generation, a man who marched under General Douglas MacArthur, only to find himself, fifty years later, sleeping in MacArthur Park. How did Douglas MacArthur get to the Philippines? And how did Pastor Amarillento end up in a park named after the general?[1]

Bound by War begins with those questions. Answering them requires a history of the soldiers and sailors who crossed the Pacific, of two nations bound together by the wars they fought there, and of the century they built together.

In November 2011, US Secretary of State Hillary Clinton announced the beginning of "America's Pacific Century." The administration of President Barack Obama, she explained, would now "pivot to new global realities" in Asia. Clinton's claim to novelty would have surprised the naval strategist Alfred Thayer Mahan, who had written in 1890 that "whether they will or no, Americans must now begin to look outward" toward the Pacific. And it would have startled the Filipinos and Americans who crossed the Pacific in uniform in the decades after America's ships first steamed into Manila Bay during the Spanish-American War. They would have known that by the time Hillary Clinton announced it, the Pacific Century was already a hundred years old. After all, they were the ones who had built it.[2]

One of the first to enlist was Gaudencio Verceies, a twenty-three-year-old hotel clerk in Washington, DC, who joined the United States Navy in 1908. Verceies soon found himself bound from Norfolk, Virginia, on the battleship USS *Georgia*. He was one of two Filipino sailors who participated in the global voyage of the Great White Fleet, the US Navy's 1908 round-the-world tour. The brainchild of President Theodore Roosevelt, the Great White Fleet was meant to send a message to the established power of Britain and the rising empires of Germany and

Japan. It was a clear symbol that America had officially embraced an imperial identity, taking up "The White Man's Burden" that British poet Rudyard Kipling laid out in his poem, written for American audiences and published in February 1899 with a now-forgotten subtitle, "The United States and the Philippine Islands." The Great White Fleet might not be the place one would expect to find Gaudencio Verceies, one of those whom Kipling dismissively described as America's "new-caught sullen peoples." Verceies spent his entire career in the Navy, and in April 1917, in an interview published on "The Student's Page" of the *Philippines Free Press*, he urged young readers to enlist in the world war the United States had just joined. "We have plenty of good food . . . and the pay is good. And then there is the opportunity to see the world, to learn about the people of other countries . . . I should say it is a golden opportunity for Filipino young men of ambition."[3]

Pacific service was also an opportunity for ambitious young Americans. In May 1898, twenty-two-year-old Joseph Evans sailed for the Philippines from San Francisco, assuring his brother back home in Oregon that "this trip is nothing but a vacation—we will have lots of fun." His fellow soldier Mark Bocek, who joined up in Baltimore in 1909, saw matters differently. "I seen a beautiful poster there, nice uniform and palm trees," he explained decades later. "They didn't tell me about the hard life. They sure didn't tell you nothing. On the other side was a pick and shovel, that you had to work." Like Gaudencio Verceies, men such as Evans and Bocek also made their history in the Pacific. Service in the Philippines transformed Americans' sense of the United States in the world. In Philippine *barrios* and jungles, Americans earned the Medal of Honor, handed chocolates to civilian children, and married war brides. The Philippines was where American forces built their first big overseas military bases, where they learned to use napalm, where they mastered the techniques of torture.[4]

What began as a Pacific moment in 1898 became a Pacific Century for both nations. Filipinos' military service didn't stop when the United

States granted Philippine independence in 1946, because America's Pacific ambitions didn't end then, either. The Philippines shifted from colony to ally and Japan from enemy to friend. The Cold War soon burned hot in Korea and Vietnam. War in Asia meant that even with independence, the two nations and their soldiers and sailors would continue to serve together. In 1947, a bilateral agreement guaranteed the United States access to twenty-three military bases in the new nation—and soon provided for the enlistment of up to 2,000 Philippine citizens a year in the US Navy. In the 1960s, planes landed at Clark Air Base from South Vietnam; American sailors arrived at Subic Bay Naval Station for leave; Philippine Army medics departed for Saigon. A generation later, Operation Enduring Freedom undertook military action not only in Afghanistan, but the southern Philippines as well. As the United States began its war on Iraq in 2003, the Defense Manpower Data Center estimated that 31,000 noncitizens wore the uniforms of the US armed forces, about 20 percent of them Filipinos. And through it all, countless other Filipinos and Filipino Americans who never wore a uniform were affected by the service of those who did: all the people who worked for or near the US military; civilian farmers and factory workers who produced food, weapons, and airplanes; spouses who kept families going during sailors' long absences at sea; young protestors demanding equal treatment for aging veterans; a woman from Burbank walking in a cemetery on a Sunday afternoon.

For both Filipinos and Americans, *Bound by War* retells the history of the United States from a Pacific perspective. The Pacific is an ocean, an array of societies living in it and around it, and a field for the projection of American power. The adjective means peaceful—the Pacific's modern history was anything but. A Pacific history tells something more than the history of the United States in the Pacific, or indeed the history of either the United States or the Philippines. Like Filipinos and Americans in the twentieth century, a Pacific history crosses the boundaries of both nations to show the connections between them:

an unbroken cord that hitched the destinies of two countries to the military and foreign policy priorities of the United States.

War shaped every aspect of the Pacific Century, from how Americans and Filipinos thought about each other to how they lived together. Those connections built Filipino America. They transformed the Philippines. And they made US power in Asia first possible, and then permanent.

For most of the twentieth century, service in the US armed forces offered the clearest path to migration and US citizenship for Filipinos who wanted it. It's not hard to see traces of this on the landscape, as some of the communities with the greatest number of Filipino Americans also happen to be US Navy towns: Vallejo, California, near Mare Island Naval Shipyard; National City, near Naval Station San Diego; Norfolk and Virginia Beach, near Hampton Roads. In 2020 the United States counts over four million Filipino Americans, one of the nation's fastest-growing ethnic groups. Many trace their family histories to a father or an uncle in a US military uniform, and when they don't, someone else's father or uncle casts a shadow. Military service also provided Filipino Americans a language of patriotism and sacrifice—and therefore of equality. Immigrants and their children used those words, not only to wage a decades-long struggle for equity for World War II veterans, but to find a place for themselves in America, making their service part of America's military history, making their protests and lawsuits part of its civil rights legacy, handing down mindsets and memories of war and the military from one generation to the next.[5]

In both the Philippines and the United States, the Pacific Century bound together high politics and ordinary soldiering. It can be seen at the highest levels in the stories of several of the nation's twentieth-century leaders: Emilio Aguinaldo, the leader of the Philippine

Revolution, who died in a US veterans' hospital with the American national anthem on his lips; Manuel Quezon, a former revolutionary soldier turned US government informant who led the Philippine independence movement for three decades; Ramon Magsaysay, handpicked for the presidency by CIA officers; Fidel Ramos, a graduate not of the Philippine Military Academy but of West Point; and Ferdinand Marcos, who presented himself as a daring guerrilla fighter with a chest full of US Army medals, only to see his heroism unmasked and his regime overthrown by a popular revolution that he watched on American television news.

Generations of military service shaped Philippine politics, and America's, too. Even at the White House. Thanks to a provision of Navy bureaucracy, the domestic duties at the US presidential residence were long managed by the US Navy, and decades of recruiting Filipinos for positions as messmen and stewards meant that for most of the twentieth century, the first person the American president saw when he got up in the morning was a Filipino sailor in an American uniform. US power in the Pacific could be exercised—or experienced—at a great distance or a very close one. The US-Philippine relationship was and is an uneven partnership, and *Bound by War* accounts for the violence and racial discrimination that Filipino servicemen experienced. Going beyond foreign *policy*, this is a history of foreign *relations*: the political, military, and personal bonds that Americans and Filipinos forged in the Pacific.

Those connections shaped US military institutions across the twentieth century. After 1898, the Philippines quickly became America's most substantial colonial commitment, and with over one hundred million people, it remains one of the United States' largest and most reliable allies. America had—and has—other territories, bases, and modes to project its global power. But after 1898 the Philippines demanded the most energy and the most money, posed the biggest questions, and set the precedents for later US actions in Asia. That relationship hardly changed after independence in 1946—if anything, it widened and deepened. As America's Asian priorities shifted, it was from the Philippines that the United States faced its Pacific rivals: Spain, Japan, the Soviet Union, and, today, China.

From the Pacific, you can watch the transformation of the American military in the twentieth century. A standing army replaced a small frontier fighting force, and a flexible National Guard took the place of an array of inept local militias. Steel ships plied the seas, refueling at coaling stations that dotted the maps at war colleges and service academies. The livelihoods of entire cities were tied to military fortunes, whether workers built B-17s at Boeing in Seattle, harvested sugar cane in Hawai'i, or packed salmon into tin cans in Alaska. There were new weapons, from nuclear warheads stored at Clark to psychological operations aimed at the hearts and minds of Southeast Asian peasants. And there were new or expanded institutions—veterans' hospitals, pension bureaus, and embassy naturalization offices—that managed the dense connections between military service, the modern welfare state, and its citizens. There were long legacies and surprising links. If you look for the only US Veterans Administration office outside the United States, you'll find it in Manila.

As the American military changed in the twentieth century, the Philippines was both its foundation and its framework. A foundation in the sense of a solid block on which everything else was built: a jungle outpost became an Army camp, which then became an Air Force base four times the size of the District of Columbia. An army borrowed from the Spanish in 1898 was sent to Japan in 1945 and replicated in Korea in 1950. Careers advanced in the Philippines—William Howard Taft and Dwight Eisenhower, Paul Wolfowitz and Paul Manafort—led to Washington's corridors of power. The Philippines provided a framework that guided and set boundaries for the United States in Asia: anticommunism in the mountains of Luzon could be exported to South Vietnam; People Power generated peaceful regime change in Manila in 1986, so why would it not do so in Baghdad in 2003?

Filipinos were part of every major policy the US military undertook, fighting with and for the nation that colonized them, and with dreams greater than food or pay or travel. They learned along the way to navigate the Pacific Century, building on its foundation, pushing against its framework, and making the century their own.

Not so different from a Manila jeepney driver. The Manila American Cemetery is a long walk from the nearest train station, and so to get there I rode in a jeepney. The streets and highways of Manila are clogged with these remarkable vehicles, and everyone will tell you the same story of where they come from: after the Second World War, the US Army sold or abandoned its fleet of jeeps, and Filipino drivers adapted them for use as informal jitneys, or jeepneys. Some drivers boast that the jeepneys they drive date from World War II, though none actually do anymore. The American Motor Car Company exported jeeps from Detroit until the 1970s, and most today are manufactured in the Philippines. To grab potential passengers' attention, drivers paint jeepneys in outlandish colors, decorating them with the names of their wives, their children, their hometowns, their patron saints. In the decades since the war, the jeepney has become for Filipinos a cherished national icon, which, when you think about it, is kind of ironic. On the one hand, there is no clearer illustration of the legacies of war and colonialism: a US Army vehicle, imported during an invasion, abandoned by the occupiers, and yet somehow still beloved. But a jeepney would be unrecognizable on American streets: it is a distinctively Filipino vehicle, built on an American platform but adapted to Filipinos' needs. In all my trips to the Philippines, I saw jeepneys in almost every color. I never saw one painted red, white, and blue.[6]

In the darkest days of the Second World War, two men briefly debated the stakes of the war that had brought them together.

Captain William Peryam had been an engineer at a copper mine before he headed to the hills to join a guerrilla unit in northern Luzon. In a memoir written just after the war, Major Thomas Jones, one of Peryam's fellow soldiers, recorded an insight on the captain's part. "I've been in this country five years before the war," he said, "and never regarded these Filipinos as anything other than a source of labor supply to be exploited as much as possible. And now, damn it, . . . the very people for whom I had nothing but a kick in the seat of the pants are now risking their lives to feed me and the rest of the Americans." Peryam insisted that "if I ever get through this war things are going to be different" at the mine.[7]

In his memoir, Major Jones then recorded another story. As the guerrillas struggled to survive in the mountains, local Filipinos offered them food and water. Then, one day, the guerrillas got the one thing they needed even more urgently: a radio man. In the 1930s, Arthur Furagganan had spent seven years in Los Angeles and picked up a trade as a radio repairman. He returned home to the Philippines just before the war, and soon after the Japanese invasion in 1942, he made his way to the mountains. When the American guerrillas asked Furagganan whether he planned to return to California after the war, he said no. "I think it's the most wonderful place in the world to live—for a white person—and the worst for a Filipino." The Americans tried to convince their beloved radio operator that "after the gallant fight in Bataan, the burden of which had been carried by Filipino troops, that things would be different in America." Furagganan was unconvinced. "Maybe just now. But you can't eliminate prejudice merely by a battle, even Bataan."[8]

The two men never lived to see the world their war was changing. William Peryam died when the Allies sunk a Japanese ship carrying him and other POWs to Japan in December 1944. Arthur Furagganan was captured by the Japanese and executed. Their service is inscribed in stone: Peryam's at a memorial in Honolulu, and Furagganan's at the

Manila American Cemetery, one of the 36,285 names whose stories remain to be told. For the lives bound up in the Pacific Century, that shared history could end in the green fields of the Manila American Cemetery or on a park bench in downtown Los Angeles. But it began in 1899, when two men—one Filipino, one American—made camp near a town called Macabebe.

CHAPTER ONE

BIND YOUR SONS

1898–1901

In June 1899, Lieutenant Matthew Batson and his servant, a man known to us only by his first name, Jacinto, made camp in the Candaba swamps about fifty miles north of Manila. Surrounded by the poorly armed but devoted soldiers of the Philippines' decades-long independence movement, the two men surely knew that America's "splendid little war" to liberate Spain's Caribbean colonies had become something else: a bitter confrontation in Asia, marked by guerrilla warfare, racial violence, and harsh counterinsurgency. When Matthew Batson enlisted as a private in the US Army in 1888, he surely hadn't expected to find himself one day in the Philippines. He almost didn't become a soldier at all. Raised in rural Missouri, Batson tried his hand at teaching and studied briefly for the bar before giving army life a chance. The next ten years brought Batson to the American West and then to Cuba, mostly with the 9th US Cavalry, a regiment of African American soldiers known as the "Buffalo Soldiers."[1]

Batson was a decorated soldier with an independent streak. His actions in one of the Philippine-American War's first battles earned him the Medal of Honor. But by June 1899, the thirty-three-year-old soldier had grown downright frustrated with the heavy-handed conduct of the war he had been sent across the Pacific to fight. Batson was unsurprised by the so-called Philippine Insurrection, reflecting in a letter to his wife that "if I was a Philipino [*sic*] I would fight as long as I had a breath left. . . . We come as a Christian people to relieve them from the Spanish yoke and bear ourselves like barbarians." Batson unburdened his thoughts not only to his wife, but to his servant as well, and at some point in May or June of 1899, Jacinto brought Batson to Macabebe, his hometown in the province of Pampanga not far from their camp.[2]

What Matthew Batson found there surprised him. Macabebe's loyalty to Spain meant it was no ordinary city. For years, it had been the largest source of military recruitment for Spain's colonial army in the Philippines. Eugenio Blanco, a colonel in that army and the city's most powerful landowner, funneled local men into the Voluntarios de Macabebe. Happy to have the troops, the Spanish protected Blanco in turn after Filipino revolutionaries launched a war of resistance against Spain. In 1898, revolutionaries surrounded the Spanish garrison in Macabebe. Five hundred Spanish soldiers, civilians, and clergy took refuge in the parish church, and 3,000 Macabebe soldiers defended them until the Spanish army rescued the town.[3]

When American troops conquered Macabebe a few months later, in April 1899, they encountered "about a thousand of the inhabitants of the place assembled upon the banks of the river, cheering the expedition lustily," and learned that "many of the Macabebes expressed themselves as being anxious to enter the American service." A delegation from the city traveled to Manila to meet with US officers, eager to transfer their allegiance from Spain to the United States in exchange for protection from revolutionary forces. The Army recruited a hundred men as civilian employees.[4]

Soon thereafter, the *Chicago Tribune* informed readers that the Filipinos "are delighted to get 50 cents a day, declaring their loyalty to the Americans." Jacinto was probably one of them, in all likelihood having previously served in the Spanish *Voluntarios*. Precisely what Jacinto showed Matthew Batson in Macabebe is unknown, but in June 1899, Batson wrote a letter to his commanding officer asking permission to organize two companies of Filipinos as soldiers—not simply as hired hands—for use in local pacification campaigns. Major General Elwell Otis, who was then the commanding general in the Philippines, hesitantly agreed. And with that began the Philippine Scouts: a colonial army that matched those of America's fellow empires, and, over time, the foundation of US power in Asia and a symbol of the partnership between the two nations.[5]

The Philippine Scouts emerged from conversations between Matthew Batson and Jacinto, carried on at times in a pidgin language that American soldiers called "bamboo English," other times conducted through their translator, a former captain in Spain's colonial army. But it wasn't an original idea. The military histories of both the United States and the Philippines made a "native" force a foregone conclusion. Matthew Batson's life story suggests the American precedents: his time with the Buffalo Soldiers ingrained a racial hierarchy, and years of low-intensity warfare in the American West made him familiar with the Indian Scouts, units of Native American soldiers recruited by the US Army in the late nineteenth century.[6]

Jacinto's experiences pointed toward the same outcome. For centuries, the Spanish had depended on Filipino troops to defend their Asian colony. The Philippine Revolution, well under way before the Americans arrived in Manila Bay in 1898, exacerbated divisions within Philippine society, forcing people like Jacinto to choose sides. For the Americans, to win the war—or even just make the war look winnable—they needed Filipino allies. In places like Macabebe, they found trained soldiers willing to take their side. Years of war had devastated large areas of the Philippines. The landless and hungry population was so tired of surviving off boiled banana stumps—as the people living around Macabebe were doing—they were willing to offer their services to any army in exchange for security. For the men of Macabebe, if food and safety required Filipino soldiers to let Batson and the Americans think the force was their idea, so be it.[7]

As they fought side by side, Filipinos and Americans spoke in a language of blood to make sense of their new bonds. The Macabebes' enemies called them *dugong aso*, or "dog-blooded"—a contemptuous term still used today—that suggested an animal's obedience rather than loyalty, brotherhood, or even self-interest. The revolutionaries called the Macabebes' service treason, but underneath the apparent contradiction of Filipinos fighting for the Americans against other Filipinos was a deeper truth. As Filipino soldiers served American interests in the Pacific, they also advanced their own nation, although not on their own terms. Instead, the war entangled two countries by linking Philippine national identity with US military priorities in the Pacific. Beginning with that conversation between Matthew Batson and Jacinto, the two nations were irrevocably bound together. This was the first time that Americans found themselves in Southeast Asian jungles with Filipino soldiers by their side. It would not be the last.[8]

In the nineteenth century, Spain maintained only a small cohort of civilian and military officials in the Philippines. Mostly, they relied on local landlords and clergy to maintain order and filled their army's ranks with Filipino soldiers, called by the Spanish *indios*, or Indians. Resistance to Spanish colonialism steadily increased, leaving Spain's small military outpost vulnerable. In 1868, the government in Madrid moved to supplement the army with a quasi-military police force, the Guardia Civil, made up of Filipino soldiers under Spanish officers. Marching through Manila in their distinctive three-cornered hats, the Guardia Civil's 3,500 soldiers suppressed Filipino nationalists, which in turn only fanned the flames of anti-Spanish rebellion.[9]

The Philippine Revolution began with a dispute about soldiers' pay. In 1872, the colonial government announced that it would replace some of the Filipino civil guards at Fort San Felipe in Cavite, a small city across Manila Bay from the capital, with a contingent of Spaniards. The Spanish soldiers would do the same service but receive European wages. Outraged, a group of 200 Filipinos, most of them soldiers in the Guardia Civil, walked out on January 20, 1872. Spain called it a mutiny, quickly crushed it, and executed three men before an angry crowd of 40,000 in Manila, setting the Philippines on an irrevocable course toward conflict with Spain.[10]

A generation later, formal petitions and sporadic rebellions had become armed insurgency. The revolution had many leaders, but after 1897 it was under the political and military command of General Emilio Aguinaldo. Born to a prosperous family in 1869 in Cavite Viejo, near the site of the 1872 munity, Aguinaldo was recruited by a cousin into the revolution's armed faction in 1895, and soon rose to military leadership, outmaneuvering his rivals and successfully turning a ragtag series of colonial uprisings into a revolution to be reckoned with. Calling on "the brave sons of the Philippines," Aguinaldo tried (with some success) to draw trained soldiers—and their weapons—from the *indios* of the Spanish colonial army into the ranks of the *Katipuneros*, or revolutionaries. At the same time, the movement's official propagandists documented the excesses of Spain's army and sought to win converts to the Katipunan by providing security, food, and animals to ordinary people.[11]

With their empire collapsing all around them, from Havana to Guam to Manila, the Spanish launched a last-ditch effort to suppress the revolution by force. They expanded the Guardia Civil and in 1895 set up a new branch, the Cuerpo de Vigilancia y Seguridad, a secret police service that recruited both Spanish and Filipino agents. The Spanish reinforced Filipino troops with about 22,000 *peninsulares*—soldiers from the Iberian Peninsula—who landed in waves over the course of October 1896 to the cheers of Manila's Spanish settlers. By January 1897, the Spanish had 36,000 soldiers under arms: most were *peninsulares*, along with a few thousand recruited from elsewhere in Europe. About 6,000 were Filipino soldiers, whom the Spanish transferred from Manila to guard other, less rebellious regions. To Aguinaldo's delight, many deserted along the way: as the revolution expanded, the Spanish Army now confronted a new force of Filipino soldiers that they themselves had trained—wielding skills and weapons they had obtained in Spanish service.[12]

The Spanish were hardly unique in using colonial subjects to police the outposts of Asian empire: the British, French, and Dutch already did the same. After 1898, Americans would look to them for guidance but drew most of their lessons from their own experiences. In the nineteenth-century American West, the US Army regularly turned to cooperative Native American soldiers, first recruited into service in an official capacity in August 1866, and only phased out as a policy in 1897. Most performed manual labor, but some acted as informants, interpreters, or as scouts—a word that Matthew Batson would have known well when he proposed the formation of the Philippine Scouts. The term would have been equally familiar to US Army generals, twenty-six out of thirty of whom had seen service in the so-called Indian Wars of the previous generation.[13]

This was not the first time the US Army had tried to find Filipinos to fight for them. In the first days of the war against Spain, they hoped to delegate the war to the Filipinos—by arming General Emilio Aguinaldo—only to see it backfire. In the spring of 1898, Aguinaldo was almost completely unknown to US officials, but he seemed like a natural ally. For years, the United States had watched as Cubans challenged Spanish rule over their homeland. Some Americans wanted to help Cuban revolutionaries and civilians imprisoned in *reconcentrado* camps; some eyed economic opportunity in the Caribbean; a few dreamed of an empire to rival the European powers. They paid little attention to political unrest also occurring in the Philippines. War with Spain followed just weeks after the February 1898 explosion of the USS *Maine* in Havana, but a conflict over Cuba then summoned the question of Spain's Pacific empire: the fortified island of Guam and the massive archipelago of the Philippines, then lightly defended by *peninsulares* and a sizeable naval force sailing outdated vessels. For America, this was a war of choice, with unexpected and enduring consequences. The United States didn't have to expand the war to the Pacific, and military and political leaders at the time didn't necessarily think they were beginning a century of US power in Asia. Stopping the Spanish Navy was tactically wise, and recruiting Emilio Aguinaldo—who knew the terrain, had troops on the ground, and held the imaginations of thousands of Filipinos—made short-term sense as well.

But when the United States declared war on Spain, Emilio Aguinaldo was not even in the Philippines. A few months before, on December 14, 1897, the revolutionary general had hammered out a truce with the Spanish at the city of Biaknabato. Aguinaldo wanted to buy time for the revolutionary troops under his command to plant and raise another season of crops, to obtain more weapons, and to continue draining the Spanish will to fight. As Spain's army lost men to malaria, dysentery, and desertion, and with Cuba in revolt as well, officials in Madrid informed General Camilo Polavieja that no more *peninsulares* could be spared for the Pacific. Polavieja seized Aguinaldo's proposed truce and sweetened it with 400,000 pesos on the condition that the general leave the Philippines. Aguinaldo agreed (although he never got all the money) and settled in the nearby British colony of Hong Kong, where expatriate Filipino politicians, intellectuals, and military strategists continued plotting revolution under the command of their twenty-eight-year-old general.[14]

Aguinaldo planned a trip to Europe to plead the revolution's cause and meet with like-minded Cuban exiles. He was already on his way on April 21, 1898, the day the United States declared war. As American consular officials scrambled to track down a potential ally in their new war against Spain, E. Spencer Pratt, the US consul general at Singapore, found Aguinaldo first. The two met on Sunday morning, April 24, for about an hour. Pratt suggested that Aguinaldo return to Hong Kong, and then, should the US Navy be ordered to attack the Spanish fleet in the Philippines, Aguinaldo would accompany Commodore George Dewey, the commander of the Navy's Asiatic Squadron. When Platt cabled Dewey about the plan, the sixty-one-year-old naval officer was enthusiastic: "Tell Aguinaldo come soon as possible." Aguinaldo hurried to Hong Kong, spent some of his Spanish money to buy arms, and contacted revolutionary leaders in the Philippines. He urged them to support an American invasion. "There where you see the American flag flying, assemble in numbers; they are our redeemers!" US naval officers were pleased, but the State Department back in Washington was not, warning Pratt not to let Aguinaldo "form hopes which it might not be practicable to justify."[15]

Dewey left Hong Kong without Aguinaldo. Secretary of the Navy John D. Long hesitated to expand the war to the Pacific, but his assistant secretary, the young Theodore Roosevelt, had no such qualms. During a brief stint as Acting Secretary of the Navy in the crucial moments of April 1898, Roosevelt ignored his boss and ordered US ships to Manila. Dewey's sailors "proceeded to daub a new coat of dark, dirty, drab paint over the snow-white that had covered our ships for thirty years," and sailed as warships for the Philippines, where the US Asiatic Squadron dispatched the Spanish fleet in just six hours on the morning of May 1, 1898. Dewey then found himself stuck. He couldn't leave Manila Bay: if he entered a neutral port, international law required that his ships and crews be interned. Nor could he stay: there were no American soldiers nearby to support a land invasion, and a halfhearted attempt would surely trigger a diplomatic crisis. International law obliged any occupying power to protect the lives and property of all Manila's residents, including British and German business owners, so if violence ensued, other imperial powers might enter the fray. If that happened, Dewey would have to hand the Philippines over to Britain or Germany—or go with to war with their far bigger navies, which would surely lead to the same outcome.[16]

Emilio Aguinaldo was Dewey's solution. His supporters could fight the Spanish without provoking an international controversy. The Filipino general boarded the USS *McCulloch*, which escorted him to Manila Bay on May 19, 1898. The two men met the next day in Dewey's quarters on board the USS *Olympia*, the Navy's Asiatic flagship. Dewey was flush with victory and eager to take advantage of Aguinaldo's forces until Uncle Sam's soldiers arrived. Aguinaldo was equally keen to use the Americans for his own purposes. The two men—who spoke through a translator—clearly misunderstood each other. What they actually said we'll never know, as nothing was written down that day. Both men published memoirs, but only later, after war had broken out, and the two accounts are impossible to reconcile. Aguinaldo insisted that Dewey had promised the Philippines its independence. He wrote that Dewey told him "America . . . needs no colonies, assuring me finally that there was no occasion for me to entertain any doubts whatever about the recognition of the Independence of the Philippines by the United States." Dewey denied there had been commitments of any kind, later calling Aguinaldo's statement "a tissue of falsehoods." But as they shook hands that afternoon, they believed they were in agreement.[17]

When Emilio Aguinaldo went ashore at Cavite on May 19, 1898, he found his hometown in ruins after two years of revolutionary struggle against Spain. The young general returned, emboldened. On May 24, just as thousands of US troops were boarding Army transport ships in San Francisco bound for Manila, Aguinaldo claimed authority to govern as dictator of the provisional government of the Philippine Republic. He sent word of the new republic to George Dewey, who—since he couldn't read Spanish—simply forwarded the unread document to the Navy Department in Washington.[18]

Within weeks, revolutionaries had formalized the Army of the Liberation of the Philippines. Men enlisted for a variety of reasons: nationalist fervor, protection from the Spanish, pressure from the revolutionaries, money. Many were recruited through social networks. When Adriano Rios joined the revolutionary forces as a sergeant, his first order was to enlist fellow townsmen. Aguinaldo's army functioned with all the trappings of a national force, including ranks, commissions, military justice, and paperwork. The provisional government's coffers were barely sufficient to make payroll, so most soldiers equipped themselves. The insurgents' rifles were good (better, at times, than those later issued to American soldiers) but in short supply. For the revolution's rank and file, military service was a sign of political commitment and a down payment on citizenship in a future Philippine republic. After May 1898, the revolutionary army promised care for wounded soldiers, benefits for veterans, and support for widows.[19]

Dewey, still hamstrung by the laws of war, quietly turned over weapons the Americans had captured from the Spanish to the Filipino army. After consolidating power in Cavite province, Aguinaldo's army marched toward Manila. For the moment, Dewey was thrilled. "The Filipinos were our friends, assisting us; they were doing our work." But he grew increasingly concerned, soon warning the Navy Department that Aguinaldo and his men had become "aggressive and even threatening." Bound together by their opposition to Spain, the two nations soon saw their interests diverge. Secretary of the Navy John Long forbade George Dewey from any communication that might recognize Aguinaldo as the head of a legitimate political entity.[20]

In June 1898, revolutionaries gathered in Cavite. They were worried the Americans might seize the Philippines, but they also wanted to prepare for the possibility that the Americans would withdraw and hand the islands back to the Spanish—or that both countries would withdraw and another imperial power would arrive. On June 12, 1898, they issued a declaration of independence. "Weary of bearing the ominous yoke of Spanish dominion," the new republic declared itself "released from all obedience to the crown of Spain" and called for a "dignified place in the concert of free nations." Aboard the *Olympia* just offshore, George Dewey had been invited by Aguinaldo to attend the festivities. Dewey declined, on the grounds that June 12, a Sunday, was his "mail day."[21]

On August 13, 1898, the official US invasion began. The battle—which one American soldier described in his diary as "a very tame affair"—followed a plan carefully prearranged by US and Spanish diplomats. The *Olympia* opened fire at 9:30 a.m., then sent a signal at 11:00 a.m. calling on the Spanish to surrender, which they promptly did. The staged conflict allowed the 13,000 Spanish soldiers in Manila to protect their political, imperial, and racial prerogatives by surrendering not to their rebellious imperial subjects but to the Americans. The deal also gave the Americans, rather than the revolutionaries, control of the colonial capital. An additional irony became apparent a day later, when news reached Manila that the August 13 battle had been altogether unnecessary: on August 12, the Americans and Spanish had agreed to end the war, but news of the armistice did not reach Manila because Dewey had cut the only cable line between Manila and Hong Kong.[22]

About 11,000 American troops entered and occupied the Philippines, nearly all of them quartered in Manila or the nearby naval station at Cavite. They were no longer looking for allies. "There must be no joint occupation with the insurgents," ordered the War Department. "The insurgents and all others must recognize the military occupation and authority of the United States." George Dewey and the Navy faded from the picture, handing over the work of the occupation to Major General Wesley Merritt of the Army. Merritt readied to enter Manila as a conqueror, but he knew almost nothing about the Philippines. He arrived with a briefing book that included—among other items marked "confidential"—several transcribed pages of the *Encyclopaedia Britannica.* Merritt named one of his assistants, Arthur MacArthur, a fifty-three-year-old Civil War veteran, as the provost marshal general and civil governor of Manila. While his son Douglas stayed home in Milwaukee to study for the West Point entrance exams, Arthur MacArthur shipped out for the Philippines. He quickly imposed martial law, much to the dismay of city residents.[23]

Crossing the Pacific with Merritt and MacArthur were enlisted men who had volunteered in the war fever that gripped the United States in the spring of 1898. When Filipino nationalist Isabelo de los Reyes disparaged "Yankee soldiers" as "simple adventurers recruited on the waterfronts of San Francisco and neighboring ports," he was on to something. Zeno Lucas signed up on May 3, 1898, while watching a parade in Portland, Oregon. H. C. Thompson rushed to the colors in Eugene after the sinking of the USS *Maine* and shipped out from San Francisco on May 25. For such men, who averaged twenty-five years of age, five feet eight inches in height, and 150 pounds, the Pacific undertaking was something between a boyhood adventure and a noble mission. Writing from Portland just days before embarking with the US volunteers, Joseph Evans assured his brother that "this trip is nothing but a vacation—we will have lots of fun." Oregon soldier Edward Kelly linked America's new Pacific venture to earlier westward expansion: "We are facing the same conditions over there that we faced on our own frontiers for so long," he wrote. Myths aside, many of Kelly's fellow Oregon soldiers had never been on a horse. Some had never seen the ocean.[24]

On December 21, 1898, as the Oregon rank and file settled in to Manila life, President William McKinley confirmed Filipinos' worst fears by declaring America's intention to annex the whole of the Philippines. The revolutionaries had been steadily establishing provisional governments in the provinces they controlled, enforcing laws, collecting taxes, and recruiting soldiers, and US troops could be found nowhere other than Manila. So McKinley's move was meant to counter the revolutionaries' obvious political power and mask America's weakness. "We come, not as invaders or conquerors, but as friends," the president announced in a declaration posted in the cities and towns US forces occupied. Filipinos could look forward to America's "support and protection. . . . The mission of the United States is one of benevolent assimilation, substituting the mild sway of justice and right for arbitrary rule." McKinley also issued a veiled threat. "In the fulfillment of this high mission . . . there must be sedulously maintained the strong arm of authority." Uncertainty evaporated: the Americans were here to stay.[25]

News of annexation, as Aguinaldo later recalled, "struck like a lightning bolt into the camp of the revolution." Apolinario Mabini, Aguinaldo's chief political partner, warned Filipinos that colonization "will unite us forever with a nation . . . which hates the colored race with a mortal hatred." McKinley's proclamation was publicly defaced, and Aguinaldo threatened a death sentence to Filipinos caught reading it. A month later, on January 21, 1899, the revolutionary government gathered at the city of Malolos, just north of Manila, and adopted a constitution for the Philippine Republic. But the time for politics was quickly passing; now there was talk of little other than war. The revolutionary cabinet split over whether to take up arms against the Americans, but in the meantime, General Aguinaldo collected weapons, trained his troops, and required them to swear to "recognize no authority but that of God and the Revolutionary Government."[26]

In early 1899, Americans and Filipinos both struggled to mobilize armies in the Philippines that would demonstrate their political legitimacy. The United States aimed at imperial acquisition through military occupation, whereas the Philippine Republic pursued national consolidation through revolutionary struggle. References to "the mild sway of justice" could not obscure American violence, nor could revolutionary appeals to the unity of "all the Filipinos" hide divisions within Philippine society. Bound by their competing national ambitions, war was the only common language the two nations could speak. Aguinaldo—America's first Filipino soldier—had been an expedient ally in the war with Spain in April 1898, neither the first nor the last time America armed and trained a useful rebel who turned on them. Very soon, he would become a formidable enemy.

At eight p.m. on Saturday night, February 4, 1899, at the San Juan Bridge just outside Manila, a group of Filipino soldiers confronted an American patrol. Private Robert Grayson of the First Nebraska Volunteers fired the first shot, and by dawn, there was no turning back. "I have tried to avoid . . . armed conflict," Aguinaldo announced in a public appeal. "But all my attempts have been useless against the measureless pride of the American Government . . . who have treated me as a rebel because I defend the sacred interest of my country."[27]

"Insurgents have inaugurated general engagement yesterday night," read the first cable to reach President McKinley. Word of hostilities stiffened the nerve of his political opponents, who were then mobilizing to stop the US Senate from ratifying the Treaty of Paris that would formally annex Spain's colonial possessions in Puerto Rico, Guam, and the Philippines. Critics argued that recent American efforts at "scurrying around the universe looking for some vague new duty" departed from the nation's republican traditions, whereas others feared a new colony would dilute the American polity with brown-skinned heathens. Some merely worried that imperialism would be expensive or might provoke war with Britain or Germany. On February 6, 1899, one day after most Americans learned of violence in Manila, the vote came. At 3:25 in the afternoon, amid a "pitiless snowstorm," the Senate ratified the treaty with a single vote to spare. Republican senator Henry Cabot Lodge wrote his friend Theodore Roosevelt that "it was the closest, hardest fight I have ever known."[28]

With the peace treaty signed, Spanish soldiers departed the Philippines—bringing some of their loyal Macabebe soldiers with them. The war against the Filipinos entered a new phase. The Americans launched a massive counterattack, inflicting 3,000 casualties in the days after the incident at San Juan Bridge. Revolutionary forces wielded substantial power. Their mix of volunteers, irregulars, and veterans of the Spanish army numbered perhaps 25,000 soldiers. The Americans had about 21,000 soldiers in the Philippines in February 1899, nearly all of them quartered in and around Manila. Many were volunteers, like the Oregon men, who had answered the call in the first days of the Spanish-American War, and their terms of service were about to expire. Congress expanded the troop strength, and the Army began pouring soldiers into the Philippines. By late summer 1899, in-country Army strength had risen to about 50,000, and it would peak that December at 71,528. White House officials believed that they had a winning strategy: overwhelming force, decisive victory, and a rapid handover of power to civil authorities, allowing the victorious troops to return home in time for next year's election. The Americans had good reason to believe that victory was simply a matter of time. The Filipinos needed only to cooperate by losing.[29]

American military officers called for even more men, but in Washington, concerns about the buildup quickly emerged. Among other things, American soldiers were expensive. The initial volunteers, quickly shipped across the Pacific in 1898, arrived wearing blue flannel, ready to eat hard tack, canned Australian beef, and dried prunes. But after the excitement wore off, morale for faraway troops required the comforts of home, few of which could be found in Manila. Fresh from the cool climate of Oregon, H. C. Thompson recalled that his fellow soldiers "would crop our shocks of hair with clippers," and the tropics likewise dictated a switch from wool to khaki, although as often as not American soldiers wore no shirts at all, leading one of the Army's more uptight generals to complain that "we are the most slouchy soldiers in the world." As soon as the War Department could manage, it shipped familiar American foodstuffs to the enlisted men, and selections of champagne, mineral water, and silverware for the officers.[30]

In the war's first days, US soldiers did not yet serve with Filipinos in uniform, but they relied on Filipinos as military laborers, hiring them to pack mules, do laundry, and serve as *cargadores*, or carriers. Employment—or outright coercion—began during the invasion. Sergeant Charles Maccubbin and his men were charged with landing a cannon and caisson during a siege. "Jim Clark of 'C' Company saw a bunch of Chinamen hiding alongside the road," Maccubbin later recalled. "He ran them out onto the street and made them take hold of the ropes, and did holler and kick. But we jabbed them with our rifles and finally I brought the gun through to a plaza." Reaching shore in Cavite just after his arrival in the Philippines, Oregon soldier Zeno Lucas headed straight for the "fruit stands in front of the barracks," where ethnic Chinese traders had been selling their wares at Sangley Point (or "Chinese Point") ever since Cavite's establishment as a Spanish naval station. "It is hard to trade with them," Lucas noted in his diary, "as they do not know the value of American money." Perhaps, but Lucas's grasp on the principles of private property was weak, too. "I borrowed a can of condensed milk from one of the natives and," he joked, "forgot to return it."[31]

American soldiers appreciated the chance to outsource burdensome tasks of military service. Assigned to fatigue duty, Zeno Lucas noted in his diary that he "carried a few boxes and sat down and let the natives do the rest. It is to [*sic*] warm here to work hard." His fellow Oregon soldier George Telfer thought that "in a country where Chinamen abound and where they carry everything—and where wages are low—it seems absurd to punish soldiers by making them beasts of burden." Officers, meanwhile, grumbled their way through a military version of what Americans at home described as the "servant problem." In 1898, Colonel F. F. Hilder told readers of *National Geographic Magazine* that Filipinos "are intermittent rather than steady workers." In letters home to his family, Ohio sailor John Willis Greenslade initially approved of his "Filipino boy called Mateo," who "is clean and nice looking," but after Mateo quit, Greenslade complained that his new servant "resembles a block of wood more than anything else I know of." For both Filipinos and Americans, these were transactional relationships that evaded thorny questions of military occupation and national betrayal, but they reflected American dependence on cooperative local workers and Filipino willingness to engage with the United States.[32]

As US forces refreshed and rearmed, the war moved into a second, more brutal phase. On November 13, 1899, convinced that head-to-head battle with American forces would only yield defeat, Aguinaldo and his military advisers shifted to a strategy of guerrilla warfare. Rather than massing their troops, they dispersed them to their home provinces. Ambush and close combat replaced the revolutionaries' suicidal full-frontal attacks on American forces. Aguinaldo's adviser Apolinario Mabini explained the shift in a letter to his enemy, Brigadier General J. Franklin Bell. Mabini "deplore[d] with all my soul the guerrilla and ambush system to which the Filipinos see themselves reduced," but hoped "the struggle will remind the Americans of the one their ancestors sustained against the English." To a Filipino audience, Mabini asserted that "to struggle is the only recourse open to us in order to save the national honor and arrive at a true peace." Aguinaldo went into hiding. Most of his officers had no information about his whereabouts, and thus no way to betray him to the Americans if captured.[33]

The war had turned ugly. News reports of the Filipinos' guerrilla tactics told Americans that "every Filipino was our enemy, and each barefooted chewer of the betel nut mixture a spy." Even dogs "seemed to be trained to bark peculiarly at an American." Week after week, the *Army and Navy Journal* shared with its readers lurid accounts asserting that revolutionary soldiers, "true to their Malay instincts," had stabbed men in the back, buried women alive, or forced new recruits to drink the blood of dead American soldiers. As American soldiers encountered unfamiliar and hostile people, they projected their ignorance or their own racial prejudices onto the Filipinos. One commander read Rudyard Kipling's poem "The White Man's Burden" to his soldiers, who responded with "vociferous enthusiasm."[34]

"Almost without exception," wrote one army officer, "soldiers and also many officers refer to the natives in their presence as 'niggers,'" and, he observed, "natives are beginning to understand what the word 'nigger' means." African American soldiers, about 5,000 of whom served in the Philippines with the 9th and 10th Cavalry and 24th and 25th Infantry, encountered revolutionary propaganda that pointed out the ironies of their service. Michael Robinson Jr., an enlisted man in the 25th Infantry, recalled "placards . . . left mysteriously in houses we have occupied," telling "the colored soldier that while he is contending on the field of battle against people who are struggling for recognition and freedom, your people in America are being lynched and disfranchised." One black soldier wrote home that he "felt sorry" for Filipinos who confronted the racialized hatred of the American army. Another said of the US war in the Philippines that "expansion is too clean a name for it."[35]

In the United States, uncoordinated criticisms had by 1899 coalesced into an anti-imperialist movement, a diverse coalition that included Republican isolationists and Democratic obstructionists, starched-collar religious pacifists and blue-collar workers, bleeding-heart northerners and full-throated racist Southerners, self-proclaimed "Friends of the Indian" and die-hard enemies of William McKinley. Only a few had opposed the declaration of war with Spain in the spring of 1898, and in fact many, urging humanitarian intervention to aid the Cubans, had actually voted for it. Occupation and annexation prompted the war's critics to form the Anti-Imperialist League in Boston in June 1898. William James, Jane Addams, and Mark Twain wrote on the League's behalf, while Andrew Carnegie bankrolled its undertakings. William Jennings Bryan hoped to lead it. The Nebraska populist's 1896 run for the White House had electrified much of country, and in the midst of war in 1899, anti-imperialists began to rally around Bryan's almost-certain nomination for the Democratic Party's next presidential ticket.

President McKinley tried to neutralize the anti-imperialists by hurrying the transition from military rule to civil government. The president had already sent a group of advisers to plan for civilian rule, "with the retention of a strong military arm" that would "reconcile the Filipinos to American sovereignty." The Philippine Commission, though, was a total failure: commissioners arrived in Manila on March 4, 1899, only to learn that war had broken out during their Pacific voyage. Military and naval officers, preoccupied with war and hostile to nosy political observers, undermined the commission's power or simply ignored it. George Dewey, who rarely entered Manila, kept his office onboard the *Olympia*, never attended a commission meeting, and then abruptly pulled anchor and sailed for the United States in May 1899.[36]

McKinley delegated the work of pacification to his new Secretary of War, Elihu Root, a well-connected New York corporation lawyer with no military background. President McKinley, stung by the failure of the first Philippine Commission, concerned about the outbreak of guerrilla warfare, and attentive to his impending reelection campaign, appointed a second Philippine Commission in January 1900. This commission would not merely study civil government, but implement it. McKinley summoned federal judge William Howard Taft from Cincinnati. Taft, forty-two years old, deeply ambitious, and a formidable player in Ohio's high-stakes Republican politics, thought he was coming to Washington to learn of his nomination to the US Supreme Court. McKinley had something else in mind: the first governorship of the Philippines. The smooth-talking McKinley swayed Taft by hinting that whoever brought the blessings of American law to the Philippines was sure to find a seat on the nation's highest court. Taft packed his bags and soon after arriving in Manila on June 3, 1900, wrote his brother, hopeful "that civil government shall be established. . . . The Filipinos are anxious to be rid of policing by shoulder straps."[37]

Taft doubted that Filipinos would be subdued by the stripes and stars on officers' shoulders. The Army, however, took them very seriously. They put their faith in their leader, Major General Arthur MacArthur, who had become military governor of the Philippines in May 1900. Frustrated by the Filipinos' guerrilla tactics and hesitant to bind the Army's hands by the terms of law, MacArthur and his advisers believed McKinley was endangering soldiers' lives by hastily imposing civilian rule merely to court votes in America's fall election, and military men did not trust the glad-handing, obese Ohio lawyer the president had sent out to the islands. MacArthur and Taft began their work in Manila cordially; within weeks, they had become bitter enemies.[38]

In the field, General MacArthur began a new campaign on June 21, 1900, first issuing an amnesty policy that offered "complete immunity" and thirty pesos for every rifle to any revolutionary who swore an oath of allegiance "accepting the sovereignty of the United States." Back in Washington, news of MacArthur's amnesty proclamation showed administration supporters light at the end of the tunnel. "The thing is entirely over," one general prematurely reported. About 5,000 Filipinos took the oath, but most of them were civilians or military prisoners. Cash rewards yielded just 140 rifles. MacArthur quietly allowed the policy to expire ninety days later, but in a publicity move, Aguinaldo soon issued his own amnesty proclamation for American soldiers, upping the ante to eighty pesos for a rifle, and authorizing his top military strategist General Artemio Ricarte to free any prisoner "who should promise on his word of honor not to take up arms again against us."[39]

Anti-imperialists believed a November election victory was essential, lest McKinley's reelection give Republican imperialists a mandate.

The Democrats' platform called "the burning issue of imperialism . . . the paramount issue of the campaign," but it wasn't. Anti-imperialists were crestfallen when William Jennings Bryan spent more time campaigning on the subject of free silver. Andrew Carnegie, no friend of Bryan's economic populism, suddenly stopped sending funds. Supporters of McKinley's Philippine policy blamed the anti-imperialists for prolonging the war. Wisconsin senator John Spooner read into the *Congressional Record* a letter from an American officer complaining that "the continuance of fighting is chiefly due to reports that are sent out here from America."[40]

Also eyeing the election were the Philippine revolutionaries, who hoped that they could outlast the US Army just long enough for a Democratic administration to take power. "The presidential election . . . seems like a ray of hope for cessation of this war," Emilio Aguinaldo observed in October 1900. Revolutionaries corresponded with anti-imperialists and appealed directly to American voters. Apolinario Mabini published "A Filipino Appeal" in the *North American Review*, widely read by anti-imperialists, expressing his hope that America's "spirit of justice, now obscured by ambition, will again shine in the firmament." Revolutionaries concluded that their military actions in the Philippines might swing the election. On June 27, 1900, Emilio Aguinaldo sent word to Artemio Ricarte "to employ every means . . . necessary for the success of our army in order that . . . the imperialists of the United States may have no reason to achieve a triumph in the next Presidential election." Guerrilla attacks—and casualties—did indeed increase. So did American retaliations. Faced with setbacks on the island of Marinduque, in September 1900, General MacArthur issued dramatic orders to field officers there "to regard all the male population over fifteen years of age as enemies," and to wage war on the island's entire population. "Round them up and treat them as prisoners of war . . . until the situation is entirely cleared up," MacArthur ordered.[41]

McKinley won with almost a million votes to spare. Many Americans surely voted their pocketbooks and not their foreign policies, but electoral defeat cost the anti-imperialist movement its momentum. Some of the insurgents lost faith, too. Voluntary surrenders increased noticeably in November and December, although that cannot be attributed solely to the election results, news of which did not reach remote provinces for months. Aguinaldo only learned of McKinley's reelection on January 6, 1901, and two days later, according to an aide, "arranged to issue a manifesto to the Filipinos in arms inciting them to patriotism in order that they may not be discouraged." Meanwhile, McKinley and his inner circle—which now included Vice President Theodore Roosevelt, the forty-one-year-old Rough Rider and hero of the Battle of San Juan Hill in Cuba—believed they had a free hand in the Philippines.[42]

At the same time, the troops had to come home. If members of the Anti-Imperialist League woke up the morning after Election Day with a sense of failure, they overlooked their long-term success. By questioning the establishment of a territorial empire—even if their misgivings reflected mixed and unsavory motives—the anti-imperialists checked some of the McKinley administration's boldest ambitions. Never again would the United States attempt another full-scale acquisition and incorporation of substantial territory. The hardest part about empire was going to be persuading Americans to "bind your sons to exile," as Rudyard Kipling had put it. Matthew Batson's proposal, as improvisational and expedient as it initially was, looked better than ever.

THE MACABEBES WOULD BE THE ANSWER. OFFICERS' FIELD experiments—and Macabebes' own initiatives—presented an increasingly appealing alternative to the long-term deployment of tens of thousands of American soldiers. By March 4, 1899, news that Colonel Blanco of Macabebe had offered his townsmen's services to McKinley reached rank-and-file soldiers in Manila. In June 1899, soon after his visit with Jacinto to Macabebe, Lieutenant Matthew Batson urged his superior, Major General Henry Lawton, to give the Filipinos a try. Lawton, a hard-fighting veteran of the Native American wars who had tracked down Geronimo in 1886 with the help of Indian Scouts, appealed directly to the new Secretary of War, Elihu Root, and secured permission to organize an initial two companies of Scouts. In August Batson won permission to form another two companies, and on September 10, 1899, Secretary Root ordered the Army to organize two more companies of Scouts. To be trained by US Army personnel, the Scouts would serve not as US Army soldiers, but as civilian employees of the Quartermaster Department, and would not be asked to take an oath of allegiance to the United States.[43]

When Batson returned to Macabebe that fall, he was, he told his wife, greeted with "a flag raising and a barbecue" and "treated here like a king." Within days, he recruited 108 men, all veterans of the Spanish army. Armed with Krag-Jorgensen rifles, the new force went to work hunting down insurgents. Three more companies formed in October, tasked with "clearing the swamps and esteros [estuaries] about the head of Manila Bay of robbers and insurgents." In September, the Scouts took their first casualties fighting off an ambush. As the soldiers' numbers increased over the course of 1899, they won Batson a promotion. "Word comes from the Philippines that the two companies of Macabebe scouts under Capt. Batson are doing so well that it has been decided to organize a full battalion of those natives," reported the *New York Times*.[44]

By the end of October 1899, Batson boasted to his wife that "I am king of the Maccabebes [*sic*] and they are terrors. Word reaches a place that the Maccabebes [*sic*] are coming and every Tagalo [*sic*] hunts his hole." Lawton was now talking of a division, and Batson's mouth surely watered to command it, together with the rank he would hold if the new force were officially recognized as part of the US Army—which it still was not. At the year's end, the War Department still considered "Batson's Scouts" to be civilian employees, not soldiers, and Lawton, who was killed in battle in December 1899, never saw the realization of his dream of a full division of Scouts. By June 1, 1900, the Scouts did, however, acquire a somewhat more official name, the Squadron of Philippine Cavalry. Major Batson (promoted again, although not to Colonel) was by this time in a military hospital in Massachusetts, wounded in battle. "It is too bad that this occurred just now," he wrote his wife, "as no one can handle the Macabebes like I can." Batson never fully recovered and retired from the Army altogether at the end of 1902.[45]

The Scouts' benefits clearly outweighed any lingering fears of betrayal or infiltration. Officials believed Filipino soldiers would know the enemy's personality and his territory, could survive in the tropical climate with fewer supplies than American soldiers required, and would be naturally amenable to white officers' commands. The civilian leaders of the Philippine Commission recommended their recruitment on a large scale: Governor Taft advocated ten regiments of Scouts. Nor were Army officers unaware of the political implications back in the United States. War inevitably brought battlefield losses, observed William Johnston, who later became an officer in the Philippine Scouts. But if "such blood shed be that of Filipinos, the American public will view the enterprise with much less discontent than if each death vacated a place at an American fireside."[46]

By 1900, the Scouts marched under the American flag and swore an oath to "faithfully serve the United States," but were still not quite American soldiers. Initially employed as part of service units that would labor rather than see combat, Scouts often received no more than a few days' training before being put to work. No matter: Colonel James Powell assured fellow officers that Filipinos "can stand drill and marching from the day of enlistment." Quartermasters likewise deemed Scouts capable of carrying their own loads, obviating the need for hiring additional *cargadores* for their units. They now wore uniforms (although their clothing allowance was half that of the Americans, so they often ended up paying for them out of their own pockets), and carried the same weapons as the regular Army, "to avoid the possibility of mistaking their fire for that of the insurgents." They brought over traditions from the Spanish colonial army and developed new soldier folklore along the way, including what one American observer described as "little pieces of paper with mysterious signs and crosses, guaranteed to entitle the holder to a seat in the seventh heaven."[47]

There was a final, unofficial, but crucially important part of the recruitment process. As Captain Charles Rhodes of the 6th Cavalry explained, "Each scout was, before enlistment, invited to perform some service for the local military authorities, which would place him on record . . . as being an 'Americanista,' and would, in future, commit him to service in the American cause." To supporters of the revolution, the Scouts were traitors—"monstrosities of nature" in one account—and indeed the word *Macabebe* became synonymous with betrayal. For the new Scouts, there would be no turning back.[48]

Some Scouts were Spanish army veterans who sought protection with the Americans, but Spain's former *indios* joined both sides of the revolution, so choosing the Scouts was not a foregone conclusion. Some saw a chance for advancement: Manuel Ponferrada used his prewar experience as a private in the Spanish army to wrangle a promotion to the sergeant of a company of Scouts in Leyte province in September 1900. Social ties generated group enlistments. Lieutenant John Ward noted that "for every Filipino soldier we enlist we gain numerous friends, as his immediate family and relatives—and they usually are legion—are interested, and take sides with him." Others, like the men who served Macabebe's Colonel Eugenio Blanco, owed debts to local elites.[49]

To be sure, many Scouts signed up for the three-year term of service for the money. After Lieutenant William Wilson convinced his superior officers in November 1900 that a "pay day would have considerable weight" in recruiting Scouts, he got results. By the end of December, Wilson reported that his troops were "contented and seemingly proud to be American soldiers." Privates in the Philippine Scouts earned $7.80 and sergeants made $15.00 per month. That was theoretically the same salary as a US Army soldier, but the Scouts were paid in Mexican silver dollars, the common currency of the Philippines, whereas American soldiers took their pay home in gold. So in practice, with an exchange ratio of two Mexican dollars to one American gold dollar, Scouts earned half the salary of their American companions. Army officials wanted it that way, repeatedly warning that Scout salaries should never exceed local wages; $7.80 "Mex" was more than enough. "The pay seems to be sufficient," observed one indifferent Scout officer, "because the wives of the married soldiers support themselves and their children without much or any help from their husbands." Overall, the Scouts earned more money, more consistently—and in cash—than most Filipinos in the hard times that accompanied a decade-long revolution and a violent American occupation.[50]

They ate better than most Filipinos, too, although not as well as the Americans. One officer observed that "a small daily ration of rice and fish" is "really all that the Filipino craves." Major General George Davis later explained in a report to the War Department that equalizing rations would be "a waste of money. . . . It is self evident that the wiry little Malay does not require for his physical well-being as much food as the husky Anglo-Saxon." Americans bought Filipino loyalty with wages, weapons, and food, but Scouts wanted to serve, and scouting was a job men wanted to keep. The force recorded far lower desertion rates than their regular army counterparts. Officers were choosy about recruitment, and it helped that Scouts were permitted "to bring their wives to the station of their company," a policy that also meant venereal disease rates were far lower than those among US troops.[51]

Initially, the Scouts' noncommissioned officers—sergeants and the like—were a mix of Americans and Filipinos, but language difficulties soon convinced Army brass that the Scouts needed Filipino noncoms, who were cheaper in any case. Initial legislation authorized Filipinos to serve as lieutenants, but the junior officer provisions were quickly phased out. "In time," wrote Major William Johnston, "natives may have acquired a sufficient knowledge of English and of United States Army methods of administration, to discharge their duties as second lieutenants, but that time has not come." No one ever seems to have doubted that senior officers should all be white Americans, many serving on assignment from the regular US Army. For American officers, Scout service was a less appealing post than the regular Army, but it paid more, and most attractive of all, time served counted double toward an army pension.[52]

The Scouts served in companies organized along ethnic and linguistic lines—Macabebes, Ilocanos, Tagalogs, Visayans, and others—each one attached to a specific US Army regiment. Although the nineteenth-century Army considered the Apaches and Cheyennes to be valuably "war-like peoples," and the British recruited from groups they identified as "martial races," Americans in the Philippines appear not to have valued one ethnic group over another. With one exception: Tagalog speakers, who lived near Manila and provided the most visible leadership of the revolution, were universally distrusted and rarely recruited. In the highlands, the Army coerced labor from Igorot tribesmen but did not initially hire or enlist them. While the US Navy's Asiatic Squadron routinely tapped Chinese seamen in ports and on board ships, the Army never contemplated putting Chinese Filipinos in Scout uniforms, but they did hire them. Concerned about disloyalty and infiltration, Army officers initially planned to organize Scouts in one region and then deploy them to another, but then concluded that service in home provinces leveraged Scouts' language skills and family connections.[53]

On paper, they were the Squadron of Philippine Cavalry, but few of them rode horses, even the half-sized "Chino ponies" imported from

China for use in the Philippines. Instead, the Army's Filipino recruits spent their time driving carabao, the lumbering water buffalo that carried most burdens in the Philippines. Along with other Filipinos hired as civilian laborers, Scouts did the Army's drudge work: heavy lifting, leading teams of animals, interpreting, ferrying, and navigating. Despite their moniker as "scouts," they only rarely did any actual scouting because they weren't much good at it. Unlike, say, the Apaches, the men of Macabebe were peasant farmers, not range hunters, so their local knowledge was limited to the surrounding countryside. In the Philippines, domestic service was a man's job, so civilian Filipino men did not hesitate to work as cooks, laundrymen, and valets for Army officers. But the Scouts—many of them not trained domestic servants but career veterans of the Spanish Army—sought to distinguish themselves from the poorly paid "coolies." So they seized the most military-seeming tasks they could get their hands on, at guard posts or on reconnaissance duty.[54]

By the end of 1899, Scouts were regularly participating in combat, generally in supporting roles at the rear, but at times even fighting hand to hand. The Army quickly decided that Filipinos could also be useful for counterinsurgency and interrogation. General Henry Lawton thought the Macabebes were "well-behaved" despite "that they have been maligned and are falsely accused by the insurgents, who . . . have themselves committed outrages, representing themselves to be Macabebes." Such double-crossing was not unheard of, but the way US Army officers harped on the ferocity of Scout warfare provided cover for American soldiers' own depredations.[55]

Scouts or not, the name stuck, and in February 1901, Congress codified it into law. That year's Army Appropriation Act formally incorporated the Philippine Scouts, authorizing the president "to enlist natives of those islands for service in the Army, to be organized as scouts, with such officers as he shall deem necessary for their proper control." In Washington, opponents focused on contentious provisions granting the president power to increase the standing army's size from 26,800 to

104,000 soldiers. The establishment of the Scouts, who were authorized to make up 12,000 of that expanded force (although initially their numbers were not that high) drew little comment on Capitol Hill. It did, however, draw scorn from the caustic pen of writer Mark Twain. In "The Stupendous Procession," an essay Twain composed at some point in February or March 1901 (but never published), he created a fictional "Adjutant General" who believed "it was a good idea to persuade these hungry poor devils to turn traitor to their country and become American citizens—no, not quite that—American serfs, and murder their fathers and brothers and neighbors, and burn the humble homes that sheltered them as children. . . . And besides, England does it in India and in China." Twain's critique aside, the recruitment of Philippine Scouts scored political victories at home. Electoral victory and the promise of a reduced in-country force took some of the wind out of the sails of war critics. But the Scouts' biggest victory—and their dirtiest, most dog-blooded work—was yet to come.[56]

On the morning of February 8, 1901, Brigadier General Frederick Funston opened a telegram that arrived at the headquarters of his army detachment. Born to a prosperous family in frontier Kansas, the thirty-five-year-old "Fighting Bantam" (Funston stood just five feet four inches tall) was an aggressive, self-promotional veteran of imperial warfare, equally passionate about the poetry of Rudyard Kipling and the US conquest of the Philippines. His earlier exploits with the 20th Kansas Infantry, which he commanded, had already been awarded the Medal of Honor. The news over the wire was promising. In a nearby village, American soldiers had captured some revolutionary soldiers, and the telegram hinted that one among them might be a messenger for Emilio Aguinaldo. The hard-bitten Funston, who already had a reputation for harsh measures, sent for the man, Cecilio Segismundo.

In Spanish, which Funston spoke well, the two conversed about General Aguinaldo and his whereabouts. Conversation then turned to interrogation and—although Funston later denied it—almost certainly to torture. Within hours, the Americans had learned that Segismundo's dispatches contained the information they wanted, if only they could decipher them. Bewildered by the secret code in which they were written, Funston called for Lázaro Segovia, a Spanish soldier who had joined up with the revolution, then defected to the Americans. The two men set to work. "We took off our coats and even other things, in fact, stripped for action, and with pencils and pads of paper seated ourselves around a table and racked our brains, while Patterson, our negro soldier cook, from time to time brought in copious libations of hot and strong coffee." Segovia, who knew Spanish and Tagalog, soon cracked the code and uncovered Aguinaldo's location.[57]

Unbeknownst to Funston, Aguinaldo and his men were in trouble. At their mountain hideout, the revolutionaries were running out of food and ammunition, short of manpower, and gripped by terror. They feared infiltration by Philippine Scouts, betrayal by local townspeople, or death at the hands of the nearby Igorot settlers, whose ritual headhunting practices so frightened soldiers that Aguinaldo's chief of staff, Colonel Simeon Villa, observed his men "crawling along on all fours and weeping." Despite their terror of the Igorots, the revolutionaries depended on their labor, and when they could not hire them "because they had all hidden themselves," they impressed them into service. Weakened but unbowed, Aguinaldo still eluded capture.[58]

Back at headquarters, Funston and Segovia hatched a plan. Funston and four American officers would disguise themselves as prisoners, and a group of eighty Macabebe Scouts would pose as revolutionaries. Funston ordered the men to dress in "second-hand material, as it would not do for the men to look neat," and armed the Scouts with Remingtons and Mausers—the weapons the insurgents carried, rather than the Americans' Krag-Jorgensen rifles. As Aguinaldo would later observe, Funston "had the knack of utilizing rascals and renegades for his own purposes," and Funston now gathered his men. "The little 'Macs,' as we called them, were quite enthusiastic over the whole proposition," among them the first sergeant of Company D, Pedro Bustos, "a little shrivelled old fellow." Bustos was a veteran of years of service with the Spanish; when asked by Funston to swear his loyalty before launching the mission, he assured the general that "I am a soldier of the United States."[59]

Marching nearly one hundred miles through the mountain highlands of northern Luzon, the group finally reached Aguinaldo's camp on March 23, 1901, the day after Emilio Aguinaldo's thirty-second birthday. The Scouts approached his headquarters to present the "prisoners," and minutes later ambushed the building, shouting, "Hurrah for the Macabebes!" Entering the main room, a burly Scout and former revolutionary soldier by the name of Hilario Tal Placido grabbed the short and wiry general (who weighed in at 115 pounds), threw him to the ground, and—dramatically, if not quite heroically—sat on him. The revolutionaries surrendered, and celebrations ensued, the Scouts chanting in Spanish, "What's the matter with the Macabebes? They're all right. Who's all right? The Macabebes." Funston later recalled that "there was some difficulty in getting under control the wildly excited Macabebes. . . . A lot of them insisted in throwing their arms about us."[60]

News coverage in the US press credited Frederick Funston, but it was the Scouts who had captured Aguinaldo. Funston had remained outside the building in mock captivity the entire time. But the daring raid was not without criticism. Some observed that Funston's methods violated the laws of war, which barred the use of bribery to encourage enemy soldiers to betray their own armies. Funston's defenders were quick to point out that the Philippine Scouts were not America's enemies, and thus had been paid and not bribed. Funston later dismissed the criticisms as the views of "lady-like persons."[61]

Taken into custody in his finest blue suit, Aguinaldo accompanied Funston and the Scouts to Manila. They arrived at the US headquarters at Manila's Malacañang Palace on March 28, 1901, at 6:30 a.m., with Funston proudly announcing to the pajama-clad General Arthur MacArthur that "I have brought you Don Emilio." Later, properly dressed, MacArthur met with his military adversary. Governor Taft thought Aguinaldo should be imprisoned at the former Spanish fort at Guam, but MacArthur had another idea. On April 1, 1901, the revolutionary general swore an oath to "acknowledge and accept the supreme authority of the United States" and to "act at all times as a faithful and loyal citizen," and urged his fellow revolutionaries to lay down their arms. Twenty thousand revolutionary soldiers followed Aguinaldo's lead. MacArthur, in turn, issued another amnesty proclamation and released 2,000 political prisoners in two months. Aguinaldo's capture fractured the revolutionary movement. Juan Villamor, a second lieutenant who had deserted the Spanish to join the Army of the Philippine Republic, felt Aguinaldo's actions betrayed ordinary revolutionary soldiers. "In our humble opinion, these comrades of ours were handed over like sheep used for consumption to the butcher."[62]

Decades later, in 1968, ninety-one-year-old revolutionary veteran Marcelo Canania told an oral history interviewer about the frustration and disappointment that followed Aguinaldo's capture. "Aguinaldo, he is the one that fought against America. . . . He lost and so he sold us to the Americans. That's why we have faith and, no more fight. . . . So the fight give up. We wouldn't fight anymore." Canania was wrong about the revolutionaries, who continued fighting. In the city of Cebu, General Juan Climaco insisted that "the capture of General Aguinaldo . . . should not discourage us" because "the essence of the revolution resides in its ideals and convictions." Under dispersed leadership and with limited resources, the guerrillas carried on their struggle without their original leader, who was charismatic and strategic, but never the sole source of their inspiration.[63]

But, so many years later, what made Canania choose the word "sold"? As the revolution unraveled, Aguinaldo's fellow leader Isabelo de los Reyes begged his countrymen: "My brothers, let us unite. Let us not betray one another." In his plea, de los Reyes imagined a Philippine nation forged out of common revolutionary struggle and without economic incentives. But Canania touched on the heart of the matter: that every armed force is simultaneously a utopian political project and a mundane labor system.[64]

The distance from utopia to the mundane could be traveled quite quickly. After revolutionary general Daniel Tirona surrendered to the Americans in Cagayan in January 1900, his lieutenant reported to Aguinaldo that the general, "in order to ingratiate himself with his master, the American captain, is acting as his personal servant." The junior officer marveled that Tirona was "now trying to secure for him the most exquisite meals possible, and now washing the dishes and quarrelling with the cook and private servants of the captain." Equally appalled were the people of Cagayan, particularly "the ex-officers, natives of that province," who called Tirona to his face "a thief of the blackest dye, a man of dishonor, a coward, etc." Whether denounced as dog-blooded Macabebes or insulted by the townspeople of Cagayan, Filipinos in the service of the United States quickly learned that the overlapping roles of soldier and laborer carried political weight.[65]

In "The White Man's Burden," when poet Rudyard Kipling urged readers to "go bind your sons to exile," he didn't mean some Filipino mother's sons. But the tactic worked just as well, perhaps even better. Initially reluctant to arm and train the Philippine Scouts, US Army officers soon found themselves dependent on them, especially as the War Department sent home nearly half the US Army regulars in 1901. By 1903, the 5,000 Philippine Scouts represented 40 percent of the US troops in the Philippines. By pursuing occupation on the cheap, the United States bound Filipinos' civic aims to the demands of US foreign policy, but compensated them with safety, status, and cold hard cash. Widely acknowledged as a successful improvised response to a changing war, the Scouts became something more. On the morning that

Arthur MacArthur and William McKinley read in the newspapers of Aguinaldo's capture, they must have been pleased. They had won the election, they thought the war was almost over, and they believed they had heard the last from either the *insurrectos* or the Anti-Imperialist League. But the war was going to get worse before it got better.

CHAPTER TWO

DEFENDING THE PACIFIC

1901–1914

BY THE SUMMER OF 1901, WITH EMILIO AGUINALDO CAPtured in the mountains of Luzon province, the anti-imperialists silenced at the voting booth, and William Howard Taft installed as the head of a new civil government, the American occupation of the Philippines entered a new phase. In the field, General Arthur MacArthur, who believed the election victory offered a free hand on the battlefield, went on the offensive against the struggling Army of the Philippine Republic. Meanwhile, Governor Taft launched his own assault on the republic's political remnants using a new force, the Philippine Constabulary, a quasi-military police outfit established that summer and meant to complement the Philippine Scouts. As both Americans and Filipinos soon discovered, policing was not far removed from war and had consequences as enduring as the war itself, because it wove surveillance and repression into the fabric of Filipino politics.

Nor did the war end overnight. Almost every technique the Americans used to pacify the Philippines—political pressure, amnesty offers, deportation to island penal colonies, outright torture—had been tried before by Spain. And just as the Spanish found, none of it worked. Armed resistance and underground political mobilization persisted. Brutal violence persisted, and Americans at home learned of the "marked severities" US forces were meting out to Filipino guerrillas. Consequently, a political firestorm briefly erupted in the spring of 1902. Faced with an unpopular and expensive war, Theodore Roosevelt—who had ascended to the presidency after an assassin's bullet killed President William McKinley in September 1901—accelerated the plan to end to the war and bring US troops home. By 1903, most of the US Army soldiers were gone, with the Scouts set to carry out many of the day-to-day tasks of protecting America's new colony.

The global context shifted suddenly after Japan's stunning wartime defeat of Russia in 1905. Faced with a new military and naval power in the Pacific, Theodore Roosevelt's Great White Fleet soon steamed into Manila Bay and on board were America's first Filipino sailors. Building on the foundation laid during the first days of the Philippine-American War, the United States developed new military institutions in Washington and constructed a network of forts and bases in the Philippines. Together they signaled a permanent commitment to American power in Asia. That system relied on Filipinos—the Scouts, the Constabulary, the Navy—in an elaborate hierarchy of military service that bound the two nations together.

Emilio Aguinaldo's dream of an independent Philippine Republic never went away, even as the Philippine-American War wound down to an ambiguous conclusion. Filipinos would learn to be partners in violence if not partners in power. The Pacific would need to be defended, and Filipinos would be doing the defending.

On December 20, 1900, General Arthur MacArthur launched "a new and more stringent policy" aimed at breaking the links between the guerrillas and the towns that supported them. "The more drastic the application the better," he ordered. MacArthur printed 10,000 copies of General Orders no. 100, a harsh Civil War–era military regulation governing occupation and guerrilla warfare. Promulgated in English, Spanish, and Tagalog, the text informed Filipinos that anyone aiding the guerrillas would be treated as an enemy combatant. The new orders demanded that local leaders "lead the American forces to the insurgent hiding-places," one soldier later wrote, "and if they failed to do so they would . . . suffer the consequences." MacArthur knew the order gave his ruthless measures the protections of law, the honor of civilized warfare, and a place in American military tradition. A Southerner, Captain John Jordan, serving with the US Army on the island of Marinduque, wrote his mother that "if we should go out here and carry on a war as Sherman did in his march to the sea we would bring every one of them to submission quickly." As Americans and Filipinos amplified their attacks, the Philippines descended in a downward spiral of violence that did not end after Aguinaldo's surrender.[1]

In July 1901, with Taft in the governor's chair and orders from Secretary of War Elihu Root to "get the Army out of the business of government," Major General Adna Chaffee took over from MacArthur as commanding officer in the Philippines. The sixty-year-old Civil War veteran was no stranger to military action in Asia, having just led the American forces in a multi-imperial effort to crush the Boxer Rebellion in China. But Chaffee settled into the Army's Manila headquarters at Fort Santiago with some trepidation. "The natives do not love us or our ways." As Chaffee knew well, guerrilla warfare continued, with insurgent strength concentrated in particular regions, while ordinary Filipinos hedged their bets, unwilling to accommodate themselves politically to the American colonial regime. Just after arriving in the Philippines, Chaffee announced a plan to concentrate US forces in fewer, larger garrisons. The Army would save money, and soldiers could go home. "The duty of preserving peace and order . . . has thus been remitted to the civil authorities," Chaffee announced, washing his hands of the problem.[2]

Resistance to American rule in nominally pacified areas posed a challenge for Taft's new civil government for which the governor had no easy answer. Calling in the US Army to quell unrest would be tantamount to admitting that civilian rule was a failure, and the Army lacked the linguistic and geographic knowledge needed to destroy insurgents' underground urban networks. But existing police forces were inadequate in number, training, or loyalty. Taft had many weapons in his arsenal: he severely restricted Filipinos' assemblies and publications, at times with measures so stringent that even the Army objected. Beginning in January 1901, American authorities began transporting insurgents to a Navy-operated prison colony on the island of Guam, some 1,500 miles away. Among the first deported was the political mastermind Apolinario Mabini, shipped out in January 1901.[3]

Taft needed an army that wasn't the US Army. His solution was an Insular Constabulary, a new national police force that would be staffed by Filipinos. The Constabulary was a thinly veiled army, but because they were policemen and not soldiers, they would report to Governor Taft and not—like the Scouts—to his political rivals in the US Army. The governor asked Luke Wright, the vice governor of the Philippines and head of police and prisons in the new civil government, to plan a "native police force." As a Confederate army veteran from Tennessee and a lifelong Democrat, the fifty-five-year-old Wright was an anomaly in the McKinley administration, but he was an enthusiast for the new force, and—over Adna Chaffee's objections—on July 18, 1901, the Philippine Commission established an Insular Constabulary "for the purpose of better maintaining peace, law and order."[4]

The Insular Constabulary set up headquarters in Manila in the former offices of the Spanish Guardia Civil—geographically and symbolically located in between the Army's headquarters at Fort Santiago and Governor Taft's residence at Malacañang Palace. Major Henry

Allen took command. The forty-two-year-old West Point grad stood over six feet tall and kept a meticulous uniform, even in the tropics. A fellow officer remembered him as "one of the handsomest men I have ever seen." After a brief tour of duty in Cuba in 1898, Allen was named military governor of the province of Samar in January 1900. Like Matthew Batson had done in Macabebe a few months earlier, Major Allen improvised a company of Scouts who he thought would be of "inestimable value . . . in ferreting out insurgents and criminals and in understanding . . . the natives with whom we have to deal." Allen thought that the Constabulary—and the pacification policy it supported—was a must-win for America's new venture in Asia. "Our proposition out here is small" compared with other empires, Allen told a fellow officer, "and it would be a confession of great weakness and incapacity on our part if we could not properly govern such a situation as this."[5]

Allen relished the task of building up "a little army from the cellar to the roof," recruiting a handful of dashing, energetic, gifted young officers, some of whom would later go on to successful military careers. Allen attracted some by offering American noncommissioned officers in the US Volunteers positions as officers in the Constabulary at ranks—and salaries—they could never dream of in the Army. Most Constabulary officers, though, were made of more modest stuff. American soldiers generally saw the Insular Constabulary as a dead-end job, and its command attracted a congeries of unsavory types. Among its officers were soldiers of fortune who had already served in the armies of a half-dozen other nations.[6]

Recruiting ordinary Filipinos to serve in the Constabulary wasn't easy, either. The work was not well paid: unlike the Scouts, whose wages were set by Congress, constables earned different amounts in each province. A first sergeant never made more than $25.00 a month, and a second-class private could earn as little as $10.00 a month, supplemented by a meager daily food allowance. Still, constables earned more than municipal policemen, so many left city police forces to join.

Some were veterans of the Guardia Civil who found hometown service more appealing than enlisting in the Scouts. Others came from cells in Bilibid Prison, where judges offered convicted criminals the choice of a prison sentence or constabulary service. Americans paid for the Philippine Scouts through the US military budget, but the colonial government funded the Constabulary directly from the islands' revenues, with no burden on US taxpayers. The Constabulary was cheap, and it showed: the force was never as prestigious, as well equipped, or as disciplined as the Scouts. If the Scouts were treated like second-class soldiers, the Constabulary men were distinctly third-class, without medicine or tools, outfitted with no mosquito nets, no shoes, nor even underwear.[7]

Inequalities between the two forces resulted in part from tensions between the Army and the civilian government. The Army predicted the Constabulary would endanger the islands' stability and the military's prestige with it. They feared journalists, politicians, and voters back home would attribute any disorder in the Philippines to the Army. Enlisted men disdained the ragtag men of the Insular Constabulary, joking among themselves that the letters "I.C." on the constables' collars stood for "Inspected and Condemned." Officers were no more enthusiastic. Carl Stone, a captain in the Philippine Scouts, vented his frustration in letters home. The biggest problem, Stone explained to his mother, was how the Constabulary opened the door for infiltration and espionage by Filipino *ladrones*, or thieves. "You see, we have to submit all plans to the Chief of Constabulary, and of course half a dozen niggers in his office see them, and then of course, also, the Ladrones."[8]

Army brass insisted that the Constabulary uniforms must not resemble those of the Army. Most constables wore a gray linen shirt on top of their pants, or lack thereof: constables from indigenous groups in the mountains of Luzon preferred loincloths to pants, much to the dismay of American colonial officials. Other battles were more material, particularly over weapons. When Vice Governor Luke Wright ordered 1,372 standard-issue US Army rifles for the men, Adna Chaffee refused, leaving the men of the Insular Constabulary initially to carry only revolvers and shotguns, a policy the Army heartily approved. "Do not arm them with rifles at all," one officer wrote.[9]

In December 1901, just six months after its founding, the Constabulary counted 180 officers and 2,500 men, and Henry Allen—who by now had earned the nickname "Iron Comandante"—reported that "in chasing down robber bands, the native troops, well-officered by American and native leaders, are unquestionably more efficient than American troops." By September 1902, the Constabulary had expanded to nearly 6,000 members in 225 posts across the country and captured nearly 3,000 insurgents. "The romance and adventure of the Constabulary Service," wrote Constabulary officer James Harbord, "would furnish the theme for a score of Kiplings, Remingtons, or Wisters." Another former officer agreed, calling the Constabulary's history "a romantic and a heroic tale" that would "make any man glory in the pride of his race."[10]

The Constabulary's work was both bloodier and more boring than gauzy colonial romance suggested. Allen rewarded cooperative Filipinos and smashed resisters, offering, as one officer put it, "the *curacha* or the *carcel*," the dance or the jail, "and no middle ground." Allen found many dance partners when he established the Constabulary's Information Division, a secret police force utilizing loyal Filipinos as informants. Under the direction of Rafael Crame, the Constabulary's top Filipino officer and a veteran of both the Spanish and Philippine revolutionary armies (he would eventually become the first Filipino chief of the entire Constabulary), the Information Division infiltrated underground revolutionary networks and monitored the press. Within two decades, colonial officials held records on 200,000 Manila residents—perhaps two-thirds of the city's population. "It is scarcely possible," Allen assured a superior officer in February 1902, "for any seditionary measures of importance to be hatched without our knowledge, and my policy is to hit squarely on top of the head each insurrecto individual as he bobs up."[11]

Tensions with the Army slowly subsided. In December 1902, the force was renamed the Philippine Constabulary (no longer "Inspected and Condemned"), and its men took on new, more military titles: captain, lieutenant, and private replaced typical police ranks such as first inspector and sergeant. In 1903, the men donned new khaki uniforms with red shoulder straps and trained according to US Army drill manuals. They began carrying Springfield rifles, but they were constantly short on ammunition, so they never became particularly good shots, unlike the Philippine Scouts, who were among the Army's best marksmen. The Army and the civil government were slowly learning to live together.[12]

Despite American colonial rhetoric, the Constabulary was never much of a school for the citizen-soldier. The underpaid and sometimes underqualified men who served in its ranks were frequently accused of corruption and abuse. Pardo de Tavera, one of the first Filipino members of the Philippine Commission, caused a controversy in 1904 when he compared "the violent means employed . . . by the Constabulary" with Spain's hated Guardia Civil. In a 1905 exposé, administration critic Henry Parker Willis concluded that "a general belief exists both among Americans and natives that the force is inefficient and cruel." As the Constabulary's violence, corruption, and undercover surveillance became part of everyday life, another of the Americans' expedient solutions for policing and social control had created long-term consequences for Philippine society.[13]

By February 1902, the American public had lived through three years of war in the Philippines and clearly begun to tire of it, consigning it at times to the inside pages of their newspapers. Then, suddenly, they were briefly preoccupied with the question of whether American soldiers had tortured Philippine civilians. This wasn't the first time news reports of violence had reached Americans. Even though military censors suppressed unfavorable news and never more than a dozen American reporters were actually based in the Philippines, anti-imperialists publicized every account they could get their hands on. By late 1901, returning veterans amplified them with personal testimony. Herbert Welsh, a crusading reformer and longtime critic of Native American policies, became a passionate opponent of America's imperial venture. In the pages of *City and State*, a reformist journal that he edited in his home city of Philadelphia, Welsh led the Anti-Imperialist League's effort to publicize soldier "severities." While earlier accounts in radical journals had been discounted, the stories Welsh circulated in early 1902 were better substantiated and potentially more damaging because they suggested that torture was an official policy.[14]

Mostly dormant by 1902, the League sprang back to life, denouncing what one of its members described as "a perfect orgy of looting and wanton destruction." Catholics added their voices after news accounts showed the desecration and looting of Philippine churches. News of sexual violence also raised concerns among upright Victorians who objected less to crimes that Americans were inflicting on Filipinos than what the conquest of tropical empire was doing to the moral fiber of American soldiers. During the war, prostitution and sexual violence increased. Marcelo Canania, who was a young man on the island of Cebu during the war, recalled that American soldiers would sometimes get drunk and pursue Filipina women. Fred Newell, who served on Cebu, reported the gang rape of a teenage girl. Reports of a male prostitution ring caused Herbert Welsh and his fellow anti-imperialists such distress that they declined to publicize the charges.[15]

For most American readers, accounts of violence inflicted by US forces were overshadowed by news of grim violence perpetrated against the Americans, which steeled their resolve to see the hard war through to its conclusion. Few places were as violent as Samar, an island of about 200,000 people in the Visayan region of the central Philippines, where harsh measures had stiffened Filipino resistance. On August 11, 1901, Company C of the 9th US Infantry occupied the town of Balangiga on Samar, billeting officers in an abandoned convent. The tense occupation soon turned ugly. Catalina Catalogo, a Balangiga resident, operated a shop that sold *tuba*, a fermented palm wine. On the night of September 22, two American soldiers entered her store, and although neither the men nor Catalogo spoke a common language, the soldiers took offense for some reason and attacked Catalogo. The woman's brothers set upon the soldiers, and the brothers won the fight, but Company C's commander, Captain Thomas O'Connell, retaliated by arresting 143 Balangiga men. Soon O'Connell followed up with an order assigning all adult males in the village to mandatory labor details, "follow[ing] the usual custom in requiring the people to clean up their grounds."[16]

Townspeople objected to the attack on Catalogo, the mass arrests, and the forced labor, and they turned to the guerrillas for support. A plan was under way. Soon after, a band of guerrillas appeared, asking to surrender to the Americans. Army forces garrisoning the town, who suffered from what the War Department would later term "too great confidence," incorporated the ex-guerrillas into their work details. On the morning of September 28, 1901, a group of laborers appeared, bolos in hand, ready to go to work. Then, summoned by the ringing of the local church bells, guerrillas attacked Company C of the 9th Infantry, killing 48 of 74 American soldiers in hand-to-hand combat. Army headquarters immediately ordered American troops to "make a desert of Balangiga," and they promptly did so. News reports steeled the American public's support for soldiers abroad.[17]

In response, the Army poured almost 4,000 troops (including 300 Macabebe Scouts) into Samar in the next month. Adna Chaffee dispatched Brigadier General Jacob Smith, a garrulous, hard-fighting, loud-talking Civil War veteran, along with several hundred US

Marines, to sever the connections between the guerrillas and Samar communities. In October or November 1901, Smith issued a remarkable order: "I want no prisoners. . . . I wish you to kill and burn. The more you kill and burn, the better you will please me. . . . The interior of Samar must be made a howling wilderness." Samar already was a devastated place, and faced with the human suffering of civilians, not all American soldiers obeyed the letter or spirit of Smith's orders. One official complained that Smith "makes more trouble than he allays." But twice—once verbally and once in writing—Smith conveyed his words and his intentions. He got the results he sought.[18]

News of a new policy called "reconcentration" reached American audiences in January 1902, adding fuel to the political fire. Brigadier General J. Franklin Bell had issued new orders in Batangas province the previous month. To sever the links between the guerrillas and the communities that supported them, the Army moved residents from their villages to areas guarded by American troops. Anyone outside the official boundaries was deemed an enemy. Bell's "zones of protection," which came to include as many as 300,000 people in provinces such as Laguna and Batangas, bore striking resemblance to concentration camps established by the Spanish in Cuba and the British in South Africa. "We have actually come to do the thing we went to war to banish," moaned the *Baltimore American*, although one colonel reported to the *Army and Navy Journal* that after reconcentration, "the inhabitants are most respectful and very cheerful looking . . . no indications of sullenness or discontent."[19]

American attention soon focused on the water cure, a gruesome interrogation method in which captives were forced to consume approximately five gallons of water, at which point their jailers pressed their bloated stomachs until they coughed the water up and the process began again. The method's first mention in the US press appeared in a letter by a Nebraska private published in the *Omaha World* in June 1900, but few paid much attention until journalist George Kennan Sr.

provided a lengthy and lurid description in the March 9, 1901, issue of *The Outlook*, a national news weekly. Kennan decried counterinsurgency's degrading impact on American morality, having observed that "soldiers of civilized nations, in dealing with an inferior race, do not observe the laws of honorable warfare."[20]

On January 13, 1902, anti-imperialist senator George Frisbie Hoar called for a congressional investigation "into the conduct of the war in the Philippine Islands [and] the administration of the government there." He was quickly outmaneuvered on Capitol Hill. Henry Cabot Lodge, Hoar's Massachusetts colleague and chair of the Senate Committee on the Philippine Islands, presided over the hearings that spring. Lodge saw to it that most witnesses were friends of the administration and its Pacific war. The anti-imperialists countered by bringing forth discontented Army officers, including Lieutenant General Nelson Miles, the commanding general of the Army, who had become an outspoken critic of the war. Miles told an influential journalist that President Roosevelt and Secretary of War Elihu Root were blocking his proposal to lead an inquiry into conditions in the Philippines, hinting that the two politicians were covering up news of military atrocities. As commanding general, Miles had full access to the Army's most sensitive documents, and he soon began leaking some of the most damning information to well-placed critics in Washington. Furious, Roosevelt compiled his own list of Miles's failures and sent it over to Elihu Root's office for later publication. At the head of TR's list was the 1890 massacre of Native American civilians at Wounded Knee, South Dakota, which took place under Miles's command. Wounded Knee was "enough," Roosevelt told Root, "to show the extreme unwisdom of relying upon General Miles to mitigate the severities of war."[21]

From across the country came justifications of US actions in the Philippines. Some defenders, such as Edward Burlingame, an American diplomat posted in China, flatly denied the events. Luke Wright deemed news accounts of Bell's reconcentration policy "largely apocryphal." Elihu Root complained that "yellow journal hypocrites" had convinced "millions of good people that we have turned Manila into a veritable hell." The war's staunchest supporters denounced the accusations. In a speech in March, Brigadier General Frederick Funston said of war critics that "I would rather see any one of these men hanged, hanged for treason . . . than see the humblest soldier in the United States Army lying dead on the field of battle."[22]

Others defended American actions as grim but necessary. The *Army and Navy Journal* called the water cure "far more effective than the celebrated third degree of the New York police," and overall, quite "valuable." Journalist John Bancroft Devins reported a conversation with an American clergyman in Manila who thought the water cure "had its legitimate place in the recent war here." In the Philippines, the controversy exasperated American soldiers, among them Constabulary Chief Henry Allen, who thought that Americans were "getting somewhat hysterical over the alleged atrocities and various kinds of cures that have been administered out here."[23]

Blame frequently landed on the Filipino revolutionaries, whose purportedly savage ways brought out the worst in American soldiers. In the War Department's 1902 annual report, General Chaffee attributed atrocities to "the nature of the warfare carried on by the insurgents, who pose as friends and act as enemies in the same hour." In February 1902, Secretary of War Elihu Root detailed for Senator Lodge's committee a catalogue of atrocities, all of which—except for a handful deemed "few and far between"—were the work of the insurgents. "The Filipino troops have . . . tortured to death American prisoners who have fallen into their hands, buried alive both Americans and friendly natives, and horribly mutilated the bodies of the American dead." Such actions, Root thought, excused the minor excesses of a handful of American soldiers. "Such things happen in every war."[24]

Defenders frequently pinned responsibility on America's own Filipino soldiers, insisting that it was Philippine Scouts, not American soldiers, who violated the laws of war. An early ethnographic account of *The People of the Philippines* prepared by the War Department in February 1901 warned that the Macabebes were "somewhat difficult to control when once they have their enemy within their power, to keep them from looting and inflicting cruelties." Theodore Roosevelt asserted that "nine-tenths of the cruelties have been committed by the native troops."[25]

The water cure, in particular, was attributed to the Scouts rather than to American soldiers—notwithstanding the fact that the Scouts officially were US Army soldiers. Captain Lee Hall, commander of a Scout company, told the Senate in May 1902 that he had never seen the water cure practiced by American troops, although he acknowledged his own soldiers used the method, which Hall was "quite sure" was "a native, and not an American, invention." Matthew Batson, who also testified before Congress that spring, called the water cure a Macabebe technique. In his 1901 article introducing Americans to the water cure, George Kennan described it solely as the work of the Scouts, but he hinted that it was "sanctioned, if not directly employed," by the US Army. The Scouts' racial difference and second-class military status allowed American officials—both civilians in Washington and officers in the field—to hold them to lower standards of military comportment. Some of the atrocities that made headlines in 1902 were indeed carried out by the Philippine Scouts. But American troops, fully aware of the racial politics embedded in the laws of war, also turned over the dirty work of torture and interrogation to the Scouts.[26]

When observers couldn't pass responsibility onto the Scouts, they blamed a few "bad apples," who took the fall for the entire conduct of the war. On April 15, 1902, under directions from President Roosevelt, Secretary of War Elihu Root ordered General Chaffee to conduct a full investigation. Military officers who might have suppressed such proceedings now drew attention to them to show that the Army was doing something. They hoped Major Littleton Waller would be their fall guy. The forty-five-year-old Marine officer joined the Samar pacification campaign in October 1901, just weeks after the raid at Balangiga. Waller ordered his men to "place no confidence in the natives, and punish treachery immediately with death." On December 28, 1901, Waller headed to the interior of Samar with sixty marines, two Filipino scouts, and thirty-three "native bearers," Filipino civilian employees tasked with hauling and keeping camp. Deep into the jungle and short on food and water, most of the white soldiers suddenly came down with an unidentified tropical fever. Trapped in the wilderness and surrounded by men they did not trust, the marines turned on the Filipino soldiers and servants. They confiscated their bolo knives and soon insisted that the men were hiding food. When the surviving members of the party returned to the base camp, Waller (himself among those gravely ill) ordered the summary execution of eleven of the Filipinos for "treason in general, theft, disobedience and . . . general mutiny."[27]

In March and April 1902, a court martial in Manila tried Major Waller and one of his lieutenants for the deaths of the native bearers. Waller insisted that "I am not a murderer," and argued that he had abided by General Orders no. 100 while carrying out Brigadier General Jacob Smith's orders to make the area a "howling wilderness." Waller walked away a free man, but news of his exoneration caused an uproar when it reached the United States. Adna Chaffee called it "one of the most regrettable incidents in the annals of the military service of the United States," though he couldn't have forced a guilty verdict out of soldiers sympathetic to the frontline perils of counterinsurgency.[28]

Soon enough, Jacob Smith was called to answer for the howling wilderness. At a court martial in Manila in May 1902, the Army laid no serious crimes at his doorstep, charging him merely with "conduct to the prejudice of good order and military discipline." Smith, too, cited General Orders no. 100—which authorized "justified acts of retaliation" for attacks such as the one on US soldiers at Balangiga—and compared the Samar campaign with that of Sherman's in Georgia.

The court convicted the general but sentenced him to a mere admonishment. President Roosevelt, who worried about the political fallout of letting Smith off the hook, forced Smith into retirement. In Manila, General Chaffee, who thought Smith was "of unsound mind," detained the retired general in the Philippines until the political controversy blew over, lest he tell reporters something "absurdly unwise." Smith ended up not being much of a scapegoat—nor would anyone else. Overall, the men accused of violations received notably light sentences: one soldier found guilty of administering the water cure to a Filipino priest was fined $50.00.[29]

The long and contentious spring was finally turning to summer on May 30, 1902, when President Theodore Roosevelt mounted the speaker's podium at Arlington National Cemetery to deliver a Memorial Day address. Roosevelt thanked his audience, which included Civil War veterans of both the blue and the gray, for having "left us a reunited country," while in the Philippines, "your younger brothers, your sons," were "carrying to completion a small but peculiarly trying and difficult war" against "forces which stand for the black chaos of savagery and barbarism." Treacherous attacks on American soldiers, Roosevelt regretted to say, had brought forth "acts of cruelty" from "some among them" in response. They were the "wholly exceptional" acts of "black sheep," "shamelessly exaggerated" by those "who walk delicately and live in the soft places of the earth." As his distinctively high-pitched patrician voice rolled over the assembled crowd, Roosevelt indicted anti-imperialist Democrats who criticized American soldiers while turning a blind eye to racial violence in the South, "cruelty infinitely worse than any that has ever been committed by our troops in the Philippines." He aimed his condemnation of racial violence at Democratic opponents on Capitol Hill, legislators who were not so much friends of the Filipino as opponents of the Republican Party. Nor did TR find it difficult to criticize violence in the American South while authorizing it overseas. The press—outside the white South—hailed Roosevelt's address as a "fervid defense of the army of the United States." It played an important part in bringing America's consideration of torture to a close.[30]

So did Roosevelt's announcement that as of July 4, 1902, hostilities in the Philippines were "now at an end." The declaration followed no particular battle or surrender. There were no handshakes or offerings of swords, as at Appomattox Court House two generations earlier, nor the formalities that would take place aboard the battleship USS *Missouri* four decades later. Desultory prosecutions of black sheep and bad apples had replaced an intense debate about what empire was doing to the moral fiber of American soldiers—and by extension to America itself. Meanwhile, none of the debate's participants gave much thought to the Philippine Scouts. Filipino soldiers—whether Scouts or the quasi-military policemen of the Constabulary—were marked as outsiders to citizenship, deemed "savage" in their methods of soldiering, harshly regulated by military institutions, and rarely protected by military justice. They became the scapegoats the Roosevelt administration had been looking for. Even as armed Filipinos found their racial status exempted them from laws of war that Americans claimed to uphold, the US Army folded their exceptionality into its rules of engagement.[31]

By 1904, the number of US troops in the Philippines had dropped dramatically from its peak of 71,000 in December 1900 to something closer to 13,000. "We have only a big job of policing on our hands," the *Manila Times* reported, and indeed, the colonial government devoted its energies to criminal investigation and political surveillance, wielding the weapons of war as they did so. Taft's colonial administration adopted a Reconcentration Act in June 1903 authorizing the Constabulary in areas "infested . . . with ladrones or outlaws . . . to order that the residents . . . be temporarily brought" to new locations. A tactic of counterinsurgency masquerading as humanitarian aid, reconcentration moved as many as 450,000 people in 1903, after the war was technically over.[32]

With all the powers of both the army and the police, and hundreds of Filipino informants paid out of the Information Division's secret budget, the colonial regime permeated public life in the Philippines. Between 1903 and 1908, Manila police and the Philippine Constabulary arrested nearly 65,000 people, about a fifth of Manila's residents, and while not all were charged or imprisoned, all had felt America's power. The Philippine Commission made it a crime "to advocate . . . the independence of the Philippine Islands," and further legislation outlawed secret societies, regulated the press, and forbade display of the flag of the Philippine Republic. Struggles over authority, violence, and politics would now be played out in police stations and courtrooms rather than on the battlefield.[33]

Peace had come at an astonishing cost. Historians will never agree on the number of the dead, but they all acknowledge the devastation. The US Army recorded 4,200 American soldiers killed and 2,800 wounded. The most commonly cited (if necessarily imprecise) figures for Filipino deaths are between 15,000 and 20,000 soldiers killed, and between 100,00 and 300,000 civilians either killed or sent to early graves by the scorched-earth tactics that starved many out of their homes and destroyed their livelihoods. All this weighed on the mind of Mary Brooke, a seventy-year-old woman from Metuchen, New Jersey, who traveled to the Philippines in 1903 with her son-in-law, a civilian colonial official. Writing several years later, she recounted their visit to a beautiful mountaintop in the hills of Luzon, a site where just a few years earlier American soldiers had killed the revolutionary general Gregorio del Pilar. "His body was stripped of clothing and lay unburied in the sun for four days. Can we blame them if, in their hearts, they are unforgiving?"[34]

WHETHER THE WAR WAS OVER OR JUST HIDDEN, THE TASK NOW AT hand was governing and defending the Philippines. American officials sometimes embraced the acquisition of an extensive territorial empire, trumpeting their new colonies in Puerto Rico, Guam, Hawai'i, the Canal Zone, and the Philippines as model laboratories for good governance. But in practice, the Philippines was not much of a model. Some officials learned Spanish, itself spoken only by a small minority of Filipinos, and a handful learned Philippine languages, particularly missionaries. But most Americans contentedly tucked themselves away in English-speaking enclaves, kept their eyes on any chance for personal enrichment, and passed tropical afternoons at the Manila Polo Club. As scandals plagued the colonial government, officials found reason to showcase the achievements of the Philippine Scouts and Constabulary. In 1904, Roosevelt and Taft, the new Secretary of War, even sent the Scouts to the Louisiana Purchase Exposition at St. Louis, Missouri.[35]

Pacific service offered opportunities for young officers: years later, Admiral Yates Stirling looked back at the Philippines as "the most beneficial, if not the most exciting, episode of my younger career." Officers moved back and forth between temporary base camps, the US Army headquarters at Fort Santiago in the heart of Old Manila, and Fort McKinley, a massive base built from scratch on the city's outskirts. Military men and their wives gathered at the waterfront Manila Hotel, which one American traveler recalled as "all that a hotel built in the tropics should be, cool and comfortable, with wide eaves and high ceilings." In the summers they left Manila's heat and typhoon rains, or their provincial outposts, for thirty days in summer quarters at the hill station of Baguio, which aspired to be, as colonial official Charles Elliott put it in 1909, "a regular Adirondack mountain camp."[36]

Enlisted men, on the other hand, generally viewed the Philippines as a hardship post. Many lived in isolated military stations in rural areas surrounded by what one guidebook complained of as "dirty shops and indolent people." A substantial number, though, stayed on after their enlistments ended, especially those who settled down with Filipina women. Relations between American soldiers and Filipina women were the subject of ongoing comment and controversy. While the Army turned a blind eye to soldiers who maintained a *querida*, or mistress, off base, officers frowned on men who actually married them, and some refused to allow those men to reenlist. As they shouldered the simultaneous burdens of household labor and sexual companionship, the women themselves navigated a fraught landscape of coercion and opportunity.[37]

Armed resistance to American rule had by no means disappeared, particularly in the Moro Province, which made up of part of the island of Mindanao and the Sulu archipelago in the southernmost Philippines. Most Moro Province residents were Muslims, whom the Spanish had long before dubbed *Moros*, or moors, the same term they used for the Muslims of southern Iberia. The region had never been fully incorporated into the Spanish colony; indeed, the United States initially concluded a separate treaty with Muhammad Jamalul Kiram, the Sultan of Sulu, in August 1899. In the summer of 1902, when President Theodore Roosevelt proudly announced the end of hostilities in the Philippines, he excepted "the country of the Mohammedan Moros, where the conditions were wholly different." The Roosevelt and Taft administrations—and the US military itself—thought the region should remain under direct military rule, which it did until 1913.[38]

President Roosevelt initially sent to Mindanao Major General Leonard Wood, the public face of the post-1898 Cuban occupation and acknowledged within the Army as America's leading authority on military governance. The charismatic Wood was a swashbuckling military man with a stocky build, ruddy complexion, and piercing blue eyes. Born in Massachusetts in 1860 and trained as a surgeon, Wood had joined the Army during its years of frontier "Indian fighting." He commanded the Rough Riders in Cuba, where his gruff masculinity and love of football (Wood had been a coach at Georgia Tech in 1893) appealed to the young Theodore Roosevelt. The close relations between the two men would last until TR's death.

The American soldiers Wood commanded were reluctant to serve in Mindanao. Some, like an Arkansas volunteer, resented "the monotony of seeing no one but dirty, greasy, Moro men, and the strain of the constant watching." Oregon volunteer Mark Bocek joined the Army in 1909 after "I seen a beautiful poster there, nice uniform and palm trees." A butcher, Bocek spent eighteen months in the Philippines working with civilian laborers. "We had three Moros to help us," he recalled, although he did not remember them fondly. "They was mean." The Moro Province's new military governor began by burning houses and crops. To fill the provincial treasury he introduced the *cedula*, or head tax, which for centuries Spanish authorities had been too fearful to collect from the Moros. Wood was exacerbating the conflicts he had been sent to quell.[39]

Wood's troops and the Moros faced off repeatedly, with devastating results at the mountaintop settlement of Bud Dajo, where a March 1906 battle left as many as a thousand Filipinos gunned down by machine gun fire, among them women, children, and other civilians. When news reached the United States—along with photographs of the massacre sent home by American soldiers—another brief flare-up of anti-imperialism ensued. "Brutality has been rewarded, humanity has been punished," moaned Boston reformer Moorfield Storey. Luke Wright, now the governor-general, awarded Wood a commendation, and Rowland Thomas, an American soldier, told readers in Boston that Bud Dajo "was merely a piece of public work such as the army has had to do many times in our own west."[40]

Among the perpetrators of the Bud Dajo massacre were the Philippine Scouts. Beginning in 1903, the Army began recruiting Moros into the Scouts and Constabulary, although it did so with a dose of trepidation about their loyalty. Once again, the "Moro Constabulary"—distinguished from other constables by their fezzes instead of wide-brimmed hats—proved useful in establishing order and helped Americans challenge the authority of the traditional *datus*, or chiefs. James Harbord, a colonel in the Constabulary, boasted of the civilizing influence of Constabulary service. "He is a marked man among his own people, well dressed, with money in his pocket, knows a little English, is admired by the women of his race, and is an object of pride to a horde of wild relatives in his native village." Leonard Wood had authorized the recruitment of a few dozen Scouts and Constables in 1903; after he left the Moro Province in late 1906, his successors expanded their ranks into the thousands.[41]

A few years after returning to the United States, Wood became chief of staff of the US Army. The position was a new one, and a sign of how America's Pacific commitments were remaking its military institutions. Thanks to the General Staff Act of 1903, masterminded by Secretary of War Elihu Root, the Army would now have a chief of staff, in control of both ordinary soldiers in the field and Army bureaucrats in Washington, tasked with long-term planning and grand strategy, and answering to the civilian Secretary of War. Nelson Miles, the commanding general and until that moment the most powerful figure in the Army, thought the general staff was "utterly subversive to the interests of the military establishment" because it would leave the final decisions about war in the hands of politicians rather than career soldiers. Miles fought Root at every step of the way—in fact, the men's struggles over the general staff proposal had been part of what prompted Miles to leak information about Philippine atrocities in the spring of 1902. Once again, Root came out on top, all but forcing Miles into retirement in August 1903.[42]

Some of the Army's battles were fought internally, but others were waged against the US Navy. Naval officers sailed under the sway of Alfred Thayer Mahan, particularly *The Influence of Sea-Power upon History*, published in 1890 while Mahan was an instructor at the Naval War College. Mahan had retired in 1895 to pursue his writing and hobnob with admiring politicians, and played only a minor role in post-1898 affairs, but consensus held that the Navy needed more men and more ships, and more of both stationed in Asia. Reforms moved more slowly, as efforts to coordinate the Navy's eight different bureau chiefs revealed underlying divisions. Reformers depicted "Old Navy" types as selfish protectors of bureaucratic turf, while traditionalists warned that a massive expansion of the navy would militarize American society and turn temporary colonial victories into a permanent global empire.

Both the Army and the Navy assumed the United States would remain in the Philippines—and the Pacific—for the foreseeable future. Staying there meant building military and naval bases, but the type and location depended on what kind of Asian future planners imagined for the United States. Initial proposals called for small coaling stations to support Navy ships and aid American commerce with China. The China market captured imperialists' imaginations in 1898, but when measured in cold hard cash it proved fairly small, and detouring to the Philippines for coal wasn't going to help. As the Pacific changed, and more specifically, as Japan grew more powerful, US plans for temporary coaling stations quickly gave way to dreams of large facilities to support its armies. The Philippines' location—tucked in Southeast Asia between the British, the French, and the Dutch empires—was not strategically propitious for a future conflict with Japan, but it would have to do. Temporary sites of military conquest became permanent installations.

Army and Navy planners had to decide where to build bases in the Philippines. Two options competed: a naval station at Subic Bay, on the South China Sea about eighty miles northwest of Manila near the fishing village of Olongapo, or an armed fortress on Corregidor Island in Manila Bay itself. Geography, interservice rivalry, and competing visions of the US role in the world shaped the debate. The Navy favored Subic, which featured a deepwater port and was surrounded on three sides by mountains, far not only from Manila Bay's muddy waters but from Manila's murky politics. From his position at the head of the Navy's General Board, Admiral George Dewey defended Subic vigorously. "Every dollar available," he wrote, "ought rather to be spent at Olongapo."[43]

The Army, by contrast, favored the fortification of Manila Bay. They were particularly enchanted by the defense capabilities of the small island of Corregidor, located at the mouth of the bay twenty-six miles west of the capital city. The Spanish had maintained positions at Corregidor since 1795, and few in the Army doubted the defensive potential of a place they started calling the "Gibraltar of the East." Whoever holds Manila, Leonard Wood wrote, "will, in the eyes of the world, hold the Philippines, whatever happens elsewhere." Manila was the "one place in the Philippines where we can keep our flags up and maintain ourselves," warning penny-pinching legislators that it would be far cheaper to defend the Philippines than to reconquer it.[44]

The debate was insurmountable because both the Navy and the Army needed something from one another. If the Philippines' main defense were to be a naval base at Subic Bay, the Navy would need the Army to defend the mountainous jungle territory around it, and the Army balked at that nearly impossible assignment. If the defense were based at Corregidor, then the Navy would have to locate its main fleet at nearby Cavite, a decidedly inferior port. The Navy objected not only to Cavite's shallow waters, but also to their own second-class status in this plan, which would leave the Navy poorly situated to engage in "blue-water" actions against other imperial powers on the high seas.[45]

In 1904, the solution became clear: Filipino revolutionaries no longer posed a threat, but the German and British navies did—perhaps not in Manila Bay, but certainly along the nearby China coast. Roosevelt sided with the Navy and encouraged construction at Subic. "If we are not to have that station," he wrote in February 1904, "then we should be manly enough to say that we intend to abandon the Philippines at once." The Subic Bay "naval reservation" created jobs for Olongapo's workers and linked their economic interests and political sympathies to the Navy. Construction cut down on the shrimp harvest, and dredging of local swamps destroyed rice cultivation, making it all but impossible to eke out a living through fishing or farming. Because Navy regulations banned the sale of alcohol on naval bases, bars and dram shops opened up in nearby Olongapo, and brothels followed soon thereafter. Municipal authorities promptly placed a tax on liquor, which allowed Olongapo to build better schools and facilities than other communities in the area. But early policies laid the foundation for Olongapo's dependence on an entertainment and service industry that dominated city life for the rest of the century.[46]

Most American observers ignored the base debate as an interservice quarrel. Congress, intent on reining in military expenses after the Philippine-American War, slashed budgets for both the Army and the Navy. That changed quickly after 1905, when Japan scored a stunning victory over the Russian Empire in the Russo-Japanese War, altering America's views on the Pacific overnight. Strategists who had previously wondered whether Germany or Britain might seize the Philippines pondered Japan's intentions instead. "Japan is now superior to us in the Pacific Ocean, and can take the islands whenever she wants them," fretted Leonard Wood in a December 1905 letter to Theodore Roosevelt. Japan's victory drew the attention of Filipino nationalists as well. American observers assumed—and feared—it would embolden Filipinos. News reports assured Americans that "intelligence officers are carefully observing the attitude of the native elements" for evidence of collusion with Japan. More often than not, Filipino independence advocates noted Japan's recent colonization efforts in Taiwan and Korea and watched its military ambitions with trepidation.[47]

General anxieties became intense fears in 1907 when some Americans—particularly naval officers in the Pacific—believed that the United States and Japan were about to go to war. In October 1906, in the wake of the San Francisco earthquake, the city's school board announced that Japanese children would henceforth be required to attend segregated schools for Chinese migrants. A diplomatic controversy ensued, and although it was never quite threatening enough to constitute a "war scare," President Roosevelt did ask the War Department to draw up plans for a potential war with Japan. On June 27, 1907, cabinet members and military officers met with the president at his home in Oyster Bay, New York, and agreed to fortify existing garrisons in the Philippines. Roosevelt ordered the Navy to move supplies for 10,000 soldiers to Subic and to fortify the hills around Olongapo. In Manila, Major General Leonard Wood received instructions urging him to proceed "as quietly as possible and without ostentations, so as to avoid it being inferred either at home or abroad that preparations are being made for war."[48]

Roosevelt's decision in 1907 to move troops and weapons out of Manila to defend the naval base at Subic angered the Army. That fall, Roosevelt heard complaints from William Howard Taft—now back in Washington and serving as Secretary of War—and from General Leonard Wood, who warned that if "Manila is lost we shall lose not only all prestige but also very largely the support and confidence of the Filipinos. We cannot afford to abandon Manila; it must be held." Roosevelt was convinced and switched his priorities from the Navy to the Army. Determined to defend the Philippines from Japan rather than use it to challenge European rivals, the president put Subic's expansion on hold while the Army set convict laborers to work in round-the-clock shifts fortifying Corregidor.[49]

Roosevelt, once the most vocal of imperialists, began singing a new tune. "The possession of the Philippines renders us vulnerable in Asia," he wrote Taft in August 1907. "The Philippines form our heel of Achilles." By the time he published his autobiography in 1913, Roosevelt would assert that "I do not believe that America has any special beneficial interest in retaining the Philippines." The full-throated jingoistic days of empire were over. In the end, both Subic and Corregidor lost the race to be America's premier Pacific post. That trophy went to Pearl Harbor in Hawai'i, which Theodore Roosevelt described in February

1908 as "the key to the Pacific Ocean," and which planners now imagined as the farthest outpost of America's defense perimeter. The flurry of construction in the western Pacific ground to a halt and instead workers in Hawai'i began dredging Pearl Harbor for America's largest steel ships.[50]

As US War Department planners mapped hypothetical conflicts, they bound them with different colored covers for each imagined enemy: Red for Britain, Black for Germany, Orange for Japan. There was even a War Plan Brown, which planned America's response to an armed uprising in the Philippines. War Plan Orange, first begun in the summer of 1907 in the midst of the war scare, reflected the military's new sense that the Philippines represented a liability. An early plan tasked the Army with defending Corregidor for at least sixty days, long enough for American ships to arrive from the Atlantic and defeat the Japanese navy. But even that was deemed too much to expect; later plans grew increasingly defeatist, taking it for granted that Japanese troops would overwhelm the American garrison, particularly if the Army relied on Philippine Scouts. Revised plans reflected the hope that US troops in the western Pacific would hold on long enough either to drain Japan of its resources or give the Navy enough time to withdraw to Pearl Harbor and defend America's more valuable Hawaiian base. After 1907, no one—except Leonard Wood in his more optimistic moods—seriously thought the Philippines could be defended against Japan.[51]

At their meeting in Oyster Bay in June 1907, Roosevelt's impromptu military cabinet also decided that the threat of war required shifting most of the American fleet from the Atlantic to the Pacific. An observer noted that Roosevelt "wanted the movement of the fleet of battleships to partake of the character of a practice march" so that the deployment would not provoke war. That afternoon, the idea for the Great White Fleet was born. America's ships would travel to the Pacific not for war but in peace—hence they would be painted white rather than wartime gray. But if war came, they would be in the right place for it. On December 16, 1907, the fleet left Hampton Roads, Virginia, under the command of Admiral Robley "Fighting Bob" Evans, who announced he was "ready for a fight or a frolic." The aging admiral only made it halfway through the trip, and the dangers of war with Japan quickly dissipated. The Japanese even invited the fleet to visit, and although Roosevelt worried about "possible attack by fanatics," the ships arrived in Yokohama to cheering crowds. It was a voyage of pageantry and publicity, announcing America's intention to make this new era its first Pacific Century.[52]

The Great White Fleet had all the ships it needed to sail around the world, but it didn't have enough sailors to man them. Labor shortage—and the particular racial politics of the Japanese war scare—brought the first Filipinos into the US Navy. In 1907, the Navy was painfully short-handed. Congress steadily expanded the Navy's authorized strength from 13,500 sailors in 1898 to 44,000 in 1909, and the number of ships grew, too, but as the Navy built them, they were hard-pressed to find enough people to serve on them. Recruiting officers was one thing: in 1898, the Navy shortened the course of study at the Naval Academy by a year, and poured its young officers into the Pacific. "It should teach me a certain amount of self-reliance and confidence," wrote a young Chester Nimitz to his grandfather after he was assigned to command the gunboat USS *Panay* in 1907.[53]

Finding enlisted sailors was another matter altogether, particularly as ideas about who should serve changed. In the nineteenth century, Navy recruiters scoured coastal communities looking for men who already had seafaring experience; they enrolled, as one old salt recalled, any man who could "hand, reef, and steer." The Navy's ranks thus had plenty of noncitizen sailors in a service that reflected the multinational character of maritime life. By the early twentieth century, as America's economy shifted from oceans to factories, there were fewer recruits to be found along the coasts, and fewer of them than ever were citizens—in 1890, US citizens made up just 58 percent of the Navy's enlisted ranks. The Navy continued signing up immigrants, but reluctantly. A generation earlier, Civil War admiral David Dixon Porter worried that "these men shipped for money. They had no sentiment for our flag or nationality." Porter's solution, which slowly took hold by the turn of the twentieth century, was to recruit in country towns, signing up young white men, many of whom had never seen the ocean, some of whom didn't even know how to swim.[54]

Sailors' pay compared poorly with other working-class jobs, so financial incentives wouldn't do the trick. Recruiters turned to other techniques. "The men we must have enlist largely from a spirit of adventure, a desire to see the world, stimulated by a very considerable amount of patriotic pride," one officer wrote in 1909. Naval adventure stories, illustrated books depicting the Great White Fleet's round-the-world tour, and 150,000 billboard posters stimulated imaginations and enlistments. But still the Navy lacked sailors for all its new ships, and pressures in Congress (and within the service) to "Americanize" the Navy imposed new limits on service by aliens. The US Supreme Court had recently ruled that Filipinos were not US citizens but American "nationals," which was sufficient to allow Navy recruitment beginning in December 1907.[55]

The Navy drew on three main sources for its Filipino recruits: merchant seamen, men with experience as domestic servants, and civilian employees already working for the Navy in the Philippines. Filipinos had joined the Pacific's multinational seafaring forces for centuries, and in an archipelago of 7,000 islands, plenty had expertise in fishing and interisland navigation. The Navy enlisted Filipino seamen at ports all over the Pacific, and sometimes even the Atlantic: Quintin Gonzales signed up as a musician in Santo Domingo in the Caribbean. They also drew heavily from the Philippine Nautical School, first established by the Spanish in 1820 to train seamen for commercial vessels in the Philippines, and reestablished by the Americans soon after the end of the war.[56]

Domestic servants who had worked for Spanish colonial officials before 1898 often took employment with US military and naval officers. As a boy, Johnny Garcia remembered that "soldiers would give us a real meal if we would do some odd job for them, like cleaning muddy shoes, scrubbing uniforms and various other tasks." Not long after the end of the Philippine-American War, twenty-five-year-old Marcelo Canania left his home village for nearby Cebu City. "I began looking for work, because of my interest to speak English. . . . I work for officer in the army because that's mighty important." Canania continued in such positions in domestic work for American soldiers until leaving for the United States in 1917. Maria Garcia Cardoz, orphaned at sixteen, found a job as a nurse for the wife of an American officer. When he asked her to return to the United States with the couple, she leapt at the chance. "I was about 20 at the time and . . . the prospect of a trip to America thrilled me no little." Plenty then jumped from domestic service to direct enlistment in the Navy.[57]

Civilian employees at American naval stations also volunteered. By 1906, the Navy officially employed at least 3,000 Filipinos at Cavite Navy Yard, with many more in domestic, hospitality, and entertainment jobs just off base. The Navy's Surgeon General reported in 1907 that at Olongapo "demands for laundry work are now being partly satisfied by a Chinaman," but "many men have to send their clothes out to native washerwomen." A 1907 guidebook for visiting American sailors praised Cavite's employees. "The little brown men of the Islands . . . work over forges and lathes of modern workshops. Peace reigns supreme. The bloody part is forgotten." Wisconsin representative Theobald Otjen, who observed Filipino workers at Cavite in 1906, understood why: "The fact is, the Philippine workman . . . is as loath to lose his job as any other workman."[58]

Filipinos in the US Navy served almost exclusively in the messman branch, established in 1893 and responsible for feeding the sailors. Some were cooks and kitchen staff in the galleys, whereas others were stewards, personal servants assigned to every officer on board ship. They encountered a racial hierarchy that was very much in flux. In the eighteenth and nineteenth century, white and black sailors had mixed (albeit uneasily and unequally) on US ships, but at the dawn of the new century a move to whiten the Navy was under way. Some of that came as domestic practices of Jim Crow went to sea with white southern sailors—the Navy segregated its mess facilities in 1905. The change also reflected working conditions on board the Navy's new ships. Sail ships were rough-and-tumble experiences for everyone, and even the captains had calloused hands. In the new coal-fired steel ships, officers tended more toward gentility than saltiness. "Annapolis seems to make the worst kind of snobs of them," complained one anonymous letter in 1906. With class privilege came the assertion of white supremacy: in 1901, the Navy quietly told its recruiters to stop scouting the docks of the eastern seaboard for African American recruits.[59]

Chinese and Japanese men also served as messmen, particularly in the Navy's Asiatic Squadron, where Chinese stewards were prized as the best servants in the service. Citizenship requirements for enlistment exempted Chinese and Japanese aliens because of their "special value." In the era when the Navy paid little attention to the formal citizenship status of its sailors, their service raised few eyebrows, except when ships docked in the United States and Chinese sailors—who were barred by law from entry—had to remain on board. But a key shift in the Navy's racial makeup accompanied the voyage of the Great White Fleet, as Japanese stewards suddenly loomed as a security threat. Some feared subversion from within; others thought that Japan would make a political issue of the Japanese stewards' lowly status, just as they had done with the San Francisco school children. The Japanese were quickly transferred off the ships of the Great White Fleet before it left from

Hampton Roads on December 16, 1907. Five days earlier, new orders authorized the service of Filipinos in the messman branch. The order came so soon before departure that only two Filipino sailors joined the cruise, including Gaudencio Verceies, a twenty-two-year-old musician with "a restless disposition and a yearning to see the world," who quit his job in a Washington, DC, hotel to join the Navy that year.[60]

In 1907, there were just 397 Filipinos in a navy of 33,027; that same year counted 356 Chinese, 354 Japanese, and 1,484 African American sailors. By 1912, just five years later, the numbers of Chinese and Japanese had dropped to 258 and 210, respectively. African American enlistment stayed steady at 1,438—but since total Navy enlistment had increased from 33,027 to 47,515, the proportion of black sailors had declined. So had their work conditions, as the Navy steadily segregated them into bottom-rung positions. The vast majority of black sailors served in the messman branch; the rest shoveled coal in the sweat and danger of the boiler rooms. Meanwhile, between 1907 and 1912, the number of Filipinos in the Navy jumped from 397 to 1,125, and soon a hierarchy emerged among the messmen, with Filipinos dominating the steward positions in service to officers, and African Americans in the kitchens. The handful of remaining black petty officers found themselves transferred to landside jobs. "We knew that the end of a colored man being anything in the navy except a flunky had arrived," one recalled. America's new navy—and its Filipino sailors—proved increasingly critical to the defense of American interests in Asia.[61]

Rear Admiral Richard Wainwright observed in 1914 that "in holding the Philippines we are an Asiatic power, . . . provided we hold them strongly." Wainwright acknowledged that the United States could do little to defend the Philippines should the Japanese "throw a large force into the islands before our fleet could arrive." But having observed the Philippine Scouts, he thought that a "territorial army seems to me to be the solution of the problem," and he urged expansion of "native" forces. The cost "would not be great," and it "would be a valuable part of our educational system in the Philippines." Nothing, he noted, "could be better adapted to fit the native races for self-government than a short term of military training."[62]

The experiences of the Philippine Scouts, the Philippine Constabulary, and the first Filipino sailors in the Navy reflected three different paths to military training—and three different formulations of US power in the Pacific. None quite matched up with Admiral Wainwright's vision of Filipino military service as part of the colonial undertaking that President William McKinley called "benevolent assimilation." For the Scouts and the Constabulary, there was steady work and modest pay but no claim on equal treatment by Uncle Sam. Sailors toiling in kitchens and attending in ward rooms likewise found few chances for upward mobility in the Navy but saw the promise of geographic mobility outside it. By 1914, America's Filipino soldiers and sailors served a power transformed by more than a decade of colonial war: a government more thoroughly controlled from Washington and the executive branch, a nation more able (and more willing) to intervene by force in sovereign states without exercising formal control over them, an empire that mobilized colonized people into its armed forces without extending to them the privileges of citizenship. A nation, apparently, at ease with the contradictions of being an empire and a republic. The world war would test the assumptions and the exclusions of America's imperial army. It would also reveal just how incomplete the changes were that military reformers embarked on between 1898 and 1914. Among the military's color-coded scenarios was War Plan Black, which prepared the United States for war with Germany. But in April 1917, War Plan Black had not been updated in years, and as world events brought the United States into war, no one even thought to take it down from the shelf.[63]

CHAPTER THREE

PACIFIC OUTPOST

1914–1934

IN SEPTEMBER 1914, SHERMAN KISER, A SECOND LIEUTENANT in the Philippine Scouts, established a Boy Scout troop in Zamboanga, one of the archipelago's southernmost and most tropical cities. In "the shade of a grove of cocoanut palms," he gathered the city's "brown-skinned lads" to hear his "description of a Boy Scout and an exposition of Scout laws." Kiser then clad his eager recruits in the "khaki Scout uniform of lightweight material" and campaign hats. "The 'little brown brothers' were now ready for the Scout oath," a visiting journalist observed, marveling that "they had become clean little Scouts." In the farthest corner of the US empire, one of its junior officers was turning the sons of America's former enemies into its newest supporters.[1]

But Lieutenant Kiser's scout troop was short-lived. Later that year, fear gripped American settlers in the Philippines as news broke that supporters of former revolutionary general Artemio Ricarte had infiltrated the Philippine Scouts and were planning a revolt. "The Viper" was the last unreconstructed revolutionary leader left from the days of 1898, living in exile in Japan and calling for "the immediate restoration of the Philippine Republic by whatever means." On December 24, 1914, a small group of Ricartistas launched an ill-fated attempt to overthrow the American regime by firing on police from a hideout in Manila's Botanical Gardens. The colonial government crushed the Ricartista plot and tightened its fist, ordering the Philippine Constabulary to keep close watch on weapons and ammunition coming into the country.[2]

In Zamboanga, Lieutenant Kiser would have been told that "all semi-military organizations"—including the Boy Scouts—were now required to apply to the governor-general's office for recognition, because "people have been misled by their marches and drills." Colonial officials also sought to dispel rumors that the Philippine Scouts were disloyal. Quite the contrary: the trustworthy Scouts had acted as *agents provocateurs* to provoke and undermine the Ricartistas. In the confusing events of late 1914—when the Philippine Scouts could be trusted but the Boy Scouts could not—Pacific partnership revealed an awkward juxtaposition of empire and republic. The Boy Scouts used the trappings of American military culture to train Filipinos for citizenship and eventual independence. The Philippine Scouts existed to suppress it. This was not the only such moment of confusion. Just a few years after requiring the Boy Scouts to register as a dangerous organization, the colonial government recruited them to sell Liberty Loan war bonds to support the First World War. And in a further twist, one of the bond drive's most enthusiastic customers in June 1917 was Emilio Aguinaldo, the defeated commander of the Philippine revolutionary army, who, unlike Artemio Ricarte, was said to be "among the first Filipinos to subscribe."[3]

As both Filipinos and Americans tested the strength of their ties, war in Europe and a growing rivalry with Japan bound them ever more closely together. It was not supposed to be that way: the 1916 Jones Act promised the Philippines eventual independence, and Filipinos formed the Philippine National Guard, with the aim of replacing the Scouts and Constabulary with a fully trained army for a sovereign nation. Philippine independence slipped out of reach before it was ever seriously pursued. As US military officers confronted the problem posed by Japan, Americans found they needed Filipino soldiers and sailors more than ever. They would have to recruit them on new terms. War generated a new social contract that linked military service to rights, benefits, and citizenship—and no longer merely wages. Filipino soldiers marched away from Matthew Batson's camp in Macabebe and toward an uncertain future in Asia.

Woodrow Wilson's election in 1912 heralded a fresh start to America's Pacific policy. Running in a three-way race against Theodore Roosevelt, the hero of San Juan Hill, and William Howard Taft, the former governor-general of the Philippines, Wilson represented an alternative. On the campaign trail, he advocated Philippine independence to appease two key constituencies—southern Democrats and progressive anti-imperialists—who agreed on little else but the error of William McKinley's imperial ambitions. In a postelection speech in his hometown of Staunton, Virginia, the Democrat announced that while "the Philippines are our present frontier, . . . we . . . are presently, I hope, to deprive ourselves of that frontier."[4]

The new president began by appointing Francis Burton Harrison as governor-general. A thirty-nine-year-old New York congressman of blue-blooded southern heritage (Harrison was the son of a Confederate officer) and a Fifth Avenue playboy millionaire with little military experience, Harrison must have struck the dour teetotaler missionaries and military martinets who had made the colonization of the Philippines their lives' work as a naïve amateur. The old Philippine hands had not expected a steady backbone under Harrison's tailored linen suits.

In his inaugural address in Manila in October 1913, Harrison told the audience that "every step we take will be taken with a view to the ultimate independence of the Islands." Republicans in Congress and the American community in Manila soon worried that Harrison would ruin their balance sheets, pull the US out of the Philippines, and hand the islands over to the Japanese navy. The vocal assault on Harrison by pro-imperialists ended up winning Harrison support among Filipino independence advocates. So did his actions, especially a policy of Filipinization that placed Filipinos in colonial government positions.[5]

Harrison also proposed ending the Moro Province's unique status under direct US military rule rather than civilian control by the colonial government. Policy toward the predominantly Muslim region urgently needed reform in 1913. Resistance had continued there long after peace came to the rest of the Philippines, with tensions inflamed by the disastrous efforts of the province's most recent military governor, Brigadier General John J. Pershing, who had left the Philippines just weeks after Harrison's inauguration.

Pershing had arrived in the southern Philippines four years earlier, in November 1909. The general was forty-nine years old, stocky in stature and prickly by nature, a meticulous dresser, the veteran of years of "Indian fighting" in the American West (much of it in command of a regiment of African American "Buffalo Soldiers") and three years of prior service in the Moro Province. As a youth, Pershing applied to West Point to get away from his hardscrabble upbringing in Laclede, Missouri, and graduated in 1886 near the top of the class. Army brass soon saw his potential: in 1906, after his first tour of duty in Mindanao, Pershing was promoted from captain to brigadier general, leapfrogging over 862 other officers. The promotion was dogged by controversy, both because it followed so soon after his marriage to the daughter of the chair of the Senate's Military Affairs Committee and because of rumors that Pershing had—as many American soldiers did in the Philippines—taken up with a *querida*, or mistress, and fathered two children by her.[6]

Back in Mindanao, violent assaults on Muslim Filipinos' culture continued—although despite later rumors, Pershing never soaked US Army bullets in pigs' blood nor condoned such action by subordinates. But Pershing did decide that it was time "to teach the Moros the meaning of government," and in September 1911 he ordered a disarmament policy that banned not only firearms but any edged weapon over fifteen inches long. Muslim Filipinos objected for political reasons and economic ones—Pershing handed down his order at harvest time, and his ban extended to agricultural tools.[7]

Pershing faced bitter resistance, which—just as it had for his predecessor Leonard Wood—culminated in an ugly mountaintop massacre, this time at Bud Bagsak in June 1913. About 1,000 Moro Filipinos on the island of Jolo had fled to the mountaintop settlement several months earlier, and the US military feared those gathered at Bud Bagsak were plotting the slaughter of Americans. By February 1913, Pershing had a plan that called for a dramatic exercise of force and a restrictive press policy. He worried nonetheless that "loss of life among innocent women and children would be very great."[8]

Civilians fled the mountaintop in advance of the assault, but not all of them. Then, beginning on June 11, 1913, seven companies of Philippine Scouts—chosen specifically to include Muslim men recruited in Mindanao—attacked Bud Bagsak. The 51st Company of Scouts scaled "the sheer side of the mountain by climbing hand over hand on bejunco vines for a hundred feet or more." Frustrated by what he later reported as "very tenacious" resistance, Pershing abandoned his "Moro-against-Moro" approach, added US Army regulars to the force, and even took up arms on the front line himself. By June 15, American forces had lost fifteen men in battle but gunned down close to five hundred Moros, including women and children. Resistance at Bud Bagsak fell silent.[9]

Pershing reduced troop strength in the southern islands, handed daily command to the Scouts and Constabulary, and left the Philippines in December 1913, just six months after the massacre at Bud Bagsak. The new governor's conciliatory Moro policy was far better received than Pershing's lessons in the meaning of government, and violent agitation for independence or local self-control faded away as anticolonialism took a more institutional form.

For all practical purposes, there was only one political party in the Philippines, the Nacionalistas, led by Sergio Osmeña, the party head and the Speaker of the Philippine Assembly. His younger colleague and rival Manuel Quezon headed to Washington in 1909 as one of the Philippines' nonvoting resident commissioners in the House of Representatives. (To this day, US territorial representatives cannot vote in Congress.) Quezon, later described by one observer to be "as dapper as Jimmy Walker and as shrewd as sin," was a skilled politician who had ascended the ranks of the colonial government. The young lawyer joined the revolution in 1898 and served briefly as an aide to Emilio Aguinaldo. Imprisoned by the Americans during the war, Quezon quickly turned and joined the Constabulary as an informant. Not long after—handpicked for the ballot by Philippine Constabulary officer James Harbord—Quezon won the governorship of Tayabas province on his way to a seat in the national assembly. Charismatic, magnanimous, and always impeccably dressed, the thirty-one-year-old Quezon made an impression in Washington far beyond his years or his (at that time) limited English. But he displayed his faults as well: a preference for backroom deals at odds with his public statements and a touch of impetuosity. Quezon himself admitted that "I can't make up my own mind and follow it for five minutes."[10]

Quezon and Osmeña viewed Woodrow Wilson with guarded optimism, the same approach they took toward William Atkinson Jones, the powerful chair of the US House Insular Affairs Committee. Supporters of Philippine independence included southern Democrats like Jones (a Virginia Democrat and a veteran of the Confederate Army), who had never been enthusiastic about the Philippine colony or friendly to the Filipinos. Representative George Burgess of Texas announced on the floor of Congress that if the Japanese wanted the Philippines, "I would offer them to them as a Christmas present." Mississippi senator John Sharp Williams wanted "to get rid of the Philippine Islands and . . . did not care what happened to them."[11]

Military and strategic issues were on everyone's minds. The outbreak of the First World War in Europe in August 1914 heightened uncertainties about the Philippines' status, and Artemio Ricarte's uprising that December exacerbated them. Woodrow Wilson urged action on the Jones bill, concerned about Japan but tactfully citing only "the general world situation." For their part, Republicans insisted that Filipinos were not ready for self-government and that world events required the United States to keep its Pacific colony, not to release it. Ohio's Warren Harding won national attention for a Senate speech in January 1916: "I do not want it said that this great nation, aspiring to a place in the councils of the world, . . . is so miserably afraid that it wants to cast aside some of its possessions to avoid some of the dangers of war." Not all were so eloquent. Elihu Root, now a senator from New York, dismissed Jones's proposal as "chuckle-headed."[12]

Congress finally passed the Jones Act, which did not grant independence, but promised it "as soon as a stable government can be established therein." That unspecified future date disappointed Filipino nationalists and American anti-imperialists alike, and set the stage for ongoing conflicts over the meaning of stability. When Woodrow Wilson signed the Jones Act on August 29, 1916, some 40,000 gathered in Manila to celebrate, and Manuel Quezon returned heroically from Washington. A new bicameral legislature with expanded male suffrage convened in October. Members reelected Sergio Osmeña as Assembly Speaker and installed Manuel Quezon as president of the new Philippine Senate.[13]

Woodrow Wilson believed the promise of independence for the Philippines would appease activists in Manila and southern segregationists in Washington, and might even improve relations with Japan.

It certainly didn't mean an end to US imperial actions abroad. During his first administration, Wilson oversaw military interventions in Haiti, the Dominican Republic, Nicaragua, Cuba, and Mexico, operating freely in regions where the United States faced fewer threats from imperial rivals. The world war rendered Philippine independence an ambivalent prospect just as Filipinos saw its first possibilities. The Jones Act was an empty promise on the Americans' part, but it was a promise nonetheless. Filipinos intended to hold them to it.

World War I changed the two nations' relations because it transformed the US military. First, it remade the US Army, as wartime legislation created a bigger, more flexible, and more federally controlled force. In June 1916, Wilson signed the National Defense Act, authorizing a standing army of 175,000 soldiers, and giving the president greater authority over the state militias of the National Guard. Later that year, he signed a Naval Act that aimed to build "a navy second to none" through the construction of over 150 new vessels. Then war mobilization emptied the US Army's Philippine barracks as call-ups quickly summoned the Army's only experienced troops to France. Americans who remained on post in the Philippines after 1917 looked with envy at fellow officers who were closer to the front and the promotions that combat promised. The number of American troops in the Philippines declined from 13,795 in 1917 to 5,255 just two years later, a large fraction of them African American soldiers with the 9th Cavalry. The Philippine Scouts expanded from 5,702 to 8,159 in the same years, extending finally from battalions to regiments, but they hardly made up the difference.[14]

The war also brought the generation of 1898 from the jungles of Luzon to the fields of Flanders. John J. Pershing had left the Philippines while Europe was still at peace; a few years later in France he tapped former Philippine comrades as advisers and subordinates. James Harbord had helped establish the Philippine Constabulary in Mindanao and Sulu as a young Marine officer in 1903. He duly impressed his boss, who remembered the young officer and in May 1917 appointed Harbord chief of staff of the American Expeditionary Forces (AEF). The Constabulary's founding commander, Henry Allen, brought his policing experience to bear as the commanding officer of the American occupation of the Rhine after the war. Even Bishop Charles Henry Brent, the former Episcopal bishop of the Philippines who had converted Pershing to the Episcopal Church, became head of the AEF's chaplain corps. By contrast, Major General Leonard Wood, who had once held Pershing's post in the Moro Province and also jockeyed for the top role in the AEF, languished as the commanding officer of a military training camp in Kansas.[15]

Officers of the Philippine Constabulary left for France as well. In 1917, nearly the entire officer corps resigned, in part because a year earlier, in a deliberate effort to push American officers out, Governor-General Harrison had slashed the Constabulary officers' wage supplement. Now military necessity gave Harrison the political opportunity he wanted, and he replaced the departing American officers with Filipinos. By the war's end, 256 of the Constabulary's 358 officers were Filipinos, among them Licerio Geronimo, a former revolutionary soldier and the man who had killed General Henry Lawton in 1899, and Rafael Crame, the Constabulary's new commander. As a young man, Crame had served with the Spanish colonial army, then briefly joined the revolution before signing up in 1902 for the Constabulary, where he made his name gathering intelligence for the PC's Information Division. The Constabulary would now be primarily in Filipino hands, but ones loyal to the colonial government and bound to support US interests as if they were their own. Two decades of colonial counterinsurgency had generated an institution that blurred the line between soldiering and policing.[16]

Even before the US entered the war, the Philippine economy boomed, with expanded markets for basic commodities such as rice and sugar, and skyrocketing demand for copra, a coconut oil used to generate the glycerin in the explosives used on the western front. Some of those profits went to buy Liberty Loan war bonds; in Manila, the *Philippine Review* boasted of Filipino participation in loan drives, calling it a sign of "unflinching devotion and loyalty to their Mother Country." War changed not only the colonial economy, but colonial politics as well. Independence activists soon saw an opening by making the most of Filipino support for the war effort.[17]

Filipinos attended Liberty Loan parades in Manila, and they also joined them in the continental United States. At New York City's July Fourth parade in 1918, the Filipino contingent included a marching band of sailors from the Brooklyn Navy Yard, along with two hundred civilian Filipino New Yorkers on a float decorated with a "palmy landscape" designed to show "the Filipino people looking to the United States as the exponent of liberty and democracy." When Jesus Garcia died of leprosy at the Salinas County Farm in California and left a bequest of $140.95 to the government "in order that President Wilson . . . might succeed in bringing everlasting peace," Wilson noted in private correspondence that it was "one of the most touching letters I ever received," and publicly expressed "gratitude that the simpler people . . . in the Philippines should have acquired in this short time such a friendly sentiment towards this country."[18]

Jesus Garcia was one of a small number of Filipinos who migrated to the United States in the years after the Philippine-American War. By April 1917, a few hundred students attended American colleges and some farm laborers settled on the West Coast. The war accelerated this trend: a group of California growers confronted by a labor shortage recruited Filipino contract workers to replace men heading off to war. But in 1917, by far the largest community of Filipinos outside the Philippines was in Hawai'i. Sugar planters began contracting Filipino laborers from the Ilocos region in 1906, and the colonial government in

Manila depended on hefty recruiting taxes the sugar companies paid. War pinched the labor supply in Hawai'i at the same time demand for sugar boomed, drawing thousands to Hawai'i. The islands' Filipino population multiplied from 2,361 in 1910 to 21,031 just a decade later.[19]

Whether in Hawai'i or California, Filipino men who lived in US territory outside the Philippines found themselves subject to the Selective Service Act. The May 1917 law required every draft-age man in the "territorial United States" to register. Because nearly all of the Filipino migrants in Hawai'i were men between the ages of eighteen and forty-five, they were disproportionately represented in initial Selective Service registrations, making up 49 percent of Hawai'i's. Class One, those immediately eligible for military duty. Most were soon exempted after sugar plantation work was deemed "necessary" to the war effort, but over the nineteen months of the war, as many as six thousand Filipinos joined or were drafted into the regular US Army—not the Philippine Scouts—and served together with other Americans. After September 1917, the Army made no effort to segregate Filipinos from other draftees, especially because, outside of Hawai'i, there were so few of them.[20]

Filipinos were as numerous in the US Navy, where America's domestic politics and its international ambitions combined to open a path to service by thousands of Filipino sailors. After two decades of naval construction overseen by Republicans, Woodrow Wilson appointed a Secretary of the Navy whose job was to rein in spending and, with it, imperial expansion. Josephus Daniels was a reformer, but not all of his ideas were wise. The puritanical secretary drew press attention for burning "a bushel of [recruiting] literature which showed young men going into tropical climates and associating with women half-dressed," for replacing grog with ice cream, and for trying (unsuccessfully) to require sailors to wear pajamas. Less visibly, Daniels dramatically increased the recruitment of Filipinos into the messman branch after 1917. His motivations reflected his southern proclivities: Daniels believed Filipinos would help eliminate African American sailors from the Navy. On August 4, 1919, Daniels codified an unwritten policy into law when he officially closed the door on new black sailors.[21]

Secretary Daniels's 1917 call for Filipino recruits "resulted in many Filipinos offering themselves at the recruiting station." One postwar writer estimated that "six thousand Filipino lads voluntarily enlisted in the American navy," and he quoted an unnamed source (probably a Manila newspaper) that noted these sailors were "so obedient, industrious and loyal that the navy department has adopted the policy of replacing with Filipinos all aliens on American warships." A postwar study of Filipino sailors at the Brooklyn Navy Yard revealed them to be uniformly young, unmarried, and educated at least through the primary school level. Most signed up in the Philippines, including Crisanto Guevara, "a Filipino of 30 years of age, weight 130 pounds, and with no physical defects," who wrote that after reading Daniels's announcement, "I did not hesitate a moment in volunteering . . . to defend the right of the noble American nation."[22]

When war began, seventeen-year-old Johnny Garcia lived on a small rice farm north of Manila. Then "came the war and the excitement of America entering it and the drive for recruits," Garcia recalled in a 1937 interview. His mother initially refused, "but when she finally learned that I could have part of my pay, about $20 a month sent home to her, she couldn't get me and my brother off fast enough." So many rushed to the Cavite Navy Yard to sign up that the Navy started assigning would-be stewards to positions (at paltry civilian wages) as domestic servants in the homes of American navy personnel in what it called a "training" program. Only the most reliable workers made it off the list and into the Navy, many of them handpicked by American officers about to ship out. For most young Filipinos, getting into the US Navy required social capital, education, and personal connections.[23]

Officers gave each other advice on commanding messmen and stewards. K. C. McIntosh of the USS *Kansas* gave his fellow officers point-by-point instructions on selecting and training messmen. "Pick as your candidate a man with a sense of humor," he wrote in a 1919 service journal. "One must never forget," McIntosh observed, "that if the average mess attendant had a mentality above that of a normal ten-year-old, he would not be a mess-attendant." Discipline followed racial lines. While African American sailors "should be punished, if possible, in the presence of every other negro aboard ship," the Filipino "should be punished privately." Filipinos, for their part, soon learned—or learned to present—a genial and easygoing persona to satisfy white naval officers.[24]

In the 1910s and 1920s, the Navy limited the messman branch to 5 percent of the overall force, and Filipinos soon filled nearly all the positions. Kitchen work was grueling: the air was "surcharged with steam at least ten hours a day," as one officer observed. Strict discipline, language barriers, years away from home, and a rigid color bar made for solitary, even lonely lives. That did not stop men from signing up. Florentine Calabia, a cousin of the revolutionary leader Emilio Aguinaldo, left school at the age of fifteen to join the US Navy. "It is Calabia's ambition to go to Harvard," reported the *Los Angeles Times*, although at the time of his interview, Calabia was taking night classes while serving as a messman at the Navy's submarine base at San Pedro, California. Immanuel Tardez had two years' experience as a stevedore on the Manila waterfront when he joined the US Coast Guard as a messman in 1925. "Life about the boat was a joy compared to the squalor of my home in Manila." After a year and a half "chasing gun runners and dope smugglers off the Philippines," Tardez transferred to a ship heading back across the Pacific. "I was anxious to see something of the world and I thought that this would be a swell opportunity." Working as chief cook on a patrol boat off the coast of Seattle turned out to be less interesting than Tardez had expected. "I became so tired in fact that after six years in the service I did not re-enlist." But, he noted, "I came out of the service a full fledged American citizen . . . with over $800 in my pocket."[25]

Filipino elites took a different path into the Navy but also found their professional advancement reached a dead end. Beginning in 1916, four Filipinos a year attended the US Naval Academy in Annapolis, and two Filipino students enrolled annually at West Point. Because Filipinos were barred by race from the Navy's officer corps, and the Philippines had no distinct naval force, study at the US Naval Academy offered limited opportunities for Filipino advancement. Jose Emilio Olivares, the first Filipino graduate of Annapolis, graduated in 1923 with a commission he could not use. Some left without a uniformed position; others did what the West Pointers did and took commissions in the Philippine Scouts, although the Navy phased out even this option by 1931. Daniels's policies slowly started to have their intended effects. The Navy never kicked out its African American sailors, nor the Chinese or Japanese messmen who had preceded the Filipinos. As those men retired or left the service, the Navy simply replaced them with Filipinos. The slow purge continued: by 1932, of the Navy's 81,120 sailors, only 441 were African Americans, and 115 of those were members of a Navy band stationed in the US Virgin Islands.[26]

Navy life was not as glamorous as the recruiting posters had made it out to be. "My experiences in the navy during the war is nothing to think about," recalled Johnny Garcia. "There was plenty of work to do and . . . very little action." Garcia shared something else in common with other stewards, too, as he followed in their well-trod paths of migration. "I came to Los Angeles and am now working as a houseboy," he told an interviewer in 1937. So did Immanuel Tardez, who got a job as a cook for a Hollywood actor. "I get a great kick out of this," he admitted. "I would like to be in the movies but I think I had better stick to my job. . . . It is better to have a full stomach than to try and realize one's ambitions."[27]

Plenty of ordinary sailors, though, believed that Filipino naval service could be leveraged for more than a full stomach: namely, for US citizenship. The recruitment of Filipinos into the US Navy, along with

Selective Service policies that drafted Filipinos directly into the US Army, combined to make Filipinos' puzzling political status—neither citizens nor aliens but US "nationals"—visible both to drill sergeants and federal judges. Ever since 1790, naturalization as a US citizen had been restricted by law to "free white persons." After the Civil War, section 2169 of the Revised Statutes of the United States expanded that provision to accommodate "aliens of African nativity and . . . persons of African descent," which sounded inclusive but wasn't. Few black immigrants ever naturalized under the new clause, but it did bar Chinese and other Asians, which is exactly what it had been intended to do.[28]

To aid immigrant soldiers, a new law, the Naturalization Act of May 9, 1918, enabled immediate naturalization for men in uniform, and some 155,000 servicemen—nearly all of them recent European migrants—took advantage of the law. The act clarified the terms of citizenship for European immigrants but muddied them for Asian Americans. As written, the 1918 law offered immediate naturalization to "any alien" in service; but did that provision override existing laws excluding Asians on the basis of race? Veterans of Japanese ancestry led a legal charge to claim that the 1918 Act had effectively overturned the 1870 racial restrictions, but in *Toyota v. United States* (1925), the Supreme Court ruled definitively that the restrictions of section 2169 excluding Asians from naturalization trumped any wartime modifications.[29]

But there was one exception. Among the Naturalization Act's many provisions was one explicitly permitting the naturalization of any Filipino "who has enlisted or may hereafter enlist in the United States Navy or Marine Corps or the Naval Auxiliary Service, and who, after service of not less than three years, may be honorably discharged therefrom." Filipino sailors were quick to take advantage of the new law and beat a path between the Navy base at San Pedro, California, and the US Federal Courthouse in downtown Los Angeles. Among those making the journey were Carlos Pausa Treas, a twenty-six-year-old cabin steward who had joined the US Navy in Cavite in 1913, and

Jose Ricafrente, a musician also from Cavite. By 1919, Joaquin Ramirez Baltazar, a thirty-one-year-old cook with a decade's service at San Pedro, went by the name "John," perhaps a relief to the naturalization officer who tried three times to spell his name correctly on the form. Many sailors brought their wives with them. Marie Mores was born in Santa Barbara, California, and thus already a US citizen, but Margarita Llorente accompanied her husband, Juan, from the Philippines. While their spouses served at sea, navy wives built some of the first Filipino communities in the Navy towns of the continental United States.[30]

Filipino soldiers and sailors were unique among Asian American servicemen in having the right to naturalize. The new law also opened up for them a clear path from military service to US citizenship—something not available to the Scouts or the Constabulary. War challenged the world's imperial system and oriented the US Army away from colonial counterinsurgency to global domination, and, for Filipinos, firmly linked American citizenship to military service. The premise that the United States owed something to the colonial subjects who served under its flag presupposed a relationship different from the previous generation's guardianship of the white man's burden. This was, at last, a meaningful social contract. It was also the idea behind the Philippine National Guard.

As an unincorporated territory, the Philippines didn't have a branch of the National Guard. But on March 17, 1917, as war clouds gathered, the Philippine legislature authorized the formation of one. The proposed Philippine National Guard was Francis Burton Harrison's pride and joy. The governor-general believed it would serve as the cornerstone of his Filipinization policy, and Senate president Manuel Quezon likewise saw in the Guard the citizen-soldiers of an independent nation. The two men also hoped that President Wilson would federalize the Philippine National Guard, not only for political reasons, but an economic one: the Guard was going to cost a lot of money, and there was not enough in the colonial treasury to pay for it. Leaders encouraged ordinary Filipinos to enlist in the rank and file of the new Guard, and they hastened to add their own names to the list of the officer corps, which would mix both American and Filipino soldiers. Now two forces—the Guard and the Constabulary—promised advancement to Filipino officers. The Philippine Scouts, which continued to restrict its commissioned officer corps to white soldiers, seemed a remnant of the previous generation's racialized war of occupation.[31]

Many Filipinos also hoped the Guard would form the nucleus of a real army for an independent Philippines. After all, Quezon explained, the Jones Act made independence conditional on stability, and "no government can be stable without an army." The new force answered some practical questions. If independence came, the new Philippine Army would be unable to draw on the Philippine Scouts: Scouts were part of the US Army, and each soldier's enlistment with Uncle Sam expired on a different date, so transferring them en masse to a new force would be impossible. Nor would the Constabulary suffice: even if it often acted like an army, it was structured as a national police force, and if it transformed into an army, the new nation would then face a shortage of police. The Guard offered an ideal means to train thousands of new troops, both officers and ordinary foot soldiers, and by showing that Filipinos could defend their own nation, also represented a symbolic step toward independence. "The national guard is peculiarly a Filipino organization," boasted the *Philippines Free Press*.[32]

Manuel Quezon met with Woodrow Wilson at the White House in June 1917 to discuss the Guard, and the president expressed what Quezon later remembered as "unconcealed enthusiasm" for the new force, convinced that "sending the militia to the front would cause real surprise throughout Europe." In December, back in the Philippines, Quezon notified Wilson that 25,000 men stood "ready and anxious to fight under the American flag." Even some in the US Army expressed enthusiasm: Major General Hunter Liggett, then in command of the Philippine Department, promised the new soldiers 24,000 rifles, although he departed for France before delivering them. In a wartime oratory contest at the University of the Philippines College of Law, student Francisco Africa claimed that "with the organization of the *Philippine National Guard*, the world of the twentieth century sees among the list of its heroes a new type of warrior, noble and valorous—*The Filipino Soldier*." Africa was right: the Guard would make the Filipino soldier, as a citizen-soldier, a reality, and he would have a claim to stake after the war.[33]

Membership in the Guard was open to "any able-bodied man of good reputation between the ages of 18 and 45." The officer corps included both Americans and Filipinos, and plenty volunteered. At their head marched Francis Burton Harrison, who was appointed the major general of the Guard and proudly donned its uniform, spurs and all. Veterans of the Scouts or the Constabulary joined up as officers at ranks that had been barred to Filipinos when they served in the colonial forces. News of the force spread across the Pacific. "Under American officers who . . . understand those people," noted a Hawaiʻi newspaper, "we believe that a Filipino army would give a good account of itself in Europe, and we would like to see the experiment tried out." The *New York Times* suggested that since the soldiers "talk both Spanish and English"—which was only the case for the Guard's officers and not even very many of them—the Philippine National Guard "would be particularly useful for patrolling our Mexican border." That, in turn, would free American soldiers to fight in France. Bishop Brent agreed: the Guard would be unsuited for service in France "owing to the cold climate," but along the border "they could tell the Mexicans what the United States has done for them and their country, and, I believe, could become a great . . . peacekeeping force." Less concerned about the cold, others imagined Filipino troops joining the US intervention in Siberia, including Secretary of War Newton Baker, who wrote Wilson in July

1918 of his plans to send American and Filipino soldiers from the Philippines to Vladivostok. In August 1918, two regiments—of US Army regulars but not the Guard—left Manila for Russia.[34]

Despite their enthusiastic endorsement of Filipino service, military officers and Wilson administration officials hesitated when it came time to establish the Guard. Regular Army soldiers who had waited years for promotion opportunities and battlefield glory dreaded the prospect of staying behind in the Pacific to train troops who would likely never see combat, and with more American troops leaving the Philippines on every ship out of Manila, army officials wondered whether they could really spare experienced officers for training. The Guard also offered the Army few of the advantages that had prompted the formation of the Philippine Scouts sixteen years earlier. Colonel O. W. Ketchum of the Army's War Plans Division objected to such a force unless it "offered greater value, greater availability for service or greater economy"—none of which it did.[35]

The bigger obstacle was Jim Crow. The National Defense Act clearly stated that federalized Guard troops would carry their ranks with them into the US Army, so federalizing the Philippine National Guard could potentially mean placing Filipino officers in command of white men. Woodrow Wilson had brought to Washington an administration committed to Philippine independence, but he also drew the color line within the federal bureaucracy. Equally committed to white supremacy and global warfare, and dependent on the votes of southern Democrats on Capitol Hill, Wilson and his officers confronted an impossible dilemma: either leave power in Manila in the hands of an armed and trained Filipinized military unsupervised by the "older and stronger brother" of the US Army—or incorporate the Filipino troops.

Rather than confront this dilemma, they avoided it. Civilian politicians in Washington dragged their heels, military officers in Manila dug theirs in, and only a few insistent voices joined Governor-General Harrison's demand for action. On January 26, 1918, Wilson finally signed legislation authorizing the Philippine National Guard, but recruitment and training stalled. Brigadier General Robert Evans, commanding officer of the Army's Philippine Department, steadfastly opposed the Guard. He ignored orders to train its officers and sent experienced American officers back to the United States, along with 25,000 Springfield rifles that the Filipino soldiers had hoped to use. He ordered 1,000 other outdated rifles dumped in Manila Bay and refused to give the Filipino soldiers tents to sleep in, although there were many to be had in storage.[36]

Harrison, fed up, finally obtained Evans's transfer in August 1918, and his replacement was more sympathetic to the Guard. Under the command of Lieutenant Colonel Dennis Quinlan—who had been among the earliest officers of the Macabebe Scouts in 1899—the Philippine National Guard organized eight companies in just three short months, slowed only by fear that concentrating recruits from across the archipelago would exacerbate the influenza epidemic that reached Philippine shores in October 1918. A force of 576 officers and 14,235 enlisted men gathered for training just outside Manila on November 18, 1918. That date was, of course, a week after the armistice ending the war with Germany. Although the United States was still technically at war, and the Guard had been called into service in wartime, for all practical purposes the question of Filipino military service was moot. The day was nevertheless a festive occasion, with the bands of the Philippine Constabulary and the African American 9th Cavalry marching in front. Even the local YMCA sent a contingent of volunteers to screen films and lead Bible study. The troops ultimately trained for three months, one paid for by the US government and two more funded out of the colonial budget.[37]

The soldiers of the Philippine National Guard demobilized on February 19, 1919. To some, it had been a great success. Journalist Leandro Fernández explained that "although the Philippine division was never sent to the front, it nevertheless was mobilized in Manila and mustered into the Federal service and given one month's intensive training at

Federal expense." Governor-General Harrison agreed that "the moral and physical training afforded, and the patriotic feeling aroused, were of the utmost benefit to the islands." On a symbolic level, it was surely a victory: nearly 15,000 Filipinos marched as uniformed soldiers of Uncle Sam—often under Filipino officers—thereby heralding the future army of an independent Philippine Republic. But the Philippine National Guard was also a failure, as everyone attending the opening ceremony could plainly see. The men paraded with broomsticks in place of the Springfield rifles that the Army never gave them, and their ill-fitting surplus uniforms prompted laughter from spectators in the stands. Independence advocate Maximo Kalaw blamed "a persistent group of men" who "saw fit to frustrate the offer of the Filipino people and prevent our division from leaving the Islands."[38]

Despite the efforts of Filipino nationalist leaders and the thousands of soldiers who enlisted, the Philippine National Guard created neither citizens, nor soldiers, nor citizen-soldiers. The disappointing history of the Philippine National Guard showed the contradictions—and the impossibilities—of the Filipino soldier. Military mobilization brought forth Filipinos' demands for new rights of citizenship as reward for risks undertaken, but ran up against the barriers of race and empire. For their part, the Wilson administration wanted it both ways: Filipino citizen-soldiers who would symbolize an enlightened imperial policy without upsetting the racial order. But a turning point had been reached as Filipinos increasingly defined for themselves the terms of their soldiering and its political meaning. The Guard's success was not in getting to France, but in tying Filipinos' political aspirations to US policy in the Pacific.

A SOVEREIGN NATION—ESPECIALLY AN ARCHIPELAGO OF THOUSANDS of islands—would need not only an army, but a navy. In October

1917, the Philippine legislature issued four million pesos in bonds to fund a submarine and a destroyer to be built "under the direction of the government of the United States, and at the expense of the treasury of the Philippine Islands . . . for service in Philippine waters or elsewhere." The destroyer, the USS *Rizal*, named after José Rizal, the hero of the Philippines' nineteenth-century revolutionary struggle against Spain, would be donated to the US Navy for the war effort. In a cable to Woodrow Wilson, Governor-General Francis Burton Harrison hoped the *Rizal* would "afford an opportunity for young Filipinos . . . to acquire expert education in the handling of these modern types of war vessels." Wilson found the proposal "truly gratifying," and Navy Secretary Josephus Daniels was equally enthusiastic. "I will heartily assist to make it possible for the people of the Philippine Islands to do this," he told Secretary of War Newton Baker. Daniels hoped the future destroyer would see action rather than languishing in the Philippines where "there would be nothing gained."[39]

On a foggy morning in January 1919, a ceremony at San Francisco's Union Iron Works launched the destroyer. The high-profile event brought out "an avalanche of moving picture operators" and a "bevy of stunning and winsome 'yeomanettes,'" along with Philippine resident commissioner Jaime de Veyra, who hoped the *Rizal* would "do its bit in avenging" the 1915 sinking of the *Lusitania*. Draped in the American flag, the ship was christened to shouts of "Viva Filipinas!" and "Viva America!" from shipyard employees and a "merry bunch of Filipino buck privates" from nearby Camp Fremont. Filipino journalist Juan Salazar was duly impressed: "Verily, Filipinas was there heart and soul to do her full share in the world struggle against Kultur!"[40]

At the Mare Island Naval Base in nearby Vallejo, the *Rizal* crew trained, for once, to do more than cook dinner or set the table. A few months later, in May 1919, she set sail, with officers detailed from the US Naval Academy and an all-Filipino crew of 114 enlisted men and petty officers. Many were handpicked from the Navy's kitchens and its officers' servant quarters, others from the ranks of the Philippine Constabulary. Few had much experience at sea. The maiden voyage was a rousing success, but a later journey proved less grand. In October, Harrison learned that the ship's engines had burned out on a recent voyage and wired to Washington that the *Rizal* "met with misfortune on the Cruise due, it is believed, to the inexperience of her crew in handling vessels of her type." Navy officers ended the training program and reassigned the sailors to the messman branch. The world war's brief and temporary experiment in racially egalitarian military service was over. The Navy kept the ship—which saw service in the Asiatic Fleet—but in the years that followed, officers spoke of the *Rizal* as convincing evidence that a racially integrated Navy would be disastrous for national defense.[41]

Filipinos' service in the Philippine National Guard or on board the USS *Rizal* brought different disappointments, though they shared one similarity: the Guard was a fundamentally political institution, and the *Rizal* likewise sailed on a political voyage. Migrations to Hawai'i or California collapsed the carefully drawn boundaries between empire and republic, and as Filipinos encountered new racial barriers, their military service was a new weapon in their political arsenal. But it was not enough. Increasingly, Filipinos sought alternatives to militarism and military service.

FILIPINO SOLDIERS AND POLITICIANS FOUGHT SO HARD TO BE INcluded in America's war effort so that they could capitalize on one of the war's few noble aims: what Woodrow Wilson called "the rights of nations great and small and the privilege of men everywhere to choose their way of life and obedience." In May 1917, Governor-General Harrison made the relationship between Filipino self-determination and the US war effort perfectly clear to crowds at Manila's Liberty Loan parade. He pointed out that "the United States was fighting in the cause of the smaller nations, and that only thus would it be able to secure to the Filipinos the blessings of complete liberty and permanent independence."[42]

Many on both sides of the Pacific assumed that Philippine independence would be part of any comprehensive postwar treaty, and that the League of Nations would be able to protect the new republic. Ever since the Jones Act promised independence, Filipinos confronted the puzzle posed by the US military presence in the archipelago. Were Republicans right that without American troops and bases, Philippine independence would be merely an invitation to Japan? Or did new international institutions such as the League of Nations offer Filipinos a new path toward a meaningful nationhood? Could they realistically hope to become an independent country without an army? And if they were to create an army, how would they pay for it?

In the fourth of his Fourteen Points, Woodrow Wilson urged that "all well-defined national aspirations . . . be accorded the utmost satisfaction." He was talking about Europe, but he found listeners around the world. From Manila, nationalists such as Conrado Benitez reminded Americans that "the people of the Philippines purposely refrained" from independence talk during the war. Now it seemed only fair to be heard. "How," asked Manuel Quezon, "could you . . . give your recognition . . . to the independence of Czecho-Slovakia, Poland, Jugo-Slavia, and others, and withhold them from the Philippines?" As representatives of a people with "well-defined national aspirations," Quezon and Sergio Osmeña thought it only natural that they should attend the Paris talks, and in the Philippine Assembly, Representative Tria Tirona introduced legislation petitioning Woodrow Wilson to send a Filipino delegate. Francis Burton Harrison supported the proposal, but Wilson flatly rejected the idea. Other than carving up the German colonies and handing them over to victorious powers under nominal mandates, the Paris Peace Conference left colonialism untouched. It was up to Lenin and the Bolsheviks—pointedly absent at Paris—to speak of "the liberation of all colonies, the liberation of all dependent, oppressed, and unequal nations."[43]

During his 1919 national tour in support of the Treaty of Versailles, Wilson spoke often of his hope that an independent Philippines could join the League of Nations. "They will be safe from the outset," he told a Kansas City audience that September. "Every great nation in the world will be obliged to respect . . . the territorial integrity and political independence of the Philippines. It simplifies one of the most perplexing problems that has faced the American public." But on March 19, 1920, the US Senate rejected the treaty, and the United States never joined the League of Nations.[44]

Japan emerged from World War I with a stronger navy and control over former German colonies in the western Pacific. Asia's balance of power—and Filipinos' place in it—became the new decade's central strategic concern in the Pacific. Few Americans were heartened to learn of the 1921 publication of Japanese general Sato Kojiro's fictional account titled *Dream Tale of a Japanese-American War*, although Americans also published their own war fantasy literature in the same years. And the US Congress exacerbated tensions when it voted in 1924 to exclude all Japanese immigrants, much to the consternation of Japanese diplomats and the Japanese press.[45]

Japanese officials repeatedly disavowed any interest in the Philippines, and few in Japan spoke openly of plans for southward expansion. Vicente Bunuan, a staff writer for the Philippine Independence Mission, observed that the Japanese "do not thrive in our country, for the climate is too warm for them." In January 1927, the editors of the *New Republic* agreed, noting that "the Japanese are as ill-fitted for life in the tropics as are the inhabitants of Connecticut." Most Americans didn't pay much attention. With so many race-mongers, war-mongers, and self-interested military or naval officers arguing in Washington, it was hard to know which authorities to believe. It was easy to downplay or simply ignore any warnings about Japan, and many Americans—already indifferent to their empire—were content, as journalist Clare Boothe Luce put it, to think Manila was "something you take when you don't want chocolate."[46]

Filipinos had no such luxury of indifference. Cognizant that defense costs could cripple an infant republic, only a few argued for a large-scale military buildup. Among them was Carlos Romulo, an aspiring journalist then studying at Columbia University. The young Filipino student—who would go on to be one of the twentieth century's leading advocates of Pacific partnership—insisted that "we need an army and a navy." Veterans of the Philippine National Guard called for "a system of compulsory military service," but full-throated militarism played badly with Filipino voters. "Why not bring us to the farm, not to the military camp?" one student asked in 1932. Miguel Cornejo, a member of the Philippine legislature, on record supporting a 50,000-man army and a twenty-four-ship navy, found himself accused of pro-Americanism and defeated at the polls.[47]

Some politicians—particularly those enmeshed in the American colonial establishment—steered a middle course, unconcerned about Japanese invasion but fearful that an immediate departure of American troops would undermine Philippine security. In 1922, Manuel Quezon reportedly told an American journalist that "we would gladly consent to America holding permanent military bases here of any kind. . . . Naturally we want the protection that an American fleet . . . would give us." Others argued the Americans could best aid Philippine national defense by leaving. In a January 1931 speech before a gathering of progressive internationalists, Washington-based independence lobbyist Vicente Bunuan urged independence, despite the Philippines' weak military. "The Philippines are in more danger under the United States than if they were independent. Your naval and army authorities agree that the Philippine Islands are your weakest link in your line of defense." But, he asked, "if we were independent, and there was war between the United States and Japan, there would be no need for Japan to go there. Would there?"[48]

Eager for a new partner outside the US empire, a small number of Filipino nationalists listened hopefully to the rhetoric of pan-Asian unity emanating from Japan. Writer Pío Duran called for the Philippines to seek shelter behind Japan's "protecting shield." Duran dismissed annexation fears as "the product of white propaganda" and thought the Japanese—the Filipinos' "brothers of the North"—would "preserve Asia for the Asiatics" and advocate for "Oriental equality elsewhere." Anything else, he warned, "would duplicate here in the Philippines the case of the negroes in the United States." Other Filipino nationalists eagerly supported Gandhi's anticolonial struggles in India. Solidarity proved elusive: pulling on the threads of pan-Asianism tied knots between Chinese republicanism, Korean anticolonialism, Japanese imperialism, and Filipinos' own ambivalent relationships with other Asians.[49]

The most radical internationalists looked to the Communist Party. During the 1920s, Soviet leaders began building ties directly with anticolonial leaders in Asia rather than working through the Communist parties of the imperial powers. Southeast Asian radicals responded enthusiastically. Ho Chi Minh, who arrived in France in 1919 only to be rebuffed in his attempt to win Vietnam's freedom at the Paris Peace Conference, spent most of the 1920s immersed in international communism. In 1925, Tan Malaka, a communist organizer from the Dutch East Indies, made the first connections between the Communist Party and radicals in the Philippines, and by 1930 the Communist Party of the Philippines was actively organizing within Manila's trade unions.

Moderates wary of both Japanese militarism and international communism, pinned their hopes on the new League of Nations, arguing that its international umbrella would offer surer shelter than Japan's shield or anything the United States was likely to provide an ex-colony. Vicente Bunuan called the League of Nations a sign of a "higher and more noble" age. "I know what some of you are mentally saying regarding the League," he told his Philadelphia audience. "Just the same, you cannot but admit that it is . . . an asset especially to small nations unable to protect themselves." Journalist Jose Melencio agreed: "The rights of small nationalities have been vindicated and safeguarded." Throughout the 1920s, Filipino nationalists continued to look to the League as a model for international engagement that held out the promise of multilateral security for an independent Philippines. But as long as it remained a colony of the United States, the Philippines could not join the League.[50]

Filipinos also paid close attention to the naval treaty negotiations convened by President Warren Harding in Washington between November 1921 and February 1922. Representatives of Britain, Japan, the United States, and several other powers met to discuss limits on naval construction along with diplomatic matters in East Asia left unresolved by the Treaty of Versailles. They agreed to a naval strength ratio known as "5:5:3," under which the total tonnage of Japan's navy could measure just three-fifths that of the navies of either Britain or the United States. In exchange, the British and Americans promised not to expand or fortify their bases in Asia. Most Americans cheered the treaty's limitations and the US Senate quickly ratified it. Kawakami Kiyoshi, a Japanese journalist who wrote frequently for American audiences, viewed the treaty as an "auspicious" improvement of US-Japanese relations. Isauro Gabaldon, one of the Philippine resident commissioners in Washington, reminded readers that if America summoned the specter of war with Japan after 1922, it would "belittle the efficacy of its own handiwork, the new treaty."[51]

If Filipinos were optimistic about peace in the Pacific, the US Navy was not. American naval thinkers continued to view the Philippines as vulnerable and thought the United States had to defend the colony aggressively if it ever hoped to use Philippine bases in a war against Japan. Naval officers thought the Washington Treaty tied their hands. "Had I been a Japanese naval strategist," wrote Captain Frank Schofield in 1923, "I would have done all I could to keep America from fortifying further her naval positions in the Philippines and Guam"—which was precisely what the treaty did. But in the 1920s, a reduced

American naval presence would have been a fact of life whether there had been a treaty or not. With the German navy gone, the British now an unquestioned ally, and the Japanese considered a serious threat only by war planners, Congress refused to fund the Navy even at the reduced levels the Washington Treaty negotiated.[52]

Despite the penny-pinching, some construction continued. Treaty provisions barred fortification of naval bases, but Americans could still augment army installations. Corregidor's post prison officer detailed convict laborers to Manila to gather empty bottles and scrap metal to pay for barbed wire. At Fort Stotsenburg in central Luzon, the Army built up air facilities in preparation for a new kind of war. After September 1919, the base carried a new name—Clark Field—after Harold Clark, a young aviator who had never visited the Philippines but had died in a crash in the Panama Canal Zone. On the maps of Washington negotiators, Philippine bases were pawns in a global chess match. In real life, they were home for thousands of America's colonial subjects. As soldiers and sailors left, jobs dried up, and stores shut down. Residents of adjoining towns of Olongapo and Cavite and *barrios* such as Corregidor's San José blamed the treaty for emptying their pocketbooks. Congress's limited budgets meant that the Army and Navy had no funds of their own to build entertainment and recreation facilities for soldiers and sailors, which allowed bars, brothels, and dance halls to expand in Manila, Cavite, and elsewhere. In Olongapo, next to Subic Bay, sailors found a gymnasium, a movie theater, dance halls, and bars such as Gordon's Chicken Farm, which served hundreds of sailors and marines every night. An entire industry of recreation and consumption emerged, tying base communities ever closer to US military forces.[53]

Another diplomatic conference in London in 1930 extended the cuts agreed to at the Washington Naval Conference eight years before. "Big Navy" supporters concluded that President Herbert Hoover's budget cutting and disinterest in naval affairs was selling national security treasonously short. Hoover, indeed, was fiscally cautious, and when briefed on the secret Orange Plan for war with Japan, he responded only that he thought it ludicrously expensive. But complaints fell on the deaf ears of an American public with a distaste for foreign adventure or military expenditure—particularly after the stock market crash of October 1929. Further reductions in the Navy's budget followed the Senate's ratification of the London Treaty in July 1930, although given the Great Depression, they would have happened anyway. Isolationists in the Senate dismissed naval warnings about Japan as saber-rattling meant to drum up votes for naval expenditures.[54]

Along with Depression-era budget cuts came naval disarmament: American diplomats in London agreed to give up 4 battleships, 52 submarines, and 123 destroyers, among other ships. The press reported that officers wept as they faced the prospect of scuttling dozens of precious destroyers, but there is no record of tears at Mare Island in California on November 11, 1931, when the Navy scrapped a 1,030-ton destroyer known simply as the USS *DM-14*. That day—marking the thirteenth anniversary of the armistice ending the First World War—few probably remembered the *DM-14*'s original name: the USS *Rizal*.[55]

IF THE *Rizal* WAS FORGOTTEN, THE WAR'S HEROES WERE NOT. ON June 3, 1917, a twenty-five-year-old laborer in the Southern Pacific Railroad shops in Sparks, Nevada, registered for the draft. Tomas Claudio had been a mere child when the Philippine-American War passed through his hometown of Morong, not far from Manila. As a youth, he was enamored of military affairs and had a talent for drill, which he learned from an "American soldier-teacher" at his school, then worked part-time as a prison guard in Manila after dropping out of high school. Soon Hawai'i beckoned, and in 1911, Claudio headed to Oahu for work in the sugar fields, then jumped around the Pacific, canning salmon in Alaska and working as an elevator operator in

Stockton, California, before finding work in the Reno post office, and then with the railroad in rural Sparks. On draft day, a confused registrar marked him down both as an "alien" and as a "citizen or subject" of the United States. No matter: he was in uniform by November 2, 1917. "I was told that I could be exempted, since I am a Filipino," he wrote on November 30 to his sister Adela in Manila. "But I replied, 'Because I am a Filipino, I feel all the more that it is my duty to enlist.'" He shipped out for France just six weeks after enlisting and first saw battle at Cantigny in May 1918. He wrote his sister that "if fortune is against me, you will have the consolation of knowing that you had a brother who knew how to fulfill his duty to his country." His death on June 29, 1918, in Oise, on the eve of the Second Battle of the Marne, was the Philippines' first combat loss. In November 1918, the newly established barracks of the Philippine National Guard were christened Camp Tomas Claudio, and in June 1921, US colonial officials in Manila gave Tomas Claudio the belated honors of a fallen hero.[56]

Soon after the war, just outside Camp Claudio, the US Navy established a recruitment station, drawing many of the enlisted men of the Philippine National Guard into the messman branch of the Navy. They joined a wave of young civilian men and women making the journey across the Pacific. Ocean travel was easier and jobs were plentiful. By 1933, with political uncertainty in Asia, a new president set to take power in Washington, and economic depression bringing racial violence to farm fields in the American West, the US Congress started talking again about Philippine independence. The United States was now unable and unwilling to mount a full-scale defense of the Philippines. In the decade to come, faced with the threat of invasion by Japan and discrimination in the United States, Filipinos would have to defend themselves.[57]

CHAPTER FOUR

DEFENDING THEMSELVES

1934–1941

On December 25, 1933, a group of veterans gathered at New York City's Camp Thomas Paine for Christmas dinner. Their meeting place was not a military installation, but a ramshackle collection of hovels on the banks of the Hudson River. During the previous presidential administration, they had named it "Hoover City"; now a reporter described it as "a ruined city, a Pompeii of the poor." At noon on Christmas, thanks to "the grace of God and an anonymous donor," a group of eighty-four veterans, along with ten others "who were not veterans, just hard up," gathered for the camp's third annual dinner.[1]

Among Camp Thomas Paine's residents was Estanislao Labo, who had left his home city of Macabebe in 1917 to join the US Navy, serving on board the USS *Nevada*. Fond of stray animals, Labo and his makeshift menagerie were camp favorites. "His 'buddies' are agreed that when Labo was born, early in the twentieth century, all of the dying Victorian virtues entered his heart." But although everyone in the camp liked Labo, none of the other men could have known him well because Labo barely spoke English. As he sat outside his "picturesquely lopsided shanty," he hailed everyone who passed with the honorary title of "General."[2]

A year earlier and a few hundred miles away, an actual general had set his sights on a different encampment of veterans. On June 17, 1932, under orders from President Herbert Hoover, Major General Douglas MacArthur, who had recently returned from the Philippines to take up his position as the Army's chief of staff, dispersed 40,000 World War I veterans and their families then camping on the banks of Washington's Anacostia River to demand the immediate payment of a veterans' bonus. Armed with machine guns (which they did not use) and tear gas (which they did), Army soldiers overran the camp as MacArthur warned his aide Major Dwight Eisenhower that "there is incipient revolution in the air." By day's end, four were dead, as many as a thousand injured, and the Bonus Army's encampment had been burned to the ground.[3]

In both the United States and the Philippines, soldiers and veterans found that a postwar culture of disillusion, along with a global depression and national belt-tightening, meant that Americans had little interest either in maintaining a large military force or caring for the veterans of their last war. Nor was there much commitment to defending America's largest Pacific territory, or extending equal rights to the Filipino Americans who began migrating in large numbers to the United States during and after the war. In the uncertain world created by the First World War, and with increasing danger of a second, Filipinos on both sides of the ocean found they increasingly had to defend themselves—against both invasion by Japan and racial discrimination in the United States. The first task prompted a desperate effort to build an army from scratch; the second led to strikes and lawsuits and attempts to sway public opinion. For most Filipinos in the 1930s, they were separate efforts: uniformed soldiers and military planners went one way, highlighting their loyal service and urging military aid and support for a soon-to-be-independent republic. Lettuce pickers and hotel busboys went another, carving out a place for themselves in North America's political, economic, and even romantic life. These were different struggles, but they were two sides of the same coin.

In the years after World War I, Filipinos found it necessary—and possible—to cross the Pacific to fulfill their ambitions. By the 1920s, Filipinos had better reasons than ever to leave the Philippines. Agricultural modernization pushed small farmers and fishers to Manila, but that city's fragmentary industrial sector offered few jobs. "The migrating Filipino sees no opportunity . . . in the Philippines," the *Manila Times* noted in 1929. "Offer a job at 25 pesos a month, not a living wage in Manila, and you will get a thousand applicants. . . . Is it any wonder, then, that the lure of pay ten times as great in the United States draws the Filipino like a magnet?"[4]

Imaginations fired when labor recruiters from the Hawaiian Sugar Planters' Association arrived in the Visayan Islands and showed movies of happy Hawaiian cane workers, or when residents of the Ilocos provinces opened their mail to find cash sent back from siblings in North America. Some migrants wanted an education. Others simply wanted to get away: one Los Angeles resident interviewed in 1937 explained that he left his hometown in Mindanao with nothing more than $3.00 and an extra set of clothes after he had killed a man. "I don't ever want to go back to the Philippines." Most, though, expected to earn some money and return home a few years later.[5]

If ship schedules made the trip easier and good wages increased its attractions, citizenship and immigration laws made it possible in the first place. Since the turn of the century, Filipinos were unique among Asian migrants, and in the period from 1924 to 1934, doubly so. Nearly all Chinese had been formally excluded for generations; in the Gentlemen's Agreement of 1907, Japan agreed to limit emigrants from Japan lest the US Congress explicitly block them. The Immigration Act of 1917 created an "Asiatic Barred Zone" that permitted only Japanese and Filipinos. And then, in the Immigration Act of 1924, Congress excluded nearly all Japanese migrants. Filipino immigrants were explicitly protected by section 28 of that act, which stated that "citizens of the islands under the jurisdiction of the United States shall not be held as aliens." Only Filipinos—defined as neither citizens nor aliens, but as US "nationals"—could still migrate freely. "There's no limit during those days," recalled Mariano Angeles. "You just come in and there's no limit, you can stay as long as you like."[6]

Hawai'i was often the first stop. The sugar industry boomed during the war, and the exclusion of Japanese workers after 1924 left labor shortages that Hawai'i's planters thought only Filipinos could fill. About 28,500 Filipinos entered the territory between 1907 and 1919; another 29,000 arrived in just the next five years; between 1924 and 1929, over 44,000 more entered the islands. The 1930 census counted 63,000 Filipinos in Hawai'i, about 18 percent of the territory's total population. By then, Filipinos made up 69 percent of the men in the sugar workforce, and one study observed that they were "continuing to prove themselves quite desirable workers." Some earned enough to go back to the Philippines, but most took one look at their average wage of $1.00 to $1.50 a day in Hawai'i, learned they could earn $2.50 to $3.00 a day doing similar work in California, then jumped their contracts and headed east.[7]

Some made the journey alone, others with relatives or members of their *barkada*, a group of childhood buddies linked loosely by kinship and tied tightly by shared sacrifice. Social ties helped unskilled migrants find work. When Vic Bacho arrived in San Francisco in 1927, his brother, who had migrated three years earlier, was waiting at the dock for him. The two traveled to nearby Stockton to look for work together.

"The many Filipinos on El Dorado Street reminded me of . . . Manila," Bacho recalled. Alfonso Yasonia, who migrated to San Francisco at the age of twenty-two in 1928, recalled traveling with "about 300 other Pinoys on the boat" and staying a week in San Francisco before he, too, headed for Stockton. "I saw a Filipino restaurant so I go in to eat breakfast. I was there about twenty minutes when somebody walk in and hollers, 'Who want work?'"[8]

For agricultural workers as well as those in military service, labor was always in motion. "I didn't have no homebase," recalled Fabian Bergano of his life in the 1920s. The work year might begin in March planting in the inland valleys of California or Washington State, then workers moved from crop to crop until harvest, starting with fruits and berries in May and June. Vegetables took up July and August, and then it was time head back to eastern Washington to pick apples or hops in the fall. Filipinos picked nearly all of America's asparagus and 80 percent of its lettuce, along with sugar beets, cauliflower, celery, figs, lemons, oranges, grapes, and rice. Some Filipinos mixed farm and nonfarm labor, planting all spring and then taking domestic work in summer camps or resort hotels. Others left in late summer for seasonal work in the Alaska fisheries, where cannery jobs lasted until December. Nearly everyone was out of work in January, February, and March. They spent long, unpaid winters in the Little Manilas that emerged near other Asian migrant neighborhoods in Seattle, San Francisco, and Los Angeles, as well as in smaller cities such as Fresno, Stockton, or Spokane. Then the cycle began again: in the middle of February, when it was time to plant asparagus, the Filipino population in Stockton would jump from 1,000 to 3,000 in a matter of days.[9]

A notch up the labor ladder from agricultural "stoop work" was domestic service. It rarely paid as much as farming, but offered steadier employment. Some Filipinos worked in restaurants or hotels as bellhops, cooks, barbers, janitors, and elevator operators, others as butlers or chauffeurs. Eddie Manzoa worked in the galley of a Japanese merchant fishing vessel until he got so fed up with the job that he jumped ship in San Pedro, California, and found work as a personal servant to a family in Beverly Hills. "The pay was much more than I was making and I also would get better food and lodging. I did not hesitate to take the job." A substantial proportion of Filipino migrants came to the United States to further their education, but only a few were able to earn college degrees. And even those who earned advanced degrees often found themselves unable to use them: the bar associations of most western states excluded noncitizen lawyers from membership, while other professional associations maintained more informal color bars.[10]

By the 1930s, Filipinos were bypassing Hawai'i and its dead-end sugar jobs. The 1920 census counted 5,603 Filipinos in the continental United States, almost exclusively on the West Coast, but just ten years later the Filipino population numbered approximately 56,000. Employers believed Filipinos offered clear advantages over other Asian migrants: they spoke English significantly better (although not always well), were familiar with American institutions, and were reportedly uninterested in unions. And employers knew that as colonial subjects, Filipinos were already socialized into American racial norms and hierarchies.[11]

After the Great Depression hit, calls to exclude Filipino migrants reached a volume far out of proportion to continental America's actual Filipino population. It came down to jobs. As Filipinos entered the service industry, they often displaced elderly white men for whom positions as elevator operators or night watchmen offered what passed for old-age security in the years before the New Deal. Sometimes they displaced white women, or they worked next to them—either situation caused consternation to white male workers. Dozens of incidents of mob violence ensued. An attack on a dance hall in Watsonville, California, on January 19, 1930, sparked four days of rioting as white locals targeted Filipino migrant laborers. Hundreds were injured, and twenty-two-year-old lettuce picker Fermin Tobera was shot. Tobera's death became a transpacific rallying cry: his body was brought back to the Philippines, where a crowd of 10,000 mourners gathered for a hero's burial and a day of "National Humiliation." Concerns about race, crime, public health, agricultural protection, economic competition, and social disorder had turned Filipinos into a "problem." And as the Depression worsened, Philippine independence appeared to be the only solution.[12]

NATIONAL POLITICAL ASSOCIATIONS, ORGANIZED LABOR, AND EUgenic scientists amplified anti-Filipino voices from the West Coast, and the economic nationalism that gripped the United States in the first year of the Depression shifted a few votes on Capitol Hill toward exclusion. In Congress, Illinois representative Adolph Sabath proposed that "what the United States should do without further delay is to grant the Filipino people . . . independence . . . after which restriction would automatically follow." Then in September 1931, Japan invaded Manchuria, and the idea of extricating America from political commitments in Asia became even more appealing. As Theodore Roosevelt Jr., the president's son and a former colonial official, noted, with independence, "we could screen our base motives with a generous gesture."[13]

In December 1932, in the middle of what Filipino observer Vicente Villamin called "the last and lamest lame-duck Congress in the constitutional history of the United States," both houses hurriedly passed legislation granting independence to the Philippines. Known as the Hare-Hawes-Cutting Bill after its three Senate sponsors (particularly Harry Hawes, an economic isolationist from Missouri), the hastily written bill reflected the urgency of the Depression and a conglomeration of special interests. A generation earlier, Democratic senators and Filipino independence advocates collaborated on the wording of the 1916 Jones Act promising independence. This time around, Congress had little time for—or interest in—consulting Filipino politicians. The bill set out a three-step plan for decolonization. First, Filipinos would convene a constitutional convention to plan a nominally distinct political entity that would have wide powers of self-government under an American-supervised dominion status. That entity, the Philippine Commonwealth, would operate for ten years until full independence, after which Philippine products would face stiff tariffs at American ports and only a handful of Filipino migrants would be eligible for entry. The bill also featured a vaguely worded clause—mostly lifted from previous Democratic Party platforms and unchanged by the last decade's international negotiations over Pacific base fortifications—reserving to the United States "such land or other property which has heretofore been designated for military and other purposes." All the Americans' military and naval bases would remain in US hands—perhaps even as US territory—after independence.[14]

Every provision in the bill—trade, immigration, security—guaranteed that Filipino independence advocates would actually oppose it. From Manila, Philippine senate president and independence leader Manuel Quezon urged President Hoover to veto the bill, and led the charge to defeat it in the Philippine legislature (which, by law, also had to approve it). With Franklin Roosevelt about to move into the White House, and Democrats about to take control of both houses of Congress, Quezon surely thought the next administration would yield a bill more favorable on every count. Eager for a way to kill Hare-Hawes, Quezon knew the bases—a contentious issue in the Philippines—would do as well as any other topic. Tapping Filipinos' emerging fear that American bases invited attack by Japan, Quezon made the military basing provisions the center of the veto campaign, denouncing them before audiences in Manila as "destroy[ing] the very essence of independent existence for the Philippines," and securing a "no" vote in the Philippine legislature in October 1933.[15]

A few months later, in early 1934, Congress revisited the topic. The new independence bill, sponsored by Maryland's Millard Tydings in the Senate and Alabama Democrat John McDuffie in the House, differed from Hare-Hawes in only one way: rather than reserving American military and naval bases, it announced that the United States would leave "all questions relating to naval reservations and fueling stations" for future negotiation. Roosevelt urged passage of Tydings-McDuffie, insisting that "our nation covets no territory; it desires to hold no people over whom it has gained sovereignty through war against their will." Philippine Resident Commissioner Pedro Guevara applauded, noting that "now that the international situation in the Far East appears gloomy and confusing, the message of the President will certainly encourage a more stable situation in that part of the world." Tydings and McDuffie had other motives. The Maryland senator expressed his view that "it is absolutely illogical to have an immigration policy to exclude Japanese and Chinese and permit Filipinos en masse to come into the country." Representative McDuffie was more even more direct: "our hope is that we may get entirely out of the islands."[16]

"We are willing to take it as it is now," Quezon announced, and on Capitol Hill, so few spoke against the bill that when Tydings-McDuffie came up in the House on March 19, 1934, members recorded only a voice vote in its favor. Three days later the Senate adopted it, unchanged, by a vote of 68 to 8. On March 24, 1934, surrounded by US cabinet officials and Philippine politicians, President Roosevelt signed the bill, promising Manuel Quezon that he would attend the independence ceremonies in 1946. Filipino nationalists put on a good show as "blowing of whistles and ringing of bells greeted news of the action in Manila," but given the act's trade, immigration, and defense provisions, celebrations were notably subdued. Tydings-McDuffie kept the United States in control of the Philippine economy, turned recent Filipino migrants into legal outsiders, and left the biggest questions of defense—whose job it was and how it would be paid for—unanswered even as Japanese armies were on the march. It hardly felt like independence at all. For decades, anticolonial advocates on both sides of the Pacific thought this day would never come. None of them could have foreseen how ambivalent they would feel on the day that it did, and no one carried more of the burden than Filipinos who wore Uncle Sam's uniforms.[17]

Tydings-McDuffie triggered an overhaul of America's colonial military, beginning with its revision of citizenship and immigration laws. Although citizens of the new Philippine Commonwealth owed "allegiance" to the United States, they would hereafter be "considered aliens for the purposes of the immigration . . . laws of the United States." Like other nations, the Philippine Commonwealth now fell under the quota restrictions of the 1924 Immigration Act, and Congress assigned the Philippines a quota of just fifty migrants per year. Following a decade of nearly unrestricted migration, Filipino subjects found America's gates locked, even though they still owed allegiance to its flag and none other.[18]

Filipinos in uniform wondered whether there would still be a place for them in the US armed forces. Army and Navy officials concluded that once Filipinos were officially aliens, they would no longer be able to enlist, even though full independence was twelve years away. Filipino cadets at the US Military Academy had long been restricted to commissions in the Philippine Scouts; now West Point officials warned them that if Congress dismantled the Scouts, they might receive no commissions at all. The Navy feared that independence would dry up its supply of stewards and messmen, and in January 1933 began enrolling African Americans for service after maintaining a thirteen-year-ban on black sailors. The policy unfolded gradually, and, lest news reach the press, quietly. "To be attended with the least possible publicity," was all that the Navy bureau chief responsible for the policy had to say about the proposed shift. Officers were unenthusiastic about the change, complaining that "the colored boys eat twice as much, work half as hard, and break 25 per cent more crockery."[19]

"I feel we ought to hang on to the Filipinos till the last," insisted Captain Leigh Noyes, the head of the Navy's training programs. Lloyd Prewitt, one of the first new African American recruits, recalled in a 1998 interview that "when we arrived, the messmen were all Filipinos. After we were there about two weeks they transferred out the same number of Filipinos." By 1941, the change was undeniable: Filipino stewards (many of whom had naturalized as citizens) continued to reenlist and their numbers stayed steady, but the number of African Americans in steward and mess positions inched up. The Navy had visibly changed, and in a guide written for general readers in 1941, Kendall Banning explained it. "If little Miss Priscilla Public has trouble in translating the language of the Navy uniform and even hesitates in making a distinction between an admiral and a mess attendant, here is one infallible rule: The mess attendants are always colored; the admirals are always white."[20]

Some Filipino sailors purged from the service had better luck elsewhere. Naval officials sympathetic to the plight of the stewards—personal servants who often shared intimate quarters with the officers—pressed an idea to assign them as civilian laborers at the US Naval Academy in Annapolis. The school's kitchens had been staffed for decades out of the pockets of the midshipmen, who sometimes tapped Filipino ex-Navy men, but usually hired local African American workers. Cognizant that the shift would throw dozens of black men out of work, the NAACP's local branch filed a formal protest, but Filipinos soon made up the full complement of 150 messmen.[21]

Independence also weighed on the minds of the US military's civilian employees in the Philippines. In August 1935, a group of thirty

Filipino workers at the Cavite Navy Yard sent Manuel Quezon a petition. The men had all worked for the Navy at Cavite for thirty years or more, and on their behalf Quezon wrote Navy Secretary Claude Swanson urging him to grant the Filipino employees the same retirement benefits as American civilian employees. As Quezon pointed out, it was a matter of rewarding those who "have always stood faithfully by the United States Navy throughout the whole period of American occupation of this country." Three years passed before the Navy gave Quezon a perfunctory, dismissive response.[22]

Filipinos who were already in the United States found themselves caught in the middle after Tydings-McDuffie. Migration made their status as citizens uncertain and as workers vulnerable. Uncertainties reinforced one another: racist laws excluded Filipino Americans from mainstream culture, and that cultural distance justified legal restrictions in the minds of white observers. One New Deal report on Los Angeles, concluding that Filipinos would never succeed as American workers, deemed Filipinos "the one race which is incapable of being assimilated into the population of the United States." Excluded by race from many unions, discontented Filipino workers found their only option was to quit, which confirmed employers' view that they were unreliable.[23]

In the United States, Filipino migrants typically lived in substandard temporary housing: barracks, rooming houses, and so-called bachelor hotels, often located in poor and racially segregated neighborhoods in or near the Chinatowns of western cities—whether the sizeable Filipinotown that emerged along Main and Weller Streets in downtown Los Angeles or the smaller enclave on the industrial west side of Fresno. "It is generally conceded," wrote D. F. Gonzalo, a Stockton-based Filipino minister, "that these are not wholesome places." Journalists and social scientists blamed poor housing and low rates of property ownership on Filipinos' moral failure despite the fact that many western states barred Asian immigrants from owning land.

Laws initially written to block Chinese or Japanese land ownership were extended to Filipinos, as voters in Washington State did in a 1937 referendum.[24]

Bored by their cramped rooms in dingy boardinghouses, working-class Filipino Americans turned to city streets and the pool rooms, gambling dens, and dance halls that lined them. Filipinos quickly earned reputations as gamblers, drinkers, fighters, and ladies' men, confirming middle-class white Americans' uneasiness about urban mass culture. Reflecting on the January 1930 race riot in northern California, the *Literary Digest* asserted that "the Filipinos got in trouble in Watsonville because they wore better clothes, danced better, and spent their money more lavishly than the Americans." Mainstream venues were off-limits: in a 1978 interview, Johnny Latosa recalled that Stockton, California's Fox Theater explicitly drew the color line by posting a sign reading No Filipinos Allowed. Although most Filipinos were Catholics, their associational life did not generally include California's Catholic churches, which often excluded them. "There isn't a church in town that wants the Filipinos to come," reflected a Stockton clergyman. "Most of the Filipinos," one migrant observed in 1930, "go to Chinese gambling houses because they have no other place to go."[25]

Filipinos' transience, together with what commentators called "the woman problem," made them seem a dangerous threat. D. F. Gonzalo attributed "maladjustment" to the fact that "in America Filipinos are the only people who do not have their own women with them." Sociologist Emory Bogardus fretted that the lopsided gender ratio "represents a serious situation." The Filipino population that migrated to the West Coast of the United States in the 1920s was over 90 percent male, all but guaranteeing that Filipino men would find romance across the color line, and conflict when they crossed it. Couples were harassed, taunted, or refused accommodation. Matters were slightly less explosive when Filipino men courted other women of color. "Most of those who have married have preferred Mexican girls," observed

D. F. Gonzalo, who was told by an informant that "you can go anywhere with her without being subjected to the inquisitive glances of people. You go with an American (white) girl and the people will look at you and then look at her from head to foot."[26]

Marriage created legal as well as cultural conflict. Some states merely folded Filipinos into existing bans on interracial marriage. The registrar of Virginia's Bureau of Vital Statistics decided that Filipinos would be "classed as colored," while Louisiana, by contrast, recorded Filipinos as white. In Maryland, relations between Filipino messmen at the US Naval Academy and African American women in Annapolis prompted state legislators to ban marriages between "Malays" and those of any other race. In April 1933, California legislators incorporated "members of the Malay race" in the state's anti-miscegenation provisions, leaving New Mexico, Washington, and Hawai'i as the only exceptions in the American West, with the 1936 defeat of a proposed law in Washington partly the doing of Filipino activists in that state.[27]

By the mid-1930s, economic hardship motivated Filipinos in the United States to fight back, and increasing familiarity with American legal institutions empowered them to do so. They challenged miscegenation statutes, land laws, and barriers to unionization, and asserted rights as veterans. When they spoke out, they rarely asserted their citizenship explicitly—often because they weren't citizens—but claimed as US nationals to be entitled to the same rights as US citizens.

Filipinos' most successful challenges to alien land laws took place in Washington State. In Seattle, Pio De Cano, a powerful labor contractor and self-appointed community leader, purchased a tract of land in 1939 to build a meeting house for the Seattle Filipino Community Club. State officials prosecuted De Cano, but he argued before the Washington Supreme Court that Filipino nationals were not "aliens," and in February 1941, he won. Voluntary associations like the one De Cano ran began to play an increasingly important role in Filipino American life, particularly as a link between working-class Filipinos and the small Filipino middle class. Fraternal lodges provided social connections and economic protection in hard times; a thriving press published community news and international politics in several languages. In Brooklyn, Navy veterans set up a Filipino community center both to aid local arrivals and change white Americans' views, hoping "to awaken these misguided individuals to the fact that racial prejudices have no place in true society."[28]

Unions challenged employers' assumptions that Filipinos were compliant workers. In late 1932, just months after the Bonus Army was dispersed from the Mall, a group of Filipino students and workers organized the Cannery Workers' and Farm Laborers' Union in Seattle. Seven thousand strikers crippled the lettuce harvest in Salinas in 1934 until farmers broke the strike. A successful action by asparagus workers in Stockton in February 1937 filled the ranks of the Filipino Agricultural Laborers' Association, which counted 30,000 dues-paying members by 1940. The American Federation of Labor, a long-avowed opponent of Filipino labor, granted a charter to Filipino and Mexican farm laborers in Field Workers Local 30326 in February 1937. The Pullman Company hired its first Filipino employees in the fall of 1925 in the hopes of breaking up the Brotherhood of Sleeping Car Porters, a union of Pullman's African American workers. But after the Brotherhood started winning victories—and advocating for Filipino workplace rights—Filipinos joined it.[29]

Filipino veterans highlighted their military service in the hopes of gaining access to social benefits or better jobs. They also had a special citizenship status. Thanks to the wartime provisions of the Naturalization Act of 1918, Filipino veterans with three years of service could naturalize as US citizens. No other Filipinos could, and not all eligible veterans did; in the 1920s many saw little to gain from doing so. As "nationals," their entry was unhampered and for many the talk of Philippine independence that filled the air fostered hopes of returning to their reborn homeland with enough savings to buy land and settle down. "I consider myself an American citizen, although I have never signed any papers," reflected one Navy veteran. "I will sign the papers any time they want me to do so."[30]

The Depression changed all that. Military service and US citizenship enabled employment in the civil service and the post office. A Chicago clergyman observed that "Filipinos discovered the civil service through their experience in the navy, where many of them served during the World War. Here they became accustomed to taking examinations for promotion. It was only a step further to try out the civil service examination. . . . This economic security has made them desirable husbands, and some of them have married Polish girls and have established comfortable homes." Filipino veterans found little support in these years from the American Legion, which at several of its annual conventions adopted resolutions calling for the exclusion of Filipino migrants, and even urged their dismissal from the federal civil service. In a few communities, Filipinos could join American Legion posts. Elsewhere, as in Los Angeles and Chicago, they organized their own; Chicago's post bore the name of Tomas Claudio, the Philippines' fallen hero of the First World War.[31]

Among the Filipino veterans fighting for their rights was one who never appeared before the US Supreme Court when it heard his case. In April 1900—before there even was a force called the Philippine Scouts—Santos Miguel began working for the US Army as a translator, then made his way into the Scouts as a quartermaster. In October 1931, more than thirty years later, he retired as a master sergeant in the 45th Infantry after a career long enough to see his son join him in the unit. Given the Scouts' high rates of reenlistment, many thirty-year veterans like Miguel would be retiring soon. When his commanding officer filed a pension claim on Miguel's behalf, the US Comptroller General's office denied it, arguing that pensions for Scouts were "not authorized even by the remotest implication of the laws." Following a two-and-a-half-year fight made possible by a legal defense fund collected by fellow Scouts,

Miguel's case reached the Supreme Court. In the Justices' view, the February 1901 law that established the Scouts authorized the president "to enlist natives of those islands for service in the Army," and the Court saw no reason to doubt that they were "in" the Army. "Statutory provisions so clear and precise do not require construction," wrote Justice George Sutherland for a unanimous Court. It was a victory, but only of sorts. The Army—which didn't even file a brief on Miguel's behalf—may well have brought the suit as a test case to gain clarity in benefits administration. Nevertheless, Santos Miguel soon received his pension, and his checks kept coming until he rejoined his Scout unit in December 1941. He died in battle in Bataan the next year.[32]

Filipinos in North America who were neither veterans nor citizens found themselves out of luck when they applied for government jobs or federal relief. The vast majority of Filipinos worked in agriculture or domestic service, the two sectors of the economy not reached by Social Security or most other New Deal workplace protections, and not until October 1939 did Congress adopt legislation making Filipino nationals eligible for welfare benefits. At the same time, through the Repatriation Act of July 1935, Congress tried to decrease the number of Filipinos claiming relief in the first place. The law funded Filipinos' travel costs from anywhere in the continental United States to Manila, and while one of its sponsors, California's stridently anti-immigrant Representative Richard Welch, promised that "there are no strings attached," there was one very big one: "No Filipino who receives the benefits of this Act shall be entitled to return to the continental United States except as a quota immigrant"—at a time when the quota was just fifty persons a year. Congress touted the law—designed to reduce relief rolls and modeled after a similar program aimed at Mexican migrants—as a humanitarian measure.[33]

The policy was a total failure. By July 1935, the national economy had begun to recover, and many unemployed migrants saw no reason to return to their semi-independent and thoroughly impoverished homeland. Mostly, though, Filipinos objected to the policy's permanent exile provisions. "This compulsory feature is distasteful to the Filipino," observed sociologist Emory Bogardus. "The more they think and talk about it, the more resentful they feel, and the more they urge their fellows not to accept the plan." When Berkeley Walker reported on interviews he conducted in Los Angeles's Little Manila for the Works Progress Administration, he admitted having trouble understanding "the lower class boys." But one thing came through clearly: "they all said they were going to pay their own fare when they go home." In the law's first year, Congress authorized funds of up to $300,000 to cover returnees' trips, at a time when a one-way ticket to Manila cost about $87.00. The money went largely unspent, even as Congress extended eligibility for the program until December 1940. In the end fewer than 2,200—most of them not destitute—chose repatriation, a rate far lower than voluntary return migration in the years before 1935.[34]

Conflict over repatriation shows how fully the stakes of American citizenship had changed since the 1920s. Before 1934, Filipino immigrants lived relatively easily with their in-between status as "nationals," and many who could have naturalized as citizens chose not to do so. It was time-consuming, expensive, and for transient workers, hard to do: immigration officers didn't follow workers around as they moved from Los Angeles to Stockton to Alaska. And before 1934, formal citizenship offered few obvious benefits. By the late 1930s, however, as Filipinos needed help from the New Deal government—or simply wanted to stay in the country—it became important for them to establish their status more clearly.

On November 15, 1935, a crowd of more than 250,000 people—some of them recent repatriates from California—gathered in Manila to witness the birth of the Philippine Commonwealth and the inauguration of Manuel Quezon, its new president. Quezon had defeated a field of candidates that included his longtime rival Sergio Osmeña and the former revolutionary general Emilio Aguinaldo, who threatened (but did not carry out) a violent demonstration against Quezon on Inauguration Day. For Filipinos, the Commonwealth brought more autonomy but not yet full independence. Thanks to Tydings-McDuffie, the new Commonwealth included some lingering colonial structures. One level above President Quezon was the US High Commissioner, a civilian official appointed by the American president, who had full authority to overrule the new government. The stars and stripes still flew over the presidential palace of Malacañang.[35]

The armed forces of the new Philippine Commonwealth likewise remained under American control during the long transition to independence. But Filipinos did not have the luxury of waiting until 1946 to address national security. Mindful of defense issues and eager to demonstrate national sovereignty, the Philippine legislature's first undertaking was a national defense bill, introduced just days after Quezon's inauguration. The task of planning and training the new Philippine Army—indeed even the writing of the national defense bill—rested in American hands. President Roosevelt announced that Douglas MacArthur would head the US Military Mission to the Philippines, established by Tydings-McDuffie. MacArthur headed to Manila on the SS *President Hoover*, a crucial voyage for the fifty-five-year-old soldier. His devoted mother, Pinky, who had never traveled to the Philippines while her husband Arthur MacArthur was commanding US forces in the Philippine-American War, now accompanied her son Douglas, but she fell ill on the journey and died soon after arriving in Manila. On board ship, the recently divorced MacArthur also met thirty-six-year-old Tennessee native Jean Faircloth; the two married in April 1937.[36]

MacArthur brought with him to the Philippines his right-hand man, Major Dwight Eisenhower, who in 1935 was a mid-career soldier with an excellent reputation as an administrator but little combat experience. Dwight and his wife, Mamie, had lived abroad before: Mamie as a young woman with her businessman father, Dwight as a soldier, and the two of them together in the early 1920s in the Panama Canal Zone. Eisenhower later recalled that he was "not ecstatic about the prospect of going to the Islands." Mamie was no fan of the tropics and initially stayed behind, to Eisenhower's dismay. "I was out there a year alone," he recalled, "and I did *not* like it." A year after Dwight's arrival, Mamie and their son John joined Dwight in a modest suite (with no air conditioning) at the Manila Hotel. They entered the social world of military Manila, and Eisenhower grew close to President Quezon, with whom he shared a passion for card games and sailing on the presidential yacht.[37]

In the national defense bill, Eisenhower proposed a Philippine Army (PA), a small standing army of 10,000 soldiers, supplemented by the 5,000 men already in the Philippine Constabulary, and a large reserve force that would be built up over time through universal military service. All men between twenty-one and fifty would be eligible for conscription, with draftees undergoing five and a half months of military training. The plan called for some nine hundred officers to be recruited over time, from either the Philippine Constabulary, which the Commonwealth government controlled, or the Philippine Scouts, which everyone assumed would be phased out with independence. The defense bill proposed a "mosquito navy" of just thirty to forty torpedo boats, an air force of sixty planes and one hundred trained pilots, and a small coast artillery force to staff the guns at Corregidor Island. These branches could only hope to slow a potential Japanese invasion, not to stop it.[38]

The national defense bill divided Philippine politicians. Assemblyman Camilo Osias warned that "we are embarking upon a saturnalia of extravagance," and urged expenditure on health and education instead. "We are appropriating money for imaginary enemies from outside." Indeed, $8 million a year—nearly a third of the Commonwealth's budget—was a heavy burden for a nation of fourteen million people struggling through a global depression, especially considering that it left alternatives such as primary school education largely unfunded. Assemblyman Maximo Kalaw, among the leaders of the charge for the Philippine National Guard a generation before, rejected Osias's doubts. "I am afraid that his philosophy is nothing but the result of the pacifistic theory which we heard in America when we were students." But "under the stormy clouds of Asia, with Manchukuo, China and the restless teeming millions of India and the militarism of Japan,—how can we . . . have a doctrine of pacifism?"[39]

The US military considered the proposed legislation with a fortress mentality cultivated on Corregidor and a dose of racist skepticism about Filipino soldiers' abilities. The Army's War Plans Division described the plan as "wholly ineffective." Dispersing units and equipment throughout the islands, they argued, would render them useless in an attack, and mass conscription and five months' training offered little military benefit while draining the treasury. But anything more could endanger US-Japanese relations: because Tydings-McDuffie gave President Roosevelt authority to call out the Philippine Army, extensive training—especially under US leadership or paid for with US funds—might look to the Japanese like the war preparations of an imperial army.[40]

The National Defense Act passed in December 1935, and attention soon focused on turning blueprints into an actual army. MacArthur dismissed Eisenhower's initial $25 million defense plan as too expensive. Returning to the drawing board, Eisenhower slashed the budget. Philippine soldiers would have to make do with hand-me-down American weapons from World War I, and substantially lower pay—"little more than cigarette money," Eisenhower later recalled. Unlike most US Army war planners, MacArthur thought the Philippines—armed with its citizen army, tiny navy, and a few airplanes—could actually defend against any enemy "no matter how ruthless and powerful." The plan, MacArthur explained, "reposes responsibility for ultimate defense, not in a costly professional force that could conceivably be made the instrument of autocracy, but in the people themselves." MacArthur aspired to an army that would not need the United States. "Don't make any mistake. The Philippines are going to be independent and they are going to stay independent," MacArthur told an American reporter in the summer of 1936. "The American army in the islands is just window-dressing; the Philippine army will be something."[41]

Draft registration succeeded beyond expectations: initial news reports on the first call in April 1936 for all men turning twenty that year noted that some 150,000 Filipinos had registered, far more than had been expected. There was some resistance in provincial areas. Muslim Filipinos in Mindanao murdered a draft officer and appended a note: "We need none of your military training. Give us rifles and we will show you how to fight." When news of the draft reached California, it hardened Filipinos' resistance to repatriation: sociologist Casiano Coloma noted that rumors circulated in Los Angeles that Filipinos who accepted the federal government's repatriation offer would be conscripted into the Philippine Army upon arrival back in Manila.[42]

When Eisenhower announced that 25,000 World War I–era rifles would soon be delivered for new recruits, the veterans of the Philippine National Guard—who had waited in vain for weapons a generation earlier—may have wryly noted the irony. But no one smiled when they confronted the shortages of funds, weapons, and facilities that plagued the new force. The Commonwealth government had neither the money nor the facilities to train thousands of men. The original plan aimed to call 40,000 men a year for five and a half months of training, starting with 20,000 men in January 1937, and another 20,000 that July. But in May 1936, Eisenhower urged MacArthur to cancel or postpone the plans because the officers—and even the camps—were not yet ready to receive the recruits. MacArthur would have none of it, and gave his aide what Eisenhower later recalled as "one of his regular shouting tirades." So Eisenhower cut the budgets again, trading his initial vision of a grand army of the Pacific for a poor man's jungle force. The Philippine Army would be a lean, barefoot force taught "conservation of ammunition, simplicity in supply, messing and camping arrangement, and development of the utmost endurance and hardihood."[43]

The Philippine Army's new recruits wore makeshift khaki uniforms, canvas sneakers, and bamboo helmets. Often armed with nothing more than broomsticks, PA troops paled in comparison either to regular US Army soldiers or to the Philippine Scouts. They earned a lot less, too: $9.00 a month for a Philippine private, about one fourth what a good factory job in Manila would pay, albeit more than most rural farmers could hope for. Five and a half months of training meant little more than rudimentary drill and basic education in literacy and sanitation. Labor on the army's model farms—described to the press as vocational training for the recruits—was desperately needed to supply their meager rations, which soldiers supplemented by roasting the pythons that plagued the half-constructed camps. Philippine Army officers begged for more money and more men. "The inadequacy" of the force "is very keenly felt," one reported.[44]

The other services proposed in the initial plan made equally slow progress. In 1935, the Commonwealth transformed the Philippine Constabulary training school into the Philippine Military Academy, with the aim of training future officers. The Constabulary, established decades earlier as a quasi-military police force distinct from the US Army and reporting to the colonial government, was folded into the Philippine Army in May 1938, a move designed to provide officer material for the new Philippine Army. The Navy was particularly vexing. As a maritime nation, the Philippines obviously needed a navy, but in practice, it couldn't afford one. Others—some recalling the failed voyage of the USS *Rizal*—doubted whether Filipinos had the skills to man their own navy, having depended for so long on Japanese crews on Philippine merchant ships.[45]

Meanwhile, Jerry Lee, a thirty-two-year-old big-talking Texan who seven years earlier had joined the US Army Air Corps on a lark, found himself in charge of training the new Philippine Constabulary Air Corps. On his first day, Lee found a single aircraft and a "field no bigger than a postage stamp." Maps recorded the locations of some eighty-five landing strips, but many were in poor condition or altogether unserviceable. Lee's flight students at Clark Field just north of Manila mastered the task faster than Lee had expected of recruits who, for the most part, didn't even know how to drive a car. Lee even found time to teach Dwight Eisenhower how to fly.[46]

As Eisenhower struggled to help the Philippine Army make ends meet, Douglas MacArthur intervened more assertively in Philippine politics. On August 24, 1936, President Quezon commissioned Douglas MacArthur as the Field Marshal of the Philippine Army in what Dwight Eisenhower would later recall as a "rather fantastic" ceremony. Eisenhower, fearful that the move would alienate MacArthur further from US military officers, urged his commander not to accept the position. "Why in the *hell* do you want a *banana* country giving you a field-marshalship?" he asked. Frank Murphy, the High Commissioner, found MacArthur impossible to deal with; by late 1936 he complained of the "growing menace" posed by MacArthur's military mission and urged FDR to recall MacArthur from the Philippines. Interior Secretary Harold Ickes and Army Chief of Staff Malin Craig both agreed: Ickes noted in his diary that MacArthur "comes pretty close to being a dictator." Craig changed his mind, wisely reminding the president that recalling a popular general in an election year could pose political problems, so MacArthur stayed in his post a little longer. In August 1937, President Roosevelt informed MacArthur that his tour of duty with the US Military Mission would soon end, but if Roosevelt thought that the old soldier would simply fade away, he was disappointed. MacArthur officially retired from the US Army on December 31, 1937, but continued to serve as the field marshal of the Philippine

Army, working some two or three hours a day while he and Jean enjoyed their privileged lives in a penthouse suite at the Manila Hotel. The MacArthurs had made a new home.[47]

Dwight Eisenhower, on the other hand, wanted very much to return to the United States and get away from the conflict with his equally ambitious and short-tempered superior officer. President Quezon, who had come to rely on Eisenhower's military advice and trusted his political sensibilities, tried to retain him. First, he facilitated the Eisenhowers' move into a larger suite at the Manila Hotel. Its opulence—and, finally, air conditioning—overwhelmed them. Mamie wrote her parents in August 1939 that "I feel very much like Mrs. 'Rich Bitch.'" At one point, Quezon even offered Eisenhower an honorary annuity policy that was just a hair short of a $100,000 bribe. Eisenhower turned it down, agreeing to stay on until October 1939, but even as Manuel Quezon argued that "the Philippines could not be defended even if every last Filipino were armed with modern weapons," Eisenhower's mind was already elsewhere. Eisenhower left in December 1939, and immediately distanced himself from MacArthur, casting his lot with his new boss, Army Chief of Staff George Marshall. Ike would not see Douglas MacArthur again until 1946. MacArthur, who frequently referred to "that traitor Eisenhower," didn't miss him.[48]

In Tydings-McDuffie, the United States had promised to build the Philippines an army, and there were some—particularly Douglas MacArthur—who not only believed America owed it to the Philippines but thought it could be done. Then war began in Europe in September 1939, and US attention and funds went elsewhere. The two nations nevertheless remained bound together by their military relationship. As MacArthur settled in and Eisenhower packed his bags, the officers and enlisted men of the Philippine Army found themselves largely on their own. National hero Emilio Aguinaldo came out of retirement to support the National Defense Act. "If there is to be any salvation for us," he wrote, "we have to work for it with our own efforts." With the threat of war reshaping Philippine politics, that would prove hard to do.[49]

GLOBAL EVENTS POLARIZED PHILIPPINE POLITICS. AS PRESIDENT Manuel Quezon implemented the National Defense Act, his efforts at preparedness militarized everyday life, prompting fears that the new Philippine Army would become the private force of a military dictatorship. Under Quezon's leadership, the Philippine legislature authorized mandatory ROTC training at universities in 1935; military drill appeared in Philippine schools, where civics textbooks taught youth that "in times of war the loyal citizen must . . . be ready to make the supreme sacrifice of dying for it." By 1937, Quezon sponsored draconian sedition and censorship laws, consolidated his personal control over the Philippine Constabulary (despite plans to move it from civilian to military control), and expanded the PC's secret service division. He cultivated ties with the commanders of both the US and Philippine armies, including the PA's chief of staff, who called for "compulsory labor camps" as part of the "service" proposed in the Commonwealth constitution and the National Defense Act.[50]

Quezon's cozy relationship with Philippine fascists amplified fears of dictatorship. Some, like Manila business executive Andrés Soriano, found Spain's General Francisco Franco an appealing model. A wealthy descendant of one of the country's powerful Spanish-speaking families, Soriano owned a vast conglomerate of gold mines, banks, and the San Miguel Brewery. Like many of his elite *ilustrado* relatives, he was also still a Spanish citizen: Soriano was one of a handful who in 1899 took advantage of complex provisions in the Treaty of Paris allowing peninsular Spaniards to retain their Spanish citizenship. In the late 1930s, Soriano donated 500,000 pesos to Franco's cause, and was photographed in July 1941 giving the fascist salute at a Falangist rally.[51]

Others joined the Manila Falange, including politician Manuel Roxas, who headed up the law firm that did most of the Soriano family's work before 1941. The mother of Joaquin Elizalde, one of the Philippines' resident commissioners in Washington, headed the group's Women's Division. Also on board was the hierarchy of the Catholic Church, which was increasingly active in politics, particularly through the work of Catholic Action, a right-leaning youth group. The Falangists probably never counted more than eight hundred members in their ranks, and the intricately divided and fratricidal world of the Spanish Civil War offered few appealing options for Filipino elites. They were never really interested in returning to Spanish colonialism anyway: their political efforts sought to interject a blustery anticommunism, rather than a gauzy colonial nostalgia, into Philippine politics. Bluster aside, by the late 1930s, national politics included a powerful right-wing bloc with anticommunist opinions, militarist visions, and close connections to both Quezon and MacArthur.[52]

Filipino fascists squared off against an increasingly strident communist movement. The colonial and commonwealth governments came down hard on the Communist Party of the Philippines, using every means of surveillance and suppression in the toolkit of the Philippine government. American colonial officials outlawed the party in September 1931 and arrested its leaders. The Commonwealth period brought more of the same. "I will throw anyone in jail who advocates communism," announced President Quezon. Underground organizing continued. A few Filipino leftists joined the Spanish Civil War on the opposite side from the Falangists. Most remained in the Philippines to defend radicals' basic political rights as their numbers dwindled.[53]

As communists organized in the cities, an armed peasant movement gathered strength in the countryside, particularly in areas hit by the Depression-era collapse of the agricultural economy. The Sakdals mobilized farmers' economic discontent, their longstanding opposition to American rule, and their passionate hatred of the Constabulary, which by the mid-1930s had become a corrupt institution that regularly extracted wealth from ordinary Filipino peasants. Founder Benigno Ramos organized the Sakdal movement in 1930, partly in response to protests that rocked the Philippines after the racial violence in Watsonville, California, that year. Ideologically committed to an anticolonial Pacific unity, Ramos pursued connections with Japanese pan-Asianists and soon drew the attention and support of General Artemio Ricarte in exile in Japan. In May 1935, a Sakdalista faction seized government offices and Constabulary posts in a dozen towns near Manila and set up what news reports called "a sort of socialistic regime." The Philippine Constabulary immediately crushed the uprising, killing over one hundred people. Broken but unbowed, the Sakdals continued as an underground movement throughout the 1930s.[54]

Communists rebuilt their forces, especially after the launch of a Popular Front movement that allowed them to operate openly until the outbreak of war in Europe. Joining them at an October 1938 convention was Sol Auerbach, a Communist Party organizer from the United States, who had been sent to facilitate the group's official entry into the Communist International. In fact, Filipino communists had already established far denser connections between Manila and Los Angeles than Auerbach could hope to build with the $4,000 allocated by the CPUSA. Leftist union organizers such as California's Karl Yoneda joined West Coast labor journalists Carey McWilliams and Carlos Bulosan to build their own alliances across the ethnic divisions that divided agricultural laborers. The Popular Front period expanded those left alliances into groups such as the Pacific Coast Congress against War and Fascism, where "workers of five different races—Negro, Chinese, Japanese, white and Filipino—clasped hands on the stage and spoke a pledge not to fight each other in any imperialist war." The Japanese invasion of China in 1937 brought further alliances between Filipino radicals, Chinese communists, and American leftists in the Friends of Free China. Militarism was not the only way to forge connections across the Pacific in the 1930s.[55]

Filipino leftists in the United States found themselves increasingly under scrutiny and surveillance. As Americans learned of the role played by fifth columnists in the Nazi invasions in the spring of 1940, aliens—especially radical ones—became suspect, and on June 14, 1940, Congress passed the Alien Registration Act. Known as the Smith Act after its sponsor, Virginia senator Howard Smith, the new law required all aliens fourteen years or older to register, state their political beliefs, and submit photographs and fingerprints to local police. Impending war turned the small number of Filipino radicals into dangerous un-Americans. But new laws passed to control alien radicals made all Filipino immigrants seem like threats to the nation. Having been excluded, rejected, and partially repatriated, the Alien Registration Act was a final slap in the face of Filipino migrants.[56]

Aimed primarily at communists and fascists believed to be lurking in the ethnic enclaves of East Coast cities, the Smith Act reflected an important shift in how the federal government thought about immigrants. Just two weeks before its passage, President Franklin Roosevelt signed legislation transferring control of immigration from the Labor Department to the Justice Department. According to Roosevelt, there was nothing to fear from the fact that the government believed immigrants were better off regulated by those trained to capture criminals than officials devoted to the needs of workers. Registration carried no "stigma or implication of hostility," he noted, and the program would be implemented "with a high sense of responsibility," but with "those aliens who are disloyal and bent on harm to this country, the Government, through its law enforcement agencies, can and will deal vigorously."[57]

No one knew for sure if the Smith Act even applied to Filipinos. The Tydings-McDuffie Act noted that residents of the Philippines would be treated "as if they were aliens" when it came to immigration, but did that mean that all Filipinos—even those who had moved to North America before 1934 and therefore never "immigrated" from one country to another—were now aliens subject to the Smith Act? Secretary of the Interior Harold Ickes, a sympathetic New Deal liberal whose department's Office of the Territories held authority over Philippine affairs, promised "to do everything possible to secure relief" for "Filipino citizens unjustly discriminated against by reason of this law," but the Justice Department insisted Filipinos must register.[58]

Registration began in late August. "We should abide by the law and register—now!" editorialized Stockton's *Philippine Journal*, and most did, dutifully lining up at the special registration stations that Stockton officials established "in the Filipino quarter." But opposition groups insisted that since Filipinos "owe allegiance to the United States Flag," they could not be aliens. The Resident Commissioner's office ordered thousands of red-white-and-blue lapel pins marked with the word "Philippines," which Filipino newspapers urged readers to wear to "prove that you are not an alien." Despite that effort, the *Commonwealth Journal*, a Portland newspaper, blamed the resident commissioners in Washington. "Surely," wrote editor Julio Mensalves, "we do not suspect for a moment that [they] will be registered and finger-printed under this act!"[59]

Dozens of groups rallied against the act, among them the Filipino Anti-Imperialist League, which included radical Filipinos in Brooklyn, and Los Angeles's Committee for the Protection of Filipino Rights. The American Committee for the Protection of Foreign Born (ACPFB) coordinated the efforts. Headed by Carey McWilliams, a California-based labor advocate and supporter of Filipino rights, the ACPFB's Los Angeles branch supported legislation sponsored by New York representative Vito Marcantonio that would exempt Filipinos from alien registration. But the bill stalled in Congress, and with Marcantonio under scrutiny for his own leftist politics, it soon died.

Secretary of State Cordell Hull urged the postponement of debate until after Philippine independence.[60]

Whether the Smith Act applied to Filipinos or not, it silenced the activism of civil rights unionists who had done so much in the previous decade to challenge Filipinos' second-class status in America. War mobilization ended the fluid world of Pacific migration, temporary labor, and fuzzy citizenship that had brought so many Filipinos to North America. As they fought in the United States to defend their political rights, progressives took the lead, only to find by the late 1930s that the threat of war put their dreams on hold and subjected their loyalties to scrutiny—often at the hands of forces that were seeking to build up the Philippine military and defend the country from a possible invasion. The two efforts at self-defense worked at cross purposes until war brought them together.

Cordell Hull probably wished in September 1940 to adjourn debate on the status of Filipino immigrants because he was preoccupied with the threat of war, but it proved impossible to shelve thorny questions of decolonization to focus on geopolitics and national security. Once again, the argument emerged on both sides of the Pacific that immediate American departure was the Philippines' best means of national self-defense. "The American flag may . . . be an invitation to invasion," wrote journalist Vicente Albano Pacis in a Manila paper in October 1939. Diplomat Nicholas Roosevelt had opposed independence in the 1920s, but by 1935 he told a meeting of the National Republican Club in New York that the United States must leave, "lock, stock, and barrel." The longer Americans stayed, he warned, "the greater the danger of our being involved in a war." In October 1940, New Dealer Hugh Johnson called the defense of the Philippines "a grotesque absurdity" and urged Americans to "get out of this dangerous and extravagant busybody Oriental kibitzing."[61]

In Washington, Tokyo, and Manila, diplomats, politicians, and military planners turned their attention to Japanese migrant communities in the Philippines. There were not that many Japanese in the Philippines—maybe about 30,000—but of all the Japanese settlers in Southeast Asia in 1940, two thirds were in the Philippines, most of them either in Manila or the southern city of Davao. Some had been drawn to the colony because America's 1924 Immigration Act excluded Japanese migrants from Hawai'i and the West Coast. Indeed, the Japanese government regularly criticized US immigration restrictions, which Japanese Ambassador Saito Hiroshi deemed "a question of discrimination" and a "needless affront to the Japanese sense of honor." But the restrictions multiplied. In March 1935, the Philippine Commonwealth adopted its own version of an Alien Land Law to prevent Japanese settlers from acquiring territory—even as Filipinos were battling identical legislation in California and Washington State. An Immigration Act passed in May 1940 restricted Japanese migration to the Philippines to five hundred persons a year, and in yet another irony, an Alien Registration Act followed in June 1941. Repeal of these immigration laws were among the demands presented by the Japanese diplomatic delegation at the White House on the eve of December 7, 1941.[62]

In the relatively tranquil 1920s, the only commentators who warned of a Japanese menace were eugenic scientists, manila hemp dealers, and naval fetishists, often crying wolf with the aim of scuttling Filipinos' independence efforts. When such rhetoric renewed in the 1930s, many therefore ignored it. Douglas MacArthur insisted that Japan did not "covet" the Philippines, and in 1940 Manuel Quezon assured an applauding audience at the University of the Philippines that "we have nothing to fear from Japan." Sensible observers rejected alarmism. "You must remember in those days nobody respected the Japanese military very much," American diplomat Claude Buss recalled. He couldn't bring himself to believe it. "It was awful hard on a beautiful day in July 1941 to think of war while playing golf."[63]

Planning for the defense of the Philippines—and paying for it—wouldn't be easy. Filipinos needed to ready themselves for war, but they could not prepare too visibly, which could send the wrong message to Japan at a moment of international tension. Quezon's critics thought the president was using war mobilization as a means of grabbing power, which he was, but that made it impossible for liberals to resist Quezon's creeping authoritarianism without opposing his necessary war mobilization measures. Having already taken personal control of the Philippine Constabulary, Quezon put loyalists in charge of the Philippine Army as well. Previously warm relations with Douglas MacArthur cooled, and the two men began communicating only through their secretaries. The president continued his elaborate plans for the construction of a new capital to be named—of course—Quezon City. In the fall of 1940, Quezon forced through passage of an Emergency Powers Act giving him near-total control of the Philippine government. Meanwhile, officials in Washington did nothing to rein him in. Interior Secretary Harold Ickes thought that although Quezon might be "a budding dictator," he was "very alert and intelligent," and noted in his diary that Franklin Roosevelt "thinks he has been doing a good job." Distracted by war, Roosevelt turned a blind eye to Quezon's policies and conveniently made do with Quezon's promise not to exercise the emergency powers. Quezon retreated to the protection of his bullet-proof car.[64]

When Quezon wasn't seizing power for himself, he was demanding concessions and resources from the United States. Quezon reminded Americans that the Tydings-McDuffie Act reserved decision making over the Philippines' military and diplomatic affairs to the US government. He told the Philippine Assembly that therefore "it rests exclusively with the United States, and not with us, to determine whether we shall be at peace or at war." Later, Quezon publicly announced that the Philippines could not defend itself, and, arguing that "the defense of our country remains primarily the responsibility of the United

States," reallocated funds that had been earmarked for Philippine air and naval defenses. Some of the leftover money funded a campaign to increase domestic production of foodstuffs that the Philippines would otherwise have to import. Some of it went to pay for the designs for Quezon City.[65]

As war loomed, talk turned to air raid shelters, refugee camps, and gas masks, and now Quezon argued that civilian defense, too, was a US responsibility. "The protection of the civilian population of the Philippines is as much the primary responsibility of the Government of the United States as is the military defense of the Islands," he told High Commissioner Francis Sayre in April 1941. But Sayre claimed that America's hands were tied, since "the United States lacks jurisdiction to take action in . . . essential 'passive defense' measures." Claude Buss tried to aid the Civil Emergency Administration (CEA), established in March 1941, so "that they might dig air-raid shelters, . . . store up medicines and food." But it was obvious there were nowhere near enough supplies to feed and clothe the civilian population in wartime, let alone protect them from an attack. In a world already at war, civil defense supplies couldn't be found on the open market, let alone paid for, and there was neither time nor ships to transport equipment to the Philippines. A brochure for air raid wardens put out by the CEA in 1941 touted the efficacy of pneumatic sirens, but noted that their purchase "seems to be out of the question."[66]

On July 24, 1941, the Japanese Army marched unopposed into Saigon in the Vichy French colony of Indochina, leading observers in both the Philippines and the United States to conclude that war in the Pacific was inevitable. Troop buildups in the Japanese colony of Taiwan troubled those who had believed (or merely hoped) that the Japanese had no interest in the Philippines. "There we were," recalled Claude Buss, "right in the middle of it." On July 26, President Franklin Roosevelt recalled Douglas MacArthur to the service of the US military, and placed the sixty-one-year-old general in control of the United States Armed Forces in the Far East (USAFFE). The new force combined all the US and Philippine forces in the region, including both the US Army and the Philippine Scouts, as well as all the Commonwealth forces—the Philippine Army, the Constabulary, and the Air Corps—and placed them under US command. "I want Douglas to be in charge," Roosevelt told a military adviser. For MacArthur, who had been alienated from both the US War Department and the Philippine Commonwealth government (including his old *compadre* Manuel Quezon), the appointment validated his long-held views on Philippine defense and tipped the balance of power in his favor and away from both Roosevelt and Quezon. Beforehand, Claude Buss noted, "Quezon was the master in that relationship," but now that MacArthur was in charge, "Quezon found himself forced to listen to him. . . . When MacArthur became the active military commander in the Philippines, we really had the feeling that war was coming."[67]

On the same day, July 26, 1941, the US government moved the Philippines firmly onto a war footing. Roosevelt used the authority of Tydings-McDuffie to incorporate the Philippine Army into USAFFE, announcing his intention to "call and order into the service of the United States for the purpose of the existing emergency . . . all of the organized military forces of the Government of the Commonwealth of the Philippines." This choice—to make one American army out of an array of forces—was a decision made in Washington based on military necessity, not the end point of Filipinos' long political struggle over race, citizenship, and military service. But it had the same outcome: Filipino soldiers were now officially American soldiers.[68]

Mobilization began immediately, but as the soldiers of the Philippine Army—now under USAFFE command—swore oaths to "bear true faith and allegiance to the United States of America," logistical complications and miscommunications in multiple languages posed obstacles. Two torpedo boats arrived from Britain in December 1941, after most of the US Navy's Asiatic Fleet had already been withdrawn.

The US Army Air Corps began transferring B-17 bombers and P-40 fighters to Clark Field. Recruits of the new Far East Air Force arrived in November 1941 without any airplanes, warned by their commanding officer that "men, you are not a suicide squadron yet, but you are damned close to it."[69]

If equipment was in sorry shape and short supply, so were the troops. The Philippine Scouts reached a peak enlistment of 12,000 men in July 1941. Their numbers actually declined in the next few months as MacArthur wielded his new USAFFE authority to reallocate troops, assigning experienced Scouts in groups of forty officers and twenty NCOs to each division of the Philippine Army. This left the Scouts—the best-trained force in the Philippines—in organizational disarray. By December 1941, five years after the National Defense Act, the fledgling Philippine Army had trained 130,000 men, but not well. Some of the men had completed their five and a half months of training without ever firing a rifle. The number of Philippine Army soldiers in uniform shot up from 4,168 men in 1940 to 22,532 in December 1941, as the force prepared to face an increasingly strident enemy knowing there would be little backup from the United States. With the Battle of Britain raging and an undeclared naval war under way in the Atlantic, Roosevelt moved US Navy vessels out of the Pacific to defend shipping in the Atlantic. Questioned on this by MacArthur, FDR admitted that he had no intention of defending the Philippines.[70]

As Douglas MacArthur shuttled back and forth between his apartment at the Manila Hotel and his office next to Quezon's at Malacañang, he knew there was little that Philippine civilians realistically could do to prepare for war. He refused to train Philippine Army recruits for guerrilla warfare, for fear that soldiers' battlefield morale would evaporate if they knew there was a backup plan. MacArthur applauded the "psychological reaction which resulted from the voluntary submission of the public will," after a citywide blackout drill on November 21, 1941. "The High Commissioner's office kept saying that everything was fine," recalled Bessie Wilson, an American in Manila. "Soon no ships were allowed out; there was no transportation even if you wanted to leave. We had a strange feeling of impending disaster."[71]

So did Franklin Roosevelt, who on December 4, 1941, dashed off an official note to Premier Tojo Hideki asking why Japanese troops were massing at Camranh Bay in French Indochina, just eight hundred miles from Manila. "Such aggression could conceivably be against the Philippine Islands," he wrote. "I should like to know the intention of the Japanese government." By the time Roosevelt received a response, he had learned from military intelligence that staffers at the Japanese consulate in Seattle were burning their files. At a cabinet meeting on Saturday morning, December 6, 1941, the frustrated Secretary of State Cordell Hull announced that Japanese diplomats "didn't mean business."[72]

In the years after the war, politicians, military officers, and historians parceled out blame for the failure to defend the Philippines. Soldiers and sailors in the Pacific—both Americans and Filipinos—felt betrayed, first by Republican administrations that cut budgets and dismissed their warnings about Japan, then by Roosevelt's explicit Atlantic priorities. Filipinos blamed the United States for dragging them into the war, and their own leaders for playing politics with war mobilization. There was simply not enough money, or time, or good will. Filipino internationalists' hopes that Japan would make no moves on an independent and neutralized Philippines may have had a chance of being realized in the 1920s, but as war-minded leaders crowded out other voices in Tokyo, the diplomatic option disappeared. A real defense, like the one Manuel Quezon wanted, with a rapid buildup of US soldiers and enormous deliveries of weapons from America, might only have provoked Japan sooner. And while Leonard Wood had been right when he warned back in 1904 that it would be cheaper to defend the Philippines than to reconquer it, massive expenditures to protect an almost-former colony were politically infeasible in either

Washington or Manila. The Philippine Army did the best it could with the money and soldiers it had, and Chief of Staff Basilio Valdes assured MacArthur and Quezon that a meaningful national defense would be in place by the summer of 1942. No one knew that they would not have that long to get ready.

CHAPTER FIVE

DEFEATS

1941–1944

ON THE SUNNY SUNDAY MORNING OF DECEMBER 7, 1941, MANY of Hawai'i's Filipino sugar workers were attending mass when Japanese planes attacked the US naval base at Pearl Harbor. Virgilio Menor Felipe, on the other hand, was walking off a hangover. "'Japanee [*sic*] planes bombed Pearl Harbor!' people shouted, hurrying from house to house like chased chickens," he recalled. But Felipe kept walking back to the sugar workers' barracks. "We thought someone was pulling a stupid joke. . . . Within minutes, our plantation boss came galloping on his horse with a .45 strapped on his belt. 'We've been attacked by the Japs, boys.'" That afternoon in Washington, US Secretary of the Navy Frank Knox didn't believe the news, either. "My God! This can't be true," he exclaimed, after months of watching Japanese maneuvers in Southeast Asia. "This must mean the Philippines."[1]

In Manila, it was 2:40 a.m. on Monday December 8—just across the international date line from Hawai'i—when word reached the waterfront headquarters of the US Asiatic Fleet: "Air Raid on Pearl Harbor.

This is no drill." At the nearby Manila Hotel, Lieutenant General Douglas MacArthur lay fast asleep in his penthouse suite for another hour until his chief of staff, Brigadier General Richard Sutherland, heard the news on the radio and woke him. Only two hours after that, at 5:30 a.m., did the War Department's official confirmation arrive. But by that point, it was too late.[2]

Clark Field, the US Army base fifty miles north of the colonial capital, was meant to protect the Philippines from attack, and in the months after Japan occupied southern Indochina in the summer of 1941, the United States hurriedly fortified it, alerting soldiers there on November 28 that Clark was "on a full war alert." As soon as news of Pearl Harbor reached Clark Field, Major General Lewis Brereton, the commander of the Far East Air Force, proposed launching Clark's planes to strike Japanese aircraft on Taiwan, just five hundred miles away. MacArthur, though, waited for an official act of war by the Japanese. Frustrated, Brereton tried to make his case directly to MacArthur, but Sutherland blocked him.[3]

No matter: if Brereton could not bring the war to the Japanese, the Japanese would bring the war to him. By 9:20 a.m., bombs struck US military installations at Baguio, just one hundred miles north of Clark Field, and the general knew he was next. Fog in Taiwan had delayed the bombers' takeoff, which bought the Americans some time they didn't use. When warnings of incoming planes reached the Far East Air Force at 11:30, and were relayed to Clark, base commanders did not notify the 5th Bomber Command, whose planes sat on the landing strip in close formation. The Japanese air group—nearly one hundred strong—arrived around 12:30 p.m. "Surprised to find the American aircraft lined up on the field," as one officer later recalled, the Japanese destroyed nearly half the planes at Clark, killing more than fifty men and taking out the Far East Air Force in a single strike.[4]

That day, people in the Philippines felt abandoned by America and fearful about their future, but after years of anticipation, war scares, and defense bickering, only a few felt much surprise. Gregoria Espinosa, a civilian nurse working for the US Army Nurse Corps at Manila's Fort McKinley, later wrote that "I was not so excited as I should have been." Colonel Richard Mallonée later recalled only "a grim, thoughtful silence." The next three and half years of war imposed political, economic, and moral burdens as Filipinos had to reconcile the competing political visions of two empires with their own national ambitions. War presented small dilemmas and large ones, from whether to buy rice on the black market to whether to take an oath of loyalty to Japan. The Imperial Japanese Army shattered US colonialism in the Philippines and defeated the colonial army that defended it, but it did not quite destroy the foundation on which American power in the Pacific stood. Ultimately the trials of war confirmed the bonds between the two nations. Across Southeast Asia, Japan invaded already-colonized places: Vietnam, Indonesia, Singapore, Burma. In most of those places, local forces fought Japan and their European colonizers at the same time. In the Philippines, Americans and Filipinos fought side by side.[5]

Challenges—less extreme but also transformative—awaited Filipinos on the other side of the Pacific. Separated from their compatriots and their homeland, Filipino Americans' ongoing struggles for political and labor rights—in California farmyards or Alaskan canneries—took on new meanings during the war. For Filipinos in the United States, military service in US Army uniforms posed dilemmas of national loyalty that mirrored those of guerrillas in the jungles of the Philippines: whether to speak up when refused service in a restaurant, whether to take an oath of citizenship as a United States citizen. During World War II, African Americans urged not only "V for Victory," but a "Double V": victory abroad over Germany and Japan, and victory over racism at home. Filipino soldiers often experienced a "Triple V": a political battle for equality in the United States; a war to be won on the battlefield for America; and another, for themselves, to liberate their homeland from the Japanese. Achieving the Triple V contributed to making Filipino migrants into Filipino Americans, and it did so in a distinctively military fashion, adapting their political ambitions to US military priorities.

Americans had to rethink those priorities and their role in Asia, too. After the Japanese invasion, and particularly after the dramatic stands taken by American and Filipino troops at Bataan in April 1942 and Corregidor that May, many Americans rediscovered the nation's Pacific colonial outpost, a place they had been content in previous years to leave in the hands of naval officers, missionaries, and sugar planters. Public attention transformed not only how Americans thought about their decades-old Pacific empire but also about their Filipino neighbors. It changed how Filipinos thought about themselves. Fighting together—on board ships at Pearl Harbor, in the last days at Bataan, at hot dusty training camps in central California, with no sense of how long the war would last or if it would ever be won—Filipinos and Americans changed each other.

WAR—THE REAL THING AND NOT A DRILL—CAME QUICKLY TO the Philippines. As air raids began in Manila on December 9, US military officials willingly opened the quartermaster's warehouses to supply civilians, knowing there would be no merchant ships arriving now that Japanese submarines patrolled the harbor. Thieves broke into the Red Cross to steal medical supplies; anyone with a car, or even a horse-drawn *calesa*, fled the city. Farther south, Santiago Pamplona Dakudao, a doctor who lived and worked among the Japanese community in Davao, hoarded food and medicine, and hurriedly planted a fresh crop of rice and corn, while Philippine authorities rounded up the city's Japanese. In his diary, Dakudao noted that "Filipino laborers who had grievances against their former Japanese masters took the opportunity to inflict bodily harm on them and looted their houses or stores as the poor Japanese were escaping their misfortune."[6]

Across the Pacific, threats of violence between Filipinos and Japanese also filled the air in the days after Pearl Harbor. Warned that "Filipino laborers could be seen sharpening their cane knives," Hawai'i's military commander took to the radio on December 11, appealing to residents to refrain from violence against their Japanese neighbors. A month later, the *New York Times* reported that "only with difficulty" had "widespread casualties been prevented" in California's Salinas Valley, although one Filipino farm worker noted that "if you change your mind and want the Japanese cleaned out, you just send the word to me . . . and our men will do the rest." *Life* magazine's December 22, 1941, issue featured a disturbingly detailed photo essay informing readers "How to Tell Japs from the Chinese" as Filipinos went to great lengths to distinguish themselves from their Japanese neighbors. Philippine Resident Commissioner Joaquin Elizalde announced the availability of 30,000 red-white-and-blue lapel pins featuring the word "Philippines" for migrants to wear—the same pins he had ordered a year earlier as a protest against the inclusion of Filipinos in the Alien Registration Act.[7]

On December 22, just two weeks after Pearl Harbor, the Japanese Fourteenth Army under General Homma Masaharu landed at Lingayen Gulf in the northernmost part of the Philippines. Rear Admiral Kemp Tolley would reflect in hindsight that it was "absolutely a lead pipe cinch" that the invaders would come ashore at Lingayen, but the Japanese faced little resistance there from green Philippine Army recruits. The Philippine Scouts, who had trained for years for this day, were elsewhere. Some patrolled the roads between Manila and the beachhead at Lingayen. Others, their units broken apart and both officers and men reassigned to the fledgling Philippine Army, were already retreating to the Bataan Peninsula northwest of the capital. Glicerio Valdez, a Philippine Scout sergeant, left his post at Fort McKinley for the countryside in Pampanga, and later rushed from there to Bataan. Nurse Gregoria Espinosa made her way to the island fortress of Corregidor soon thereafter. They all loosely followed War Plan Orange, a defense plan crafted years earlier by the US War Department, which assumed that a tough defense of Bataan by US Armed Forces in the Far East (USAFFE)—the combined strength of the US Army, the Philippine Scouts, and the Philippine Army—could hold off the Japanese until the US Navy arrived from Honolulu. With nearly two dozen ships sunk or damaged at Pearl Harbor, that plan was obsolete, but military officers followed it anyway.[8]

On December 26, to protect civilians, MacArthur declared Manila an open city, a largely empty gesture. "The Japanese weren't interested in destroying Manila," recalled Robert Lee Dennison, then serving as a captain in the Navy's Asiatic Fleet. "They wanted the city, not a bunch of rubble." But the declaration did require USAFFE soldiers to evacuate. The vast majority, following War Plan Orange, retreated to Bataan; some scattered to defend other locations. Douglas MacArthur swapped his command post at the Manila Hotel for the US Army fort at Corregidor, taking with him the civilian leadership of the Philippine Commonwealth, including President Manuel Quezon and Vice President Sergio Osmeña.[9]

On December 28, 1941, with Japanese troops on the march throughout the archipelago, President Roosevelt addressed the people of the Philippines via shortwave radio broadcast from San Francisco. "In this great struggle of the Pacific, the loyal Americans of the Philippine Islands are called upon to play a crucial role," he intoned. Roosevelt assured Filipinos that the transfer of independence scheduled by the Tydings-McDuffie Act for July 4, 1946, would not be postponed, giving his "solemn pledge that their freedom will be redeemed and their independence established and protected." Many shared journalist Maximo Kalaw's sense that Filipinos "felt they had been duped" by the "tone of misinformed optimism" that preceded December 7. When the Japanese marched into Manila just after the new year, they faced no resistance and inflicted little damage, rounding up about 4,000 US and other civilians and interning them for the duration of the war, most at the University of Santo Tomas. There was no time for optimism now.[10]

FACING A RAPID JAPANESE ADVANCE ALL ACROSS THE ARCHIPELago, about 80,000 USAFFE soldiers dug in on Bataan. Regrouping, holding out against the Japanese, and waiting for reinforcement could only work for so long—and was impossible with so few supplies and no reinforcements on the way. After January 4, men lived on half-rations and civilian handouts; within a few weeks they would eat the 26th Cavalry's beloved horses. The soldiers fell back, then held the line against the Japanese. They were hopeful and might have been more so if they had known that Japanese general Homma was just as short of men as they were: Japan redeployed troops from the Philippine invasion to attack the nearby Dutch colony of Indonesia. Dubbing themselves the Battling Bastards of Bataan, the soldiers knew they were orphans, left with "No Papa, no Mama, no Uncle Sam." No Douglas MacArthur either, as the general watched from Corregidor, just a few miles off Bataan in Manila Bay. In February, in desperation, the American and Filipino soldiers of USAFFE retreated again.[11]

With the Philippine Commonwealth effectively doomed, civilian officials including Quezon and Osmeña evacuated Corregidor, eventually making their way to Washington to establish a government-in-exile. MacArthur, for his part, intended to stay on, but on February 22, Roosevelt ordered him to withdraw to Australia. Handing overall command to Major General Jonathan Wainwright, MacArthur left on March 11. "On the dock I could see the men staring at me," he later wrote. "I raised my cap in farewell salute." Days later, at a train station in Adelaide, he told a reporter, almost in passing, "I came through and I shall return." Afterward, to a Melbourne audience, he repeated the phrase, more forcefully, and would begin intoning it incessantly, a promise both to the Filipino people and to himself. General Homma made sure MacArthur would not return soon. On April 3, with fresh reinforcements from Japan, his 14th Army began a new offensive to seize the peninsula, and defeat was now inevitable. About two thousand men (including Wainwright) escaped to defend the island fortress of Corregidor for a few more weeks, while 76,000 men, now under Major General Edward King Jr., held on at Bataan for a few more days before surrendering on April 9.[12]

General Homma knew that international law required him to hold the surrendered troops—64,000 Filipinos and 12,000 Americans—but practicality dictated they be imprisoned somewhere other than Bataan, which had been devastated by months of battle. So Homma announced the men would march to Camp O'Donnell, an unfinished Philippine Army camp some one hundred miles away. They would walk the first sixty-six miles from Mariveles to the railhead at San Fernando before boarding train cars, then the final eight miles to the camp, again on foot. General King, speaking for his sick and hungry men, begged Homma to send the prisoners by truck, but Homma—who was short on vehicles and had been stunned to capture so many prisoners—said no.[13]

The men set out at gunpoint on April 10 on what would come to be known as the Bataan Death March. There was little food or water: the Japanese had planned for 25,000 healthy soldiers to surrender no earlier than April 20, and now confronted three times as many men, starving and plagued with dysentery and malaria. (The Japanese 14th Army itself had 81,000 troops in country, just a few thousand more than had surrendered at Bataan.) Because USAFFE soldiers were slow to surrender, many of the first captives waited for days at a concentration point that had not been stocked with any supplies at all. Marching at a grueling pace, even those men who were relatively strong could barely keep up. Some fell out along the way; others died in the rail cars during the journey's second half. Random violence and torture, meant to break the prisoners' will, took the lives of some. Overall treatment was inconsistent, ranging from confiscation of weapons to seizure of every personal possession. A handful escaped into the jungles, and some Filipino locals took great risks to share food and water. More often than not, the men marched alone. Somewhere between 7,000 and 10,000 of the men died before they arrived at Camp O'Donnell. Another 1,600 Americans and 16,000 Filipinos died in the two months after they settled in the camp.[14]

At times, the march generated the ultimate brotherhood between its American and Filipino soldiers, bonds more genuine and more enduring than anything Matthew Batson and Jacinto had imagined in Macabebe in 1899. But the march also revealed how thin—or even fictional—the ties of brotherhood had been all along. On the march and then in the camps, the Japanese separated Filipino and American soldiers. For some of the American officers and noncoms of the Philippine Scout 91st Division, surrender meant summary execution by the Japanese, and American soldiers faced extensive cruelties, generally worse than those meted out to the Filipinos. The march also prompted a brutal race war in which Americans and Filipinos, in language laced with racial epithets, stole one another's food, blamed each other for poor preparation and battlefield losses, and accused each other of cozying up to the Japanese. Some Americans pulled rank—or, if they were enlisted men, played the race card—ordering Filipinos to carry their packs, treat their wounds, and feed them from scarce rations. Filipino civilians, for their part, heckled the marching soldiers—"That's what you deserve!"—and mostly sold, rather than bravely donated, their food and water. None of this was commemorated after the war. Today, memorials at every kilometer along the route depict the silhouette of an American soldier bending down to aid a Filipino comrade.[15]

Meanwhile, the Japanese, who quickly understood the bitter divisions among the men, sought to divide and conquer by turning the Filipinos against their American officers. Warning them at the time that "you are exposing your life in danger without any remuneration," and reminding them later of "the inhuman and discriminatory attitude of the Americans in the Battle of Bataan," the Japanese hoped ex-USAFFE soldiers would be valuable converts to their utopian vision of a Greater East Asia Co-Prosperity Sphere: a Pacific liberated from European colonialism through Japanese political and military leadership. But from the beginning, the Japanese were also motivated by their manpower needs. They expected turned USAFFE soldiers to form the core of a Filipino native soldiery that would keep order in the Philippines, freeing up Imperial Japanese Army soldiers for service elsewhere on Asia's front lines.[16]

News of the collapse of the US and Philippine forces—the surrender at Bataan on April 9 and then General Wainwright's final capitulation at Corregidor on the morning of May 6—reached the handful of USAFFE soldiers still holding out elsewhere. Many ignored Wainwright's order to put down their weapons and took to the hills to form guerrilla units. Glicerio Valdez and a few others fled Bataan in civilian clothes, but were soon "confronted by a group of Japanese soldiers with fixed bayonets," who uncovered their military status and took them prisoner. Major Thomas Jones of the Philippine Scouts, hiding near Baguio, encountered a group of Philippine Army men who, he later recalled, "had been ordered by their American instructors to discard their uniforms and to return to their homes. It was a disheartening spectacle." Others, exhausted and sickened from living on half-rations, could simply do nothing but wait for another day. There would be new armies and new battles.[17]

In the United States, after the fall of the Philippines, there came nothing but silence. No radio broadcasts from Corregidor, no letters or telegrams from soldiers or family members. Filipinos in North America also found that politics changed quickly. On the eve of the war, US immigration officers had excluded Filipinos, and federal police had scrutinized them. Now, with stories of Bataan and Corregidor reminding

Americans why Filipinos were living and working among them, the fight was on. As partners in war, Filipinos had value and soon a voice.

They wanted to work—but stumbled over the controversial Alien Registration Act that had been extended to Filipinos in the fall of 1940. After Pearl Harbor, employers regularly dismissed noncitizen employees, particularly in the burgeoning defense industry. As industrial mobilization heated up—and even more so as young men started to leave in uniform—the ban on alien defense workers chafed at employers and employees alike. Filipino American newspapers protested the policy; Filipino unions petitioned employers and the War Department. Individual workers, many of them veterans of the Philippine National Guard or the Philippine Constabulary, sought documentation of their service and asked whether it entitled them to a coveted veteran preference that could get them in the door at defense plants. Ramon de la Peña, who had served three years with the Constabulary, asked "Is it consider my 3 years in military in this Country?" M. de Ocampo hoped that a letter from Washington would "clear up his case to some ignorant employment office." The Interior Department consistently ruled against the Filipino veterans, but bosses at the Mare Island Naval Shipyard in Vallejo, California, deemed service in the Philippine National Guard sufficient evidence of veteran status. On June 25, 1941, months before Pearl Harbor and in response to African American activists, President Roosevelt issued Executive Order 8802 establishing the Fair Employment Practices Commission and requiring "the full and equitable participation of all workers in defense industries, without discrimination because of race, creed, color, or national origin." On March 6, 1942, Roosevelt followed up with another executive order explicitly stating that Filipinos, as American "nationals," were eligible for jobs in defense plants or with the federal government.[18]

But a signature in Washington, DC, did not always mean a job in Washington State. "Go back to the plantation," Fausto Cardenas was told when he looked for war work in Honolulu. In the early years of the war, and particularly in "closed shop" workplaces where employees had to be union members and unions admitted only white laborers to membership, defense jobs went overwhelmingly to white workers. Equal employment required agitation by Filipino labor leaders. Seattle's Julius Ruiz, a labor organizer and journalist, went on a national speaking tour, pressing wartime employers to open factory gates. "The Filipinos in America are loyal to the United States and the democratic system of government, but they are tired of so much dishwashing," he told a Los Angeles audience in October 1942. "They would like to have a more important share in the war effort, and be treated as equals." Ruiz pointed out that Filipinos in cities such as Detroit worked in war plants, but "this is not true on the Pacific Coast." He assured his listeners that "we are willing to shelve the independence issue for the duration, but we would like to have a fair break in war-plant employment. . . . We want to do everything we can to help win this war."[19]

By the war's end, more than 2,000 Filipino men worked at Pearl Harbor Navy Yard in Honolulu. In Seattle, Genevieve Laigo earned $1.00 a day as a maid before the war; her husband also worked in domestic service. "And then when the war broken then we went to, I went to Boeing, he went to the shipyards." Her paycheck shocked her. "Boy I was on top of the world. . . . It was 35 cents but when the war broke we have a union so it went to 62 and one-half cents." Gone were the hardships of the Depression. "I get everything I want," explained Marcelo Canania, who worked the assembly line for Douglas Aircraft Company in Los Angeles. "I buy everything to wear. I got plenty of money. They paid me well and I saved my money. So I had no complaint." One Filipino worker in Hawai'i recalled that "we had something jingling in our pocket, too you know. We bought beer by the quart, not the bottle. We had a good time." As Seattle resident Toribio Martin later recalled, "I think the American people . . . recognized the usefulness of the Filipino." Filipinos would find themselves useful to the US Army as well.[20]

When Filipino volunteers showed up at military recruiting stations in the days after Pearl Harbor, they initially found the doors closed as firmly as those of the defense plants had been. The US Army would only accept citizens of the Philippine Commonwealth if they joined the Scouts, which could only be done in the Philippines. The Navy had ceased new enlistments by Filipinos in 1932 in anticipation of Philippine independence—although Filipinos who reenlisted were still serving as messmen and stewards and were among the 2,000 naval personnel who died on the morning of December 7 at Pearl Harbor. At first, the Selective Service Act drafted only "citizens of the United States and all aliens residing in the United States." Filipinos, as "nationals," were neither citizens nor aliens, so they were exempted, although they still had to register. On the first day of Selective Service registration in October 1940, the *Washington Post* proudly noted that automaker Henry Ford's grandson "stood side by side with a Filipino domestic at a municipal building in suburban Detroit."[21]

Overwhelmed by protest letters from eager recruits, Resident Commissioner Joaquin Elizalde petitioned for changes in military manpower laws. He quickly got his wish: on December 21, 1941, two weeks after Pearl Harbor, Congress revised the Selective Service Act to authorize military service by "citizens of the Philippine Commonwealth." On January 3, 1942—just one day after Manila fell to invading Japanese forces—Selective Service informed local boards that Filipinos "shall be reclassified in the same manner as citizens of the United States." A few weeks later, Ereberto Brabante and Prudencio de la Cruz registered in New York City, happy to sign up for Army rather than the Navy. "We're not unpatriotic. It's just that we want to fight, not cook," Brabante explained. "I was in the United States Navy eight years as a steward. In the Army they'll give me a gun instead of a tray."[22]

WITHIN DAYS OF THE JAPANESE INVASION OF THE PHILIPPINES, Filipino community leaders in the United States proposed an all-Filipino battalion for the US Army. A volunteer force would achieve multiple ends: uniformed service would demonstrate Filipinos' patriotism to Americans; their language and cultural skills would be helpful to the US Army in any effort to retake the Philippines; and it would give Filipinos the opportunity to participate as partners in the liberation of their homeland. Among those leading the charge was Captain Mariano Sulit, a retired officer with twenty years' experience in the Philippine Scouts. The idea of an all-Filipino battalion must have been dear to Sulit's heart. As a student at the University of Vermont in 1918, he had enlisted in the US Army, but just before his unit was about to leave for France, Sulit was pulled out of the ranks, reassigned to the Philippine Scouts, and transferred to the Philippines, where he served for the next twenty years. On January 12, 1942, at a San Francisco conference, Sulit explained that "Filipinos everywhere . . . are clamoring to get a crack at the Japanese."[23]

On February 19, 1942, while USAFFE forces stood their ground on the Bataan Peninsula, Secretary of War Henry Stimson, a former governor-general of the Philippines, announced the battalion's formation "in recognition of the intense loyalty and patriotism of those Filipinos who are now residing in the United States. It provides for them a means of serving in the armed forces of the United States, and the eventual opportunity of fighting on the soil of their homeland." He ordered the War Department to begin recruiting soldiers—men who would train and serve as proper GIs, not as Philippine Scouts. The "Filipino Battalion," as it was initially called, was not a segregated unit like those in which African American soldiers served during World War II. Men seeking to serve in its ranks needed to enlist in the Army, and then to volunteer specifically for the new unit undergoing training at Camp San Luis Obispo in central California, although many draft boards sent Filipino soldiers directly into the new force whether they wanted it or not.[24]

The Filipino Battalion's commanding officer was Lieutenant Colonel Robert Offley, a career military officer and West Point grad who was born in the Philippines while his father served in the Philippine-American War and boasted that he spoke "passable" Tagalog. The soldiers—a vast majority of whom spoke either Ilocano or Visayan—may not have understood everything the colonel said, but they definitely caught the meaning of his curses. Offley was known for "interspersing his homilies with well known Tagalog phrases that would scald a cow." Many other officers were Filipinos. The minister of Stockton, California's United Filipino Church even signed up as the unit's chaplain.[25]

Filipino journalist Ernesto Ilustre recounted the soldiers' training regimen. "There is hardly any group of soldiers under the American flag more happy and more contented than these Filipinos," Ilustre wrote. "They adore their superior officers, they pay close attention to their military training, they like the California climate, and they just relish the Filipino dishes served to them Army style, rice and all." A writer for *American Legion* magazine found the high quality of the food unsurprising, since the "former personal chefs of Henry Ford, Leopold Stokowski, General George Marshall and Mae West are among the men now turning out meals for the Pinoys." The men "being put into combat shape by Uncle Sam are exceeding even the most optimistic expectations," Ilustre wrote, and would soon prove adept at jungle warfare, too. After all, he asked, "have not our very own fathers . . . perfected the guerilla method of fighting during the Spanish-American War?"[26]

News of the new battalion traveled quickly, reaching Filipino communities all across the country, and so many men signed up that Army officials expanded it into the Filipino Infantry Regiment on July 13, 1942. The regiment had outgrown Camp San Luis Obispo and now trained in temporary quarters at the Salinas Rodeo Grounds, not far from agricultural communities such as Watsonville, where Filipinos regularly worked. Soon, one regiment wasn't enough. On October 22, 1942, transferred from the rodeo grounds to nearby Fort Ord and renamed the First Filipino Infantry Regiment, the force was supplemented by a second regiment. The First shipped out for Camp Meade, near Sacramento, while the Second trained at Lompoc's Camp Cooke. Eventually some 7,000 men would join the "First and Second Fil."[27]

In the summer of 1942, while the men trained at the Salinas Rodeo Grounds, some of them would have known that just a few months earlier, the stadium had served as an assembly center for Japanese Americans from the Monterey Bay area. The wartime incarceration of 120,000 persons of Japanese descent affected Filipinos' own experiences on the job, around city streets, and even within their own families. Global events uncovered local fault lines between Filipinos and Japanese. On western farms, Filipino migrants often worked for Japanese labor contractors or on Japanese farms, and tensions carried over into residential neighborhoods, where Japanese ownership of housing, stores, pool halls, and movie theaters fostered resentment. Calls for boycotts of Japanese businesses filled the streets of Stockton, California, after December 1941, but they were nothing new: similar boycotts had followed a controversy there in February 1930 when the Saikis, a Japanese American family, rejected their daughter's marriage to Felisberto Tapia, a Filipino. By early 1942, pressure to intern America's Japanese population built until it became overwhelming. Opponents were few and far between.[28]

On February 19, 1942, President Franklin Roosevelt issued Executive Order 9066 authorizing the War Department to designate regions of the country "from which any or all persons may be excluded." That area would soon comprise nearly all of the three West Coast states. From his headquarters at the Presidio in San Francisco, Lieutenant General John DeWitt, a sixty-one-year-old career soldier and a veteran of the Philippine-American War, oversaw the process. His proclamation on March 24, 1942, established a curfew for those of Japanese ancestry in most West Coast areas. Just a few days later, on March 27, DeWitt announced full-scale evacuation.

When the news reached Mamerto and Mary Ventura, living in Seattle's multiethnic International District, it hit hard. Mamerto Ventura migrated to the United States from the Philippines in 1928, earned a college degree at Washington State College, and married Mary Chiyo Asaba, a Japanese American woman born on nearby Bainbridge Island in 1917. War now threatened to separate the couple, so they hired a lawyer. After their polite inquiries requesting exemption for mixed-race couples failed, on April 13, 1942, they filed the first known courtroom challenge anywhere in the United States to Japanese internment. Mary Ventura insisted that she was "loyal and devoted to the Constitution, laws, institutions, and customs of her country," and asserted that she was subjected to "unlawful and arbitrary restraint . . . only and solely because she is of Japanese descent."[29]

Two days later, federal district court judge Lloyd Black rejected the couple's claims, and the Venturas' case set a dangerous precedent. When Seattle resident and University of Washington student Gordon Hirabayashi challenged the War Department's curfew as a violation of the Fourteenth Amendment's equal protection clause, his case, too, was dismissed—by none other than Judge Lloyd Black, who cited as the controlling authority his own ruling in *Ex parte Ventura*. Hirabayashi appealed to the US Supreme Court, which unanimously upheld the curfew, despite the warning of Justice Frank Murphy—the former governor-general of the Philippines—that the order went to "the very brink of constitutional power." Hirabayashi spent three months in prison near Tucson, Arizona. As for Mary Ventura, the record is unclear. She was surely removed from the city in the spring of 1942, but was probably permitted to return sometime after March 1943: a Seattle church leader noted that "six or seven wives of mixed marriages" were among the first Japanese allowed to return to the city.[30]

As West Coast Japanese left, positions opened up in hotels, restaurants, and domestic service. Filipinos had shared those jobs with Japanese immigrants in the past. Now they found they worked next to African Americans, who moved to western cities in substantial numbers during the war. On fruit and vegetable farms, sudden labor shortages created openings for Filipino workers. Some Japanese American landowners asked Filipino employees to work their farms for them. In the Santa Clara Valley near San Jose, California, Johnny Ibarra took over the farm of his former boss, Yoshio Ando, charging merely a token sum to cover the property tax bill. Filipinos on Washington's Bainbridge Island tended the farms of their Japanese partners or bosses; some even moved into their houses. But generous cooperation between the two groups was hardly the norm: boycotts, hate strikes, and threats were more common. Overwhelmed, many Japanese simply abandoned their lands. In the month of March 1942 alone, Japanese farmers gave up nearly one third of the 200,000 acres that they farmed in California.[31]

Faced with shortages of both farm operators and agricultural laborers, the federal government stepped in to keep the farms running. In April 1942, with incarceration under way and an urgent need to plant the season's vegetable crops, the federal Farm Security Administration (FSA) hatched a plan to resettle San Francisco's Chinatown residents in the Santa Clara Valley about an hour south of the city. The War Department agency in charge of Japanese internment announced that noncitizens could apply for FSA loans to take over abandoned farms and that with "an honorable discharge from the armed forces of the United States," Filipinos were eligible to apply. As they collected checks from the FSA to manage land they were still barred by law from owning, Filipino farmers could reflect that war had forced the US government to include them in the privileges of citizenship—at the same time the government excluded and incarcerated another group of Asian migrants. War divided Filipinos and Japanese, drawing lines dividing ethnic groups, communities, and, as Mamerto and Mary Ventura learned, even families.[32]

"You are a disgrace to the name Filipino," labor leader Victorio Velasco told slack workers in late March 1942. "You can only redeem yourselves by *snapping out of it* and finding yourselves a job." Before the war, Filipinos' labor cycle of seasonal migration and frequent unemployment had marked them as unreliable workers. Now transience threatened to undermine the war effort. The solution—devised on the fly by federal officials and Filipino union bosses—helped make Filipino Americans partners in war mobilization. In the fall of 1942, the federal government introduced "manpower controls" in critical industries, essentially tying workers to their jobs. With a "release," a worker could go to the US Employment Service for a new job, or join the military. Although the rules were widely evaded, job-hopping without a release was difficult, particularly in closed-shop unionized workplaces, and Filipino workers often found they could not quit. A few years earlier, such steady work would have been a godsend, but in the middle of the war—with prices rising faster than wages—labor controls made it hard for agricultural "stoop" workers to make ends meet.[33]

In Hawai'i, wartime labor policies had even more drastic effects. "If you saw the Big Island then—ay, you can believe in the power of America," Virgilio Felipe later recalled. "Everywhere you looked, there was nothing but soldiers." Almost 80 percent of Filipino workers in Hawai'i were employed on the sugar plantations. War sent sugar prices through the roof, but wages remained frozen; workers were locked into their jobs and faced heavy penalties for absenteeism; and with martial law in effect throughout the islands since 11:30 a.m. on December 7, 1941, criticism of the policy was nowhere to be found. "They guarded you at work, at the movie house, in the street with MP's and police, and required permission to go do what you felt like doing," Felipe recalled. "Even the good-time girls could hardly sneak into our camp anymore. Made you think, maybe we were prisoners of war."[34]

Filipinos' agricultural work kept America's soldiers fed. Moving food around the globe for sixteen million soldiers and sailors posed logistical problems of nutrition, spoilage, and cost. Soon, the Army had an answer: canned salmon. Now generally thought of as a luxury food, salmon (or, as GIs called it, "goldfish") was the tuna of the 1940s: cheap, nutritious, and easily portable. In June 1942, the Army announced that it intended to purchase the entire "pack" of salmon, herring, sardines, and mackerel that year, despite labor shortages and military threats to the canneries after the Japanese seized Attu and Kiska in the Aleutian Islands in June 1942.[35]

Filipinos had begun working in Pacific Northwest canneries in 1911 and by the late 1920s were the largest ethnic group in Alaska's diverse salmon workforce. "Very seldom will you meet a Filipino along the Pacific Coast who had never been to Alaska," observed a Juneau newspaper. Canneries operated on a contracting system: managers told labor contractors—some of them Japanese, some Filipino—to show up in Alaska on a certain date with an agreed-upon number of men. It was the contractor's job to hire and transport the workers, and to provide housing and food, the cost of which was taken out of the workers' pay at the end of the season. This arrangement rested enormous power in the hands of contractors, and prewar strikes had often aimed at breaking the contractors' monopoly and winning union authority over hiring.[36]

Most Filipino union workers carried the membership cards of the Cannery Workers' and Farm Laborers' Union (CWFLU), founded by Filipino migrant Virgil Duyungan in 1933 and affiliated by the 1940s with the Congress of Industrial Organizations (CIO). The union won some victories in the 1930s, but it was the war that truly transformed the contracting system, as gutting and packing fish became "vital" to the war effort and Japanese middlemen disappeared. Filipinos could not easily be replaced by other unskilled workers, as was the case elsewhere. In the Lower 48, women had always worked in canneries, and as men left for war (or for better-paying wartime factory jobs), Filipina, Chicana, and southern European women stepped into cannery work in places like Oregon and Washington. Alaskan canneries hired more Native American men and women during the war, but there were few other local residents, and transporting West Coast women to Alaskan work sites was not an option. Existing sites housed workers in shoddy all-male barracks where beds were nothing more than wooden planks. Acquiring scarce construction materials in the middle of a war—and then moving both the materials and the construction workers to Alaska in time to build women's barracks by canning season—was deemed out of the question. Nevertheless, the troops needed canned salmon, and feeding them required keeping Filipino men on the cannery lines—regardless of whether they would have preferred to be in uniform or working in better-paying factory jobs in Seattle. Salmon jobs had become war jobs.[37]

Selective Service regulations technically gave employers—not unions—authority over who received a necessary worker exemption. But cannery owners turned the job over to the union itself, if for no other reason than that they rarely shared a common language with the men who worked for them. Selective Service in Washington, Oregon, and California officially recognized the Cannery Workers' Union as a "co-employer," and soon after, the CWFLU started writing to local draft boards across the West Coast with all its newfound authority. In March 1942, Local 7 told the Los Angeles board to defer Agapito Badbada at least until September, so that he could go to Alaska and help "put up a big pack of a vital defense food." A month later, they asked a Seattle board to defer Severino Munar, "an experienced key man in the fish house." By the middle of the war, draft boards across the country wrote directly to the CWFLU for information on the whereabouts of missing registrants, and union leaders such as president Trinidad Rojo even received special gasoline rations to help recruit and transport cannery workers. "Well, it is not because, not of Trinidad Rojo," he later recalled, "it is because of Mr. Salmon. Mr. Salmon's priority is very high."[38]

Partnering in power established the union's authority among Filipino workers, and as the wartime federal government regulated ever more aspects of American life, new political avenues opened for Filipinos. Prudencio Mori, a Cannery Workers official, urged the Office of Price Administration, which regulated housing costs and oversaw wartime rationing, to address the housing shortage his union's members faced. "These hotels in Chinatown in which most of our members are living are exorbitantly charging room rents to exploit unnecessarily people who are ignorant or much too busy to fight for their rights," he wrote in December 1943. Mori's description of his union brothers as too busy and too ignorant to fight was a calculated gesture. Filipinos had waged the same political battles over jobs and housing in the 1930s. Now, during the war, they got different results, even if it meant hitching their political aspirations to America's war machine.[39]

Far from the heat of California and the chill of the salmon cannery lines, Carlos Romulo set out deliberately to tie Filipinos' ambitions to American security. The forty-three-year-old journalist was also an officer in the Philippine Commonwealth Army, serving as an aide-de-camp to Douglas MacArthur and fleeing to Washington to join the government-in-exile, while his broadcasts from the Malinta tunnels of Corregidor and publications in the *Philippines Herald* won him the Pulitzer Prize in 1942. With easy access to Congress, the War Department, and the media, Romulo propagated a compelling story of shared sacrifice and citizenship.[40]

Romulo assured Americans that their empire was different. "In other countries in the Far East natives were reduced to the level of animals, but in the Philippines, from the beginning, the Americans regarded us as men." The sacrifices of Filipinos were American sacrifices, he argued, and the people who made them were at heart, as they were in law, American soldiers. A gifted writer and a savvy politician, Romulo knew exactly what he was doing. Time and again, Romulo masterfully took the political edge off decades of Filipino resistance, turning the nationalist struggles of Filipinos for the liberation of their homeland into a heartwarmingly American undertaking "against the enemy that was theirs and America's." His distortion of Philippine history and Philippine politics fit Filipinos into wartime America at a time when, he passionately believed, Filipinos needed America if they were ever going to establish their country as an independent nation. It worked marvelously—and it gave the US-Philippine relationship a new urgency in a world at war.[41]

"We suddenly became important because . . . we are the only Free Filipinos in the world," editorialized Stockton's *Philippines Mail* in December 1942. "We now count for something useful, something honorable and desirable." A few John Wayne movies didn't hurt, either. In the United States, the government needed Filipinos as workers, and decades of exclusion, uncertainty, and denial faded, at least for a moment. Across the Pacific, a similar struggle was under way, as another empire struggled for the hearts and minds and labor of Filipinos.[42]

THE JAPANESE OCCUPATION FORCES NEEDED LOYAL COLONIAL subjects, too, and tried to bind them to a new but not so different empire. As soon as the Imperial Japanese Army established control in Manila on January 2, 1942, officers of its civil affairs division, the Japanese Military Administration (JMA), began recruiting Filipino civilians for a Philippine Executive Commission to carry out daily governance. Civil servants, teachers, and postal employees kept their jobs, and little changed at the top. Of those Philippine politicians who remained after Corregidor, most assumed their JMA-assigned leadership roles, including the Executive Commission's head, Jorge Vargas, who, on January 23, 1942, offered Japanese officers a champagne toast of *mabuhay*, or "welcome." Only one official, Supreme Court Chief Justice Jose Abad Santos, was executed for refusing to join up.[43]

The Japanese found a handful of enthusiastic partners. Some nationalist politicians, happy to see the Americans withdraw in defeat, welcomed the Japanese as fellow Asians and true liberators. But plenty of Filipino nationalists were disappointed to find that the Japanese were no better than the Americans or Spanish had been before them. JMA administrators, for their part, couldn't simply appoint the most vocally pro-Japanese politicians to official positions, because unconnected political unknowns would lack authority among the Philippines' unenthusiastic civilian population. So rather than installing figures such as Artemio Ricarte or Benigno Ramos—both of whom had, in previous decades, taken up arms against the American colonial regime in avowed solidarity with Japan—the JMA recruited the political leaders of the former Commonwealth, men and women who had already made their careers navigating between a distant imperial power in Washington and the emerging mass politics of Philippine farms and streets.[44]

Across the Philippines, labor shortages followed from massive wartime population movements. Cities had emptied in the initial weeks after the invasion, but as violence wracked the countryside, rural Filipinos sought safety in urban areas. Manila's population nearly doubled during the war. At first, the Japanese hired Filipinos directly or used Japanese contracting firms as middlemen. Rather than commandeering rice from Filipino farmers, they bought it with occupation currency. The Japanese also harnessed labor from their POW and internment camps. Captain Tomibe Rokuro, who spent the war years managing the civilian internment camp at Baguio, reflected that it "was small and we did have a family-like atmosphere" conducive to managing the camp's labor needs, while an October 1944 report from the civilian internment camp at Santo Tomas boasted of 50,000 "man days" provided by the internees in that month. Wartime labor included domestic service and sexual labor, either paid, informally coerced, or managed by the Imperial Japanese Army's sex slavery or "comfort women" system. In early 1942, Hara Tamechi, captain of a Japanese destroyer, allowed the 300 men on his crew three hours of shore leave in the southern city of Davao. The men came ashore to find houses euphemistically labeled "Japanese military recreation center," with "many soldiers and sailors [already] queuing up in front of them."[45]

The Japanese governed at the local level through the Kapisanan sa Paglilingkod sa Bagong Pilipinas, or Kalibapi, the Association for Service for the New Philippines, a quasi-political party modeled on a similar organization that mobilized the Japanese home front. Established in December 1942, the Kalibapi sought to build a "New Philippines" by "invigorating" Filipinos with "oriental virtues" such as "hard work, . . . loyalty, [and] discipline." At its head was Benigno Aquino Sr., a powerful landlord from Tarlac, who soon accompanied Japanese officials in a William Howard Taft–like inspection tour to persuade locals to "collaborate with the new order." By 1944, the Kalibapi claimed some 1.5 million members—largely because membership was a precondition for most available civilian jobs.[46]

The Kempeitai, a military police force deployed throughout the Co-Prosperity Sphere, kept order. In the Philippines, the Japanese adapted the Kempeitai to the Philippine Constabulary, and recruited Kempeitai men from it, but the JMA never quite made peace with the Constabulary. On the one hand they considered constables the core of a "de-Americanized force" and boasted of ex-POWs in their ranks, including Brigadier General Guillermo Francisco, installed as the PC's wartime head. And yet the Japanese also feared arming the Constabulary, worried (rightly) that it was honeycombed with spies and guerrillas, so they never provided the Constabulary with adequate arms to bring order to an occupied and divided country, nor even enough ammunition to protect themselves: Filipinos in the Kempeitai carried only about six or seven rounds, and each bullet had to be accounted for at the end of the day.[47]

War and occupation destroyed the institutions of the US colonial government. Hospitals closed and schools were out of session for more than a year; some children stayed away for the duration of the war. As Filipinos dealt with shortages and policies that put Japanese soldiers' needs ahead of their own, they adapted, even learning enough Japanese to stay out of trouble. They focused their attentions where they had to. The most resented figures were not the Japanese soldiers stationed at distant urban headquarters, or political leaders who spoke to them over the radio, but those closer at hand: the captains of the labor details, the tax collectors, the Constabulary. Hated more than anyone else were the black marketeers, men and women cynically dismissed by Filipinos as practitioners not of the larger-than-life crime of *kolaborasyon*, but of something more tawdry that they called *buy-and-sell*.[48]

The Japanese grappled with the same difficulties that Filipinos faced—shortages of food, medical supplies, and manpower—and others too: resistance by guerrillas, frustrating noncooperation from local civilians, and fear of reinvasion by the United States. "Since we could not rule by power," Captain Tomibe later recalled, "the only way was to appeal to human warmth and mutual trust." Their colonial rule was at best improvisational, and eventually simply desperate. That did not stop them from filling the pages of the *Manila Tribune*, the occupied city's official newspaper, with florid rhetoric promising to redeem the Philippines from US colonialism. Japanese occupiers made grand gestures of renaming streets and revising school textbooks, and shipped a few elite Filipino students to Tokyo to study, efforts akin to those the Americans had made forty years before. Miki Kiyoshi, the architect of the Greater East Asia Co-Prosperity Sphere's ideology of pan-Asian unity, suggested that the Japanese owed an "older brother's guidance" to the people of the Philippines, and even came to the Philippines to give lofty speeches at POW camps. Not everyone was buying it: "They tell us we are their brothers," one young man recalled. "Then they beat us."[49]

For the Japanese, decolonizing the Philippines was ultimately a step toward recolonizing it as part of Japan. When they sang the praises of "Oriental civilization," they had Japanese culture in mind. This had particular valence for Filipino prisoners of war, who were most intensely targeted by Japanese propaganda. The Japanese released many of them after POW Rejuvenation Schools that inculcated Japanese war aims, told Filipino soldiers they had been "misled by America," and assured them they could now be "reliable brothers." Taken prisoner at Corregidor on May 6, 1942, Gregoria Espinosa signed a loyalty oath two months later, walked free, and returned to nursing. Ex-POWs offered the JMA fertile ground for labor recruitment, not because the ex-soldiers had embraced Japanese ideas, but because the released prisoners were displaced young men in search of work and often found themselves released far from their homes. Some 3,500 were said to have joined the Imperial Japanese Army following their political rehabilitation.[50]

Over the course of the war, several hundred thousand Japanese soldiers served in the Philippines. Some of the Filipinos' new "older brothers" may have brought with them from Japan some knowledge of Southeast Asia gleaned from publications of the Philippine Society in Japan, a small publicity group established in 1935, or the writings of Enosawa Hisashi, a prominent Japanese settler who published dozens of articles explaining the two cultures. Many had relatives in the Japanese settlements in Davao. Other soldiers, veterans of colonial service in Korea, Manchuria, or Taiwan, carried their conquering mindsets to the Philippines. Most, though, knew little or nothing about the country and imposed distorted understandings of tropical societies. Captain Hara, shocked to see Filipinos walking barefoot, acknowledged he "was intrigued by the native scene" he encountered in Davao.[51]

In a mirror image of the Filipino soldiers who were then in Uncle Sam's armed forces, a component of the Imperial Japanese soldiers in the Philippines were Koreans. During the war, the Japanese recruited some 240,000 soldiers from Korea, about half as volunteers and half as conscripts, along with soldiers recruited from Taiwan. In the Philippines and elsewhere, they worked as dockworkers, interpreters, and prison guards. Fifty years after the Americans mobilized *chinos* and *cargadores* to get their imperial job done, so, too, did the Japanese.[52]

By the time the Japanese had set up these new governing institutions, it was already too late. They did not have enough resources to claim Filipinos' loyalty through patronage, and they would soon find themselves rivaled by the increasingly powerful guerrilla armies.

Some of the first guerrilla units were formed by Filipino and American soldiers who evaded capture at Bataan or elsewhere to start again from scratch. Filipino POWs released by the Japanese also joined guerrilla groups. Glicerio Valdez survived the Bataan Death March, left Camp O'Donnell in August 1942, and made his way to his home village of Alcala, where he and fellow veterans set up a small guerrilla unit. In Ormoc, on the island of Leyte, the prewar commander of the local Philippine Constabulary unit, Lieutenant Blas Miranda, headed to the mountains in early 1942 and emerged by August to consolidate his leadership of the Western Leyte Guerrilla Warfare Forces. Leadership within units such as these generally deferred to the authority of prewar (and thus American-approved) ranks, as when rival guerrilla groups in Leyte selected Colonel Ruperto Kangleon as the head of the forces on that island in early 1943. Kangleon was a model officer of a US-oriented guerrilla group. A former Olympic athlete and a 1916 graduate of the Philippine Constabulary Academy in Baguio, Kangleon served as a PC officer until joining the new Philippine Army in 1936. He escaped a Japanese POW camp in Mindanao in December 1942 and made his way by outrigger canoe to Leyte.[53]

Wendell Fertig, an American civilian mine operator living in Manila at the outbreak of the war, made his way in 1942 to Mindanao, intending to do "any damn thing but surrender." Asserting (falsely) that MacArthur had named him a brigadier general and issued him orders, the charismatic Fertig assembled a guerrilla army, installed himself as its commander, and proceeded to govern a fictional polity known as the Free Philippine Government of Mindanao. US-oriented guerrilla units such as Fertig's operated on a colonial model, with strict control by white officers and subservient service by Filipino troops, along with an understanding that liberating US territory from Japanese control was an American colonial obligation, not a step toward Philippine national self-determination.

By contrast, radicals in central Luzon province north of Manila formed the Hukbo ng Bayan Laban sa Hapon, or Hukbalahap, the People's Army of Resistance against Japan, tapping peasants' opposition both to the Japanese invaders and the Filipino landowners who were profiting by collaborating with them. Their military commander was Luis Taruc, a small, wiry, intensely political man who would become the face of twentieth-century Philippine communism. Born to a peasant family in 1913 in San Luis in Pampanga, just ten miles from the Candaba swamps where Matthew Batson had formed the Philippine Scouts, Taruc began as a moderate socialist, then joined the Communist Party by 1939. For the Huks, overthrowing Japanese fascism was a first step toward socialist transformation. Guerrilla war was communist revolution and the enemies were anyone who stood in its way, regardless of which flag they marched under.[54]

The guerrillas' only shared aim was the defeat of the Japanese. Men like Kangleon fought with the US empire; Fertig fought for the US empire; Taruc and the Huks fought against it. With Japan's occupying forces stretched thin, the guerrillas easily claimed the upper hand in many regions of the country, despite having few weapons, not a lot of food, and no communication with MacArthur in Australia until late 1942. (Indeed, initially fearing the messages were bait from Japanese codebreakers, Americans left the guerrillas' first contacts unanswered.) Utilizing tactics from armed insurgency to sabotage to passive noncompliance, Filipino guerrillas made military pacification and day-to-day administration challenging for a Japanese army spread too thin to impose its will by force of arms. The guerrillas also kept a close watch on Filipinos who remained in public office, pressuring them to cooperate with the resistance and against the collaborators.

Taruc and the Huks put ideology front and center. By contrast, some guerrilla groups were merely gangs of desperate men and women living by plunder. Among such gang leaders was Felipe Culala, the powerful boss of a small band known as Dayang-Dayang, who ransacked the Luzon countryside until rivals from the Huks assassinated her. Every guerrilla group depicted its rivals as mere "bandits," but nearly all them could be characterized that way. Especially in the war's early days, before leadership was consolidated, guerrillas had no alternative but to extract their livelihoods from local communities. Over time, though, the better-organized guerrillas acted more and more like governments, issuing currency and imposing price controls, running schools, authorizing marriages, and keeping order, while extracting taxes from local populations. In this, they were forming not only armies, but military-dominated societies, tapping extant labor and family networks and providing patronage to their rank and file. By contrast, the US-oriented and American-dominated USAFFE remnants focused on building military units that looked like the US Army, with an eye toward long-distance cooperation with, and eventually official recognition from, MacArthur.[55]

The violence between rival guerrilla groups could be as intense as anything the guerrillas faced from the Japanese, especially the battles waged between the USAFFE remnants and the revolutionary Huk forces. In such situations, the Japanese retreated, letting the guerrillas attack one another. On the island of Samar, guerrillas faced off against the Philippine Constabulary, Filipino men conscripted by the Japanese Kempeitai. Rather than target Filipinos serving in Japanese uniforms, the guerrillas resisted their commander's plan to attack the PC. Guerrillas sympathized with the constables' politically difficult position and calculated that assassinating the Constabulary men who were halfheartedly chasing them would only lead to their replacement by Japanese soldiers, who might be more ruthless, and would surely be better armed than the PC men with their seven-bullet rations. It was a wise calculation: as guerrilla resistance and civilian noncompliance increased over time, so did Japanese counterinsurgency campaigns, including the establishment of "provincial pacification committees" throughout the countryside.[56]

In the imagination of Douglas MacArthur and his fellow US Army war planners, the guerrillas were still a colonial army, brave and loyal brown brothers under the command of daring and valiant white Americans, waiting for orders as if nothing had happened at Pearl Harbor or on the march in Bataan. Or indeed as if nothing had changed since William McKinley had proclaimed America's aim of "benevolent assimilation." But it had. The bonds of war forged decades before endured even in the darkest days of the war, and Japanese propaganda proved unable to sever them. But Filipino soldiers themselves tied those bonds together in new ways. The guerrillas in the jungles—even the communists—knew that in 1942 there was no path to national self-determination without the US Army. Guerrillas chose their fight, and more often than not, they chose to fight with the United States, and not simply for it. Whether anyone knew it or not, the days of the Philippine Scouts were numbered. All the more so on the other side of the Pacific, where the First and Second Fil marched under the American flag, preparing for America's reconquest of its largest Pacific colony.

On October 15, 1942, Resident Commissioner Joaquin Elizalde addressed the assembled soldiers at Camp San Luis Obispo in California. "Every Filipino must be proud at the sight of this Filipino Unit," he claimed, "because it represents the hope of all of us to retake our country from the Japanese invader—with our own hands." The Filipino unit was a "symbol of revenge, the continuation of the glorious and heroic spirit of Bataan." After recounting the social and economic sufferings of Filipinos living under occupation, Elizalde noted that "every one of us, every red-blooded Filipino, must save them. . . . While the Japanese are in our country, our independence is a myth."[57]

Carlos Romulo meanwhile complained that Filipinos' contribution to the American war effort was not being taken seriously enough. "Not an American seemed to realize the blood-given right of the Filipino soldiers to the American uniform." The First and Second Fil were new and different soldiers. Ever since 1901, the Philippine Scouts had been part of the US Army but held a second-class status. Most of the men who served alongside Americans in Bataan in April 1942 were soldiers of the Philippine Commonwealth Army that Douglas MacArthur and Dwight Eisenhower had designed. The Philippine Constabulary had never reported to the War Department, and the guerrillas were known in Washington only by rumor and reputation. But the men of the First and Second Fil were regular US Army GIs, who wore the same uniforms, drew the same pay and benefits during the war, and looked forward to GI Bill benefits afterward.[58]

Wearing US Army uniforms didn't always change laws or mindsets. Alejo Filomeno of the First Filipino Infantry Regiment explained to Colonel Offley that before he shipped out for the Pacific, he wanted to marry his girlfriend, Jessie Chavarria, a Mexican American woman from Texas, but California law forbade their marriage. This was not the first that Offley had heard of the issue. The colonel chartered a bus to Gallup, New Mexico, in a state with no anti-miscegenation statute, where Filomeno and Chavarria—along with dozens of other couples—married under color of law, and rode the bus they called the "Honeymoon Express" back to their base. Everyday discrimination continued as well: a group of soldiers of the Second Fil on leave from Camp Beale in northern California were refused service at a restaurant in nearby Marysville. Colonel Offley gave the Marysville Chamber of Commerce a piece of his mind, but the soldiers were skeptical that change would follow. "We of California had never really believed that Americans would change their stripes," observed Manuel Buaken, one of the men. Here was Filipinos' "Triple V": a war against Japan, for the Philippines, and within the United States.[59]

When American news accounts highlighted one part of the Triple V—that Filipino soldiers served in uniform in pursuit of US citizenship—they oversimplified what was actually a contentious undertaking. Within the ranks of the First and Second Fil, naturalization was an official requirement, but as Manuel Buaken explained, the discrimination experienced by soldiers in places such as Marysville "tarnished the golden privilege of citizenship. There has been much discussion in our ranks as to whether it has any meaning for us." His fellow soldier Jose Trinidad asked "what good would it do to become citizens of America if we are still brown-skinned inferiors? I would rather not."[60]

Neither would Mariano Angeles, who objected to the policy and its inequities. "Before World War II," he recalled in an interview a generation later, "we Filipinos are fighting for our, you know, being to, become a citizen see." Rather than celebrating the rapid transformation of federal policies toward Filipinos, Angeles "resented it. . . . I resented why do they have to become an American citizen now . . . only to the service men see?" In the past, "when we ask to become American they even describe us as barbarous and things like that. And trouble citizens. So I told them, . . . why only even to the soldiers?" After voicing his objections, Angeles was "called to the intelligence officer twice in 50 minutes." He continued to object. "Why do they have to give only to the soldiers rather than to all?" he asked. The captain had an easy answer. "You know you are now in the Army. That's why." But Angeles was unconvinced. "So they mean to say that when my future is to die, that is the time when I, they give me my, they give me the privilege to become American, so 'Hell no.'"[61]

Angeles walked out of the office without taking an oath of allegiance to the United States, but while Manuel Buaken and Jose

Trinidad debated the meanings of citizenship, their sergeant laid down the law: "If you don't want to be American citizens, you'll do K.P. the rest of your life. I personally guarantee that." So they joined a group of more than four hundred soldiers naturalized at Camp Beale on February 20, 1943, in a public event that drew reporters, politicians, and top army brass. "They become officially now what they have long been in their hearts," Captain Chandler Sprague told the crowd that afternoon. "Americans."[62]

In an April 1942 editorial, published just days after the surrender at Bataan, the *Chicago Tribune* boasted that "when we go back to Bataan, as we're going to do, Filipino battalions are going with us." The paper equated service in the First and Second Fil with the struggles of Filipino guerrillas fighting the Japanese occupation and noted that a "loyal population" in the Philippines "awaits the coming of the new Filipino army in training on American soil, and when these fighting men come home they will have the help of the guerrilla forces that are keeping up the battle from the mountains and the jungles." Two years later, as they shipped out to join America's reconquest of the Philippines, many of the soldiers in the First and Second Fil surely did think they were "going home." But even while Captain Sprague told them were, in their hearts, "Americans," the article revealed that service in US Army uniforms could not erase the assumption that Filipinos did not belong in the United States.[63]

By 1943, the Japanese hold on everyday life in the Philippines remained fragile. Just like the Americans forty years earlier, the military government alternated between carrots and sticks. Amnesty offers and financial incentives alternated with raids on guerrilla holdouts—among them a May 1943 reinforcement of troops in Mindanao, and 5,000 soldiers sent to Leyte in late 1943 in what the Japanese themselves acknowledged was a "reinvasion." Japan pursued a strategy of vengeance that writer Maximo Kalaw called "collective responsibility for individual acts." In a flourish of historical irony, the Japanese even adopted the water cure. The final push for conquest had failed, and retreat seemed to be looming on the horizon.[64]

Then, in the fall of 1943, Japan made a bold political move: it granted independence to the Philippines. By establishing the Philippine Republic, the Japanese hoped to appeal to Filipino nationalists, discredit American imperialism, and capture the attention of other occupied Southeast Asian areas such as Burma, Malaya, Indonesia, and Indochina. (Indeed, a month earlier, in August 1943, Japan had announced plans for Burmese independence.) Japanese Premier Tojo Hideki, who visited the Philippines in the spring of 1943, announced that independence would follow once order was restored and the Filipino people had returned "to their true Oriental spirit," terms not so different from the conditional promise in America's 1916 Jones Act.[65]

Independence ceremonies took place on October 14, 1943, in front of the legislative buildings in Manila. The crowd of 300,000—bigger than had turned out to mark the Jones Act in 1916 or Tydings-McDuffie in 1934—included Emilio Aguinaldo, hero of the Philippine revolution between 1898 and his 1901 capture. Out of the political limelight for some time, Aguinaldo had emerged in the war's earliest days, when he broadcast a radio appeal to General Douglas MacArthur to surrender, and later insisted that "to oppose the white man and gain freedom and independence, the colonial races must join together." Today, the president of the ill-fated First Philippine Republic in 1898 raised the Philippine flag to introduce the Second. "The birth of the glorious new Philippines is now a consummated fact," announced Japanese military commander Lieutenant General Kuroda Shigenori. "I can well imagine your profound joy at obtaining independence."[66]

No Americans were present at the independence ceremonies, but James Reuter, an American priest in Manila, recalled that some

Filipino seminarians who attended the day's events "wept when they saw that flag going up by itself. . . . When they came back . . . it was apparent that they were deeply touched, so much so that they gathered by themselves, talking Tagalog. We felt that they were separated from us by some emotional barrier." The international press dismissed the new republic (American columnist Walter Lippmann sneered that for the Quislings and Lavals of Europe, at least "there was a reasonable prospect of making their treason pay"), but in the Philippines serious debate ensued, asking whether 1943 marked the abjection of Filipinos' national aspirations or their fulfillment.[67]

At the head of the new Philippine Republic stood President José Laurel. Brilliant, reckless, and uncompromisingly anti-American, Laurel was the ideal president for the Japanese puppet state. His opposition to US rule stemmed from his memories of the American invasion in 1898, his resentment of American cultural influence, and a disdain for American democratic institutions he acquired while studying at Yale Law School from 1917 to 1920. By contrast, Laurel admired Japan's rapid economic growth and its rhetoric of pan-Asian unity. From his office at the Malacañang Palace, Laurel announced that "because I like my country to be free, I do not like America to come back." But he played it carefully. Fulsome praise for Japan—whether Laurel believed it or not—would not have appealed to Filipinos living under the occupation's political and economic hardships. And with armed guerrillas in the hills just outside Manila, full-throated declarations of Filipino nationalism would have raised Japanese suspicion. In such contexts, anti-American rhetoric was the safest bet: the Japanese were pleased to hear it; it resonated with the Filipino people, many of whom felt abandoned by their American colonial rulers; and Laurel sincerely believed it. "We are wearying with the pretensions of the 'White man's burden,' which more often than not has only served to cloak exploitations of weaker peoples," he wrote in a November 1943 issue of the *Manila Tribune*.[68]

To be sure, the Philippine Republic was a propaganda move aimed at transforming a conquered country into a liberated ally. It was also a useful governing tactic, because it allowed Japanese officials to turn over day-to-day responsibility for policing and civil affairs. Filipino politicians, in turn, knew that independence was not just a political fiction: it would likely mean fewer Japanese soldiers around, offering them more control over increasingly scarce resources, which would give them the upper hand as they competed with the guerrillas for political legitimacy. "The offer of independence could not have been rejected," Laurel wrote in his memoirs. "Our ancestors had fought for it."[69]

As a president, José Laurel was a largely—and at times deliberately—ineffectual figurehead. For him and for every Filipino serving in the wartime republic, necessity was the mother of everyday collaboration. Many made do as best they could, dragging their feet or feigning sickness when ordered to take on unpleasant tasks. A few kept up contacts with guerrillas in the mountains while working secretly on behalf of the underground movement. Nevertheless, Laurel also was, for better or worse, a puppet of the Japanese occupation, and the Philippine Republic existed at the pleasure of imperial Japan. On the same day as the declaration of independence, the two nations signed a pact of military alliance in which the Philippines agreed to "afford all kinds of facilities for the military actions to be undertaken by Japan," basing terms not so different from those the United States had imposed on the Philippine Commonwealth a decade before. Laurel also tipped his hand about the regime's priorities in his inauguration speech, when he emphasized for Filipinos that "the common denominator is hard work."[70]

Work became the most common topic of government propaganda. Guillermo Francisco and J. C. Quimbo, two former USAFFE officers serving with the Japanese-controlled Constabulary, wrote an open letter to the civilian population of the Visayan Islands. Appealing to national sentiment, they noted that "for the first time in 400 years" Filipinos had "been given a chance to work out their own salvation," and therefore "all hands should be in the fields and in the factories, working for the New Philippines, not fighting against its peaceful progress." Francisco and Quimbo did not want Filipinos to lose this opportunity, warning that "any further resistance is not only futile but would be classified as outlawry. . . . As soldiers and compatriots, we think too much of you to see you being annihilated."[71]

Independence did nothing to conceal the fact the life was growing increasingly grim, with shortages of food and medical supplies, and raids by both Japanese and Filipino soldiers on storehouses and barnyards that left ordinary civilians helpless. What "Mickey Mouse" Japanese occupation currency could not buy, the black market supplied, stoking uncontrolled inflation. Hunger generated a barter economy, with urban dwellers "glad to work for a bowl of rice or a mess of camotes." Japanese soldiers were no better off, ordered to buy their rice from locals but not to seize it, lest they antagonize civilian populations and thereby push them into the ranks of the guerrillas, who by March 1943 had established clear lines of communication and supply with the Americans.[72]

Allied preparation for reinvasion required coordination with the guerrillas. General MacArthur, frustrated at initial failures, tapped Colonel Courtney Whitney to head up the Philippine Regional Section of the Allied Intelligence Bureau for the Southwest Pacific Area. Whitney, an acolyte of MacArthur and an advocate of aggressive guerrilla war, reported to MacArthur's chief of staff for intelligence, Colonel Charles Willoughby, who was more cautious, fearful that open warfare would lead to the guerrillas' slaughter and convinced the guerrillas' chief value was reconnaissance. But MacArthur sided with Whitney and pumped in weapons, money, and medicine. By late 1943, the guerrillas could even evacuate wounded soldiers to Australia. USAFFE top brass wanted guerrillas they could work with, which required guerrillas who either shared their values or willingly took their orders. That meant they tapped guerrilla units commanded by men they had previously known in the Scouts or the Philippine Army. MacArthur sent

Lieutenant Commander Charles Parsons behind the lines to Mindanao to bring guerrillas there under US command, and tellingly, the first ones Parsons recognized were the guerrillas organized by Wendell Fertig—the force that looked and acted most like America's prewar colonial army. In Leyte, US officials coordinated with the US-oriented unit under the control of Ruperto Kangleon rather than the homegrown forces assembled by Blas Miranda, an army of nationalists who resented MacArthur's abandonment and responded to his promise of "I Shall Return" with the reminder that "We Remained!"[73]

The practice was self-reinforcing. After establishing connections in March 1943, MacArthur initially ordered the guerrillas to "lie low," but guerrilla officers insisted they needed to start attacking to win some victories in order to bolster morale and recruit more troops. MacArthur and Whitney agreed, hoping guerrillas could at least hem the Japanese in to the towns where they were garrisoned. As soon as Kangleon and other US-connected guerrillas started receiving shipments of American weapons and food, they began winning battles. Enlistment in their units boomed, and further victories followed. Locals knew that if they joined failing guerrilla units, they were at risk of starvation, capture, or betrayal, but if they joined successful units, they would be armed and fed and maybe someday paid. If they were killed, someone—possibly even Uncle Sam—might care for their widows. Men soon deserted independent guerrilla units and flocked to the ones the Americans favored. Much to their distress: US Army officers also came to understand that guerrilla armies were contending for political authority over the Filipino people, and consistently sought to hold guerrilla numbers down and keep power out of local commanders' hands. MacArthur wanted no rivals when he returned.

Cigarettes and chocolates proved the crucial means of exchange. They were effective recruitment tools because guerrillas could easily resell them on the black market. But not only that. Stamped with the US flag and MacArthur's words ("I shall return"), they conveyed that the guerrilla units handing them out were the real deal. Thus, political supremacy emerged in the end not from which guerrillas were most committed to liberating the nation, but which were best able to tap into American coffers and deliver the goods to a starving people already adept at tactical loyalty. This process, in turn, shaped Filipinos' understandings of military service for generations. In the decades after the war, as guerrilla leaders took up political positions in the independent Philippines, they mobilized veterans into legions and promised them continued financial and social security. On election day, politicians reaped the rewards of loyalties established in the darkest days of the war and reiterated afterward. It started with cigarettes and chocolate.[74]

Reinvasion—or, as the Americans called it, liberation—was now just a matter of time. In Washington's grand strategy sessions, Roosevelt thought it best to send allied forces around the Philippines, a view shared by many if not most of his strategists. "There wasn't any naval officer I know," recalled Robert Lee Dennison, "who didn't think bypassing the Philippines was the way to do it." But Douglas MacArthur would have none of that: at a meeting in Honolulu in July 1944, the general persuaded FDR that recapturing Manila would weaken the Imperial Japanese Army while serving propaganda purposes in the Philippines. MacArthur tapped a loyal general, Walter Krueger, to lead the invasion. And he made a place—albeit a subsidiary one—for Filipino soldiers in the reinvasion.[75]

In the meantime, as American goods circulated in the countryside and rumors of an American invasion spread, the tone changed from resignation to anticipation. At Baguio, after guerrillas gained access to supplies and ammunition, Captain Tomibe could feel the difference: "The eyes of the natives changed from friendship to hate." Something was coming.[76]

CHAPTER SIX

LIBERATIONS

1944–1946

On September 22, 1944, the Philippines declared war on the United States. Manuel Roxas, a former Philippine Army officer and Douglas MacArthur's prewar confidante, signed the declaration on behalf of the nominally independent Philippine Republic that Japan had established a year earlier. In a radio address that evening, President José Laurel urged Filipinos "to render every aid and assistance to the Imperial Japanese Government." Not since 1899, when revolutionaries fired on American soldiers at Manila's San Juan Bridge, had Filipinos tried officially to sever the bonds that had joined them to the United States. Five days earlier, the first American air raids had hit Manila, well-supplied guerrillas were growing bolder by the day, and US forces gathered offshore a few hundred miles away. "Liberation" was imminent, and from Guadalcanal to Tarawa to Guam, US troops were recovering America's Pacific Century from Japan one hard-fought island at a time. The declaration—which was Japan's idea, not José Laurel's—accomplished little.[1]

Filipinos' national aspirations now rested in the balance between Japanese occupation and American invasion. More than two years after the fall of the Philippines, American and Filipino soldiers were about to renew their bonds in battle by fighting together against Japan. The United States continued to depend on Filipino soldiers—guerrillas in the mountains and the GIs in the First and Second Fil—to prepare the way for invasion. From that necessary but uneven military partnership, Filipinos demanded concessions that took the form of promises: national independence for the Philippines, veterans benefits and citizenship rights for ordinary soldiers. It would remain to be seen whether America would deliver after the war. But for now, one promise—MacArthur's vow that "I shall return"—was about to be fulfilled.

AT 10:00 A.M. ON OCTOBER 20, 1944, THE SOLDIERS LANDED NEAR Tacloban on the island of Leyte. Lieutenant General Walter Krueger and the 6th Army—132,000 strong—faced just 16,000 Japanese troops. General Douglas MacArthur watched the initial landings from aboard the USS *Nashville* as Filipino US Navy stewards and messmen below deck kept the ship running. That day, the 6th Army opened a beachhead just wide enough to allow MacArthur to stage his watery landing for the newsreel cameras and announce: "People of the Philippines, I have returned." In Washington, President Roosevelt boasted that "we and our Philippine brothers in arms . . . will drive out the invader." Victory proved slow. With 45,000 Japanese troops rushed over from other islands to shore up defenses, Leyte was not fully conquered until Christmas.[2]

Tacloban residents waved US flags and shouted "Americanos come!," hopeful for an end to the war's deprivations. "It was thus I saw my countrymen again for the first time," reflected Filipino journalist Carlos Romulo, who accompanied Douglas MacArthur during the invasion. Also among the cheering crowds were thieves, swindlers, prostitutes, and refugees. Japanese withdrawal prompted widespread looting and violent reprisals against collaborators. Guerrilla leader Ruperto Kangleon, put in charge of Leyte's makeshift military government by MacArthur, was powerless to stop the lawlessness, or even to keep Filipino civilians from fleeing into active combat areas. Guerrillas, for their part, rushed to the Americans as well. Some reestablished their prewar Philippine Scout or Philippine Army units. Other guerrillas sought out the US Army looking for arms and authority.[3]

The soldiers of the First and Second Fil—the US Army's Filipino volunteer regiments—came ashore at Leyte, too. In June 1944, the First Fil sailed from California for New Guinea, where Australian Army officers taught them jungle warfare tactics. Filipino draftees who had trained in Hawai'i were surprised when they found themselves sent to New Guinea and incorporated into the First Fil. "When I was shipped to the jungle," one recalled, "I saw the other members of the regiment. I thought, what the hell is this? I didn't want to be part of the Philippine Army. Some of us were real peeved." Others were proud: "I was kind of glad, when I wrote home to my dad, address at the First Fil. . . . He was surprised, then glad, there was such a thing." Officers plucked about five hundred men from the ranks for the First Reconnaissance Battalion, which did secret intelligence work in advance of the US invasion. "Before we landed on Leyte," boasted an American officer, "we were in a spot where if a Japanese buck sergeant, anywhere in the Philippines, even went to the latrine we knew about it in half an hour."[4]

Most soldiers, though, drew assignments less daring than secret reconnaissance missions. The First Fil did guard duty and participated in mop-up operations against Japanese troops on the Philippines' outer islands. Many of the Second Fil's men arrived in country only after the fighting was over, detailed to Philippine Civil Affairs Units (PCAUs), or "pea-cows," that helped restore the prewar government and aid refugees. Aurelio Bulosan, brother of writer Carlos Bulosan, found the

First Fil enthusiastically greeted by the guerrillas. "Altho all of you Filipinos have been away from this land," a guerrilla told him, "I always knew that you will come back to fight for your people and for the things America stands for."[5]

On October 23, three days after the landings, a massive naval battle raged offshore in Leyte Gulf, and the first kamikaze planes took off from Clark Field near Manila for suicide attacks on US ships. That day, Sergio Osmeña announced the restoration of the Philippine Commonwealth government that the Tydings-McDuffie Act had established in 1934 and that military defeat had displaced in 1942. He was its new president, having stepped into the role after the death of President Manuel Quezon in August 1944. Osmeña moved quickly to feed hungry people and establish law and order. He also sought to incorporate the guerrillas into the US Armed Forces in the Far East (USAFFE), the umbrella force established under MacArthur's command on the eve of the war. Just a week after the invasion, on October 28, 1944, Osmeña inducted all officially recognized guerrilla groups (some 70,000 men and women) into the Philippine Army (PA). He had full authority to issue the executive order and plenty of practical reasons to do so—it was the only way legally to put the guerrillas under MacArthur's control. But given that the Philippine Army was already a formal component of USAFFE, Osmeña's order had the unstated—and very deliberate—effect of placing the guerrillas into the service of the US armed forces. General Douglas MacArthur approved of Osmeña's action and, calling for "equal pay for equal risk," used his field command authority to equalize pay rates among all USAFFE soldiers, although US War Department officials later overruled him.[6]

By now, with the American invasion under way and the Japanese retreating and regrouping, the guerrillas had no trouble filling their ranks. Some joined hastily as rumors of invasion spread; others concocted stories to persuade Americans that they had been guerrillas all along. Some names were retroactively added to the muster rolls to reflect clandestine service during years when paper records could have led to betrayal, or when there simply wasn't any paper to be had, or after the guerrillas had learned to read and write their names. Other rosters extended to reflect personal loyalties or kinship ties. The final word on recognition rested with US Army officers. Some were guerrillas themselves, tasked with coordinating between their ragtag forces and the 6th Army juggernaut, and sensitive to the complexities of the guerrilla situation. Others were bureaucrats far away in Washington who knew little and understood less.

As refugees fled to the American lines, they offered their labor in return for food, shelter, and medicine. "The Filipinos were eager to help the fight in any way they could," Carlos Romulo reported. "Physical labor was all they had to offer, and labor was a commodity most needed by the invading forces." In fact, US Army brass were hesitant to hire too many or pay too much, lest they accelerate the inflationary spiral already gripping the countryside. The PCAUs coordinated the work. Captain Abner Pickering told a group of workers in Tacloban, "We need labor. You will get paid for the work you do in Philippine currency and with it you will be able to buy the rice and the other products we will bring." But, he assured them, "you'll do it as free men!"[7]

The Japanese continued to mobilize locals for the epic battles still to come. When the Philippine Republic declared war on the United States on the eve of the Leyte landings, President José Laurel refused to institute a military conscription law that would draft Filipino men into the Japanese forces. Top officials in Tokyo wanted it, but Japanese officers in country were relieved, fearful of arming and training tens of thousands of Filipino troops, many of whom, surely, would defect to the guerrilla armies. Laurel's anti-conscription stand disappointed the Japanese, who wanted both a military draft and labor conscription as well. Through local neighborhood associations, through the official Labor Recruitment Agency, and then at a point of a bayonet, they got the workers they needed.[8]

Under Japanese command, labor battalions transformed into defense leagues, and then into last-ditch armies, as a few thousand Filipinos took up arms with the Japanese against the American and Filipino invaders. On November 14, 1944, just weeks after the Leyte landings, the Japanese military announced that it would "make use of part of the armed strength of native units who have friendly feelings toward us." At least 5,000 Filipinos served in the Kalipunang Makabayan ng mga Pilipino, or Makapili, the Alliance of Philippine Patriots, a Japanese auxiliary force recruited by the dedicated pro-Japanists Benigno Ramos and Artemio Ricarte after Laurel rejected conscription. The extent to which service in these militia regiments for "home defense" was voluntary remains unclear. Some men joined the Makapili out of nationalist fervor, or were mobilized by leaders such as Ramos. Some needed food to eat; others were impressed into service. The men served as guides and scouts, doing reconnaissance work and manual labor for the Japanese forces as they fought off the American armies.[9]

By January 1945, two months after the American invasion, the Japanese were on the run but not yet defeated. Officials in Tokyo ordered a retreat from far-off conquered territories and an all-out defense of Japan's home islands, now under regular attack from American bombing runs. But the Japanese would not—or simply could not—evacuate all their troops with them from Southeast Asia, so soldiers had to fight to the last man. Some two thirds of the Japanese in the Philippines died before the fall of 1945—including half the 38,000 Japanese civilian settlers, nearly all of whom were mobilized into the armed forces in some form. Filipinos who had cast their lot with the Japanese faced difficult times. José Laurel was evacuated to Japan. Irreconcilable to the end, Artemio Ricarte, the Viper, took to the hills of Luzon with a remnant of loyal troops, and was never heard from again.[10]

The invasion was now under way from all directions. On January 9, 1945, Krueger's 6th Army landed 68,000 men at the Lingayen Gulf in the north, where they faced no Japanese opposition, in part because the radical Hukbalahap guerrillas had already cleared the Japanese from the area. The US 8th Army under Lieutenant General Robert Eichelberger began closing in on Manila from the south, as Major General Charles Hall and the 11th Corps blocked the escape routes Japanese forces might have taken had they tried to repeat the defensive Bataan Peninsula campaign of three years earlier. The Japanese didn't make that mistake, choosing a strategy of "resistance in depth" that slowed American reinvasion and guaranteed that Filipino civilians would bear its brunt.[11]

Violence exploded. Increasingly fearful, the Japanese incarcerated male Filipino civilians en masse to preempt uprising or retribution. For their part, ordinary Filipinos worried about both Japanese retribution and American bombing. They had good reason to worry, as Lieutenant General Oscar Griswold advocated dispersing Japanese troops with the newly invented defoliant napalm, only to be told initially by MacArthur the idea was "unthinkable." It wasn't, in fact, unthinkable at all, at least at Corregidor, the US Army's island fortress captured by the Japanese in May 1942. A surprise US paratrooper invasion of "The Rock" caught Japanese defenders off guard, but what really cleared them was napalm—delivered by air, from flamethrowers, and from demolition squads that trapped Japanese soldiers in caves. During the island's reconquest in February 1945, US forces overwhelmed 5,000 Japanese soldiers, but took only twenty prisoners. Events on neighboring fortified islands were equally grim, with Japanese soldiers burned alive by petroleum, napalm, and phosphorus grenades.[12]

As the invading American and Filipino forces approached Manila, the Japanese leadership fled to the Americans' former colonial summer capital in the mountains of Baguio far outside the city. In Manila, a power vacuum ensued, with no clear lines of authority and no easy means of communication. Frightened, desperate, and under attack, the Japanese soldiers and sailors who remained in Manila unleashed one of World War II's most gruesome assaults on any civilian population. Life had been hard for the city's residents throughout the war, but the so-called Rape of Manila brought an unprecedented wave of violence over the course of several days in February 1945. Japanese soldiers and sailors were nominally under the command of General Yamashita Tomoyuki in Baguio, but on the ground, they answered primarily to Admiral Iwabuchi Sanji, if they answered to anyone at all. None were spared: one of the most callous attacks targeted Manila's Red Cross hospital. By the end of the battle on March 3, 1945, over 1,000 US soldiers and 16,000 Japanese had been killed. That was just a small part of the story. As many as 100,000 Filipinos—in a city with a prewar population of 700,000—were dead. Many were slaughtered by the Japanese; most were collateral damage from the aerial bombardment and artillery shells the Americans used to displace the Japanese from dense urban areas. Americans had destroyed what they crossed the Pacific to rescue. Then they called it liberation.[13]

Little wonder, then, that Manila residents did not immediately hail MacArthur as their national savior, and that after the battle ended no one bothered to organize a victory parade. On February 23, MacArthur walked through the smoldering ruins of the Manila Hotel. In his former suite, he found the broken shards of a vase given in 1905 by the Emperor of Japan to his father, Arthur MacArthur. Japan's Greater East Asia Co-Prosperity Sphere, too, lay shattered that day. Never again would Japan challenge US power in the Pacific, and soon it would emerge as a reliable American ally. But in the ruins of the Manila Hotel that day, even as visionary a general as Douglas MacArthur could not have known the outlines of the Pacific Century's next phase.[14]

Where the Philippines fit in that Pacific Century was just as uncertain to President Sergio Osmeña. By February 27, 1945, the flags of the United States and the Philippine Commonwealth once again flew over the presidential palace at Malacañang. From its balcony, Osmeña, who had spent the war years in Washington, surveyed Manila's devastation.

Perhaps no other capital city—not even Tokyo or Berlin—had suffered as greatly. Only a few buildings in the city center remained, and on that morning smoke clouds still gathered over the neighborhood. Block after block had been destroyed; bridges and ports and electrical systems had ceased to function; hunger and disease ran rampant. Reconquering the Philippines had devastated the country. At a formal ceremony that day, MacArthur felt not triumph but what he later described as "the culmination of a panorama of physical and spiritual disaster." He could not even finish his speech.[15]

The war continued. American forces battled the Japanese at Iwo Jima in February and March, and at Okinawa for three months after that, and fighting continued in the Philippines until June 1945. Nearly 250,000 Japanese died as the 6th Army faced what would turn out to be the US Army's largest land battle of the Pacific War. As USAFFE consolidated control, most of its soldiers believed they would soon move on to join an impending invasion of Japan. The US Army poured men and materiel into the country, including tens of thousands of military jeeps. With the world's most powerful supply chain in their hands, the army could deliver American jeeps directly from Detroit instead of buying British vehicles in Hong Kong. So in the middle of the invasion, Osmeña's provisional government announced on March 10, 1945, that Filipinos would henceforth start driving on the right hand side of the road. In matters large and small, US military priorities called the shots.[16]

The invasion of Japan never happened: news reached Manila of the atomic bombings of Hiroshima on August 6 and Nagasaki on August 9, and then of the Japanese surrender on August 15. Yamashita himself surrendered at Baguio that day, while other Japanese soldiers held out for weeks, or even years, to come. Soon planning focused on postwar reconstruction, not only of the Philippines but of the entire Pacific. On August 28, just days after the war's end—and with a handful of Japanese snipers still holding out in the jungles and in Manila's alleyways—MacArthur departed for Japan to oversee the US occupation. For American GIs thousands of miles from home, the war's end couldn't come fast enough. When soldiers grumbled about the slow pace of demobilization and convened mass meetings in Manila, US officials fretted about the "considerable communistic influence in the leadership of these demonstrations" and hurried them home. The jeeps, in the rush, were left behind.[17]

For Filipinos who had survived three years of war, there was unfinished business. Cries for retribution targeted collaborators who had fought with Japanese forces or profited from the Japanese occupation. Collaboration policy unmasked the complications of national loyalty in the wartime Philippines and demonstrated the extent to which US military needs would continue to shape postwar Philippine politics. President Franklin Roosevelt had promised swift justice for wartime collaborators. On June 29, 1944, FDR insisted that "those who have collaborated with the enemy must be removed from authority and influence over the political and economic life of the country." His successor, Harry Truman, agreed, and MacArthur likewise promised "to run to earth every disloyal Filipino who has debased his country's cause." Filipino radicals added their voices of denunciation, particularly the communist guerrillas of the Hukbalahap, who hoped that exposing the collaborators' wartime malfeasance would build popular support for revolution. Behind the headlines, though, popular sentiment was hard to read, and people were uneasy. The fact was, of course, that thousands of Filipinos had made compromises with the occupation government and feared an aggressive policy managed by Washington crusaders. Many adopted a quiet, wait-and-see attitude. As Filipinos busily assembled their guerrilla credentials, the black market price of paper soared.[18]

In March 1945, before the Japanese were fully defeated, the Philippine Army announced the formation of a Loyalty Status Board to investigate collaboration. Thousands claimed that they had been guerrillas all along, so the board tightened the chain, requiring suspected collaborators to document that they had joined the guerrillas at least one month before the Allied landings at Leyte. A second body, the US Army's Counter-Intelligence Corps (CIC), sifted out possible collaborators from among the tens of thousands of Filipinos who came under American invaders' control. The CIC intended to turn them over to the Filipino People's Court, a special civilian court that would try Filipinos accused of collaboration. By September 1945, some 5,000 were in detention, including nearly all the leading political figures of the prewar era, and even two of President Sergio Osmeña's sons.[19]

The thinly stretched occupying US Army—its men loudly eager to head home—could not hold or feed 5,000 alleged collaborators for the time it would take to try them, and so the Army began releasing them. CIC detainees walked out of US custody with a "clearance," meaning they had been temporarily released, not that they had been cleared of any charges. (None, indeed, had been filed.) This bureaucratic misnomer would confuse the issue of collaboration for years to come. Even President Osmeña treated the CIC's release decisions as de facto exonerations. Hamstrung and overwhelmed, the CIC more or less gave up punishing collaborators—most of them anyway. Through a remarkable feat of bureaucratic gymnastics, the CIC defined the leftist Hukbalahaps not as guerrillas but merely as "civilians with guns," and used the occupation's authority to hunt down some of the war's most dedicated anti-Japanese fighters. "The campaign of slander had no limit," Huk leader Luis Taruc fumed.[20]

US and Philippine military leaders were now actively using collaboration policy to intervene in Philippine politics. Most notoriously, the Loyalty Status Board issued a hasty "clearance" to Manuel Roxas, the man who had signed the Philippine Republic's declaration of war against the United States. American forces had announced Roxas's wartime capture in the hills near Baguio as the "liberation" of an ally, rather than the surrender of a treasonous enemy. (Notably, the press described others captured in the raid as members of the "collaborationist cabinet.") "I have known General Roxas for twenty years, and I know personally that he is no threat to our military security," MacArthur said of his longtime personal friend. "Therefore we are not detaining him." Later, Loyalty Status Board members announced—again without offering evidence—that they "had personal knowledge" of Roxas's loyalty. Roxas trotted out the "clearance" as state-sanctioned affirmation of his wartime bona fides, and walked free. He returned to the abandoned schoolhouse on the city's outskirts where the Philippine Senate was meeting, his eye on President Osmeña's job.[21]

Finally, in September 1945, the Filipino People's Court began adjudicating wartime "crimes against national security." A team of special prosecutors, headed by the passionate and principled Solicitor General, Lorenzo Tañada, prepared the cases in a bombed-out shell of a building in central Manila. Tañada, described by an American observer as "a young energetic man with a broad smile and apology for the surroundings," was an able attorney trained at both the University of the Philippines and Harvard Law School. He was himself untainted by the collaboration question, having spent the war years in quiet exile in the countryside. Tañada commenced work with great fanfare, intent on prosecuting "those individuals who engaged in acts and activities in cooperation with and in aid of the enemy."[22]

The People's Court was doomed from the start. It faced an impossible task: there was no budget to pay for the courts and too few people to staff them. Tañada's photogenic do-nothing young assistant attorney, Ferdinand Marcos, was no help. The Department of Justice, bombed out of its official headquarters, operated from makeshift offices in a former cigar factory, with no clerks, very little paper, and no typewriters. Under pressure from accused collaborators, some witnesses were reluctant to testify, while others refused outright or disappeared. Crucial evidence had already been destroyed, much of it purposefully. The courts had no clear legal mandate nor much precedent to rest on. Tañada, on observing that "the country did not have a single book on treason," ordered some shipped from Washington. With a March 25, 1946, filing deadline approaching, thousands of cases had been registered, but only a handful completed. It was hardly an exaggeration, then, when one observer described the People's Courts as "pitifully inadequate."[23]

In the meantime, the independence that had been scheduled in the 1934 Tydings-McDuffie Act for July 4, 1946, was just around the corner. First, the Philippines needed to hold the presidential election that had been preempted during the war. Manuel Roxas gathered campaign funds from wealthy landowners and the tacit support of the Americans. Roxas's Liberal Party claimed it would "prosecute mercilessly those guilty of collaboration," but everyone knew the Nacionalistas—led by sitting president Sergio Osmeña—were the only ones serious about prosecution. On April 23, 1946, Manuel Roxas won the election. The new republic's president, vice president, and a majority of its congress had all served in the former Japanese occupation government.[24]

In the April elections, voters in central Luzon sent Luis Taruc, the political commander of the Hukbalahap guerrillas, to the Philippine legislature along with five other communist leaders. On the campaign trail, leftists advocated land reform, recognition and benefits for guerrillas, and an end to ruthless militias. They kept collaboration on the agenda, mobilizing class consciousness against former *buy-and-sell* men who had profited during the war years. For the armed soldiers of the Hukbalahap, the war was not over. Confronting the chaos of reinvasion and the discredited politics of most of the Philippine elite, the Huks believed they had the upper hand both politically and militarily. They had mastered the terrain of the jungle and the rules of engagement, and commanded a loyal army with nearly as many soldiers and weapons as the beleaguered Philippine Army. And they knew the Americans would be leaving soon.[25]

With American blessing (and pressure), Manuel Roxas and his legislative allies refused to seat the elected representatives. Soon the Hukbalahap met not only political opposition but military repression, led by Mariano Castañeda, a Philippine Army officer and a graduate of the US Army Infantry School at Fort Benning, Georgia. Roxas gave official imprimatur to the Civil Guards—anti-Huk militias controlled by the plantation owners—as "temporary police." Roxas demanded that the Huks disarm, and they again refused. "I cannot tell them to give up their arms," said Luis Taruc, "unless I know that the MPs and the USAFFEs will not torture and kill them, and this I do not know." Fear of communism—and the real threat posed by communist movements—would take center stage on the agenda of the postwar Philippines. And just offstage was the US military.[26]

With independence just ten weeks away, US colonial officials were packing their bags, and most of the American soldiers had left. The possibility of mass prosecutions of collaborators rapidly faded, and soon even the crusading Lorenzo Tañada accepted an offer to run for the Philippine Senate, making a graceful exit from his increasingly distasteful and impossible task. In the midst of wartime disorder—starvation, unemployment, a suffocating black market—Filipinos had made difficult decisions, but they did not reflect permanent loyalties. It proved possible to switch sides: to march in a Japanese parade and head for the guerrilla camps in the hills; to work for the occupation government and rush to the Americans when they returned. To American observers, such moves appeared opportunistic or disingenuous, signs of bold-faced treason or cunning Oriental duplicity or brown-skinned simple-mindedness. But tangled loyalties and difficult choices had been part of Philippine political life for decades.[27]

Filipino soldiers were the most visible figures of the fragile republic about to celebrate its independence. Stories of guerrilla resistance and American connections shaped relations between both nations. During the war, when rival guerrilla groups contended for mass loyalty, the most successful ones were those that attached themselves to the US military and its resources. Collaboration policy generated the same dynamic. Lorenzo Tañada and his colleagues wanted to restore the nation's values and discredit those who had cozied up to a foreign power—Japan. But that did not fit with the priorities of a different foreign power—the United States. Proximity to power, not to principle, decided the outcome of the Philippines' collaboration dilemma.

For Filipinos in the United States, described by one commentator as "legally undesirable heroes," an unfinished piece of business remained: the law of citizenship. The soldiers of the First and Second Fil were regular GIs and had been naturalized en masse, often over their objections. For others, their status was murky, and independence made clarity necessary. After July 4, 1946, Filipinos would no longer be "nationals" but aliens—and as Asian aliens, they would be racially ineligible for citizenship according to laws on the books since the 1790s. Two days before independence, President Harry Truman signed legislation, cosponsored by Representatives Clare Boothe Luce and Emmanuel Celler, making citizens of the Philippine Commonwealth eligible for US citizenship, and naturalization rates shot up in its wake. But if Luce-Celler made a big difference for Filipinos in the United States, the law offered little to aspiring migrants in the Philippines, merely raising the country's annual immigration quota from 50 to 105.[28]

Among those would-be migrants were war brides. The men of the First and Second Fil were among the Philippines' most eligible bachelors in 1945: not only were they dashing liberators, but as US servicemen, they earned substantially more money than Philippine Army soldiers, let alone the guerrillas with their "Mickey Mouse" Japanese currency. "More money, more pay, we were cocky," one recalled. "We knew the war was over, when we were fighting the Philippine Army." Hardened guerrillas who had survived jungle warfare resented the *musiceros* of the First and Second Fil who arrived in town with chocolate, cigarettes, and rice, and earned full US Army wages while playing in a band or doing manual labor. But the soldiers' appeal wasn't just money. Dressed in better uniforms and fed on four years of good food (including, of course, canned salmon) while their guerrilla comrades were lucky to eat one hundred grams of rice in a day, they were also probably better looking. Soon, so many had gotten hitched that the Army set up a separate housing section for the First and Second Fil's married soldiers.[29]

The War Brides Act of 1945 and War Fiancées Act of 1946 were designed to allow Filipino American soldiers and sailors to sponsor spouses outside the restrictive immigration quotas. Some of them weren't really war brides, but women who had been separated from their husbands by nearly twenty years of depression and war. And romance wasn't always involved. "Actually, there was no courtship," recalled war bride Sixta Vinluan. "His people and my parents talked about the marriage. I had no part in the talks at all." Although the soldiers of the First and Second Fil were US citizens, bringing spouses back to the United States was complicated. Bob Tabafunda left Bainbridge Island, Washington, to serve in the First Fil, and married Maria Soriano in the Philippines in 1945; she migrated only three years later. The War Brides Act didn't apply to soldiers in the Philippine Army or to guerrillas, as guerrilla veteran William Patterson learned when immigration officials attempted to deport his Filipina wife and their children, who came with him to the United States just after the war. "The Japs couldn't separate us during the war but I guess the United States will," Patterson complained. Mariano Angeles, who had replied "Hell, no," when his commanding officer told him he had to be naturalized, ended up becoming a US citizen after all. He wanted to return to the United States with his wife, whom he met in the Philippines during the war. "I applied for it because I like to have my family come over here."[30]

For those Filipinos who served in the Philippine Army or as guerrillas, citizenship was also unfinished business. During the war, there hadn't been much time to think about eligibility for US citizenship or reason to pursue it. But after President Sergio Osmeña's declaration on the Leyte beaches incorporating into USAFFE the 120,000 Philippine Army soldiers and 70,000 recognized guerrillas, Filipino soldiers qualified for new rights of naturalization, and a handful began to claim them. They cited a 1942 amendment to the Nationality Act of 1940 that promised noncitizen soldiers serving outside the "territorial United States" rapid naturalization. Soldiers and veterans needed to file their paperwork while in service "during the present war," which for the act's purposes officially ended on December 31, 1946. Worldwide, over 140,000 service personnel from dozens of countries gained US citizenship this way during the war, including a few Filipinos serving as far away as Iceland.[31]

Not very many of those soldiers were naturalized in the Philippines. On August 1, 1945, months after the reestablishment of the Philippine Commonwealth and days before the Japanese surrender, the US government authorized George Ennis, vice consul in Manila, to carry out the naturalizations authorized by the 1942 amendments to the Nationality Act. But that authority—and its implications for immigration rates—soon came under scrutiny. Although no evidence survives to prove it, officials in both the United States and the restored Philippine Commonwealth may have agreed that mass naturalization would open the doors for large-scale emigration of Filipino veterans to the United States, a result that neither government relished. As Attorney General Clark said, "it would be a political embarrassment and a drain of manpower to have a mass exodus of the young Filipino ex-fighting men and women going to the United States on the eve of independence of the new nation."[32]

Soon there was a solution worthy of *Catch-22*, the Second World War's memorable novel of military bureaucracy. On September 13, 1945, just days after Japanese officers surrendered to the United States aboard the USS *Missouri*, US Commissioner of Immigration Ugo Carusi wrote to Attorney General Tom Clark asking that the naturalization "situation . . . be handled by revoking the authority previously granted" to the vice consul "and by omitting to designate any representative authorized to confer citizenship in the Philippine Islands." Clark approved the maneuver, and by the end of October, Ennis had departed Manila. Nearly 200,000 soldiers who marched under the American flag and had a legal right to claim US citizenship suddenly had nowhere to turn. Only in August 1946—after formal Philippine independence—did the Immigration and Naturalization Service return, and during a brief window between August 1 and the December 31, 1946, filing deadline, a naturalization office operated in Manila. Some 4,000 Filipinos acquired US citizenship, all of them veterans of the Philippine Scouts—officially part of the US Army since 1901.[33]

None of this troubled Arizona senator Carl Hayden, who argued that USAFFE soldiers fought "because they fervently desired freedom for their country and not with the idea of acquiring the right to go to another country. . . . It would be the worst kind of public policy practically to invite them to . . . come to the United States, where, as immigrants, they would have to begin at the bottom of the economic ladder to make their way upward." For legal justification, US authorities pointed out that—at least before July 4, 1946—the Philippines was not yet outside the "territorial United States," and thus provisions meant to ease soldier naturalizations "abroad" didn't apply to the Philippine Commonwealth. The US Justice Department's maneuvers foreclosed large-scale naturalizations and thus mass migrations, but also denied basic rights to Filipino soldiers who had marched next to American soldiers at Bataan. This was not America's finest hour.[34]

Then came a second broken promise. Filipino veterans were going to be expensive. In October 1945, Senator Carl Hayden queried VA Director (and wartime general) Omar Bradley about the status of USAFFE veteran claims. Bradley affirmed the VA's position that USAFFE soldiers were considered to have been in the "active military or naval forces," and estimated that the lifetime benefit costs of 190,000 veterans would run to approximately $3.2 billion. Hayden, chair of the Senate Appropriations Committee, balked. "Three billion dollars is a substantial sum of money," he observed, noting that "no one could be found who would assert that it was ever the clear intention of Congress that such benefits as are granted under the . . . GI Bill of Rights . . . should be extended to the soldiers of the Philippine Army."[35]

So under Hayden's leadership, Congress set itself the task of trimming veteran expenditures, blocking Filipino immigration, and strengthening the Philippine military, all at the same time. Hayden, together with Senators Richard Russell of Georgia and Charles Brooks of Illinois, a subcommittee drafted what would become the First Supplemental Surplus Appropriation Rescission Act, known simply as the Rescission Act. The law authorized a one-time lump-sum payment of $200 million directly to the government of the Philippine Republic to settle benefit claims. But there was a quid pro quo. The final version of the Rescission Act included a provision—inserted by the Senate Appropriations Committee following an off-the-record debate—stating that "service before July 1, 1946, in the organized military forces of the Government of the Commonwealth of the Philippines, while such forces were in the service of the armed forces of the United States . . . shall not be deemed to be or to have been service in the military or naval forces of the United States . . . for the purposes of any law . . . conferring rights, privileges, or benefits." Filipino soldiers were not American soldiers, at least when it came time to pay benefits. The law thus blocked individual claims by USAFFE veterans, even though the Rescission

Act contained no guarantees that any portion of the allocated $200 million would be spent by the Philippine government directly on veterans benefits. No GI Bill, no college loan, no home mortgage, no medical care, no widow's stipend, not even a flag for a soldier's casket. This was not America's finest hour, either.[36]

Harry Truman very much wanted to veto the bill, but mindful of the pressures of a belt-tightening postwar Congress, cognizant of the desperate financial plight of the Philippine military, and aware of what he called the "practical difficulties in making payments to Philippine Army veterans," he signed the Rescission Act on February 18, 1946. Appending a signing statement, Truman insisted that there existed "a moral obligation of the United States to look after the welfare of Philippine Army veterans," and asked the Veterans Administration to prepare legislation to rectify the situation. "The Government of the Philippines is in no position today, nor will it be for a number of years, to support a large-scale program of the care of its veterans." Truman, meanwhile, assured "our comrades in the Philippines" that the issue "is receiving attention and is being expedited as much as possible," becoming the first of a dozen presidents to promise action at some future date.[37]

Congress presented the Rescission Act as a deal between the United States and the Philippines—even though while the bill was under consideration, no one on Capitol Hill consulted Philippine politicians in Washington. After the fact, they protested vigorously. Former Philippine Army Chief of Staff Basilio Valdes and guerrilla hero Macario Peralta led a delegation from the Philippine Veterans Legion, but arrived in Washington on March 17, 1946, too late to make a difference. Carlos Romulo, now serving as the Philippines' resident commissioner in Washington, worried that the modest reforms that Truman administration officials later recommended would give "officials in Washington the opportunity to say that they have discharged their obligations to the Filipino veterans while in fact many major discriminations . . .

remain." On Romulo's advice, the Philippine government refused the $200 million backpay settlement. The US Congress, in turn, declined to act on the remedies that Truman and the VA proposed. For Filipino veterans, the Rescission Act was a broken promise and would remain unfinished business.[38]

But in the eyes of the State Department, America's debt to Philippine Commonwealth veterans had been paid. High Commissioner Paul McNutt, the highest-ranking official in the colony—already scheduled to depart from Manila—saw the Rescission Act as a lost opportunity. Veterans, he warned, were "violently aroused" and the United States might lose "good will." Instead, he suggested, "retention in American hands of the paymaster's role for Philippine veterans will insure the United States a powerful hold on an important segment of the Philippine public for years to come." Senator Carl Hayden wasn't having any of that. "The best way to proceed is to wipe the slate clean," he insisted. "The best thing the American government can do is to help the Filipino people to help themselves. . . . What the Filipino veteran needs is steady employment rather than to depend for his living upon a monthly payment sent from the United States." Filipino veterans, for their part, called it "discrimination"; one wrote that he mourned the "forgotten veteran" and observed he was a "disillusioned, sadder and wiser man." The language of dependency, delay, and discrimination would set the tone for decades to come.[39]

When they read about the Rescission Act, veterans of the First and Second Fil might have felt lucky, with GI benefits in their pockets and war brides beside them. But equality eluded Filipinos in the United States at the war's end, too. At war defense plants, unions had fought to keep out workers of color, so when employment contracted after V-J Day, seniority rules meant that Filipinos were among the first let go. Veterans sometimes faced obstacles in finding housing, jobs, and loans that were theirs on paper to claim. Cosmé and Lorraine Libadia sensed discrimination when Cosmé applied for naturalization. "I do feel at this time too that occasionally those that were married to the white girls were, had to go through a little more to get their paper, their citizenship papers," Lorraine Libadia recalled. But nevertheless, new jobs, more money, and a fuller integration into American public life slowly followed.[40]

Veterans' preferences helped. Filipinos who had worked at defense plants found that wartime naturalization meant the jobs were still theirs. In Seattle, Genevieve Laigo, who had been thrilled to earn 62.5 cents an hour at Boeing, stayed on the job after the war. Boeing changed her life; it also changed her citizenship status. She applied for naturalization "because they announce it because we cannot work at Boeing, only after the Filipino get their independence. . . . So we went to school, so I got mine." Sylvestre Tangalan had worked for Boeing during the war, and then been laid off after V-J Day. After a series of other jobs, "I thought I was to go back to Boeing, which I did and never left Boeing since then," he explained in an interview three decades later. Camila Carido's husband never returned to his job picking asparagus in the fields near Stockton, finding work instead as a civilian employee at McClellan Air Force Base near Sacramento. Fabian Bergano found a job as a pharmacist at the VA hospital in Seattle. After Mariano Angeles returned to the United States with his wife, he worked at the post office for the next twenty-four years. Almost none of the second-generation Filipino Americans from Hawai'i who served in the First and Second Fil returned to the sugar plantations.[41]

While USAFFE veterans in the Philippines were denied their rights by the Rescission Act, and Filipinos in the United States experienced the uneven benefits of postwar life, soldiers and sailors still in uniform wondered what independence would mean for Filipinos in the US armed forces. In the new atomic age, did the United States still need the Philippine Scouts? Actually, they needed their manpower, so in the immediate aftermath of the war, the US Army decided to keep the Scouts on for just a little while longer. On October 6, 1945, the Armed Forces Voluntary Recruitment Act authorized expansion of the Scouts from 12,000 to 50,000 men. Known informally as the New Philippine Scouts, its men eagerly enlisted for service "in the occupation of Japan and of lands now or formerly subject to Japan, and elsewhere in the Far East." The provision's sponsor, none other than Arizona senator Carl Hayden, reflected on "what a magnificent body of troops the Philippine Scouts were." Nebraska senator Kenneth Wherry asked whether the New Philippine Scouts would be a means to "reduce the number of our own men." "Obviously," Hayden replied, going on to assure fellow senators that legislation for the New Philippine Scouts "does not change the citizenship of those enlisted. . . . Each scout will remain a citizen of the Philippine Islands." In the end, about 38,000 joined the New Scouts, making up a substantial fraction of the 262,000 soldiers in America's Asian occupation force.[42]

From his headquarters in Japan, Douglas MacArthur appreciated that reestablishing the Pacific colonial army would also reduce the number of African American and Puerto Rican soldiers serving in the region. US Army officers denigrated black and Latino soldiers and their segregated units. Filipinos and Pacific Islanders blamed them for unrest, protest, and misconduct during occupation and reconstruction. Filipinos, as they had in the US Navy a generation before, played a critical role in triangulating the fraught white-black color line that the US armed forces brought with them into the Pacific War. The New Philippine Scouts headed for Okinawa in 1946 and quietly relieved African American units stationed there. Most did manual labor, reconstruction, and police work.

MacArthur's management of the color line, though, created its own problems. A July 1946 memo by two generals fretted that reliance on the Scouts would discourage white enlistment and warned it could yield a majority-Filipino force in the Pacific. They urged MacArthur to prevent "the undesirable situation which can occur if the opportunity to enlist in [the Regular Army] remains open to substantial numbers of naturalized ex-Philippine Scouts." MacArthur struggled to find an alternative. US Army officers tried importing "U.S. laborers belonging to the White race" for jobs on Pacific islands, but acknowledged they could not afford to pay enough to entice them. Japanese ex-soldiers were off limits for reasons of international law and public relations. Filipino soldiers would have to do, and the New Scouts would stay on the job in Japan and the Pacific for the next four years. Joining them after independence were tens of thousands of Filipino contract workers recruited for jobs in Guam, first by the US Army and then by the Army's civilian contractors. Whether Filipinos would remain brothers in arms with the US armed forces was never in doubt. But as workers set up a stage at the Luneta, Manila's main plaza, in preparation for the independence celebrations, it remained to be seen on what terms Filipinos would fight in American uniforms.[43]

On July 4, 1946, thousands gathered in the rain at the Luneta to watch the flag of the new Philippine Republic unfurl. Asia's first republic faced a painful postwar future. The Japanese were gone—although rumors circulated that holdouts had been spotted deep in the jungle or on remote islands. But the country's infrastructure was destroyed, and an American economic survey estimated the cost of living had multiplied by eight times between 1937 and 1945 as wartime shortages initially prompted inflation and GI spending then accelerated it. Violence and crime persisted, exacerbated by the proliferation of American and Japanese weapons. The ambiguous and abrupt end to collaboration trials bequeathed a pervasive sense of cynicism. But at the Independence Day celebrations—Filipinos' third declaration of independence since 1898, and thanks to the Japanese, their second flag-raising in three years—Manila resounded with optimistic assertions of a new national destiny and renewed Pacific partnership. President Truman sent a message hailing the "great experiment in Pacific democracy" and observing that "our two countries will be closely bound together for many years to come." US Interior Secretary J. A. Krug cautiously praised Filipino soldiers, who "joined with the armed forces of the United States against a common enemy," carefully choosing the word "with," which accorded with the newly adopted Rescission Act, rather than "in," which would have recognized the veterans' rights. Broken promises accompanied the achievement of an independence first promised by Woodrow Wilson in 1916.[44]

Douglas MacArthur returned briefly from Japan for the ceremony, where he announced "the end of empire." As an entity of formal territorial control, yes. There would be no more High Commissioners sent out from Washington wielding veto power over the will of the Filipino people. Only one flag—the Philippine flag—flew over Malacanang. But the institutions of US power, from .30-caliber M1 rifles to jeeps driving on the right side of the road, remained. So, too, did decades-old assumptions that Filipinos could be recruited into the US armed forces without being treated like US citizens. A new chapter in America's Pacific Century was just beginning, and the Cold War would write it. Anticommunism would keep the two nations bound together. It was a powerful force, and before the Cold War had fully begun, it was already wielding its influence: it excused collaboration as it erased the Huks' guerrilla service; it empowered veterans organizations while silencing leftist critics; it made it necessary for the US military to remain in the Philippines and possible for Filipinos to stay in the US armed forces. The war's end brought a violent "liberation" to millions of Filipinos and broken promises to thousands of Filipino soldiers. But the ties connecting the two nations were stronger than ever, and would soon be put to use in a new conflict.[45]

CHAPTER SEVEN

ALLIES

1946–1965

In the years after World War II, US Defense Department officials looked toward the Pacific from the windows of the Pentagon, their recently constructed headquarters just outside Washington. America's view of postwar Asia comprised not only its former colony of the Philippines, but a new set of power arrangements and partnerships. Japan, living through occupation and reconstruction, was on its way to becoming one of America's most reliable allies while China lurched toward civil war and revolution. The Soviet Union had emerged as a formidable adversary with ambitions in the region. In the rural Philippines, leftist Hukbalahap guerrillas battled for hearts and minds.

But to ordinary Filipinos serving as US Navy stewards or working at US military bases, not everything had changed. Military institutions the United States had created in 1898 to dislodge the Spanish Empire and suppress the Philippine revolution—and then expanded to defend America's Pacific outpost from Japan—were being retooled for a global war against communism. That new war would be planned from the Pentagon, but there was no better place from which to fight it than the Philippines, with its long history of American connections, a shared anticommunist ideology, two really big military bases, and thousands of willing naval recruits. The bonds of war that had tied the two nations together since 1898 were put to the service of the Cold War in the Pacific.

There would be a new rhetoric of partnership, aptly captured in a classified memorandum prepared for the US National Security Council in December 1949, which advocated that US foreign policy should "appeal to the Asiatic nations as being compatible with their national interests and worthy of their support." As sovereign allies and "free Asians," Filipinos found Americans needed them as much as ever, both as military partners and as symbols of partnership. During the Cold War's first two decades, Americans and Filipinos continued to fight together, first against communists in the Philippines and Korea using forces trained at bases that the US Navy and Air Force expanded during the 1950s. Then, Filipinos and Americans collaborated again as they trained South Korean soldiers and South Vietnamese police, firm in the belief that what they had built in the Philippines could be transferred elsewhere in the Pacific. Americans built on the foundation of the colonial past they shared with Filipinos, intent on establishing a US-dominated order in postwar Asia—determined, in other words, to achieve the Pacific Century.[1]

Independence posed difficult questions for the armed forces of both nations. What would happen to America's forty-year-old colonial army, and to the Philippine Scouts who served in it? Should the newly independent Philippines rebuild the army that Douglas MacArthur and Dwight Eisenhower had designed for them in the 1930s? Or, after the disaster of Bataan, should Filipinos start from scratch? Any new force, to be sure, would be used to fight communists. But where—at home or overseas?

All told, the new army looked a lot like what MacArthur had proposed in 1936. After independence, the Armed Forces of the Philippines (AFP) consisted of an army of 40,000 soldiers, most of them volunteers, an air force with a few dozen planes, and a tiny navy. The Philippine Constabulary (PC), the quasi-military police force established by William Howard Taft in 1901 and taken over by the Japanese in 1942, disintegrated after the Americans invaded in 1944. In 1948, it was reestablished and restored to its status as a civilian police force rather than a supplementary army. The AFP fulfilled the dreams of Emilio Aguinaldo in 1898 and the Philippine National Guard a generation later, in that the Philippine Republic now maintained its own standing army. But economic realities, enduring colonial assumptions, and a serious communist threat meant that the Philippines built the military force the United States wanted and was willing to pay for, which in turn required Filipinos to continue to align their security needs with America's geopolitical ambitions.[2]

Those ambitions required military bases. On March 14, 1947, US and Philippine officials gathered at the Malacanang presidential palace, where, with "the festive atmosphere of a farewell ball," the two nations signed the Military Bases Agreement (MBA). The pact granted the United States access to twenty-three military and naval installations in the country. The two nations agreed that the ruined island fortress of Corregidor at the mouth of Manila Bay, rendered obsolete in the atomic age, would be reserved for some future use, perhaps as a memorial or a penal colony. Filipinos pressed the United States to turn over any facilities in Manila, including Fort McKinley, the US Army's longtime headquarters. American diplomats wanted bases for seafaring and air power projection, not forts to protect against an insurrectionary army, and readily acceded. The MBA was America's deal. On issues from criminal jurisdiction to US personnel's exemption from Philippine taxes to the ninety-nine-year term of the agreement, American negotiators achieved almost everything they wanted.[3]

Former president Sergio Osmeña called the MBA "a virtual nullification of Philippine independence." Radical journalist Amado Hernandez thought the pact reduced the status of the Philippines "to that of a banana republic" and warned fellow Filipinos not to trust the United States. "Uncle Sam is not a Santa Claus. In fact, he has a reputation as a smart horse-trader." While some argued the Philippines could not survive without the United States, Hernandez pointed out that from 1942 to 1945, it had done just that. "American bases," he noted, were "haunting reminders"—all the more frightening after Hiroshima—"that the monstrous experience of the past might visit us once more."[4]

The two countries negotiated the MBA during the window between V-J Day in 1945 and the Chinese communist takeover in 1949, a period when some at the Pentagon—including General Dwight Eisenhower, now serving as the Army's chief of staff—concluded that the Philippines no longer had "a very important place in the defensive alignment we are building in the Pacific." Planners hoped the MBA would help to withdraw large numbers of US Army soldiers from the Philippines, leaving the Navy at Subic and handing Clark to the US Air Force, established as a separate branch of the Defense Department in September 1947. But with uncertainty in Asia, a lingering sense of colonial obligation, and awareness that the days of the European empires of Britain, France, and the Netherlands were numbered, Americans certainly had no intention of leaving the Philippines altogether.[5]

They would stay to teach and advise. The Joint US Military Assistance Group (JUSMAG), set up on the eve of independence in 1946, trained Filipino soldiers in the AFP for operations against domestic insurrection. Americans transferred—which is to say, abandoned—vast quantities of surplus US military property that had been moved to the Philippines in 1945 in anticipation the invasion of Japan. The AFP grew accustomed to using American weapons, and strings JUSMAG attached to its aid meant the AFP could buy nothing else. Ownership of the military equipment Filipinos trained on rested with the United States, and even though the Philippine Republic paid JUSMAG's budget, the law forbade the Philippines from buying military weapons (or even basic supplies like ammunition) from any nation other than the United States. Military aid and technical training reflected a new vocabulary of alliance, but this was colonialism by another name.[6]

Leadership development continued as well. The Philippine Military Academy reopened in 1947 to train the AFP's future officers. Nevertheless, Filipinos still enrolled at Annapolis and West Point. JUSMAG officers handpicked future midshipmen and cadets—among them a bright young recruit by the name of Fidel Ramos, who arrived at the US Military Academy as a plebe in the fall of 1946. JUSMAG also sent officers and enlisted men to US military technical schools. If this, too, represented lingering colonialism, ambitious Filipino officers didn't acknowledge it. One Philippine Army tank officer simply observed in 1947 that the US Army Armor School at Fort Knox was the "best and only place for these officers and men to be trained."[7]

Even as the United States helped the Philippines rebuild its military, the US armed forces were changing too, shifting from global combat to the reconstruction of Germany and Japan and adjusting to the new possibilities of atomic warfare. It was also time to confront the color line the services had maintained for the past decades. After April 1942, African Americans had entered the US Navy in greater numbers, but they trained in segregated units and filled messman or manual labor positions. Black sailors and politicians called for the full integration of the force, but when questioned about it during the war, Secretary of the Navy Frank Knox summoned the memory of the USS *Rizal* and its all-Filipino crew: "This had not worked and there was no reason to believe Negroes could sail ships either." Knox's assistant,

Adlai Stevenson, pressed him on the matter, and after James Forrestal replaced Knox as Navy Secretary in May 1944, some modest changes followed, but not many. In 1945, more than half of the African Americans in the Navy served in the messman branch together with Filipinos who had enlisted before 1932, when the Navy stopped recruiting new Filipino sailors.[8]

On July 26, 1948, President Harry Truman issued Executive Order 9981, mandating "equality of treatment and opportunity for all persons in the armed services without regard to race, color, religion or national origin." Truman also requested a full-scale study by federal attorney Charles Fahy to document discrimination and recommend policy reforms. In its 1950 report, the Fahy Committee found "no specific facts" supporting racial discrimination against Asian servicemen, and deemed Filipinos' second-class status the product of restrictions on citizenship, not discrimination on the basis of race. The committee made no mention of the recently adopted Rescission Act that excluded most Filipino World War II soldiers from veterans benefits. Truman's boldly worded integration order set no timetable, offering "due regard to the time required to effectuate any necessary changes without impairing efficiency or morale." Many half-hearted efforts and a war in Korea followed before soldiers and sailors served together in significant numbers.[9]

After independence, the US Army also phased out the Philippine Scouts. Their final days brought misty-eyed recollections and soldierly tributes. The *New York Times* spoke rhapsodically of "our Philippine . . . brothers-in-arms," fondly recalling "the bonds of comradeship" and baseball teams "made up of both Filipinos and Americans." Of the 29,000 remaining Scouts, some 3,000 were US citizens or had joined before July 4, 1946, and thus were eligible to transfer over individually to the US Army. The rest were mustered out in July 1949. So, too, were the thousands of New Philippine Scouts recruited right after the war for the occupation and reconstruction of Japan. The Army affirmed a policy "of not recruiting and using organized foreign troops as a part of the American military establishment." But buried in the 1947 Military Bases Agreement was a clause that authorized 1,000 Filipinos per year to enlist directly in the US Navy. Largely overlooked at first, when the Navy was trimming its rolls and didn't need more sailors (Filipino or otherwise), this provision would transform Filipino armed service and remake the landscape of Filipino America in the decades to come.[10]

DURING THE COLD WAR, AS ANTICOMMUNISM SHAPED POLITIcal rhetoric on both sides of the Pacific, Filipino veterans in the United States—domesticated by their war brides and settled in the West Coast's new suburbs—appeared to take on new roles as Cold War Asian Americans. Observers, and Filipino migrants themselves, found it easy to describe this process of "settling down" as natural, but it reflected the culmination of two decades of political struggle. Even after the war, Filipino Americans had to fight for rights to own land, to join unions, or to marry across the color line. And appealing to their Cold War neighbors as good American citizens required them to silence dissenting voices within their own communities.

After independence, Filipinos were now by any definition foreigners, subject to an annual immigration quota of just 105 per year. More than ever, armed service opened doors for migration that independence had closed. This was even more true for women than for men, thanks to the War Brides Act of 1945 and related laws. A 1948 family reunification law allowed Filipinos who had lived in the United States for at least three years before the war to sponsor their wives and minor children as "nonquota" immigrants. Far more Filipinos arrived in the United States through military family reunification than would ever enter under the limited national quotas. Migration rates were actually higher after independence than they were before the war. The steady fall of anti-miscegenation statutes and alien land laws lowered barriers to suburban settlement.[11]

World War II veterans fanned out from grim urban Chinatowns to booming suburbs in California and other states, although whites-only restrictive covenants meant that Filipinos tended to settle in racially unrestricted, lower middle-class suburbs, choosing the dusty south side of Stockton over its leafy north side, or inner-ring suburbs such as Daly City, just south of San Francisco, or National City, just south of San Diego. Experience as navy cooks and personal servants meant lavish dinners in those suburban kitchens. "Our pioneer-generation parents," recalled Juanita Tamayo Lott, "looked for houses with big dining rooms." Family structured everyday life, and while there were plenty of uncles, not all of them were related by blood. Lopsided sex ratios during prewar migration—followed by years of immigration restriction and a world war—meant that many Filipino American children had multiple *manongs*, or elders, in an extended kin network.[12]

In the United States, Filipino veterans' military mindsets, firm anticommunism, and devout Catholicism made them familiar to Cold War suburbia. Community circled around church and school and veterans' groups; hometown associations, fraternal societies, and beauty pageants offered entertainment. The American Legion slowly welcomed Filipino veterans. Some joined racially integrated Legion posts, but wherever Filipino vets' numbers were large enough, they formed their own. In Stockton, veterans gathered at the Filipino Trinity Church in January 1948 to establish the Santo Tomas Post of the American Legion. In Los Angeles, Michael Padua headed up that city's Manila Post; women guerrillas, such as Julia Peters Garces, established a ladies' auxiliary at its headquarters at 819 Temple Street in December 1949.[13]

When Filipino American sociologist Valentin Aquino studied postwar Los Angeles's Filipino community in 1952, he observed a remarkable transformation. Once confined to Little Manila, barred from citizenship or landholding, and refused in some cases legal permission to marry, Filipinos were now a geographically dispersed and demographically settled population. In a study of 270 migrants, Aquino found that 92.5 percent were US citizens, and a remarkable 81 percent owned their own homes. Respondents told Aquino of discrimination in the housing market, but advocacy by the Legion's Manila Post "has been very instrumental in suppressing some of these oppositions." Filipino civic associations fought for veterans' access to property, and the federal government helped them pay for it. "Almost all the Filipino veterans of World War II who have houses now obtained them through the help of the Veterans Administration," Aquino observed.[14]

For many Filipino veterans, the postwar years offered a path to the middle class, but not all Filipinos joined the wave of domestic settlement. Discrimination remained in employment and housing, and as inner cities experienced crime and urban decay, Manilatowns turned from temporary seasonal settlements to permanent homes for the aged and poor. Some continued to work in the Alaska canneries, but there were fewer jobs to be had. After the war, cannery owners invested their wartime profits in mechanization, and postwar job cuts followed. By 1961, the seasonal migrations to Alaska had dwindled from 4,000 men to just 500.[15]

Filipino salmon packers turned to the Cannery Workers' Union and its Seattle-based Local 7 for help, but the union's strident leftist positions had brought it under federal scrutiny as well as internal investigation by the Congress of Industrial Organizations (CIO). In 1949, as it fought to survive the red scare, the CIO purged its left-leaning locals, including the Cannery Workers. The Cold War meant that military service offered political and economic rewards for loyal anticommunists, but now there was no one left to fight for the *manongs*. As the United States and the Philippines both moved into the Cold War, communism became the central issue shaping the political experience of Filipinos in the two countries. By the late 1940s, Local 7 was fighting for its life. So were the Hukbalahap.

Luis Taruc, the charismatic guerrilla leader who had mobilized thousands to fight Japan during World War II and continued to lead a revolutionary movement from the mountains of central Luzon, toured Huk camps in 1948. He "found the soldiers extremely bitter. Their experience in three years of fighting against the Japanese and the puppets had made them militant. . . . They told me that they did not feel like always running away, that they were not cowards and that they wanted to fight." Taruc and the Huks brought that fight to the Philippines' new president, Elpidio Quirino, who entered Malacanang after President Manuel Roxas died of a heart attack at Clark Air Base in April 1948. Raised in modest circumstances in the province of Ilocos Sur, Quirino studied law at the University of the Philippines and had sat out the war, although his wife and three of his children had died at the hands of the Japanese. Like Roxas, Quirino was openly pro-American. "There's no better friend in the whole world," he told Filipinos. Few respected Quirino at the time, and almost none praised him later. The US ambassador, Myron Cowen, called Quirino "incompetent, vain, stubborn, and unwilling to listen to his close advisers." American military observers thought him complacent and naïve about the communist threat. On June 21, 1948, after meeting with Luis Taruc at Malacanang, Quirino announced an amnesty for almost all Huk soldiers. Taruc took up his long-delayed seat in Congress, collected two years of back pay, and announced plans to star in a movie. American observers were horrified.[16]

The ceasefire soon broke down, and under pressure from JUSMAG, Quirino adopted his predecessor's hard line. Taruc, now with a price on his head, rejoined the guerrillas, vowing he would "never submit to any peace imposed by imperialist-feudal guns and bayonets," and telling the *Manila Times*, "I do not think that to be a true Filipino I must lay down my life for American military bases and for the right of American imperialism to exploit my people." Huks saw themselves as the descendants of the revolutionaries of 1898 and the true veterans of World War II. "Everyone else took to the hills during the war," one Huk explained in March 1947. "We fought right here." They disparaged private armies as mercenaries and the Philippine Scouts as puppets. They called each other comrades.[17]

Huks waged small-scale guerrilla attacks and attempted to infiltrate the AFP. American observers claimed that "the No. 1 target then, and now, is the United States," but Huks only raided US forces when they needed money or guns, noting that "Washington is our arsenal." For most supplies, Huks relied on their People's Home Defense Guard. "Wherever we went," locals "would wash and iron our clothes, run errands, buy us cigarettes, get us illegal unit patches for disguise Constabulary uniforms." The movement's wartime manifesto insisted that "forcing the people to work for the army is forbidden," but in reality Huks raised revenues by seizing cash, crops, livestock, and even typewriters.[18]

Meanwhile, their adversaries in the Philippine Constabulary also sometimes forced local women "to do their cooking and washing" and operated graft and extortion rackets that helped constables align their meager salaries with the skyrocketing cost of living. The Constabulary and the Huks often targeted the same communities. "Many no longer keep pigs or chickens," one farmer observed. "Huks come and take them one day and the constabulary want some the next." Some landlords or mayors reached uneasy truces with local guerrillas. "Oh, we have many Huks here," plantation manager Miguel Franco explained in July 1950. "Plenty of Huks, but no trouble." Meanwhile, the US State Department fretted that Constabulary men were so embedded in local politics that they refused to fight, and had grown "so lax as to intermarry with Huk women."[19]

By 1951, Huks had at least 10,000 and perhaps as many as 15,000 armed soldiers. Thousands more joined allied political organizations such as the National Peasants Union and the left-leaning Congress of Labor Organizations. Landlessness, poverty, nationalism, and intimidation by local leaders pushed Filipinos into the Huk ranks. One Huk soldier reflected that "almost all of us have had our houses burned and our families thrown in jail," while another wanted "to stop the civilian guards and PC from beating up my family." Motivations were not always ideological: "Many of the guerrilla soldiers are boys still in their teens who left the farm because of wretched conditions," correspondent Albert Ravenholt observed in 1951. "Others are veterans of the war against Japan who resented the U.S. Army's failure to award them the back pay and recognition given many of the more respectable guerrilla units." Communist ideology was never absent, particularly among the party elite, but the aims of Huk leaders and the rank and file sometimes diverged.[20]

The Huks attracted sympathizers who craved alternatives to the Cold War Pacific's rigid politics. Luis Taruc's 1953 memoir featured a foreword by civil rights activist and performer Paul Robeson, who had learned about the Huks from radical pineapple workers in Hawai'i and felt their struggle showed that "the answer is the people, in them lies the eternal wisdom." Dozens of American and Filipino military deserters—including fervent communists, AWOL servicemen, and intelligence plants—joined the Huks in the mountains. William Pomeroy served in the Philippines during World War II with the 5th Air Force Bomber Command, and then, inspired by connections he forged in Manila's wartime radical underground, later returned to the Philippines as a civilian. In April 1950, already a committed communist (although no longer a Party member), Pomeroy and his wife, Celia Mariano, joined the Huks, where he did propaganda work until his capture in 1952. "I could not remain a mere spectator in the Philippines without being a traitor to my conscience," he explained.[21]

By the Philippines' election day in November 1949, communist insurgency was expanding. At the polls, veterans flocked to Quirino, who boasted that his connections to the Americans would deliver US dollars, and on the eve of the election, Quirino traveled to the United States to drum up economic guarantees. Quirino won, but America's obvious intervention in the election proved embarrassing on the world stage and supported radicals' claims that the Philippines remained an American colony. For the Huks, there was now no turning back. In January 1950, the Huk leadership called for "an all-out armed struggle, for the armed overthrow of the imperialist-puppet regime." On March 29, while President Quirino again went to Washington in search of aid, Huks raided government buildings, targeting local Constabulary units and urging Filipinos to stop the "imperialist forces of America." Fear gripped Manila. "Why doesn't the President do something?" asked an office worker.[22]

Asserting that "no quarter will be shown," Quirino tried to crack down, even asking the US Defense Department for shipments of napalm. American advisers at JUSMAG had another idea: move the 12,000 men of the Philippine Constabulary into the AFP, turning them from the civilian police they were on paper into the soldiers that anti-Huk campaigns had already made them. US officers also knew the policy would enable the Pentagon to evade restrictions on using military foreign aid to fund domestic police forces. Quirino, though, understood it would remove the PC from local political control (and a patronage network that he controlled), so he dragged his feet. Americans pressed Quirino harder, withholding funds in early June 1950 on the grounds that the "Constabulary, combined with the vicious system of Civil Guards, has gotten seriously out of hand." Eventually, Quirino gave in.[23]

Repeatedly shouting that the emperor's clothes were American military fatigues, the Huks undermined the Quirino administration's claim on legitimacy. They also pushed the desperate Philippine government toward the US military, which in turn aligned the newly independent nation ever closer with the strategic interests of its former colonizer. Quirino had initiated a shift larger than anyone saw at the time. Under the pretext of emergency, the AFP now regularly marched through the countryside, treated civilians as military enemies, and, "as a guarantee of order and honesty," policed elections. It was a recipe for continued ties to the United States—and for fratricide among Filipinos.[24]

THEN, ON SUNDAY, JUNE 25, 1950, NORTH KOREAN TROOPS INvaded South Korea across the 38th parallel. President Harry Truman immediately dispatched General Douglas MacArthur to command the United Nations' military response. In Manila, Secretary of National Defense (and former guerrilla leader) Ruperto Kangleon assured the public that the Philippines was "sufficiently strong . . . to meet any eventuality." President Quirino lobbied the United States for more military aid. "The bases were not just intended to be idle military reservations," he said in Manila on June 28. "Now is the time to develop them." But would the Philippines send soldiers to Korea? If so, should the recently dismantled military formations—USAFFE or the Philippine Scouts—be revived, or would that reestablish the colonial relationship that Filipinos had fought so long to undo?[25]

Military leaders, including Secretary Kangleon, warned that sending the AFP to Korea would drain manpower from the country and jeopardize the war against the Huks, who urged Filipinos to "refuse to be butchered in Korea." At first, Quirino announced the Philippines would not deploy troops but send supplies: coconut oil, rice, medicine, and seventeen Sherman tanks. Hawkish politicians seized on Quirino's hesitation, disparaging the president's foreign policy as "effeminate," while Carlos Romulo—America's favorite Filipino soldier and Pulitzer Prize-winning journalist, now installed as the Philippines' foreign secretary—pressed Quirino to "fight side by side again" with the Americans. Romulo insisted that United Nations commitments complemented the "more intimate, and in a sense, a more compelling consideration" of the "battle-tested comradeship" the two nations forged during World War II. Representative Diosdado Macapagal likewise argued that Filipino "soldiers will fight in Korea not as troops of any country but of the UN," and thus the Philippines would join America's Korean coalition as a partner, not a colony.[26]

American aid assuaged financial fears. On August 3, President Truman asked Congress for $30 million to support "friendly countries" in Southeast Asia, and in Manila, President Quirino changed his tune. "We have a definite stake in the Korean war . . . to stop Red aggression there and thereby prevent it from engulfing us and the rest of the world." A few days later, Quirino insisted that "though our country needs its available troops to put down its political dissidents at home, . . . we are not going to dodge our responsibility." On August 7, 1950, the Philippine Congress authorized the Philippine Expeditionary Force to Korea (PEFTOK). President Truman was "very happy to hear" the news: "We want all our allies in the fighting and shooting part of this unpleasantness."[27]

At a massive sendoff rally in Manila in September 1950, Quirino praised the men of PEFTOK's 10th Battalion Combat Team (BCT) as the "first to carry the flag of your own sovereign nation abroad." At any given time there was never more than one BCT—about 1,300 soldiers—in country, but given that the entire Philippine Army had about 30,000 soldiers, that was no small commitment. The men who arrived in Korea on September 19, the third of twenty-two nations to join under the UN flag, were mostly career soldiers, often with combat experience in both World War II and the ongoing anti-Huk campaign. Many had signed up for voluntary PEFTOK assignments to earn the enlistment bonuses that doubled the salaries of officers and more than doubled the salaries of enlisted men.[28]

Filipino soldiers again marched under Douglas MacArthur's command. Fed on specially issued Filipino "F-rations"—which substituted two thirds of a pound of rice for GI bread—PEFTOK soldiers played a relatively limited role in the Korean conflict. In an ironic legacy of the Spanish-American War, they were initially assigned to serve with the "Borinqueneers," the 65th US Infantry Regiment recruited from Puerto Rico, on the mistaken assumption that Filipino soldiers spoke Spanish. Denigrating PEFTOK men's "siesta complex," US officers ignored their combat potential and initially assigned them to labor battalions. When it became clear in November 1950 that the 10th BCT would be broken up into guard duty companies under the command of the US Army's 187th Airborne Regimental Combat Team, PEFTOK's commanding officer, Lieutenant Colonel Mariano Azurin, urged the Philippine government to withdraw the force. Eventually they did see action, including the disastrous defeat for UN forces at the Imjin River in April 1951.[29]

The Philippine expedition's hero was twenty-four-year-old Lieutenant Fidel Ramos. Born in Lingayen to a leading member of the Philippine Congress, Ramos graduated from West Point just eighteen days before the Korean War began. In the early morning hours of May 21, 1952, Ramos's platoon watched as US forces pounded an otherwise impregnable Hill Eerie with artillery and napalm. Then Ramos led a daring and successful raid on the hill. He returned to Manila marked by both US and Philippine officers as a young soldier with a promising military future. Equally ambitious, though with his eye on politics rather than the army, was the young Benigno Aquino Jr., scion of a powerful political family, who spent nearly a year in Korea as a newspaper correspondent.[30]

With communist insurgency at home, the Korean War rarely grabbed Manila headlines until April 1951, when President Harry Truman dismissed General Douglas MacArthur after the general publicly contradicted the president by calling for an escalation of the war. Filipinos overwhelmingly sided with MacArthur. Senator Macario Peralta called his sacking "the greatest Russian victory since the last war," and President Elpidio Quirino invited MacArthur for a "most-deserved rest." PEFTOK troops, though, barely registered in the American press during the war or in soldiers' memoirs afterward. Even Douglas MacArthur paid little attention to PEFTOK. Nor did he consider offers by veterans of the Philippine Scouts to rejoin his command for the war in Korea. The 31,000 members of the National Federation of Philippine Scout Veterans—many of them mustered out of the Scouts against their will only a year earlier—volunteered "to fight once more for the democracies headed by America," and retired civilian employees of the US Navy at Cavite passed a unanimous resolution supporting UN efforts in Korea. Across the Pacific, a Filipino group in Los Angeles wrote to President Quirino offering aid as an "indirect way of reaffirming our loyalty to the Philippines." The US Army, having just dismantled the Philippine Scouts, was uninterested in reestablishing the force. But on the ground in Korea, a manpower crisis changed the minds of top brass, and America's Philippine past soon offered a model for its Cold War present.[31]

In August 1950, North Korean troops surrounded the US Army soldiers who had retreated to the South Korean city of Pusan. American replacement troops were unavailable and it was unclear whether allies would send soldiers in time, or, in fact, send them at all. So US forces deployed "impressment teams" to round up able-bodied men inside the Pusan perimeter. Men "who could not understand a word of English, who quickly exhausted the quartermaster stock of small size clothing, and who had never fired a rifle" now found themselves in KATUSA, the Korean Augmentation to the United States Army.[32]

Born out of necessity, KATUSA was modeled on the Philippine Scouts, and as the soldiers mastered English and marksmanship, they found a niche on scouting patrols and in interpreting and interrogation work. Over time, pressure mounted in the United States to bring

American soldiers home from the Korean stalemate, and MacArthur's replacement, General Mark Clark, begged for more. The KATUSA program, he explained, "provides the finest training" and "a savings of lives of our soldiers [*sic*] results." Matthew Batson had said much the same thing in Macabebe a half century earlier. Improvised structures like KATUSA reflected the Cold War emergency, but American power in the Pacific layered new institutions on top of old mindsets.[33]

Seven thousand Filipinos fought in PEFTOK as US allies, but even more joined the US Navy directly. Provisions of the 1947 Military Bases Agreement authorizing the enlistment of Philippine citizens were only implemented after the onset of the Korean War, as the Navy's Philippines Enlistment Program (PEP) recruited 2,000 Filipinos a year to meet the wartime needs of Navy and Coast Guard. Young Jose Monge Montano saw the appeal. "All those Navy men would take vacation in our town and married all the beautiful and highly-trained women, like the teachers, and they build big houses. So I said to myself, 'Maybe I'll join the Navy too.'" When Victor Sarmiento enlisted in the Coast Guard he was assigned as a steward, denoted with the rating "TN" for noncitizen stewards, and which Coast Guardsmen sneeringly referred to as "Table Navigator." An April 1953 law extended US naturalization rights to alien veterans of the Korean War, including Filipino US Navy sailors, offering a path to citizenship to young sailors that the Rescission Act had denied to their fathers after World War II.[34]

As noncitizens, Filipinos had few options in the Navy, but African American sailors didn't have many more. Before 1954, sailors could enlist either as a seaman in general service or a steward, and recruiters consistently directed sailors of color into the steward service. US Secretary of the Navy Robert Anderson urged caution on integration: "You can't eliminate the customs and habits of people by executive order." In September 1953, despite his hesitations, Anderson ordered Vice Admiral James Holloway Jr., the Chief of Naval Personnel, to "bring about an integrated type of service" for the steward branch, where, although it was not formally segregated, about half of the Navy's 25,000 African Americans then served. Navy recruiters found that even after eliminating the two-track enlistment policy in March 1954, few white sailors were willing to become stewards. The Korean War manpower shortage and the emerging civil rights movement ratcheted up political scrutiny, so the Bureau of Naval Personnel used the PEP to enlist thousands of Filipinos to integrate the kitchens. Navy officers quickly achieved their aim: the steward branch was, if not more white, at least less black.[35]

Whether serving under the Philippine flag or sailing under the stars and stripes, Filipinos in uniform found that questions of national sovereignty and economic incentive endured. The direct connection between American money and Filipino soldiers fighting a US-led war led some to worry that PEFTOK was a mercenary army in the service of its old colonial master. Quirino assured PEFTOK soldiers in 1951 that they fought "not merely as paid soldiers of the country but as citizens of the world." In Carlos Romulo's mind, the Philippines reaped the rewards of sending PEFTOK soldiers to fight side by side with Americans when the United States committed itself to defend the Philippines. Recognizing the "common bond" that had led the nations "to fight side by side against imperialist aggression during the last war," the Mutual Defense Treaty (MDT)—signed in August 1951 and still in force today—bound the United States to respond to an attack on the Philippines. Leftists such as Amado Hernandez denounced the treaty as "another frame-up against peace," and others noted that the wording (which only required the United States to act "in accordance with its constitutional processes") was vague. But in fact the MDT reflected a stronger commitment than the United States had stated in 1941. In response, Secretary Romulo signed the Philippines' long-delayed peace treaty with Japan. Romulo calculated wartime losses (with accuracy, if not diplomatic savvy) at $8 billion. With the Korean War in full swing and Japan's promise of $800 million in reparations, the two countries buried the hatchet.[36]

Overall, before the last PEFTOK soldiers came home in May 1955, more than 7,400 Filipinos had served in country. About 128 lost their lives in combat or were missing; another 41 POWs survived Chinese and North Korean psychological warfare. Anticommunist battles abroad shaped politics at home for both nations. American diplomats believed the bonds of Pacific partnership allowed them to wield the colonial stick as they dangled the carrot of Cold War aid. Savvy Philippine politicians, for their part, understood how much they could get—financial or otherwise—from America by waving communism's red flag.[37]

THE PENTAGON FOUND NEW USES FOR AMERICA'S PACIFIC BASES in the tense years of the early Cold War. During World War II, US forces expanded existing facilities from Pearl Harbor to Guam, conquered Japanese bases in island-hopping campaigns, and dispatched seabees to construct new posts and landing strips. Now there were new challenges in the Pacific. America's relations with the Soviet Union and China hardened into Cold War, and thinly stretched European empires increasingly passed the burdens of anticommunism to the United States. By the late 1950s, the United States maintained 450 bases in thirty-six countries. Two dozen in the Philippines complemented others throughout the Pacific: in America's fiftieth state of Hawai'i, on the US island territory of Guam, on the western Pacific island of Okinawa (under direct US military administration until 1972), and all over Japan and South Korea. The Korean War turned America's Philippine bases from a clause in the 1947 Military Bases Agreement to the anchor of a Pacific strategy. They were useful for training men, storing equipment, repairing ships, listening in to radio broadcasts, and, if the time came, for launching a military assault. Legal arrangements accompanied US basing in every host country. Powerful European allies demanded respect for national sovereignty, but in the

Philippines, decades of military control yielded basing agreements that looked more like colonial impositions than bilateral agreements.

Of the twenty-three installations covered in the Military Bases Agreement, the largest was Clark Air Force Base, a sprawling 247-square-mile installation sixty miles north of Manila in Luzon province. Clark was a home away from home for some 40,000 American service members and their families, who enjoyed libraries, theaters, schools, bowling alleys, a PX that rivaled the most modern of 1950s supermarkets, a 1,200-seat movie theater, and a fishing pool stocked with specially flown-in Minnesota bass. The authors of *A Pocket Guide to the Philippines*, a 1961 Defense Department booklet issued to arriving US personnel, emphasized ordinary airmen's role as international ambassadors. "Be prepared to . . . explain different aspects of America, why American soldiers, sailors, airmen, and marines are based in foreign lands all over the world, and—most important of all—that the United States has dedicated its tremendous military strength (of which you yourself are a part) to the protection of freedom and the preservation of peace."[38]

In 1957, at least 12,000 Filipinos worked directly on base at Clark as technicians, stenographers, and security guards. In the neighboring city of Angeles, residents were almost entirely dependent on Clark for work as entertainers and bartenders, gardeners and maids. A 1950s guide for American airmen's wives promised a "full time housegirl" for just $25.00 a month. Leny Mendoza Strobel, who grew up in San Fernando, just a few miles south of Clark, recalled "the mystique of its isolation and separation by miles of barbed wire fences." She visited the base once a year, on the Fourth of July, when it was open to visitors, and recalled a tour on "one of the army [*sic*] buses" with "a hamburger sandwich wrapped in star-spangled blue and red stars."[39]

Filipinos not only worked at Clark Air Base; they also lived on it. Despite Air Force officials' claims to the contrary—and probably without their full knowledge—some 50,000 Filipinos lived on base lands.

Clark comprised some of Luzon's best agricultural land, and given that it was about four times the size of the District of Columbia and was never entirely fenced off during this period, many Filipinos established informal "squatter" settlements. US officials called them "trespassers," but many, particularly the Aeta, an indigenous mountain tribe, had been living there for centuries.[40]

Subic Bay Naval Station, about eighty miles northwest of Manila on the South China Sea, was almost as large as Clark. Americans steadily expanded the former Spanish naval base into the Pacific Fleet's repair shop and docking station—and one of the Navy's leading recreational leave destinations. After all, one Philippine magazine noted, "the men need a shore-break once in a while, just like office personnel need coffee-breaks." As the Navy acquired more and more planes, the United States also built a naval air station at Subic; laying its 8,000-foot runway required the movement of more earth than building the Panama Canal.[41]

Subic was also surrounded by Filipino civilians, crowded into the city of Olongapo, which was not, despite Admiral Arthur Radford's 1955 pronouncement, "one of the happiest little towns in the Philippines." Olongapo wasn't just next to Subic. The city was literally on base. From 1902 to 1959, the US Navy directly governed the city, with power to police, tax, regulate utilities, hire and fire school administrators, and even "deport" city residents. In 1955, US Ambassador Homer Ferguson assured the State Department that "Filipinos recognize Olongapo cannot be run as [an] ordinary municipality," but local residents resented the Navy's direct control—and that of the Filipino city councilors carefully groomed and approved by Navy officers. US Defense Department officials boasted that wherever the military "carries out its oversea commitments," it hired local labor, "easing the soldier's burden and saving the American taxpayers thousands of dollars." Filipino labor, "employed at prevailing local wages" in Angeles or Olongapo, or recruited into the US Navy's steward branch, represented a key component of the Cold War Pacific system. Whether as base workers or as uniformed soldiers, Filipinos were partners in America's efforts to contain communism in Korea and to fight it in the mountains of the Philippines.[42]

THE KOREAN WAR AND THE PACIFIC BASING SYSTEM THE UNITED States built to respond to it meant that during the Cold War America would never forget its former colony. Anticommunism was a global way of thinking that demanded action on multiple fronts. The Philippines became America's Pacific training ground for a worldwide campaign of counterinsurgency and a home base for launching that effort across Southeast Asia. But although the Philippines faced armed communist insurgency, the United States never fought a massive ground war there as they soon would in Vietnam. They didn't have to. They had Filipinos who would fight it for them.

US military officials balked at the idea of intervening directly in the anti-Huk campaign. The return of American GIs to an independent Philippines would only feed Huk propaganda, and after the outbreak of the Korean War, there were no soldiers to spare. Instead, there were advisers, including a forty-two-year-old Air Force officer who arrived in Manila in September 1950 as part of JUSMAG. Tall, handsome, and military in bearing, Lieutenant Colonel Edward Lansdale left a career in advertising during World War II to join the Office of Strategic Services, the wartime predecessor to the Central Intelligence Agency. He served as an OSS intelligence officer in Manila after the 1944 reinvasion, and maintained his CIA connections while rising through the ranks of the US Air Force, despite never flying a plane. Assigned to JUSMAG while actually working as part of the innocuously named Office of Policy Coordination (later folded into the CIA), Lansdale oversaw America's ambitious efforts against the Huks. At his side was Charles Bohannan, a tough-talking lieutenant colonel who started his career as an anthropologist and had also first seen the Philippines during World War II. Tasked with retraining the Philippine Constabulary from a police force into an army of counterinsurgency, Bohannan advocated "unconventional" methods "limited only by the ingenuity, resources, and ethical standards of those who are responsible for them." Bohannan regretted that it had become "unfashionable to exterminate or enslave the guerrillas and the civilian population from whom they draw their support," words that made the "howling wilderness" orders that Brigadier General Jacob Smith issued in Samar in October 1901 sound mild by comparison.[43]

Just off the plane in Manila, Lansdale played a substantial (if murky) role in a September 1950 shakeup at the Philippine Department of National Defense that pushed out guerrilla veteran Secretary Ruperto Kangleon and replaced him with Ramon Magsaysay, a forty-four-year-old congressman. Born in 1907 and raised in the province of Zambales not far from Subic Bay, Magsaysay represented a younger generation. While other politicians had forged their careers in the early twentieth century's shift from anticolonial rebellion to grudging collaboration, Magsaysay grew up under US rule. Americans appreciated his wartime service with a US-oriented guerrilla unit and loved his military bearing. A year after the war's end, voters elected him to the Philippine legislature, where he soon claimed the chairmanship of its Committee on National Defense.[44]

The new secretary of defense came out swinging. At a September 1950 press conference, Magsaysay announced an outlandish Huk policy: first, to organize "a unit of Negrito tribesmen" to intimidate the rebels; second, to "import some bloodhounds"; and third, to "dump all captured and surrendered Huks on an uninhabited island and there teach them the democratic way of life." Gruff rhetoric shook up the status quo and enchanted US military officials. With advisers watching over his shoulder, and with hefty bags of cash—some of it from the Americans and the rest provided by anticommunist landowners in Huk-dominated regions—Magsaysay retooled the Huk campaign. He switched from large assaults to small sweeps and armed soldiers with the .30-caliber rifles the police used rather than tanks and artillery that Huk guerrillas could see from miles away. But despite his big talk and incessant press releases, Magsaysay didn't change much. His much-vaunted use of small units merely reflected a shortage of men.[45]

President Quirino followed the Defense Department shakeup with a political one, declaring a state of emergency in October 1950. An anti-subversive dragnet rounded up Huk leaders, along with journalists, trade unionists, and even a movie producer. In Manila, the Philippine legislature's Committee on Un-Filipino Activities launched investigations that mirrored Senator Joseph McCarthy's witch hunts in the United States. At times, the two countries' efforts overlapped, particularly when it came to immigration. Provisions of the US Internal Security Act of 1950 made communist advocacy grounds for deportation from the United States. Soon dozens of officials in the West Coast's Cannery Workers' Union found themselves under investigation, with charges against three of its leaders: Ernesto Mangaoang, Chris Mensalvas, and Ponce Torres. The men put up a fight. On appeal, most of them successfully argued that as Filipinos, when they arrived in San Francisco or Seattle, they had not "entered" the United States but had merely moved from one part of its territory to another, and thus could not be deported. In October 1953, the US Supreme Court agreed, blocking Mangaoang's deportation. But the CWFLU's legal campaign bankrupted the union and frightened new workers from joining.[46]

The stakes were higher on the other side of the Pacific. In the Philippine countryside, Quirino's emergency declaration gave the AFP, the Constabulary, and the private armies a free hand. Huks and their supporters were slaughtered, and the emergency lasted until 1953. In the Philippines, the red scare was real: there were communists, they were armed, and they posed a threat to the government of the Republic.

But Philippine anticommunism still played out on implicitly American terms and with explicitly American funds, giving the United States leverage to intervene in the domestic politics of its former colony in the name of national security.

In November 1953, with his loyalists in the Philippine Army supervising the polls, and American money bankrolling his campaign, Ramon Magsaysay won the presidency. From Moscow, *Izvestia* editorialized that the outcome showed the Philippines remained "an American colony," and given that Magsaysay spent election day on the yacht of a US Navy officer, the Soviet journalists were probably on to something. As president, Magsaysay pushed a new policy that aimed at remaking the Huks into loyal Filipino citizen-soldiers. The Economic Development Corporation (EDCOR) offered "politically rejuvenated" Huk soldiers twenty acres, a house, tools, and farm animals in the so-called virgin land of the southern island of Mindanao. Small business loans (funded by US military aid) would, Magsaysay insisted, "make the Huk a capitalist." The new president even proposed a resettlement camp in Luis Taruc's hometown of San Luis, sure to lure Huks "like a jukebox attracts teen-agers."[47]

Homesteading offered a compelling vision, but it had one problem common to frontier settlement anywhere: namely, that the empty land wasn't empty. EDCOR exacerbated tensions with Muslim residents of Mindanao, setting the region on a collision course with the Philippine government. Nor was EDCOR a new idea. A rhetoric of land ownership, a policy that announced an end to war and redefined insurgency as crime, and a media campaign that papered over continued violence in the countryside were all moves direct from William Howard Taft's playbook. Magsaysay himself acknowledged this to an American reporter: "We treat the people as you did when you came here to fight us in 1901." In the end, land reform was mostly a public relations maneuver. Not that many people actually took advantage of EDCOR—perhaps as few as 950 families—and most of those who did were AFP veterans, not Huks.[48]

Magsaysay repeatedly claimed that the Huk soldier fought for himself and his family, not ideologically for a communist revolution or patriotically for a better future for the Philippines. By insisting that Huks "never were communists, really. Just desperate men," Magsaysay erased the political content of Huk soldiering. Offering Huks "a house and land of their own," Magsaysay's policies foregrounded Huks' financial motivations but also emptied the civic content from his own soldiers' service. Perhaps cognizant of how Philippine politics worked, he sought a path whereby ordinary Filipinos in the AFP could make claims on their patronage-driven government. After all, he observed, "money does things to men in war and out of it."[49]

Politics and patronage also led Magsaysay to court his fellow veterans of World War II. Securing veterans' votes at home required seeking results in Washington, but veterans found Philippine leaders often unable to deliver the goods. Ambitious politicians paid lip service but accomplished little—among them a young congressman by the name of Ferdinand Marcos, who joined a 1947 delegation to Washington that sought, unsuccessfully, to repeal the Rescission Act. Veterans protested: in a typical incident from March 1949, some 15,000 people marched in Manila demanding "backpay," the retrospective payment of USAFFE salaries to wartime guerrillas. As one protestor carried a placard reading UNCLE SAM HAS FORSAKEN US, veterans' allies in Washington argued that American failure to reward wartime service could lead Filipinos to lose faith in the United States. Shadowy figures in Manila quietly started funding the reliable anticommunists of the Philippine Veterans Legion, whose highly visible protests meant the Huks would not be the only group recruiting discontented ex-guerrillas. The Cold War now structured the veterans issue on both sides of the Pacific.[50]

It even shaped the day-to-day operation of the Manila office of the US Veterans Administration (VA). The agency had maintained an office in the Philippines since 1922, mostly to serve American ex-service personnel. In early 1946, the VA, the Department of State, and the Department of the Interior (which exercised authority over the territory before independence) agreed that instead of accessing the government through the State Department and its consular offices, veterans in the independent Philippines would continue to visit the VA Regional Office in Manila. To this day, it is the only VA office outside the United States.[51]

VA staffers in the Philippines—whether US citizens on overseas duty or Filipinos hired locally—were never vigorous advocates for the veterans they were supposed to serve. Corruption in the Philippine government and in the VA set the tone in public and shaped the policy in practice. The evidence required to document military service to the VA or the US Army's Recovered Personnel Division offered ample opportunities for inauthentic applications and kickback schemes. American diplomats and VA officials, failing to see that their own policies incentivized fraud (or, often, participating in the corruption), attributed veterans' efforts to Filipino culture. While collecting bribes from swindlers posing as former guerrilla officers, they trotted out an occasional knowing reference to the *utang na loob*, or debt of gratitude, which they asserted led Filipinos astray from the Western bureaucratic norms that Americans purportedly upheld. While many claims surely were fraudulent—and many veterans suffered at the hands of fixers, racketeers, and predators—US government officials in Manila quickly came to assume that all of them were. Thus, Filipinos found that the one American institution in the Philippines they could have turned to in the years after the Rescission Act was persistently hostile to them. At a dead end, vets and their survivors sent heart-rending letters to US officials, begging for relief or the return of stolen benefits. By the 1950s, their letters were no longer even answered.[52]

Despite independence, advocacy for Filipino veterans continued in the United States. Filipino Americans played only a modest role in this process. In Washington, Cold Warriors—including William

Howard Taft's son, Senator Robert Taft, who had spent four years in the Philippines during his father's term as governor-general—backed the veterans' cause out of a lingering sense of imperial obligation. Congress extended some modest benefits and funded the construction of a Philippine Veterans Memorial Hospital (VMH) in Manila. Slow to open and always short on beds, the VMH was less substance than symbol: a VA administrator wrote in a 1956 brief to President Dwight Eisenhower that the hospital "is a widely publicized showplace" with a special role in supporting "United States standing in the area, where there is an ideological contest." Revolutionary hero Emilio Aguinaldo died there in 1964.[53]

Veterans' claims generally featured as a minor diplomatic squabble between the two nations, shunted off to the desks of second-tier State Department lawyers. Time and again, when American officials in the US Information Agency boasted of the extent of foreign aid to the Philippines, they included in their calculations the direct payment of veterans benefits and other pensions that individual Filipinos had earned on the battlefield. Veterans, too, spoke of foreign aid, and not of discrimination or equal rights. Their bargain, argued former senator Claro Recto, generated a "mendicant" foreign policy that brought the Philippines "step by step into an intimate, almost exclusive, association with the former metropolis."[54]

If a beggar's foreign policy linked the Philippines and the United States in a continued association, counterinsurgency paired the two nations—indeed locked Ramon Magsaysay and Edward Lansdale together in an intimate embrace. By 1953, the president and his American adviser believed they were winning the war against the Huks, although the guerrillas' ranks thinned for reasons unrelated to Lansdale's schemes or Magsaysay's public relations moves. Huks had underestimated the strength of the Philippine government and alienated their middle-class allies. The leadership's ideological purity chafed against the family-based social ties of the countryside, which often led peasants to choose kin over class. Deprived of a mass base, Huk guerrillas began to live off the land, and as their depredations blurred the line between revolutionary action and everyday banditry, popular support deteriorated further. Huk leaders saw the writing on the wall: Luis Taruc, dismissed from the party in 1952 and convinced that he was safer in jail than on the run from his former comrades, surrendered on May 17, 1954. He spent much of the next fourteen years in a Manila prison, and no Huk commander replicated his charisma or his leadership. Magsaysay and Lansdale took credit for the victory.[55]

Magsaysay died in a plane crash near Cebu in March 1957. His death turned him into a legend, one that Edward Lansdale later went so far as to have "invented." Bound by war, the men's relationship was warm, genial, and masculine, simultaneously fraternal and obviously unequal. American news accounts boasted the two slept in the same room (although reporters did reassuringly note that they kept twin beds), while Lansdale noted that "we were so close that we thought and spoke of each other as 'brother.'" Just before a public event in 1952, Lansdale harangued Magsaysay for refusing to deliver a CIA-authored script full of praise for America's "brotherly protection and friendship." Magsaysay responded to Lansdale's hectoring with a shove. Lansdale then "plugged him real hard, and he went down." The two men quickly made up. "I am fighting because I love this guy very much," Lansdale explained. After all, he later reflected, "counterinsurgency is [only] another word for brotherly love."[56]

Carlos Bulosan, the leftist Filipino writer and activist in Seattle, also advocated brotherly love, but as a revolutionary alternative to counterinsurgent fraternity. While the FBI tracked his movements and read his mail, Bulosan delved into Huk politics, corresponded with Luis Taruc, and poured his energies into *The Cry and the Dedication*, a sprawling novel composed between 1949 and 1952. The book follows the fortunes of seven Huk guerrillas in the mountains of Luzon. Comradeship across lines of class and nation supersedes the outdated relations of patron and clan, as one guerrilla describes revolutionary struggle as "one and indivisible all over the planet." Brotherhood—or more accurately, fratricide—provided the book's ending as well. In the final pages the main character Dante dies at the hands of his own brother, an anticommunist priest. Bulosan never published his novel. In the midst of the red scare, Bulosan found it difficult to find work and died, poverty-stricken and practically forgotten, in 1956. With him died one vision of an American-Filipino bond that could be forged without war. In both the United States and the Philippines, the Cold War destroyed any alternative formulations. Only militarism remained to bind the two nations together.[57]

WITH STALEMATE IN KOREA AND COLD WAR MENTALITIES IN place across the Pacific, President Dwight Eisenhower took a moment in April 1954 to explain to Americans the stakes of another conflict in Southeast Asia. Eisenhower pointed to "what you would call the 'falling domino' principle. You have a row of dominoes set up, you knock over the first one, and what will happen to the last one is the certainty that it will go over very quickly." To calm Americans' fears about South Vietnam, he offered the Philippines as the model counterinsurgent nation. The US-Philippine military relationship was the foundation on which the two nations built new structures of US power in Asia. America would increasingly commit its troops elsewhere, precisely because the Philippines continued as the sturdiest link in the Pacific chain.[58]

That September, Manila hosted the conference that established the Southeast Asian Treaty Organization (SEATO), modeled after the successful North Atlantic Treaty Organization (NATO) that gathered Cold War allies in Europe. But SEATO was not NATO: only a thin commitment bound its eight member states, each of which was already firmly in the American orbit and a recipient of US military aid. The Soviets dismissed SEATO as an American puppet show. A year later, in April 1955, political leaders from twenty-nine nations gathered at Bandung in Indonesia for the Asian-African Conference. As momentum toward decolonization accelerated, participants sought a shared foreign policy of nonalignment to challenge what American observer Richard Wright called the global "color curtain." Philippine statesman Carlos Romulo hoped to play a leading role at Bandung, only to find himself relegated to "observer" status after delegates concluded that the presence of US bases in the Philippines meant the republic was not "unaligned." Behind the scenes, US State Department aides dismissed Bandung as a "Dark-Town Strutters' Ball."[59]

Officials at the US State and Defense departments were less interested in Afro-Asian solidarity than the brotherhood of counterinsurgency they had developed in the Philippines during the previous years. Former World War II guerrillas played a key role, particularly Wendell Fertig, who joined the Pentagon's Special Forces team in 1951. Crediting his guerrilla experience as "the basis for the concept and policy of the U.S. Special Forces," Fertig set up Special Forces training at Fort Bragg in North Carolina before returning to the Philippines in 1953. Filipino veterans did similar work. West Point graduate Fidel Ramos, back from the Korean War and now a rising star in the AFP, headed up the Philippine Army's unconventional warfare committee in 1961, and the next year took over as commanding officer of its Special Forces Group.[60]

Shared experience in counterinsurgency—sustained by romantic memories of the late President Ramon Magsaysay—taught American officials that civic action programs against the Huk insurgents were, as US Army Colonel John Duffy put it, "a sound idea for developing new countries" such as South Vietnam. In 1962, Air Force Major William Thorpe told fellow airmen that the successful Huk experience offered "hope for the future," thanks to helicopters, which "proved particularly effective," and napalm, which he deemed "not altogether successful in the jungle because dense vegetation and high humidity tended to blunt searing and burning." During the late 1950s and early 1960s, hundreds of officials from Vietnam, Laos, Burma, and Malaya traveled to the Philippines to study psychological warfare and anti-guerrilla methods. For Edward Lansdale and others, training together was the key to building close relationships among military men across the anticommunist Pacific.[61]

Eisenhower's secretary of state, John Foster Dulles, dispatched Edward Lansdale to, as Lansdale recalled it, "go to Vietnam and help the Vietnamese much as I had helped the Filipinos." Lansdale brought some of his trusted allies with him. Among them were counterinsurgency experts such as Napoleon Valeriano, who had risen within the AFP with the support of US military and intelligence officials and applied the lessons of the Huk insurgency to Vietnam through the work of the CIA-sponsored Freedom Company of the Philippines. The Freedom Company, incorporated in November 1954, recruited members of the Philippine Veterans Legion to share with other Southeast Asians "the techniques of preserving their freedom." Its operatives set up South Vietnamese President Ngo Dinh Diem's Presidential Guard Battalion, and advisers even helped write the country's new constitution. In January 1958, facing scrutiny for its CIA ties, the Freedom Company folded up shop, only to undertake the same work as the euphemistically named Eastern Construction Company, offering what the US Army described as "certain professional and technical skills." On a USAID contract with a firm called International Police Services Incorporated, Valeriano traveled to Saigon in March 1964 for a briefing on Vietnam's police system from the young Foreign Service officer Richard Holbrooke. Charles Bohannan circulated copies of the 1915 Philippine Constabulary training manual, reprinted with USAID funds.[62]

Filipinos also updated William McKinley's rhetoric of "benevolent assimilation" for the Cold War era. Oscar Arellano, a thirty-eight-year-old architect and World War II veteran active in Manila's chapter of the Junior Chamber of Commerce, established Operation Brotherhood, a medical mission, after the Geneva Accords divided North and South Vietnam in 1954. That October, the first Filipino doctors, nurses, dentists, and medics—trained professionals, despite Arellano's attempt to underplay them as "just a group of amateurs"—arrived at a refugee center in Saigon and headed to the nearby city of Tay Ninh. As a medical venture, Operation Brotherhood's impact was limited, with no more than sixty Filipino volunteers in Vietnam at any one time. President Diem was nevertheless thrilled: "From a small country comes the first sign of concern and offer of friendship." The Manila Jaycees initially funded the scheme until Vice President Richard Nixon opened doors to American donors. All along, it counted on the support of Edward Lansdale and the CIA. Trumpeting what Arellano called "Asians helping Asians," Operation Brotherhood retooled the Pacific partnership into Cold War propaganda, making US power in Vietnam look humanitarian, multilateral, and most importantly, multicultural. Not that Operation Brotherhood had strictly humanitarian goals in the first place: volunteers also collected intelligence and contributed to South Vietnamese psychological warfare campaigns.[63]

Increasingly aware of what CIA operative Joseph Burkholder Smith described as "a large number of activities . . . run from Manila to try to use Filipinos as our alter egos," the Vietnamese grew skeptical, with one among them observing that the Filipinos in Operation Brotherhood "have brown faces but they wear the same Hawaiian sports shirts the Americans do." Arellano admitted that "Filipinos became the target of innuendos and attacks, as being tools of the U.S. Government," and even Diem's enthusiasm cooled: "The Vietnamese didn't need the help of a bunch of . . . nightclub musicians." Operation Brotherhood lasted just two years before Arellano decamped for Laos in pursuit of a lucrative contract with USAID.[64]

As civil war continued to split Indochina, some called for soldiers. Speaking at a 1961 Manila convention of the Asian People's Anti-Communist League, Connecticut senator Thomas Dodd advocated an "Asian Freedom Legion" of Southeast Asian troops, sure to "stir the imagination of free peoples everywhere." The CIA's Freedom Company pursued a different track, establishing the Vietnamese Veterans Legion in May 1955 in the hopes of turning former soldiers from France's colonial army into nation-building military officers—just like America's Filipino veterans were doing for the AFP. But despite Dodd's warning that soon "the whole Pacific will indeed become a Red ocean," the Asian Freedom Legion never materialized.[65]

Dodd's proposal seemed out of date because military officers in both countries had spent the previous decade developing a more modern system of counterinsurgency. The new US president, John F. Kennedy, was particularly enamored by Special Forces. He poured funds into training programs at Fort Bragg that brought Philippine officers for training stints, and heard regular briefings from counterinsurgency advisers who compared the challenges of South Vietnam with those the anti-Huk campaign had overcome. Kennedy strongly considered sending Edward Lansdale as ambassador to Vietnam and even authorized Napoleon Valeriano to train anticommunist forces to overthrow Fidel Castro in Cuba. JFK likewise updated benevolent assimilation for the 1960s through the Peace Corps, whose very first volunteers headed for the Philippines. The volunteers, one wrote, "are an effective counterbalance to the offensive displays of whoring and drinking of soldiers on R&R." Idealistic American youth were surprised when Filipinos assumed they were CIA plants.[66]

Kennedy himself took the Philippines for granted. At the White House on November 19, 1963, with his bags packed for a trip to Dallas, Kennedy met staffers to plan a major Asian trip. The president didn't see much to be gained by stopping in Manila. "The Philippines," he observed, "are pretty old hat." Kennedy's lack of interest cooled relations with his Philippine counterpart, Diosdado Macapagal. Born in Pampanga in 1910 to a poor family, Macapagal made his way through law school, kept his head down during World War II, and jumped into politics after independence in 1946. Recruited to run for Congress in 1949 against a legislator popular with Huk sympathizers, Macapagal was soon on a fast track to the presidency, where he kept a distance from the United States until August 2, 1964. That day, radio transmissions reached the US Naval Communications Station, a small listening post at San Miguel in Luzon, reporting an attack on American vessels in the Gulf of Tonkin off the coast of North Vietnam. Within days, the US Congress authorized military action by President Lyndon Johnson. A new war was under way in Asia.[67]

The previous decade's reworking of the US-Philippine relationship suggested that everything was in place for an easy victory in Vietnam: an American-led effort launched from massive military bases in the Philippines; US military strength complemented by Filipino soldiers marching as anticommunist allies rather than colonial helpmeets; counterinsurgency networks and anticommunist rhetoric that had stopped communism in South Korea and the Philippines and eliminated it from Seattle unions and Manila newspapers; all polished with SEATO's multilateral sheen and humanitarian aid from Operation Brotherhood. At a speech in Manila, Senator Thomas Dodd praised the "sons of our two nations," whose "blood was commingled" in the last war. "America does not forget her friends," he promised Filipinos, and explained that after his recent trip to South Vietnam, "I can assure you that the tide of battle has now begun to turn." In fact, the war had only just begun.[68]

CHAPTER EIGHT

QUAGMIRE

1965–1977

After Philippine independence in 1946, the colonial bonds between the United States and the Philippines had been replaced by a Cold War consensus of military fraternalism that was not so different. In the 1960s, however, the Vietnam War unwound the tightly woven fabric of Pacific partnership. At the time, the alliance looked stronger than ever, particularly as Philippine President Ferdinand Marcos consolidated his hold on power with US military support. But by the time the last American helicopters departed from rooftops in Saigon in April 1975, the United States, defeated abroad and divided at home, lurched away from Southeast Asia. Its longtime political partner was under martial law, crippled by economic instability, political unrest, and communist and Islamist insurgencies.

The shift began in 1965, as the United States escalated the Vietnam War and recruited Philippine troops to join them; as immigration restrictions lifted in the United States; and as protest movements on both sides of the Pacific called the alliance into question. Across the United States and Southeast Asia, critical moments in 1965 capture the turning point in the two nations' shared history. In Delano, California, on September 7, 1965, Filipino grape pickers meeting as members of the AFL-CIO's Agricultural Workers Organizing Committee voted to strike the next morning. "We were the first ones to sit down in the fields," explained labor organizer Philip Vera Cruz. Nine days later, when Chicano laborers in the National Farm Workers Association learned they were supposed to replace the strikers, they walked out in solidarity. Soon after, under the leadership of Cesar Chavez and Larry Itliong, the two unions formed the United Farm Workers Organizing Committee (UFW). For more than five years, the UFW's strike disrupted central California and mobilized a multiethnic labor and civil rights movement, and in the words of San Francisco Filipino activist Sid Valledor, it was "more than just the struggle of farmworkers." It was the "crusade . . . since time immemorial to be free and live as men." One of the men who would also soon stand up for his rights was Marciano Haw Hibi, a World War II veteran of the Philippine Scouts who arrived in San Francisco in 1964 and soon thereafter began meeting with a young immigration lawyer. His naturalization petition would eventually reach the US Supreme Court.[1]

On September 7, the same day Filipino workers were gathering in Delano, Captain Alberto Soteco of the Philippine Army proudly reported on his team's work at Tay Ninh in Vietnam. In the space of just a week, a few dozen volunteers in medical units under his command had treated more than 1,000 South Vietnamese civilians in a region of the country hotly contested by Vietcong forces. "We could easily detect . . . the happiness and comfort we brought to them," Soteco recalled. Charged with helping to separate Vietnamese "both physically and ideologically" from the communist Vietcong insurgents, Soteco believed medical aid represented "the first major breakthrough in the psywar-civic action operations ever launched in the country." Within a year, the Philippine contingent in Vietnam would grow to nearly 2,000 soldiers.[2]

A month later, at Ellis Island on October 3, 1965, President Lyndon Johnson signed the Immigration and Nationality Act of 1965. In the shadow of the Statue of Liberty, Johnson assured his audience that the new law was "not a revolutionary bill. It does not affect the lives of millions. It will not reshape the structure of our daily lives, or really add importantly to either our wealth or our power." For Filipinos, whose tiny annual quota of 105 migrants per year was lifted with a stroke of the president's pen, Johnson's words proved a poor prediction. The law affected the lives of millions, reshaping their daily lives and adding to the wealth and power of both nations.[3]

On December 30, as the fateful year came to a close, the Philippines' newly elected president warned of trouble ahead. In Manila, before a crowd of 80,000 on a hot sunny day, the forty-eight-year-old Ferdinand Marcos worried in his inaugural address that "our people have come to a point of despair." While the threat posed in the previous decade by radical guerrillas of the Hukbalahap had faded, ordinary Filipinos' discontent and political cynicism had grown. "Our government is gripped in the iron hand of venality, its treasury is barren, its resources are wasted, its civil service is slothful and indifferent, its armed forces demoralized. . . . We are," he concluded, "in crisis."[4]

Ever since 1898, the two nations had been bound together by shared histories of military service that prompted Filipinos' migrations and their claims to rights and resources in a search for a better future for their country and their families. The bonds of war were tested during Vietnam, questioned in the halls of Congress in Washington and Manila, and remade by a new generation of Filipino Americans. Whether in support or opposition to the war in Vietnam, Filipinos and Americans understood that US ambitions in Asia continued to set the terms for Philippine politics and shape the daily lives of Filipinos on both sides of the Pacific.

As early as April 1964, President Johnson aggressively advocated a multinational armed force for South Vietnam, telling the press of his desire to "see some other flags in there, . . . [so] that we could all unite in an attempt to stop the spread of communism in that area of the world." By August 1964, Johnson's phrase, "more flags," became the nickname for an official policy, the Free World Assistance Program. LBJ wanted boots on the ground, but America's allies treated More Flags symbolically. Several sent humanitarian aid. Canada funded scholarships for Vietnamese students. South Korea sent a delegation of karate teachers. Morocco donated 10,000 cans of sardines.[5]

Within days of the August 1964 incident at Tonkin Gulf, the Philippines sent a twenty-eight-person medical contingent to South Vietnam. PHILCON, as it was known, replicated the short-lived Operation Brotherhood experiment of the 1950s. The US State Department beamed: "There should be more Asians helping Asians. We're impressed with the performance of Fils already there, and would warmly welcome more." To deflect political controversy at home, Manila officials promised only humanitarian aid, but as men such as Captain Alberto Soteco set up medical stations in Tay Ninh, they found themselves officially attached to the psychological warfare units of the South Vietnamese Army and firmly integrated into US military efforts.[6]

If Lyndon Johnson had taken a close look at the Philippine military, he might not have pressed so urgently for its soldiers to join the United States in Vietnam. In 1964, the Armed Forces of the Philippines (AFP) was a small force of 26,000 uniformed personnel (including some of its first female recruits), who relied on the US Defense

Department for equipment, training, and about $25 million in annual aid. For Filipino youth who lacked the education, English fluency, or personal connections needed to land a coveted slot in the US Navy, enlistment was a decent career option. A 1969 sociological survey found most AFP officers were rural-born men from the lower middle class, motivated by "boyhood ambition, patriotism, and careerism." Military service enabled modest social mobility. "I could be comfortable and spare my parents of added hardships," one explained. "The military job was the first one that came along," said another, "so I entered it."[7]

In October 1964, Philippine President Diosdado Macapagal announced that the Philippines was "prepared to share in the responsibility of . . . preserving freedom in our part of the world." On a state visit to Washington, seeking political gain and the chance to see his daughter Gloria at Georgetown University, Macapagal conferred with Lyndon Johnson. The two presidents issued a statement in which they "agreed on the establishment of a joint commission" to settle "matters pertaining to Philippine veterans of World War II." Macapagal had scored points in Washington, but his suggestion to reporters that the Philippines soon "might join" the war in Vietnam would cost him at home.[8]

A few months later, in June 1965, Macapagal suggested sending 1,000 engineers and 1,000 combat personnel—nearly one sixth of the entire Philippine Army—to South Vietnam. Protestors marched with torches and burned an effigy of Uncle Sam in front of the US embassy, and opposition in the Philippine Senate crushed his proposal on the eve of his reelection campaign. Among the expedition's most vocal opponents was Macapagal's campaign rival, Senator Ferdinand Marcos, who warned that even a small combat contingent would draw the Philippines inexorably into combat. AFP soldiers, he insisted, could "hardly do anything to influence the tide of the war."[9]

The young senator was a man on the make. Born in the town of Sarrat in Ilocos Norte on September 11, 1917, Marcos studied law at the University of the Philippines and earned the top score on the nation's bar exam despite facing murder charges (later dismissed) during the testing period. His wartime record was shiny on the surface and murky underneath. Marcos boasted of guerrilla service that earned him approximately twenty-seven medals. (The total was never clear and sometimes included five Purple Hearts and the US Distinguished Service Cross.) He recounted his experiences on the Bataan Death March and even told American journalist William F. Buckley he had been subjected to the water cure by his Japanese captors. Observers would question his service during the 1965 campaign and eventually discredit it two decades later, but in the meantime, Marcos moved smoothly in Philippine politics, blessed with charisma, a winning smile, and a golf handicap of three.[10]

Drawing campaign funds from his personal connections in the Ilocos region, along with those of his wife, Imelda Romualdez, in the Visayas, Marcos rode to victory in the November 1965 presidential election on a tide of economic frustration and a wave of election violence. During the campaign, Macapagal accused Marcos of being "lukewarm" toward the United States, but Marcos—who told an American reporter that "you can't win an election by being anti-American"—soon earned the moniker of America's Boy. Marcos had campaigned against the Vietnam buildup, but quickly came to support it. Perhaps he was responding to Lyndon Johnson's notorious pressure tactics. Five US diplomatic missions arrived in Manila between November 1965 and early 1966, including, on Marcos's second day as president, a private meeting with Vice President Hubert Humphrey, who urged Marcos to dispatch combat troops to Vietnam.[11]

At first, the new president obliged with vague references to "the possibility" of joining the "efforts of the free world" in Southeast Asia, then quickly switched to more concrete terms. In January 1966, assuring Filipinos he was motivated by "neither coercion, threats, blackmail nor dollars," Marcos asked the Philippine Congress for 35 million pesos (about $9 million) to support 2,000 combat engineers and security troops to defend them—almost exactly the plan he had campaigned against six months earlier. Coming so soon after Humphrey's visit, Marcos's about-face generated skepticism. Senator Benigno Aquino Jr., emerging as Marcos's leading critic, suggested that the Philippines was joining the war in Vietnam because "the United States was already in the fray." Senator Alejandro Almendras balked at the notion of shared interests in the Pacific, recounting an incident during his wartime service two decades earlier, when a US Army officer called Filipino soldiers "monkeys." "I hate . . . the Americans for taking us for granted," he told the Senate.[12]

Marcos got his wish: on June 18, 1966, Congress authorized the Philippine Civic Action Group (PHILCAG). "We do not go to war," Marcos explained. "We go to help a friendly nation rebuild . . . its civilization." PHILCAG generated enthusiasm in the AFP ranks. From an army of 16,000 soldiers, over 10,000 volunteered, drawn by a promised boost in pay—double salary for enlisted men and triple for its officers. In mid-September, Marcos sent off the first soldiers following a ceremony at Manila's Fort Bonifacio—established in 1901 by the US Army as Fort McKinley and now the headquarters of the AFP, with a massive cemetery nearby built to honor the American and Filipino dead of the Second World War. In his address, Marcos told the initial contingent of seven hundred men that they were embarking on "a mission of mercy and of peace." There was, he solemnly concluded, "no price too high to pay for freedom." PHILCAG's journey to South Vietnam was slow. Even as American F-100 Super Sabres took off from Clark Air Base almost hourly, Filipino soldiers traveled in a Philippine Navy landing craft, lest PHILCAG face "charges that the Filipinos are flunkies of America."[13]

Their destination was Tay Ninh, seventy-five miles from Saigon in the hills along the Cambodian border—exactly where Operation Brotherhood had worked a decade earlier and where PHILCON doctors were already serving. Under the command of Brigadier General

Gaudencio Tobias and his chief of staff, the Korean War hero Lieutenant Colonel Fidel Ramos, PHILCAG soldiers began their one-year rotations. Marcos announced that PHILCAG engineers were there to build roads and cut trees and would "not fire a shot in anger." But the men carried M1 rifles and of the 2,000 soldiers, nearly half were counterinsurgency experts, many of them veterans of the Huk campaign that had only recently wound down. "We're going to clear the forest," explained one determined officer, "whether the Vietcong like it or not." The men also participated in the Vietnam War's grimmer facets: psychological warfare, intelligence, and the establishment of "strategic hamlets" through forced population movements.[14]

Despite PHILCAG soldiers' experience and political commitment, American advisers doubted their value. One in-country officer later described the refugee housing program as a "Potemkin village, which was largely to impress VIPs," and could only recall of PHILCAG soldiers that "I think they built some roads." Particularly skeptical were those who understood the quiet accounting maneuvers that moved USAID money to fund the Philippine initiative. LBJ's aide Jack Valenti asked the president, "What is too high a cost for the presence of 2,500 Philippine fighting men in Vietnam?"[15]

As the first PHILCAG soldiers crossed the South China Sea, Ferdinand and Imelda Marcos headed for Washington to collect rewards. On a seventeen-day national tour in September 1966, Marcos met with Filipino American leaders across the country. Before a joint session of the US Congress, applause interrupted him fifteen times. "One elementary fact of American history," he observed, "is that the United States was a Pacific power long before it became an Atlantic power."[16]

At the White House, Marcos demanded money for World War II veterans, whose benefits continued to be a stumbling block in bilateral relations, and left Washington with an agreement "in principle to correct injustices in the compensation rates for Filipino World War II veterans." In June 1967 the two countries hammered out a $31.1

million financial settlement of claims for veteran backpay, war damage payments, and unpaid taxes. The agreement explicitly noted that it would "have no effect on the eligibility requirements of veterans for benefits programs administered by the United States," terms that left the 1946 Rescission Act in place and allowed the State Department to deem the matter "closed"—a claim it would continue to make into the twenty-first century. The settlement, paid directly to the Philippine government, did little for Filipino veterans in the United States, but it cemented Marcos's popularity at home. It also confirmed the views of journalists, diplomats, military officers, and ordinary observers that More Flags was a contractual arrangement.[17]

Although Marcos advocated Philippine participation in the Vietnam War, he did not seem to believe that military service as a Cold War ally of the United States was the key to Philippine national sovereignty, as statesman Carlos Romulo had argued a generation earlier during the Korean War. Overall, thirty-nine countries ultimately joined the Free World Assistance Program, but only a few ever provided combat troops. Thailand sent 12,000 soldiers, far more than the Philippines, reaping much less aid from the United States in exchange. Johnson rejected Taiwan's offer, lest it trigger a confrontation with communist China. The Australian contingent peaked at 8,000, nearly a third of the country's available military forces. The largest delegation, nearly 50,000 strong, came from South Korea, whose president, Park Chung Hee, pressed the United States for economic concessions and military aid in return. Vietnam would remain an American war.[18]

SENT TO ASIA IN AUGUST 1967 TO DRUM UP MORE TROOPS, President Lyndon Johnson's adviser Clark Clifford fumed that "it seemed . . . as if the Asians were ready to fight in Vietnam to the last American." But if Clifford broadened his view, he would have seen Filipinos laboring across the Pacific on behalf of the US military. Tens of thousands lived and worked in the US island territory of Guam, and Filipino Americans kept their jobs at defense plants in Seattle, San Diego, and southern California. Clifford could even have looked right in Saigon. More Filipinos traveled to South Vietnam as construction laborers and entertainment workers than ever served as PHILCAG soldiers. Official civilian employment skyrocketed from thirty-five in 1966 to eight thousand in 1969, although numbers were surely much higher. When the Vietnam Builders, a construction firm on military contracts, ramped up its budget to $670 million—calling 1966 "as wild a period as any human being can imagine"—Filipino construction workers poured in and soon made up the company's softball league. Saigon's Truong Minh Giang Street, an area where Catholic refugees from North Vietnam had settled in the 1950s, became "virtually a Filipino quarter," and one magazine reported that "many have married South Vietnamese girls." Philippine factories that were already producing goods for America's booming consumer market now shipped them to American GIs in Vietnam.[19]

Clark Clifford could also have looked at the aircraft carriers off the Vietnamese coast or listened to the booming jets landing at Than Son Nhut Air Base, reminders that just across the South China Sea were Clark and Subic, the Philippines' real contributions to the Vietnam War. By 1967, Subic Bay Naval Station hosted more than two hundred ships a month for what Navy officers called the "Three R's"—rest and recreation for sailors on leave from Vietnam, and repair for Navy ships. Clark Air Base, home to the US 13th Air Force, served as a training ground and transit hub for airmen heading to or from Vietnam, while its enormous hospital treated the war's wounded. Airmen and sailors at Clark and Subic meant jobs for Filipinos. In 1972, the US Department of Defense, with a payroll of $170 million, was the Philippines' second-largest employer.

Base workers soon leveraged experience at American bases in the Philippines—and their reputation as what US Ambassador G. Mennen

Williams described as "willing and adaptable workers"—into higher-paying jobs with contractors elsewhere in the Pacific, especially in Guam. By 1968, at least 16,000 Filipinos worked in Guam through diplomatic agreements that offered free transportation for Filipino workers, paychecks in US dollars, and overtime wages at 1.5 times base pay—but which gave the US Defense Department and not the Immigration and Naturalization Service (INS) control over their movement. Although Filipino contract workers in Guam had entered US territory to serve the needs of the US military, they had no claims on citizenship or veterans benefits. With the bases a permanent feature of US policy in Asia, a September 1966 revision of the original Military Bases Agreement extended the pact's expiration date to 1991, then reassuringly far in the future.[20]

While critics of US military bases filled Manila's press, college classrooms, and radical underground cells, the awkward issue of pro-Americanism haunted debate about bilateral relations. Plenty of Filipinos thought fondly of America, preferred its cultural products, and agreed with Ferdinand Marcos that their country's "security is guaranteed by the umbrella of American power." A 1969 opinion poll reported that 79 percent of Filipinos "liked" Americans; three years later, another survey revealed that 76 percent of Filipinos wanted the bases to remain. To Vietnam critic and opposition senator Benigno Aquino, this was no surprise. "Almost half a century of American rule bequeathed to the Asian Filipino a trauma by making him uncomfortably American in outlook, values and tastes. . . . By reflex—they still react and respond like little brown Americans." On February 18, 1970—a day when Manila students were violently protesting in front of the US embassy—an American survey researcher asked 165 college students in the provincial city of Cebu, "If money were no problem and you had your choice of living in any country in the world, which country would you choose?" Nearly 81 percent said they would leave the Philippines, and 84 percent of those who would move named the United States as their first-choice destination. Many of them were already packing to go.[21]

WHEN LUZ LATUS GRADUATED FROM A MANILA UNIVERSITY, SHE "decided to go to the United States, because it seemed like everybody, all my friends and even the teachers in the school, wanted to come here." By 1970, the Filipino population in the United States had doubled, from 176,310 in 1960 to 343,060 a decade later, and the Philippines became, after Mexico, the second-largest sending country to the United States. Women now made up a larger fraction of migrants.[22]

According to the 1970 census, 72 percent of Filipino Americans lived in the five states of the Pacific. Migrations to Hawai'i increased after the 1965 act took effect, with some 15,000 Filipinos arriving there between 1967 and 1972—in some years making up over 75 percent of its new immigrants. The state was rapidly changing: agriculture declined, tourism boomed, and the Vietnam War fed defense contracts. Family settlements replaced the sugar plantations' bachelor barracks. Many Filipinos settled in Kalihi, a dense and poor neighborhood on Honolulu's west side. Others lived next door to the military bases spread across the state, particularly on Oahu, as the military wielded its powerful influence. In California, new migrants and the children of the first wave increasingly settled in suburbs. A 1977 community study of Mountain View, California, a new suburb near San Jose, found that more than 80 percent of Filipino Americans in that city had arrived after 1970. At times, Filipinos were difficult to track because census takers initially lumped them into "Oriental" populations, then distinguished them from Japanese and Chinese Americans as "Other," and then after 1970 assigned them with Latinos as "Spanish-surname" Americans. Seattle community activist Fred Cordova observed that "publicly, statistically, and even visually, the Filipino is forever hidden as an integral American entity."[23]

Because family reunification policies for spouses, parents, and minor children of immigrants favored Filipinos already in the United States, the 1965 Immigration Act tended to benefit some migrants more than others—most notably military and naval veterans. For navy veterans, the easiest place to settle was near where they had been stationed. Stewards and messmen created Filipino communities in navy towns such as San Diego or Vallejo in California, Bremerton and Seattle in Washington, and Virginia Beach and Norfolk in Virginia. Assignment at a US facility gave some sailors the chance to bring their families to the United States while still in service. While Filipino sailors traveled the world as cooks and stewards, their wives often lived not in the Philippines but in the United States, building up years of residency required for naturalization.

When Luz Latus arrived in San Diego in 1964, she noted that "the organizations that existed were mostly Navy-related or military-related, like the Filipino American Veterans Association." By the late 1960s, however, advocacy and social service organizations emerged that were oriented toward the US welfare state. Lyndon Johnson's war on poverty often overlooked new migrants, leading San Francisco's United Filipino Council to complain in 1969 that "Filipinos have received only token responses to the social and economic conditions which affect them." The concentration of Filipinos in San Francisco's impoverished downtown neighborhoods prompted community leaders in the South of Market Neighborhood Association to build a Filipino Education Center to teach literacy and English, which one city official praised as "something positive to help the new arrivals."[24]

Social service groups pushed their clients to advocate aggressively for themselves. Social worker Roberta Peterson noted that Filipinos "need to be made to feel that they are entitled to services." Overcoming political alienation was a challenge. In Seattle, Fred Cordova observed that "our parents have satisfied themselves in joining the silent majority." Filipinos' demands on US government agencies grew out of the day-to-day work of urban organizations and ethnic parishes, amplified by the civil rights and labor activism that swept California during the five-year strike of the UFW and its nationwide grape boycott. Even as President Richard Nixon tripled grape orders to feed soldiers in Vietnam, the UFW nevertheless forced Central Valley growers to settle in the summer of 1970. Sidestepping tensions with the Chicano-dominated UFW leadership, Filipino union organizers launched the construction of Agbayani Village, a housing complex addressing elder poverty among Filipino farmworkers.[25]

By the 1970s, a two-tiered immigration structure separated the Filipino middle class from ordinary workers. High-skilled workers had migrated to the United States in small numbers before the 1965 act thanks to navy recruitment, nurse exchange programs, and student visas, but the new law's skill preferences drew a highly educated cohort. Soon the phrase "brain drain" emerged to account for the 832 Filipinos who applied on any given day for US visas. Many were from Manila or other cities in the Philippines, distant from the mountain villages that had sent men to can salmon and pick celery decades before. Veterans—still hoping for the repeal of the Rescission Act—felt they had been passed over by a newer, richer generation of Filipino immigrants who had jumped the line.[26]

Those men, the *manongs*, slowly aged out of the West Coast's workforce or found themselves displaced by agricultural mechanization. Old age was particularly precarious for migrants who had not married or formed families, all the more so for those who had spent their careers in domestic service or farm work—jobs that left them ineligible for Social Security. Some working-class Filipino Americans invoked the immigration law's family reunification provisions as a way to recruit care and support, but inviting impoverished family members from the Philippines to West Coast cities often led to overcrowding. The 1970 census revealed that three-quarters of low-income Filipino households in San Francisco lived in the South of Market neighborhood, where construction of a convention center threated to displace their fraternal organizations, small businesses, and residential hotels. As inner cities declined and then gentrified, Filipino enclaves faced off against urban renewal, whether proposals to clear the residential hotels of San Francisco's Chinatown, to clean up the boarding houses of Honolulu, or to run an expressway through Little Manila in downtown Stockton.[27]

In January 1972, Anselmo Revelo, a staffer in the office of San Francisco mayor Joseph Alioto, reported to his boss on conditions in the city's Filipino community. He drew attention to the plight of the "oldtimers," many of them World War II veterans who had chosen to "retire in seclusion in dingy hotels with their social security in the average of $120 per month." To Revelo, the *manongs* stood outside the American polity, "quiet, deliberately ingratiating, completely subordinate and sadly illiterate about many things American." The oldtimers, though, were more politically nimble than Revelo realized. And they had younger allies, ready to connect across generational lines and see discrimination as a Pacific problem, and not just an American one. Among them was Amado David, who came back from Vietnam with a political awareness that led him not only to protest on the streets of San Francisco but to head for Delano to help the UFW build Agbayani Village. It was, for him and for many others, a war on two fronts.[28]

For Filipino Americans who served in the US armed forces, the Vietnam War cut both ways: at times tying them closer to American culture and institutions, other times radicalizing them. In a war against an Asian enemy, Filipino American soldiers faced additional challenges. Lorenzo Silvestre grew up in a military family in the Seattle area and signed up for the Marines in 1967. "Out of the whole company . . . in boot camp," he recalled, "I was the only Oriental." Silvestre recalled discrimination. "I was called names. I was called gook.

I was called monkey. . . . The dirtiest job they got in the platoon, I got 'em." Racial profiling continued in South Vietnam. "When I was on patrol, sometimes I would be by myself. They say I look like the Vietnamese so the Vietnamese won't bother me."[29]

Men like Silvestre made peace with discrimination—he came to love the Corps, and rose to the rank of master sergeant by the time he retired in 1990—but many Asian American soldiers in Vietnam struggled with what military psychologists termed "race-related stress." The men themselves called it the "gook syndrome." It included the daily disconnect between Asian Americans' ethnic pride and their orders—often couched in racist language—to target and kill Asians. They faced dangers other servicemen did not: officers more frequently sent Asian soldiers out to face the Vietcong, and on return they feared friendly fire from comrades who couldn't distinguish Filipinos from Vietnamese. In the quieter moments after the war, many reported what psychologists called "race-based remorse." Whether to survive the war or simply to fit in with other American soldiers, Asian American servicemen sometimes dehumanized their Vietnamese enemies with the same racist words American soldiers had used to describe Filipinos in 1898. No wonder, then, that some Filipino soldiers were radicalized by their tours of duty. At a July 1972 teach-in in San Francisco, Army vet Gil Carillo confirmed Silvestre's stories of how Asian American GIs were used "to play gooks" during training, and a month later he told an audience that he reached a "turning point" when he killed a young Vietnamese boy. "Why you shoot him?" the boy's father asked. "He look like you, you look like him!"[30]

While the US Army drafted Filipino Americans from the United States, the US Navy continued its policy of directly recruiting Filipino volunteers in the Philippines. During the Vietnam War, the US Navy's Philippines Enlistment Program regularly hit the 2,000 annual ceiling allocated by the Military Bases Agreement. More Filipinos than ever donned jackets and white gloves to serve meals and shine shoes for

Navy officers. In 1968, recruiters sorted through some 150,000 applicants for 2,000 spots. Many applied multiple times.[31]

Filipino recruits waved a tearful goodbye at Cavite or Subic before shipping out to the United States for training. They undertook basic training together with other sailors, but then went on for more: some at the Naval Station Great Lakes in Chicago, but most at the Naval Training Center San Diego, where they learned shoe shining, table setting, and even flower arrangement. Training success rates were remarkable—only about 1 percent of sailors washed out after San Diego—and retention rates were high, too. Naval officers estimated some 95 percent of Filipino sailors re-upped, with many reenlisting to claim US citizenship under Vietnam-era naturalization provisions, or staying on a full twenty years for a pension.[32]

The work was tedious. "It was kind of hard sometimes," steward Jeff Colet recalled, "to be a waiter, busboy, and janitorial worker without the benefit of tips." Licerio Lagda grew disillusioned: "We're nothing but a bunch of mess boys, and we're treated as feeble-minded subhumans who hardly speak English." A generation later, though, most stewards looked back on their service with great pride. "Many Filipinos are very happy being in the Navy," recalled Gregory Alabado, another career sailor. "We made only seventy-eight dollars per month, minus Uncle Sam's taxes, but we still had a grand time. . . . What more could we ask?" Years of service led Filipino sailors to embrace US Navy culture and traditions, and they transmitted an energetic American patriotism to their families at home. "Indeed, we have a new and better life in America," observed Ray Burdeos. "We learned in the military the discipline and love of country. We are honored to have payed [*sic*] our dues by serving the military in order to earn our citizenship."[33]

A US Navy personnel officer remarked in 1970 that the service offered "a better life than back in the barrios of the Philippines." By Philippine standards, it was a high-status, high-paying job, and a waiting list with thousands of applicants minimized Filipino sailors' complaints about hardships they experienced in service. Carlos Faustino, the Philippine consul in Los Angeles, defended the stewards' role. "There does not seem to be anything wrong about some people wanting to be stewards considering U.S. Navy pay as compared to that of similar jobs in the Orient." Faustino didn't want to talk about discrimination, questioning "whether it is accurate to tie-up [*sic*] the recruiting program with racial developments in the United States."[34]

It was impossible not to. Filipino sailors encountered the legacies of a Jim Crow Navy that had been only partially desegregated. Fe Trias grew up in the Philippines and eagerly joined the Navy in the last days of the Vietnam War. For her, discrimination began in basic training. "Most of my co-sailors are White. The commanders gave me all the tasks, the hardest tasks." She grew conscious of the situation. "That's why I say, 'Hey there's something going on.' But at that time, I didn't say anything to anybody." Stewards and messmen ate and bunked exclusively with one another, which effectively (if unofficially) segregated them. The steward system reflected the rapidly changing ethnic makeup of the Navy in the two decades since Filipino recruitment expanded. By 1970, there were only 1,100 US enlisted men (of all races) working as stewards, and 13,500 Filipinos doing the same.[35]

Informal segregation and racial shuffling took place at the highest levels. The White House kitchen had long employed Filipinos as cooks and stewards. In a deliberate effort to hide the fact that African Americans could be found working in the White House kitchens and grounds but not its West Wing offices, First Lady Patricia Nixon expanded the White House's Filipino contingent after 1970. At the White House and at nearby Camp David, Filipino stewards had a proximity to power that reflected the long legacies of American wars in the Philippines.[36]

At sea, Filipino sailors sometimes made alliances with African Americans, especially when they worked together in the mess. Rogelio Reyes, a Coast Guardsman, thought "that the whites generally didn't want to associate with the Filipinos," but "we found ways to get along with the blacks." In other cases, Filipinos looked down on black sailors or brawled with them, as happened below deck on the USS *Enterprise* in December 1966. As Reyes recalled of his time in the Coast Guard, any camaraderie "ended whenever we got off ship and hit the town. None of our shipmates, blacks or whites, ever spent time with us as friends or shipmates."[37]

In 1970, Admiral Elmo Zumwalt Jr. decided to tackle the Navy's entrenched racial hierarchy. Zumwalt had grown up around Filipino migrant laborers in the Central Valley town of Tulare, California, and would have met Filipino stewards as a midshipman at the US Naval Academy. They also greeted him every morning: Navy regulations assigned Zumwalt and his wife a full complement of eight full-time stewards. In June 1970 he became Chief of Naval Operations and initiated a range of reforms—announced through regular "Z Grams"—meant to bring the Navy into line with "changing social attitudes." Zumwalt beefed up the number of black recruits, who in 1971 made up just 5.5 percent of the Navy's enlisted men and just 0.67 percent of its officers. "Our orders are to sign up as many as we can," one African American recruiter explained. Zumwalt also tried to open up ratings for the Navy's 12,000 Filipino sailors, but was limited by the men's exclusion—on the basis of citizenship, not race—from rated positions, nearly all of which required security clearances that noncitizens couldn't get. Filipinos who reenlisted and naturalized could move up into clerical ratings, such as yeoman, personnelman, and disbursing clerk, but often found that barriers of language and cultural competency dragged down their scores on the Applicant Qualification Test (AQT) the Navy used for personnel placement.[38]

Persistent criticism changed steward policy. Zumwalt modestly improved conditions for Filipinos—including a 1970 directive "to stock food and produce frequently requested by minority groups" that meant generations of US Navy sailors would dine on *pancit*, a Filipino noodle dish. Simultaneously, he found himself forced to cut stewards' numbers. By 1970, the Navy had slashed its annual recruitment of Filipinos from nearly 2,000 a year to only 420, though reenlistment meant demographics changed slowly. In March 1973, the Navy reported 85 officers and 22,566 enlisted personnel of the "Malayan" race.[39]

Entrenched racism also generated a crisis on board ship. On October 3, the aircraft carrier USS *Kitty Hawk* pulled in to Subic Bay for six days of shore leave, a relief for sailors who had not been rotated out of Vietnam in nearly eight months. Among them were white, black, and Filipino sailors, divided by lines of race and rank, their tempers soon stoked by alcohol. Over the course of their stay at Subic, the men quarreled at an enlisted men's club and had to be dispersed with tear gas, then drank off base in Olongapo and fought with one another. In revenge, a white sailor hired local Filipino hit men to go after an African American sailor from the ship. By the time the *Kitty Hawk* left Subic on October 10 on its way back to Vietnam, tensions were high. The next day, they exploded in six hours of rioting between white and black sailors that injured more than forty sailors and led to the arrest of twenty-eight men.

It was the Navy's biggest racial conflict that year, but not the only one. Soon after the *Kitty Hawk* incident came a racially charged fight on the oiler USS *Hassayampa* while it docked at Subic, followed by a sit-down strike by African American crewmembers of the USS *Constellation* in November. White-gloved Filipino and African American stewards waiting on white Navy officers were now an embarrassment. In November 1972, Wisconsin senator William Proxmire critiqued "pampered and soft" naval officers who "get up in the morning to put on clothes pressed by stewards, shoes shined by stewards, all laid out in proper order. They eat at home with food cooked by stewards and then are driven to work or elsewhere by these same men." Proxmire thought the steward service undermined Defense Department claims "that the military budget is at rock bottom," but he was particularly disturbed by the program's implicit message. "Most servants, at least in the Navy, are either blacks or Filipino." The practice "smacks of racism," and, he pointed out, "opens the United States to a charge of imperialism." Three years later, Senator Proxmire got his wish. A government study recommended, over the Navy's objections, that the Defense Department eliminate the steward system. Officers would carry their dirty clothes down to the laundry and eat from a buffet rather than be served at table, saving more than $50 million a year. The lines of expectant young men outside Subic and Cavite shortened. But in the fall of 1972, Filipinos all across the Pacific had something else to worry about: martial law.[40]

In the Philippines, opposition to the Vietnam War spread much as it did in the United States: from universities and leftist publications to the halls of Congress and the nation's streets. Protestors' numbers grew, and their tone became increasingly critical both of Vietnam and cozy US-Philippine relations. Some two hundred marched against PHILCAG in January 1967. A year later, on January 23, 1968, at least 1,000 gathered in front of the Philippine Congress, burned Lyndon Johnson in effigy, denounced Ferdinand Marcos as a "puppet" and "Asian butcher," and demanded the withdrawal of Philippine troops from Vietnam. With an election looming and the war dividing the country, Marcos listened. Even as President Nixon later declared America's intention "to shift primary responsibility for Asian security to the Asians," Marcos announced in March 1969 that the 1,500-man PHILCAG force would eventually be replaced with "a smaller and less costly unit of doctors and nurses."[41]

It was only a matter of time before America's More Flags program came under scrutiny. In late September 1969, Senator Stuart Symington, a Missouri Democrat and a bitter foe of Richard Nixon, convened closed-door hearings on Capitol Hill to investigate precisely what Americans were getting for the money they spent on Southeast Asian soldiers. Testimony revealed the United States had transferred nearly $39 million since 1966, with $35 million in payments to the Philippine government and an additional $4 million in aid to the AFP. Many were surprised to learn that Filipino soldiers earned double pay for their service in Vietnam, although that had actually been reported in 1966 when PHILCAG was established. By October, with the Symington committee's key findings already leaked, Marcos accelerated PHILCAG's departure to "sometime" after the Philippines' November 1969 election, which handed Marcos a victory margin of two million votes. His opponent, Sergio Osmeña Jr., refused to concede, complaining that "we were out-gooned, out-gunned and out-gold everywhere." Osmeña warned that Marcos planned to declare a state of emergency that would give him a pretext to institute martial law.[42]

On November 18, a week after the election, Senator Symington released his findings. In response, Secretary of National Defense Ernesto Mata angrily reminded the press that it was South Vietnam, not the United States, that had invited the Philippines to send troops, and insisted that his government had "received no fee or payment of any kind for the Philcag or its personnel." To counter Secretary Mata, Symington then released copies of US Treasury checks signed by Mata himself and deposited in the Philippine Veterans Bank (PVB). It was the first public sign that Marcos was using the veterans—and their bank—for his political ends.[43]

The bank, chartered in June 1963 during the presidency of Diosdado Macapagal and opened to customers a year later, was the primary link between veterans and the Philippine government. The PVB operated as a public commercial bank but with government-appointed managers, drawing its initial capital of $20 million from Japanese war reparation payments. Policy makers decided that rather than distributing the $20 million directly—a move that would have given each veteran about $50 in cash—the PVB would issue each veteran a single share of the bank's stock.[44]

It got shadier from there, as political opportunity displaced financial responsibility. The bank couldn't issue stock certificates until the Philippine Veterans Administration developed an authoritative list of all Philippine veterans, so shares would meanwhile be "held in trust by the President of the Philippines." The bank's Japanese startup funds allowed it to operate outside the purview of either the Philippines' General Accounting Office or its national Bureau of the Budget. An outside observer gently noted that the PVB "had not yet hired an external auditor" and that "investments rose sharply in 1966," a year in which any returns on those investments would have accrued solely to its custodial shareholder, Ferdinand Marcos. The bank's day-to-day operations were administered by three hundred employees who filled positions reserved for veterans or their families. By the end of 1966, more than 16,000 Filipinos (mostly veterans) had deposited their savings as retail customers, placing their financial and political faith in the institution and its promise to care for veterans. So too did "some of the country's largest corporate depositors," wooed by bank officials and, likely, the chance to influence its largest shareholder. Some 20 percent of the bank's profits were set aside for the board, who could personally "give grants-in-aid to veterans, their widows, orphans or . . . heirs." Reflecting patronage politics more than bureaucratic precision, the veterans' list steadily grew from 500,000 to 640,000 in 1967. Then, with great fanfare, the PVB issued its first shares to ordinary veterans in late 1969, right in the midst of Marcos's reelection campaign. To ordinary veterans, Marcos's 1967 settlement of veterans' claims and the opening of the PVB surely felt like victories they thought would never come from America. In 1946, the Rescission Act stripped them of their status. Immigration officers turned them away. The VA office in Manila denied their petitions. Now, at least, they were stockholders in the Philippine Veterans Bank.[45]

Despite Marcos's reelection, Senator Symington's hearings in Washington made the renewal of PHILCAG politically impossible in Manila. Soldiers at Tay Ninh struck camp in December 1969, transferring control to the US 1st Cavalry Division. Many of the men stayed on, though, as the US Army hired Filipino engineers—including some from PHILCAG—as civilian contractors. Although the force had taken thirteen mortal casualties (including nine men killed in action), PHILCAG achieved a grand total of only four Vietcong surrenders while notching an average of five official VIP visits per week. Unlike the Philippine Scouts carrying American soldiers' packs, unlike the Philippine Army soldiers who marched next to Americans at Bataan, unlike even the soldiers who fought with PEFTOK in Korea, these Filipino soldiers were not partners in the Pacific Century, but merely symbols of it. And they came at a price America was no longer willing to pay. Too often, Americans chalked controversies up to Philippine corruption rather than US military labor practices, let alone either country's foreign policy objectives. No one saw how each country manipulated the other by exploiting the ordinary soldiers, sailors, and base workers who carried out the war's day-to-day work. Vietnam had tied the politics of both countries together in a knot.[46]

EARLY IN HIS PRESIDENCY, FERDINAND MARCOS WARNED FILIPINOS that "unless we continue to make progress and provide a better life for the people, we could be the Vietnam of the 1970's." By 1972, the country was in crisis. Amid strikes and student protests, landlessness, a 25 percent inflation rate, communist insurgency in the north, violence in the south, crime in the cities, private armies in the countryside, and guns everywhere, social unrest was impossible to hide. Marcos blamed a new adversary, the New People's Army (NPA). In December 1968, Jose Maria Sison, a former college professor from a wealthy Manila family, led a breakaway faction of Maoist-oriented leftists who were discontented with the Moscow-aligned Hukbalahap guerrillas. Sison reestablished the Communist Party of the Philippines (CPP) and reinvigorated the radical left with his charismatic if doctrinaire leadership. The NPA, founded in March 1969, comprised the CPP's armed wing.[47]

Initially the NPA posed little threat to the regime. With fewer than 5,000 armed soldiers, most of them ill-equipped and untrained new recruits lured by a monthly salary of 200 pesos, the NPA hardly resembled the hardened World War II vets who carried the Huks into the postwar period. But Marcos's ham-fisted repression stoked what one NPA sympathizer called "a revolutionary temper among a great number of our people." Among the comrades was Victor Corpus, a lieutenant in the Philippine Constabulary who defected in December 1970 from his teaching position at the Philippine Military Academy, taking a truckload of weapons with him. The NPA also included a cadre of women soldiers, among them Maria Lorena Barros, who led Makibaka, the women's revolutionary arm of the CPP. "If an armed conflict does arise," Barros explained in a 1971 interview, "we will fight alongside with the men, we should take arms if necessary."[48]

Across Manila, students joined protests that peaked during the initial academic term of 1970 and came to be known as the First Quarter Storm. Student politics ranged from moderates in the Christian Social Movement to radicals in the CPP-oriented Kabataan Makabayan (Patriotic Youth). Radicals claimed responsibility for a makeshift bomb attack that targeted US Vice President Spiro Agnew when he visited in December 1969, and after Marcos's January 1970 State of the Nation address, police cracked down on thousands of protestors, injuring more than three hundred people. Four days later, police dispersed 2,000 students who stormed Malacanang, killing six.[49]

The moderate opposition was paralyzed. Senator Benigno Aquino sought to unify them, but faced obstacles of his own making. He was seen as too closely tied to the United States—indeed, he occasionally boasted of connections to the CIA. He was from a politically powerful family in the Tarlac area—during Japan's wartime occupation, Aquino's father had been head of the Kalibapi political party that controlled government jobs. Through his wife, Corazon, he had access to the sugar wealth of the Cojuangco family. He even kept his own private army. To observers, Aquino's opposition to Marcos looked more like personal rivalry than political principle.[50]

A year later, as 3,000 protestors disrupted Marcos's January 1971 State of the Nation address, the president openly hinted at the possibility of martial law. That hardly seemed out of place in 1970s Asia, where military rule or limited democracy governed Taiwan, South Korea, Indonesia, Malaysia, Thailand, Singapore, and South Vietnam. When an explosion ripped through a rally at Manila's Plaza Miranda on August 21, 1971, killing nine people and injuring dozens (including several leaders of the opposition Liberal Party), Marcos blamed the communists, suspended the writ of habeas corpus, and authorized a roundup of CPP leaders. He even suggested that Liberal Party leader Benigno Aquino had personally masterminded the attack, and that Senator José Diokno, who opposed the suspension in court, was a communist stooge. Even at the time, many saw the work of Marcos in the bombing. The suspension of habeas corpus, warned radical leader Pablo Santos, "is merely one step towards the imposition of martial law and dictatorial rule." But press support for the action, and confirmation of its constitutionality by the Supreme Court in December 1971, must have given Marcos confidence that martial law was politically possible. In its wake, Marcos expanded the authority of the Philippine Constabulary, the quasi-military national police force that reported to him, at the expense of the Manila Police, which did not. Most boldly, in early 1972, Marcos purged the AFP's military leadership, eliminating eighteen generals, twenty colonels, and thirteen lieutenant colonels, and replacing them with more loyal men, most from his home region of Ilocos.[51]

As bombs continued to explode mysteriously—at Manila's city hall, at department stores and schools, generally late at night and injuring no one—Marcos's tone became more ominous. US Ambassador Henry Byroade briefed President Nixon and National Security Adviser Henry Kissinger on the possibility of martial law, and while sources are unclear on whether Nixon and Kissinger gave any kind of go-ahead, they certainly raised no objections. According to later reports, Marcos made his decision in early August. On September 12, 1972, the president issued another public warning. By September 21, the declaration was written, had been shared with the US embassy in Manila (despite later claims by the State Department that it did not "have any advance knowledge" of the plan), and the roundups had already begun. The public, as yet, knew nothing.[52]

Two days later, on September 23, 1972, news broke of an assassination attempt on Secretary of National Defense Juan Ponce Enrile, reporting that a vehicle overtook the secretary's car on a Manila side street late the previous night. Some thirty bullets were fired. None of them struck Enrile, who was not riding that night in his blue Ford but in the security vehicle behind it. In fact, no bullets struck anyone, no one was harmed, and none of the gunmen were ever apprehended. But Marcos now had his opportunity. Proclamation 1081 announced that the Philippines was in a state of martial law.[53]

Within hours, the Philippine Constabulary shut down provincial and municipal governments and detained thousands of regime opponents. Among them were Senators José Diokno and Benigno Aquino, whom Marcos claimed had met secretly with the NPA's Jose Maria Sison. Marcos silenced most of the media outlets that he—or his relatives—did not control, while police enforced a curfew, closed casinos, and led raids on "men with long hair and young women with short skirts." ROTC cadets fanned out into neighborhoods to enforce traffic laws and encourage Filipinos to stand in orderly lines. Before long, Marcos dissolved the legislature and packed the courts with sympathetic judges guided by a new rubber-stamped constitution. Civilian courts diverted thousands of cases to military tribunals, with Marcos holding a final say over their verdicts. Habeas corpus petitions followed, including from Senators Diokno and Aquino, who languished in prison while the Philippine Supreme Court did somersaults to avoid confronting Marcos on the constitutionality of his actions. Within a year, Aquino would find himself convicted of subversion and sentenced to death.[54]

In Washington, the White House and the State Department declined to offer any public statement on the declaration of martial law. Marcos exploited the US government's nonresponse, explaining to an American reporter that "there has been no official U.S. reaction, and there is no change in our domestic or foreign policies that would affect the U.S." Reporters observed an "uneasy calm" as "tourists packed the hotels" and noted that "it is business as usual at U.S. military bases." American military officers viewed martial law as a favorable development. "That's the best thing," commented Admiral Thomas Moorer, chairman of the US Joint Chiefs of Staff. In the Philippines, some hoped that martial law would rein in private armies and curb crime. "Martial law is okay for the poor people," explained Gerry Feliciano, a Manila taxi driver. "Now I can sleep beside my wife instead of in my cab to keep it from being stolen." With no information beyond official government announcements, most people took a wait-and-see attitude.[55]

In the years that followed, martial law promised Filipinos a glorious future: *Bagong Lipunan*, the New Society, a mix of populism, anticommunism, and Catholicism that would deliver national pride, land reform, clean government, and a modest redistribution of wealth. In the New Society, the AFP and the Constabulary would build infrastructure, protect Filipinos from the depredations of gangs and insurgents, and turn back the clock on cultural change by censoring B-grade movies and destroying pinball machines. The reality was somewhat different: populist rhetoric didn't dislodge elite rule; modest changes followed announcements of economic transformation; corruption grew unchecked. As Marcos accumulated power, he dispersed favors to allies, business partners, and foreign visitors while portraying himself as the people's champion. But there was more to the New Society than the regime's dismissive opponents acknowledged. By wrapping together promises of national greatness, popular voice, and social order, Marcos won a strong hold on power, although it was difficult to measure his support. A July 1973 referendum on his rule passed with a resounding—if suspicious—91 percent of the vote. A later referendum asking, "Do you like the way President Marcos is running the Government?" yielded a 95 percent positive response. From Constabulary headquarters, Fidel Ramos observed that "if this is martial law, it is a very just law."[56]

At the president's side stood the "Iron Butterfly," Imelda Marcos. Born to a wealthy family in the Visayan region of the central Philippines, Imelda Romualdez married Ferdinand Marcos just eleven days after meeting him and played a critical role in his rise to power by linking his Ilocano political networks with the Visayan family networks—and Romualdez family money—that she brought to their marriage. After the declaration of martial law, Imelda gained power through official appointments. In 1975, in a move designed to displace the powerful mayor of Manila, Ferdinand Marcos named Imelda governor of a newly created province of Metropolitan Manila. Then he made her Minister of Human Settlements, with access to the government's massive construction budget. Taking advantage of the rhetoric of crisis, Imelda positioned herself as Ferdinand Marcos's political successor.[57]

In a chauffeured black Cadillac with a license plate that read IM777 (her lucky number), surrounded by seven cars of bodyguards, Imelda consolidated not only power but wealth, accepting donations for lightly regulated charities under her personal control and spending lavishly from state funds. Imelda never tried to deny her spectacles of wealth.

"When I travel around the world they know I am Miss Philippines," she explained in 1979—although she was only ever Miss Manila, and even that title had been won in a contested pageant. "I cannot dress like a hobo." Known to jeweler Harry Winston as the company's best customer, she once spent $40,000 on clothes in a November 1977 Honolulu shopping spree without even trying them on. Cognizant of the media's role in his own rise, Marcos allocated $10 million a year in the mid-1970s to Doremus, a New York public relations firm, which took out full-page ads in the *New York Times* and *Fortune* magazine touting his policies. Marcos bought a lavish cultural center on Fifth Avenue in midtown Manhattan, while on the West Coast the Philippine Consulate in Los Angeles cultivated Hollywood stars.[58]

Back in Manila, the presidential couple hosted celebrities and politicians, including an ill-advised 1977 visit by UFW leader Cesar Chavez, who believed paying a call on Marcos would win favor among Filipino grape pickers in California. The Marcoses built a grand Philippine Cultural Center, with nearly a third of the monstrosity's budget diverted from Philippine War Damage funds allocated by US law to support "general education." Manila hosted the "Thrilla in Manila," a high-profile boxing match between Joe Frazier and Muhammad Ali in October 1975. A year later, to beautify Manila for an October 1976 meeting of the World Bank, the new governor (Imelda Marcos) displaced squatter communities while the Minister of Human Settlements (Imelda Marcos) launched a $200 million hotel construction boom subsidized by the Philippine Central Bank. Ferdinand Marcos topped it all off in 1975 when he made the anniversary of the declaration of martial law a public holiday.[59]

Under martial law, the Philippines was not a military dictatorship, it was a police state. Day-to-day enforcement rested with the Philippine Constabulary, leaving enormous power in the hands of the newly appointed Constabulary chief, Brigadier General Fidel Ramos, PEFTOK hero and PHILCAG veteran. In the regime he called an "authoritarian democracy," Marcos, not his generals, called the shots. Taking personal control of military appointments, budgeting, and deployments, Marcos bought military loyalty instead of earning it. First, he gave officers men to manage: the AFP ballooned from 58,000 soldiers in 1971 to 142,000 in 1983. That was still relatively small as a percentage of the population (smaller, in fact, than the proportion of Americans serving in the US armed forces), but patronage politics exploded. Many of the officers had little military experience and much to gain by sitting on corporate boards, engaging in kickback schemes, replacing elected officials who had been arrested under martial law, or extorting cash from junior officers who fleeced their enlisted men in turn. While in office, Secretary of National Defense Juan Ponce Enrile served as chairman of the Philippine National Bank and, after July 1973, also chaired the Philippine Veterans Development Corporation, a military contracting firm that hired AFP veterans. Fabian Ver, a childhood friend of Marcos, started out as Marcos's chauffeur and bodyguard, then used his insider status to rise within Malacanang's arcane palace politics to become the commander of the Presidential Security Guard and ultimately the chief of staff of the AFP. Corruption certainly predated martial law, but as Marcos eliminated budgetary controls and independent oversight, the AFP became an entrepreneurial enterprise. It was also an ineffective army. Rewarded for loyalty rather than skill, the men were better at plunder than soldiering. With a weak professional identity as soldiers and little inculcation into the military's ritual codes of honor, they carelessly mixed terror and extortion with battlefield inaction.[60]

When the AFP was actually doing its job, it could be found in the southern island of Mindanao, home to most of the nation's Muslim minority. Since the 1960s, Mindanao had experienced waves of settlement by Christian Filipinos (including a small but symbolic settlement of former Huks through Ramon Magsaysay's EDCOR program), and by the late 1960s Muslims were a minority in many of their ancestral provinces. Now, with the Christian-dominated AFP attempting to impose order, and the Constabulary in cahoots with the peasants' absentee landlords, Muslims' resistance fortified, and the region descended into civil war. Leftist Muslims established the Moro National Liberation Front (MNLF) in 1972 under the leadership of Nur Misuari. The MNLF drew from Maoist guerrilla principles, affirming that armed struggle was the "only means" to liberation. In Tripoli in December 1976, the Organization of the Islamic Conference brokered a truce between the Philippine government and the MNLF, although the hard-won deal broke down a year later when MNLF soldiers refused to dismantle their army in fear of local private armies.[61]

The nation's private militias overlapped with—and at time outnumbered—official forces. They could be a handful of bodyguards protecting a landowning family, a criminal gang hired to do a company's financial dirty work, or even a standing force charged by regional politicians to break strikes and guarantee favorable electoral outcomes. They could be quite large (Marcos himself estimated their overall numbers at 75,000) and were better armed than the insurgents in the NPA or MNLF. Prominent families and major landowners often drew men and weapons from the AFP to staff them. The rank and file included military veterans recruited for their training and deserters eager to sell their weapons.[62]

Through a complex system of patronage, the militias delivered about as successfully as the AFP, the Constabulary, or the NPA. But militia members were not citizen-soldiers in any civic sense, nor the honorable warriors that Douglas MacArthur had in mind when he preached about what a soldier represented. That became clear as a handful of Japanese soldiers emerged from Philippine jungles in the 1970s to find themselves welcomed and honored by their former enemies. Holdouts from the Second World War included men such as Onoda Hiroo, a Japanese intelligence officer left behind on the island of Lubang in February 1945 with orders to collect information in anticipation of the Imperial Japanese Army's triumphant return. After

Onoda finally surrendered on March 9, 1974, he wept openly when told that the Japanese had been defeated three decades earlier. Men like Onoda reflected a kind of military honor that seemed distant from the realities of Philippine life in the 1970s.[63]

MARTIAL LAW INITIALLY BROUGHT FILIPINO MIGRATION TO A sudden halt, as Marcos announced a requirement that all would-be emigrants needed a clearance from the Department of National Defense to keep those "sympathetic to the subversives from flying the coop." The visa lines at the US embassy soon returned, though, with political exiles joining those seeking economic opportunity. When martial law came, Carol Ojeda was a student at the University of the Philippines, her campus surrounded by "barbed wire fences and military personnel." Within a year, she dropped out of college to join the radical underground. In February 1975, after the "military had also started visiting our home frequently," Ojeda moved to Los Angeles.[64]

Martial law shaped not only migrants' decisions but their destinations. Bilateral agreements between the Philippines and Middle East governments—initially Iran, Libya, and Saudi Arabia, and then many others—sent Filipino domestic servants, caregivers, and construction workers on short-term contracts. Marcos hoped that good relations with Middle Eastern nations would smooth relations with Muslim Filipinos at home and maintain a steady supply of oil from OPEC states. The Philippine Labor Code, a 1974 presidential decree, recruited laborers and managed the monetary remittances they sent back, a portion of which the Marcos regime skimmed off their paychecks. Meanwhile, rapid population growth, urbanization, and the beginnings of globalization sent Filipinos into new industries all around the world. Just as the US Navy was slashing the steward service and its PEP enlistments, transformations in shipping technology and international maritime law opened opportunities for Filipino seamen in numbers greater than the Navy could ever offer. By turning the Philippine government into a global labor broker, the Labor Code also ensured that martial law would shape migration patterns for decades to come.[65]

Money steadily trickled back. Traveling in the province of Ilocos Norte in 1973, anthropologist Stephen Griffiths observed that remittances from Hawai'i had built two-story homes "constructed of cement blocks and expensive woods, and painted in many bright colors." Houses that "contrasted sharply with their humble neighbors" now defined the aspirations of rural Filipinos, particularly as migrants regularly returned along with their money. Some came for annual Christmas trips on low-budget charter flights from Honolulu. Others retired to the Philippines, especially when they could bring with them US military pensions or Social Security checks issued in US dollars, which supported far more comfortable lifestyles in the Philippines than were possible in the slums of Kalihi or SoMa. The rapid devaluation of the Philippine peso meant that retirees living on US dollars sometimes collected pensions worth more than seven times the median income in the Philippines. Filipino veteran retirees often settled near US base communities in the Philippines, where veteran status gave access to the Post Exchange for low-cost shopping. Even then, racial hierarchies persisted: a de facto segregation of PX facilities restricted Filipino shoppers to limited hours. In a 1975 interview in Seattle, veteran Mariano Angeles, who had only reluctantly naturalized after World War II, expressed his intention to retire in his home country: "I like to go back to the Philippines." Angeles's fellow Seattle resident Zacarias Manangan, though, was hesitant to return. "I have to look back in the Philippines, this Martial Law and I soon be here than living in a country under a dictatorship."[66]

Marcos used migration as a political safety valve, which scattered dissident Filipinos around the globe. As radical writer E. San Juan noted, "there was no real Filipino Diaspora before the Marcos dictatorship."

But because politics and economics sent emigrants everywhere and not just to the United States, diaspora became a game-changer in turn. The Philippines' first steps toward globalization started to unravel the tight bonds of war that tied Filipino military service to Filipino America. Its effects would be years in coming, and in the meantime, the Vietnam War provoked a new generation of Filipino Americans to take an explicitly American—and politically oppositional—stance in the United States.[67]

Filipino American activists connected protest of the Vietnam War with demands for an end to martial law in the Philippines. They allied with other Asian ethnic groups and increasingly identified not only as Filipinos, but in a pan-ethnic coalition as "Asian Americans." The movement spread nationally from roots in the San Francisco Bay Area. Gil Mangaoang, a third-generation Filipino American, became active at City College of San Francisco after leaving the US Air Force in 1970. On campus, Mangaoang underwent what he later described as a "re-education process" that led him to ethnic consciousness and Maoist politics. Others like him joined the Bay Area Asian Coalition against the War, founded in May 1972 as a "broad based anti-imperialist movement of Asian people against the war in Vietnam." Filipino students joined strikes for an ethnic studies curriculum at San Francisco State College and elsewhere. From 1968 to 1977, tenants, neighborhood residents, and progressives united to delay the demolition of the International Hotel, a Chinatown rooming house home to Filipino senior citizens. Others expanded ethnic consciousness in literature and art, rewrote curricula, and questioned the meaning of monuments to the suppression of the "Philippine Insurrection" that stood in San Francisco's Union Square or Portland's Lownsdale Square.[68]

Throughout the Pacific, dissenting soldiers opposed the Vietnam War and the US basing system from within, whether at radical GI coffeehouses, in the ranks, or through the Pacific Counseling Service, a leftist advocacy group that operated the GI Center for Legal Rights just outside Subic in Olongapo. As Black Power and other radical movements grew in the United States, they came to the Philippines as well. African American sailors on leave at Subic gathered at Cloud Nine, a Black Panther–oriented bar in Olongapo. In October 1972, soon after the declaration of martial law, three American activists in the National Lawyers Guild who arrived in Olongapo to defend black sailors charged in conjunction with the brawl on the USS *Hassayampa* found themselves detained in the city jail. The three men were then transferred to Philippine Constabulary headquarters at Camp Crame in Manila, where they learned, "from PC officers and confidential reports carelessly left in our sight, that it was under the direction of the US military authorities that we had been arrested and detained." One of them, Gene Parker, believed their detentions had occurred because "we had been giving help to American soldiers opposed to the Vietnam war and discrimination within the military. So we learned that our government . . . had used the undemocratic declaration of martial law to stifle and crush dissent and legal opposition to the military." They nevertheless gave in. "If we'd stayed we would have been tried by a military tribunal," prisoner Doug Sorensen explained.[69]

Martial law sharpened radicals' critiques and focused their attention on the links between US foreign policy in Southeast Asia and the Marcos regime in the Philippines. Diverse anti–martial law groups responded to Marcos's September 1972 declaration. Moderates in the Movement for a Free Philippines argued that US military aid "helped to strengthen martial law's repressive measures." Members of the Philadelphia Committee of Concerned Filipinos organized a demonstration in front of Independence Hall on October 2, 1972, while in San Francisco, hundreds gathered outside the Philippine Consulate. Human rights activists, most of them white progressives active in the antiwar movement, founded the Friends of the Filipino People. The Los Angeles chapter of the Anti-Martial Law Coalition worked out of a community center on Temple Street in downtown LA. The National Coalition for the

Restoration of Civil Liberties in the Philippines (NCRCLP) initially served as an umbrella organization. In New York, its local spokesperson, Loida Lewis, insisted that "we cannot permit the travesty of the people's will to continue unchecked."[70]

The most radical group organizing on both sides of the Pacific was the Katipunan ng mga Demokratikong Pilipino (KDP), the Union of Democratic Filipinos, founded in the San Francisco Bay Area in July 1973. The KDP included both political exiles from the Marcos regime and Filipino Americans radicalized by the politics of the 1960s. It challenged the exploitation of Filipinos as a racial minority in the United States at the same time it advocated revolution in the Philippines. "U.S. imperialism," members announced, "is the main enemy of the people of the whole world." In alliance (and tension) with the Communist Party of the Philippines, the KDP organized anti-Marcos protests, petitions, and other events, particularly in California. The KDP recruited Carol Ojeda at a Los Angeles movie theater not long after she fled Manila, but she always remained concerned that her activism might get her in trouble with INS officers, or that Marcos hoodlums might harass her in California or her family in the Philippines. Indeed, as KDP activists built transpacific solidarity, the Marcos regime was one step ahead of them, constructing even more powerful networks of political surveillance and repression.[71]

By February 1973, with US withdrawal from Vietnam under way, American troop presence in the Philippines dropped from 24,000 to 15,000. What would America's final withdrawal from South Vietnam in April 1975 mean for the decades-long bonds between the US military and the Philippines? The new president, Gerald Ford, torn between realists such as Secretary of State Henry Kissinger and a younger generation of foreign policy hawks, had to balance a show of American strength in the region with his vow to bring US troops home. "I hope that other countries in Southeast Asia—Thailand, the Philippines—don't misread the will of the American people," Ford insisted at an April 3, 1975, news conference, "to believing we are going to abandon our position in Southeast Asia. We are not."[72]

Three months later, Marcos called Ford's bluff. Privately "shocked" by the fall of Saigon, Marcos tested America's commitment by making overtures to other Asian allies, including a dramatic recognition of the People's Republic of China in June 1975 that came with a personal visit to Chairman Mao Zedong. Marcos praised China as "the leader of the Third World and a moral inspiration to all the world and mankind"—something of an irony given Marcos's claim in September 1972 that Chinese support for the Maoist NPA justified martial law. Pressing the United States further, Marcos asked in July 1975 for a review of the basing agreement. He demanded fixed payments of rent, which would be guaranteed by treaty, rather than annual appropriations of aid, which were dependent on an increasingly critical US Congress. Carlos Romulo, now serving as Marcos's foreign secretary, explained to Kissinger that Filipinos had been patient about the basing agreements "due to circumstances in Indochina," but gently observed that "now the situation has in fact changed."[73]

Ford—who had served on a US Navy ship in the Philippine Sea during World War II—traveled to Manila on December 6, 1975, along with a team of military and diplomatic negotiators that included his newly appointed secretary of defense, Donald Rumsfeld. At dinner, Marcos gave a long-winded toast to his dream of a self-reliant Philippines that could "defend our own soil with our own troops." The next day, at Pearl Harbor in Honolulu, Ford announced "a new Pacific doctrine," although his claim that "the United States is a Pacific nation" wasn't new and he offered no particular doctrine. Base negotiations dragged on, then stalled after Ford's defeat in the November 1976 elections. To Kissinger's surprise, Marcos walked away from an offer of $1 billion in aid guarantees.[74]

One topic absent from the bargaining table in 1976 were the claims of Filipino World War II veterans, deemed settled by the 1967 lump-sum payment, still on deposit at the Philippine Veterans Bank. Nor were the veterans' claims to citizenship and benefits on the agenda of the KDP or other Asian American activists, who marched against the US military and Filipinos' reliance on it. Veterans sought allies where they could, often from Marcos's supporters in the United States. The anticommunism of military migrants and their families, along with the ties that ethnic Ilocano migrants had to their fellow Ilocano at Malacanang solidified support for Marcos among the veterans. Many, veterans or otherwise, remained politically quiet, not yet mobilized by social movement activists, nor courted by urban ethnic politicians. Seattle community organizer Fred Cordova regretted that "militancy is not 'the thing' for the Filipino 'establishment' in 1970."[75]

Militancy may not have been "the thing" for the Filipino American middle class, but for Filipino veterans struggling with poverty or facing deportation, US federal courts were their last resort. Veterans filed a handful of cases immediately after the war, but not very many. Their leaders surmised that folding veterans benefits into foreign aid requests would yield better overall results than individual lawsuits, and few ordinary veterans could afford travel to the United States, hire attorneys, and file claims. Marciano Hibi, on the other hand, was already in California, and in danger of deportation. A lawsuit was his only remaining option, and on September 13, 1967, at the US District Court in San Francisco, he filed a petition for naturalization. In 1973, immigration lawyer Donald Ungar took Hibi's case before the US Supreme Court.

Hibi had joined the Philippine Scouts in February 1941, was briefly held captive by the Japanese, then rejoined his Scout unit in April 1945 after the US reinvasion and was discharged that December. Hibi argued that the postwar actions by the INS—withdrawing the naturalization office and deliberately not filling the position—amounted to misconduct by the federal government. Thus, Hibi argued, the INS should not be allowed to reject his naturalization claim by invoking the statute of limitations. Under the principle of estoppel, the government is responsible when its own conduct prevents the timely filing of a claim. Because the INS's own malfeasance caused Hibi to miss the deadline, the agency should be blocked (or "estopped") from invoking the statute of limitations against him. The Court saw matters otherwise: "We do not think that the failure to fully publicize the rights which Congress accorded under the Act of 1940, or the failure to have stationed in the Philippine Islands during all of the time those rights were available an authorized naturalization representative, can give rise to an estoppel against the Government." In an angry dissent, Justice William Douglas (joined by Justices William Brennan and Thurgood Marshall) argued that "the Court's opinion ignores the deliberate—and successful—effort on the part of agents of the Executive Branch to frustrate the congressional purpose and to deny substantive rights to Filipinos."[76]

Hibi lost his case for citizenship, but lawsuits over veterans benefits soon followed. In the early 1970s, a group of Filipino veterans and their descendants, all of whom lived in California and some of whom had naturalized as US citizens, sued the US Veterans Administration in a class-action lawsuit on behalf of 250,000 veterans and their dependents. The veterans cited the Fourteenth Amendment's guarantee of equal protection, arguing that the Rescission Act discriminated against Filipino soldiers on the basis of race. But VA attorneys explained to the federal district court for Northern California that "the differentiation between the two kinds of servicemen . . . was based, not upon ground of race or alienage, or merely to cut expenses, but, in part, upon [the] difference in their military status within our armed forces; also in part upon 'practical difficulties'" in administering benefits and "a difference in monetary and living standards between the United States and the Philippines." The VA's argument carried the day as the court rejected the California veterans' pleas.[77]

Even veterans who had established rights to US citizenship found it difficult to make their claims. As veterans and their advocates stood before US courts, turning a fragmentary guerrilla history into a proper legal record often proved impossible. The federal court in San Francisco looked askance at one veteran's submission of a photograph "standing next to a military vehicle" and dismissed the petition of another, recalled by a witness "on various occasions during the period '42 to '45 . . . in khakis and fatigues." Attorney Donald Ungar insisted of the veterans that "if they can establish their rights to be naturalized, they ought to be." With conflicting laws, fading memories, and indifferent bureaucrats, veterans experienced the same inconsistency and unpredictability they had encountered decades earlier.[78]

A rare and surprising victory came in 1975, when another group of sixty-eight Filipino veterans organized by Donald Ungar—working together with Filipino American community leader Alex Esclamado—convinced US District Court Judge Charles Renfrew to approve their naturalization claims. The new administration of President Jimmy Carter declined to appeal the ruling, so the men's naturalization was confirmed, and almost 4,000 more citizenship petitions quickly followed. Observing the scale of naturalization, INS officials appear to have regretted forgoing the earlier appeal, because two years later, faced with a similar ruling, the Justice Department appealed, and the US Supreme Court sided with the government, shutting the door once again. For men like the sixty-eight Filipino veterans who had persisted in their claims, the courts offered rare and unpredictable opportunities for justice. Nor were government agencies much more sympathetic: a 1977 study by the US General Accounting Office recommended cuts to the VA program in the Philippines, which it described as riddled with "claims fixers" and believed supported "a life of luxury" for veterans in the Philippines. The Rescission Act's unfinished business remained. But veterans had switched the arena of their struggle from Philippine voting booths to American courtrooms.[79]

By the end of the Vietnam War, the snapshots taken a decade earlier—at Ellis Island, in the grape fields of Delano, in Tay Ninh, at a Manila park—had started to fade. Tight bonds of Pacific brotherhood woven by the Cold War in the 1950s had been frayed by Filipinos' global migrations and by the war in Vietnam. Filipino soldiers and sailors continued to find work as part of the US military enterprise, but civilian migrants crossed the Pacific, too, along with their money, their political ambitions, and their social movements. By the 1970s, veterans and progressive activists—whether in Manila or San Francisco—stood at a great distance from each other. But in the next decade, a new administration in Washington would attempt to restore the cozy military relationship of the 1950s until political crisis in the Philippines brought millions of Filipinos to the streets and tested the bonds between the two nations.

CHAPTER NINE

PEOPLE POWER

1977–2001

As President Jimmy Carter walked down Pennsylvania Avenue after his January 1977 inauguration, it seemed—to Americans, to Filipinos, and not least of all to Ferdinand and Imelda Marcos—that Washington had changed. In his speech, Carter explained that Americans' "moral sense dictates a clearcut preference for those societies which share with us an abiding respect for individual human rights," and promised to make human rights a guiding principle of his administration's foreign policies. The Philippine military's close ties to the United States, forged by Ramon Magsaysay and Edward Lansdale a generation before, had once symbolized Cold War fraternalism. Now, as the Vietnam War faded from the headlines and martial law defined the Philippines in America's political imagination, the military connections between the two countries came under a new scrutiny that targeted those enduring bonds.[1]

The ties appeared strong. Five years after declaring martial law, Marcos easily outmaneuvered his opponents at home and dismissed or targeted them abroad. Opposition leader Benigno Aquino Jr. languished in prison. The regime delivered law and order along with economic growth rates between 6 and 7 percent a year. But there were signs of unrest that even Marcos couldn't hide. Political repression was no secret, as news circulated in the Filipino diaspora and in the American press. Jaime Sin, Manila's Catholic cardinal, paid high-profile visits to imprisoned hunger strikers and defended dissenting priests, nuns, and missionaries. Legal progressives joined with trade unions, women's organizations, and indigenous groups, challenging indefinite detention or practices of kidnapping and execution known as "salvaging." Armed rebels continued to gain strength in the Philippine countryside. In the United States, anti–martial law activists kept up pressure on Congress. Opponents of the Marcos regime criticized US military aid and the role of American personnel in teaching Filipino police and soldiers the techniques of repression. American aid and anticommunist fear would not be enough to keep the regime in place.

Over the course of three months in late 1985 and early 1986, Filipinos remade their history through a popular movement they called People Power. While Americans watched on television, millions rallied on Manila's main highway. Filipinos simultaneously challenged and relied on the US-Philippine military alliance—a partnership that had brought Marcos to power and that would play a role in his downfall by siding with the people in a critical moment in 1986. People Power flexed its muscles on Capitol Hill as well, where new coalitions built on the growing electoral power of Asian Americans and Filipino veterans learned a new language that connected military service and civil rights. And yet, within months of one of the largest pro-democracy uprisings in human history, old political and military connections reasserted themselves. What had been forged in 1898 proved impossible to undo. All that would change again on a September morning in the new century, but the shifts began as both nations wandered in the ruins of the Vietnam War, wondering what would become of their Pacific partnership.

In Washington, President Carter tried to put his human rights principles into action, giving a platform to advocates such as Patricia Derian, the Assistant Secretary of State for Human Rights and Humanitarian Affairs, who condemned Aquino's imprisonment during an official visit to the Philippines in 1977. But if Carter stated a "clearcut preference" for clean records on human rights, his inconsistent policies suggested otherwise. Carter applied only the softest of pressure on Marcos, insisting that ongoing military engagement gave the United States political leverage. As early as July 1977, Secretary of State Cyrus Vance noted that because "we are and will remain a Pacific nation," the United States "must balance a political concern for human rights against economic or security goals." Foreign aid to the Marcos regime, already generous, in fact increased.[2]

Carter waffled because America depended more than ever on its military bases in the Philippines—especially after the Vietnam War, as Soviet forces took over the former US air base at Danang and US naval base at Cam Ranh Bay in South Vietnam. Conflicts in the Middle East shaped bases policy, too. Carter proposed a Rapid Deployment Force aimed at supporting US military operations around the world at any time. Congress and the post-Vietnam public initially balked, but by the end of Carter's term, following the Iran hostage crisis, a second oil shortage, and the Soviet invasion of Afghanistan, he got his wish. In 1980, the United States acquired the former British naval base at Diego Garcia in the middle of the Indian Ocean. Clark and Subic, long imagined as the anchors of a Pacific strategy, now reoriented to the Middle East. "Without bases in the Western Pacific," observed Assistant Secretary of State for East Asian and Pacific Affairs Richard

Holbrooke, "our ability to support American interest [*sic*] in the Indian Ocean would be significantly limited." Even as US defense priorities shifted to the Middle East and Central Asia, enduring bonds with the Philippines made the country crucial to support of American military ambitions. Some of this was geography, but a lot of it was history.[3]

Carter inherited from President Gerald Ford the task of renewing the 1947 Military Bases Agreement (MBA). The updated pact modestly trimmed the size of the bases and placed the Armed Forces of the Philippines (AFP) in command of base security. More important was Carter's promise to pursue $500 million in aid over the next five years. Direct military aid would rise from $37 million to $60 million a year, with an additional $250 million in credits for equipment. A huge cache was earmarked for infrastructure projects in the bases' adjacent cities of Olongapo and Angeles. During negotiations with Vice President Walter Mondale, Marcos tellingly referred to the funds as support for "human settlements," suggesting he intended the money to be controlled by the regime's Minister of Human Settlements, Imelda Marcos.[4]

Marcos insisted that "I would not have agreed if I wasn't satisfied," but having rejected Henry Kissinger's $1 billion offer just two years earlier, the $500 million deal was a defeat. Nor did Marcos appreciate Carter's moralizing lectures, including a personal letter, hand delivered by Mondale during the base negotiations, urging clemency for Benigno Aquino. Released from prison in May 1980 after a heart attack, Aquino and his family settled in suburban Boston. Marcos likely believed that Aquino, ensconced in a cushy position at Harvard University, would fade from public view. By contrast, Marcos's foreign minister, the elder statesman and World War II veteran Carlos Romulo, warned that in the United States, Aquino would become the public symbol of the regime's misdeeds. Romulo was right.[5]

If Marcos couldn't see the writing on the wall, neither could his brother in arms, President Ronald Reagan. Ferdinand Marcos saw Reagan's 1980 election as "a turning point" and eagerly dispatched

Imelda to meet with the presidential transition team in New York. In the 1980s, Reagan referred to Ferdinand and Imelda Marcos as "old and good friends," but their relationship was rockier than it appeared in carefully choreographed press photographs. Back in 1969, when Reagan was governor of California, President Richard Nixon had sent Reagan and his wife Nancy to the Philippines for the lavish ceremony dedicating the Cultural Center of the Philippines. Relations between the two couples started off chilly, not least because of Imelda Marcos's deliberate attempts to upstage Nancy Reagan.[6]

Over time, though, the friendship warmed. On January 17, 1981, Marcos ostentatiously announced the end of martial law, although the implausible move left him with unchecked power and even granted immunity to Marcos and the military for any actions taken during the previous eight and a half years. His timing was impeccable, coming on the eve of Reagan's inauguration and just before a visit to the Philippines by Pope John Paul II. In Manila, the pope openly criticized Marcos, but when the pontiff refused to stay in the extravagant Coconut Palace that Imelda Marcos built to honor his arrival, no matter: the First Lady invited actress Brooke Shields instead.[7]

In his January announcement, Marcos called a presidential election for that June. Against handpicked opponents and amid widespread boycotts, he won an eyebrow-raising 88 percent of the vote, but that satisfied the new administration in Washington. Visiting Manila, Secretary of State Alexander Haig celebrated the "wonderful victory" and assured Marcos that "there is a new America, an America that understands that it must once again bear its burdens that history has placed on our shoulder." The most memorable visit came from Vice President George H. W. Bush, who attended Marcos's June 30 "inauguration." At a lunch that day at the Malacanang presidential palace, Bush reassured Marcos that the Reagan administration "will not leave you in isolation." Then he raised his glass and offered one of the decade's most-quoted toasts: "We love your adherence to democratic principle—and to the democratic processes." It was too much to swallow, perhaps even for Bush, who quietly erased the visit from his later memoirs.[8]

Most in the Reagan administration lived casually with the Marcos regime's abuses. White House staffers avidly read "Dictatorships and Double Standards," a 1979 essay published in *Commentary* by Georgetown professor Jeane Kirkpatrick, who blamed Jimmy Carter's human rights policies for the overthrow of US-friendly regimes in Nicaragua and Iran. Doubtful that "change per se in . . . autocracies is inevitable, desirable and in the American interest," Kirkpatrick offered support for regimes such as Marcos's. Reagan named Kirkpatrick as US ambassador to the United Nations and appointed Elliott Abrams—an outspoken foe of human rights movements—to Patricia Derian's old job as Assistant Secretary of State for Human Rights. Their views were echoed by the State Department's Assistant Secretary for East Asian and Pacific Affairs, a thirty-nine-year-old political theorist-turned-diplomat named Paul Wolfowitz. Together, the team advocated "quiet diplomacy" and soft-pedaled any critique of the Marcos regime, announcing repeatedly that despite violations, the White House saw "progress" on human rights.[9]

Amid renewed talk of Pacific unity, Ferdinand Marcos pressed his political ambitions. After the June 1981 elections, he reshuffled the top brass of the Armed Forces of the Philippines. His former bodyguard, General Fabian Ver, a sixty-one-year-old thug with little military expertise, became the AFP's chief of staff and not long after, head of the country's National Intelligence and Security Agency (NISA), giving him control of NISA's secret police. American officials were unimpressed. Admiral William Crowe Jr., the Commander in Chief, Pacific (CINCPAC), later described Ver as "a farce" with "almost no concept whatsoever of military affairs," a man whose "chief personal interests were in delivery dates for American equipment and in developing avenues for direct money inputs from the United States."[10]

Marcos next gave Ver control of the Metropolitan Police Command (MetroCom), keeping near the capital a force loyal to Marcos and his allies. He then supplemented the MetroCom with the 15,000-strong Presidential Security Command, a personal army stationed at Malacanang under the direct command of Ver's son, Lieutenant Colonel Irwin Ver. Marcos then implemented a series of "reforms" that forced the retirement of seventeen generals and thirteen colonels. Gone were professional soldiers, and rotating in were men personally closer—and politically connected—to the president. Although defense ate up nearly 20 percent of the Philippine budget, it did little to produce quality soldiers. Bloated by politics, the AFP topped 100,000 service members in the early 1980s, along with another 43,000 in the Philippine Constabulary and 35,000 in the so-called barangay brigades of the Civil Home Defense Forces (CHDF). Intended to mobilize civilians against insurgency, the barangay brigades were private armies by another name. By the time Marcos admitted that the CHDF "might become abusive," it already was, emboldened by the state to carry out political repression and financial plunder.[11]

One of the officers pushed out was Fidel Ramos—West Point grad, PEFTOK hero, and when he served as head of the Philippine Constabulary, the administrative muscle behind the imposition of martial law in 1972. Strong enough to threaten Marcos, Ramos found himself reassigned to a powerless position as vice chief of staff of the AFP. Ramos, though, could play army politics as well as anyone. Working connections with the faction of AFP officers who had graduated from the Philippine Military Academy in Baguio, Ramos started looking for a means to get back at Fabian Ver and the armchair generals who surrounded him. Juan Ponce Enrile, a longtime Marcos loyalist and Secretary of National Defense, assumed he would be well situated to succeed the president, and now seethed to see Fabian Ver edging him out at Malacanang. So Enrile started talking to Ramos, until Enrile learned that Ver was mobilizing a death squad to kill them both. To protect themselves, Enrile and Ramos recruited a team of discontented soldiers from within the ranks of the AFP. They gave it a progressive name: the Reform the Armed Forces Movement (RAM). But these were no human rights activists, and RAM was not so much a political movement as the private self-defense force of a dissident wing of the Philippine Army. Difficult choices lay ahead for Filipino soldiers.[12]

Who was the AFP meant to be fighting? Ongoing crisis drove recruits into the ranks of the New People's Army (NPA). The NPA kept up a blistering propaganda campaign against the regime, calling Marcos "the No. 1 Filipino agent of the US," but with some 5,000 to 7,000 guerrillas, they didn't yet pose a military threat. What the communists had over the AFP in ideological commitment and popular support, they lacked in weapons. Most of what NPA soldiers carried had been captured during raids on the AFP; some were bought on the black market from AFP soldiers, others scurried away by double-dealing members of the CHDF militias. Nevertheless, when US military observers (and CIA infiltrators) reported to the Pentagon, they depicted the ragtag New People's Army as the knife edge of global revolution, compared it with communist movements fighting in Nicaragua or Angola, and warned that the NPA threatened US bases in the Philippines.[13]

During a September 1982 state visit to Washington, Marcos and Reagan approved the forty-second set of revisions to the Military Bases Agreement. Marcos insisted that he had "no intention of begging for anything," and after quarrels with Kissinger and Carter, this time he didn't have to. In June 1983, the Reagan administration announced its plan to pursue $900 million in aid over the next five years, nearly doubling the $500 million that Carter had promised in 1979. American forces found themselves legally obliged "to abstain from any political activity," and the United States agreed, once again, to improve base conditions. Before Congress, the State Department's Paul Wolfowitz explained that $50 million would go for "improving the lot of Filipinos residing in the areas surrounding our military base facilities." Infrastructure jobs cemented relationships between the US Navy and powerful local figures such as Olongapo's navy-friendly mayor, Richard Gordon.[14]

By the 1980s, Gordon ran the city as a one-man fiefdom, and acknowledged the Navy's power. "This is a camp follower town," he observed in 1982. "The navy is here, all sorts of people are attracted here. . . . The sad fact is that . . . Olongapo has . . . no industry other than the navy." Or, as an Olongapo news editor observed, "this is the only place in the country where there are people who want war—and pray for war!" Base workers were thankful just to have jobs: traditional fishermen, constantly watched from a forty-foot Navy guard tower, hauled ever-smaller catches in Subic Bay. Others scrounged in garbage heaps. Under a bridge used by passing navy sailors, local children waited in small boats, calling, "Throw me coins!"[15]

The bases had long been a lightning rod for nationalist politics, and now increasingly for anti-Marcos activism. The 1982 Military Base Agreement negotiations marked the emergence of a unified opposition movement. José Diokno, who had been imprisoned for two years after the declaration of martial law, and Lorenzo Tañada, a longtime senator who had been the crusading prosecutor of the Filipino People's Court in 1945, founded the Anti-Bases Coalition (ABC) in February 1983. US aid could not appease ABC nationalists: "There is no price tag to our survival and dignity," Diokno argued. The bases, Tañada insisted, "expose us to nuclear attacks." Increasingly, base opponents found they were not alone. By the 1980s, the ABC tapped into a global network of peace and anti-nuclear activists from Puerto Rico and Okinawa to England and West Germany.[16]

Authorities from both countries consistently denied that the bases held nuclear weapons, but evidence kept turning up. Aircraft carriers and missile cruisers that carried nuclear arms elsewhere docked regularly at Subic, and the US Navy's announcement in March 1978 of training for "nuclear weapons accidents/significant incidents" gave the lie to claims that Subic was nuke-free. In June 1983, Gene La Rocque, a retired US

Navy rear admiral, testified to a US House subcommittee that Subic stored nuclear weapons, though the Navy denied that. Clark hosted nuclear weapons as well. American diplomat Raymond Garthoff learned during a 1975 visit to the Philippines that the US Defense Department actually wanted to remove them. Garthoff later reported that Secretary of State Henry Kissinger "had put a hold on Pentagon plans to withdraw the weapons, believing that somehow we should be able to get something from President Ferdinand Marcos in exchange for 'agreeing' to withdraw our nuclear weapons." Filipino base workers didn't need confirmation from retired admirals or diplomats. They knew the signs well. "We always know which missiles are nuclear," one Subic worker explained in 1982, "because the firemen and the Navy's safety officers show up."[17]

The bases were not only a nuclear danger, but a social disaster. "Whatever dollars and cents these bases may be bringing to the country," Tañada fumed, "should also be measured against the social costs," burdens that by the 1980s included drug abuse and AIDS. Olongapo mayor Richard Gordon dismissed criticisms as "an emotional binge," but in Olongapo, as many as 13,000 servicemen sought R&R on any given weekend, and prostitutes could be hired for as little as $7.00 a night. The city regulated the sex work industry through official programs that managed permits for more than five hundred "entertainment" facilities and required employees to pass city-administered tests for sexually transmitted diseases. By 1983, about 9,000 women were registered with city officials (at least 8,000 more worked illegally), and some four hundred to six hundred women a day marched through Olongapo's Social Hygiene Clinic, operated by city officials. The US Navy generously funded the clinic, and its head doctor was "grateful . . . for what they have given," but as a clinic employee observed, the Navy's "main concern is protecting the health of the Americans, not the Filipinos." That sexual health spending distorted public health priorities must have been apparent to anyone who walked along the shores of

Olongapo's main stream, unfondly known to navy sailors and Filipinos alike as "Shit River."[18]

In the rhetoric of the Anti-Bases Coalition, the military prostitute represented US imperialism and the violation of Philippine sovereignty. But in communities like Olongapo and Angeles, she was also a real person. Most of the women were young, rural, and poor, and arrived in Olongapo from faraway regions with few if any social connections. Some took jobs as waitresses only to discover later what they had signed up for. Others were trafficked through large-scale exploitation networks. In the landscape of poor women's labor in the Philippines, sex work and entertainment were dangerous jobs but could be among the economy's better-paying options. Theirs was a rational strategy of survival.[19]

A small number achieved mobility by marrying their GI customers. A 1979 study at Subic calculated that about 6 percent of entertainment workers married US servicemen, a relatively high percentage considering that the US military actively discouraged formal unions. By the early 1980s, officials were recording more than 2,400 marriage applications per year, and at Subic, the Navy convened a "bride school" to prepare Filipina women for life in the United States. In a 1987 study of 143 American men and Filipina women, more than two-thirds (and by one calculation as many as 90 percent) of the women had worked as "hostesses" before meeting their husbands. Some wives expressed hope that marriage would bring a "better future for myself and my children." Young American enlisted men, many of whom had joined the Navy to escape limited opportunities at home, arrived in Olongapo having endured hierarchical and coercive shipboard environments. But in the Philippines, any American was—regardless of rank—a "rich man." Some sailors seized the opportunity, reporting that "the serviceman could not marry as attractive a woman in the U.S. as he can in the Philippines." Sailors who found Filipina women more appealing than their "self-centered" and "aggressive" American counterparts also hoped intermarriage would turn back the clock on changing gender norms at home.[20]

For most of the twentieth century, Filipina sex workers who sought a better life struggled alone, shunned by their families, shamed by the church, excluded by the state, and demonized by nationalist movements. That changed dramatically by the 1980s, as feminists in the Philippines paid close attention to the bases, and—despite martial law—global feminist networks supported Filipina activists. Many held the United States responsible for the sex trade. "For as long as the Philippines remains a neocolony," wrote leftist feminist Delia Aguilar-San Juan, prostitution will "seduce these women, and their little girls after them, with the grotesque lure that is the product of a well-honed colonial mentality." Aguilar-San Juan's formulation obscured the role of Filipino men in the country's sex trade, but it mobilized anti-prostitution feminists worldwide. For decades, the military labor of Filipino men had been honored as brotherhood, but the labor of Filipina sex workers was never depicted as a family relationship. By the 1980s, though, sex workers linked their claims to a feminist movement that spanned the Pacific, aimed at dismantling sexism and militarism at the same time. Introducing a volume of poetry by the imprisoned writer Mila Aguilar, the African American feminist writer Audre Lorde wrote in 1987 that "our war is the same."[21]

The Marcos dictatorship continued to shape the migration patterns of Filipinos who came to the United States. American politics did, too. By the 1980s, the impact of the Immigration Act of 1965 was noticeable: the 1970 census counted 343,060 Americans who had been born in the Philippines; a decade later the census counted 781,894, and estimated more than a million by the middle of the 1980s. In fact, there were more Filipinos in California in 1980 than there had been in the entire United States in 1970. But population growth did not guarantee visibility. Chinese migrations grew at an even faster rate, and Japanese Americans, while small in number, drew heightened attention due to Japan's economic power in the decade.[22]

With numbers so large, multiple generations of migrants spread across the United States, and the striations of class becoming apparent, "Filipino America" was hard to characterize. Working-class labor migrants and their descendants did not always see eye to eye with the doctors, nurses, and engineers who came as part of the post-1965 professional migrations, but all struggled with explicit or subtle forms of discrimination and stereotyping. In 1986, Proposition 63 made English the official language of California, and accent discrimination targeted Filipino immigrants who often spoke English as fluently as—although quite differently from—native-born English speakers. One woman, by contrast, explained that being Filipino helped her get hired. "The managers automatically think that you will be a very diligent worker and that you will not cause any trouble."[23]

Political inclusion was slow. Filipino Americans were mostly Democrats, but not reliably so, and they captured little attention at the national level: Jesse Jackson was the only presidential candidate in 1984 who spoke openly against the Marcos regime. Filipino Americans elected far fewer public officials than their population numbers and geographic concentration would predict, but as Asian American politicians came into their own, they courted Filipino constituents in their districts. In Hawai'i, Democratic politicians were the first to woo Filipinos. Knowing that the Filipino population of the state had close ties to the Ilocos provinces of the Philippines and was mostly loyal to Ferdinand Marcos, figures such as Governor George Ariyoshi cultivated warm relations with his regime. Other eager politicians included San Francisco mayor Dianne Feinstein, who linked Manila and San Francisco as sister cities at a 1981 celebration. Aware that some 48,000 Filipino Americans lived in her city, Feinstein traveled to the

Philippines in 1981, and—to the applause of Marcos loyalists and over the protests of critics and several city council members—she handed Ferdinand Marcos the key to the city when he and Imelda visited San Francisco in 1982.[24]

As they listened to potential voters, urban politicians in San Francisco, Los Angeles, San Diego, and Honolulu began hearing complaints from Filipino World War II veterans, who wanted their help winning equal benefits and the right to naturalize as US citizens. In 1982, Oakland-based activist Lillian Galedo called veterans benefits "a 'hot' issue in the Filipino community around which little information is available," and indeed the arcane details of the 1946 Rescission Act baffled both activist groups and local constituent services offices. Veterans organizations such as Vicente Lim VFW Post 5471 in Washington loudly supported the Marcos regime at the same time that they grew increasingly assertive on veterans' political and economic rights. Helping VFW members required veteran leaders to make common cause with community organizers, many of them former 1960s radicals who had settled into urban ethnic coalition politics. (Galedo, for instance, had been active with the Bay Area's leftist KDP chapter a decade earlier.) Slowly, a political issue that for decades had rested in the backwaters of bilateral diplomacy began to shift to the arena of civil rights.[25]

Over the course of the 1980s, veterans exhausted their options in US courts, so they turned elsewhere. As they found sympathetic listeners among Asian American politicians such as Hawai'i senators Daniel Inouye and Daniel Akaka and Representative Patsy Mink, veterans contemplated legislation instead of litigation. Vets made their first attempt by trying to fold repeal of the Rescission Act into the 1986 Immigration Reform and Control Act, but came up short. Then, after movements for redress brought by victims of wartime Japanese American incarceration won a major victory with the passage of the Civil Liberties Act of 1988, Filipino veterans' advocates saw a new path to undo the Rescission Act and win equity in migration, health care, and veterans benefits.

Filipino veterans focused on Washington in part because the Philippine government was no longer a reliable advocate for them. Marcos continued to count himself among their ranks, until exposés by journalist Arturo Taca and historian Alfred McCoy revealed that Marcos's medals and indeed his entire military record was, as the US Army itself noted just after the war, "fraudulent" and "absurd." Marcos purported to have founded and led the Maharlika, a daring guerrilla unit. VA records suggested that Maharlika had sold contraband goods to the Japanese Army, while an Army document concluded that "no such unit ever existed."[26]

Marcos officials even began plundering from the veterans themselves. A presidential decree authorized him to appoint the board of the Philippine Veterans Bank (PVB) and a series of uncollected loans followed. In 1979, the PVB invested its clients' savings in a new Biglang Bahay ("instant home") bond scheme operated by the Minister of Human Settlements, Imelda Marcos. The bonds paid no interest, but one lucky bondholder would be selected to receive a dividend of 100,000 pesos in real estate. It was, in other words, a lottery, to be paid for with the funds from the 1967 veterans settlement that was supposed to cover individual claims. By 1985, the game was up: PVB directors admitted that only a quarter of the bank's funds could even be located, and the bank promptly went into receivership.[27]

In the United States, opposition to the Marcos regime included highly visible Filipino exiles like Benigno Aquino, but it had a rank and file of Filipino Americans, especially on the West Coast. Anti-Marcos activists did not always see eye to eye: moderates warned that communist revolution was around the corner, while radicals hoped to prepare the way. Others sympathized but feared getting involved. Marcos agents kept a close watch on Filipino dissenters abroad, sending photographers to protests and informants to political meetings. Marcos pressed for an extradition treaty with the United States, which anti–martial law groups warned (with good reason) would be used to target his opponents. The treaty never materialized, but the FBI did regularly interrogate Filipino Americans and Filipino exiles based in the United States. Prominent critics of the regime were assassinated. Primitivo Mijares, for instance, disappeared soon after testifying before Congress in 1975. Silme Domingo and Gene Viernes, progressive labor leaders in Seattle and activists in the left-leaning KDP, were shot dead in June 1981.[28]

By contrast, money poured from Philippine consulates into the coffers of pro-Marcos groups and the pockets of loyalists such as Leonilo Malabed, whose Mabuhay Corporation provided "security activities" on behalf of the regime. Economic pressure kept community organizations in line. Pro-Marcos publications such as San Francisco's *Filipino American* and the *Filipino Reporter* in New York boomed, while at other papers, ad revenue dried up after editors spoke out. Romeo Arguelles, the Philippine consul general in San Francisco, ran Marcos's Bay Area PR machine. He courted politicians, cultivated the Filipino American middle class, and redbaited the radicals. The Filipino community was not united, and its sense of crisis and division took a new turn in the summer of 1983.[29]

On June 23, 1983, Benigno Aquino announced he was returning to the Philippines. He knew the risks: "If I go back to the Philippines and [Marcos] decides to have me shot, he can have it done the moment I arrive." Maybe Aquino believed that recent US criticism of Marcos and political openings in Manila signaled an opportunity for an opposition leader. It's likely that the regime thought this as well, and so they plotted his assassination. Imelda Marcos met with Aquino in New York in May 1983—after finishing a $3.3 million shopping trip—to persuade him to return to the Philippines with her. When he refused, Imelda warned his fellow opposition figure and former senator Salvador Laurel that if Aquino returned, he would be killed. "She was very serious," Laurel later testified.[30]

On August 21, 1983, crowds in Manila eagerly awaited the return of the political leader widely known by his nickname, Ninoy. At the airport that afternoon were two former senators, Salvador Laurel and Lorenzo Tañada, along with Aquino's mother, sisters, and brother. Every time they turned a corner, the group found the doors barred or military officers blocking their way. "We knew time was running out and the China Airlines plane had landed," Laurel later recalled. "I was banging on the wooden door and thinking of kicking it open." Then the military told them the news. Aquino had stepped onto the staircase to deplane from his flight, surrounded by five military men, four in uniform and one in a civilian *barong*. Nine seconds later, he was dead. He never reached the tarmac.[31]

The White House issued a bland statement of regret, expressing its trust that Marcos would "swiftly and vigorously track down the perpetrators," and indeed Malacanang quickly placed blame on a lone rogue communist, a man who had been killed outside the airport just after the shooting. One visitor later recalled that when he arrived at the US embassy for a prefuneral briefing, "of all the people I spoke to . . . the only one who thought the Marcos government wasn't responsible was the CIA station chief." San Francisco mayor Dianne Feinstein, who had cast her lot with Marcos and his consular cronies in the hopes of winning the Bay Area's Filipino vote, cancelled the Manila–Sán Francisco partnership. "Clearly the present situation makes the normal functioning of the sister city relationship impossible," she announced. President Reagan, more reluctantly, postponed a state visit to Manila scheduled for November 1983, offering a range of excuses. Joan Quigley, Ron and Nancy's astrologer, had warned that the trip's timing was unfavorable, and Reagan joked with reporters of Nancy's fears following his own assassination attempt: "She's a little gun shy."[32]

Popular unrest exploded after Ninoy's assassination: labor unions, civil society groups, and churches spoke out; armed insurgency gained strength in the countryside; capital flight precipitated an economic crisis. That October, the Philippines announced it could no longer pay its debts, and devalued its currency. Inflation rates hit 50 percent by mid-1984, accompanied by shortages of oil and food. The Marcoses continued their international shopping sprees and Marcos handed out sweetheart deals to family members, political allies, and a former fraternity brother. Investors grew particularly wary after the Central Bank of the Philippines revealed that it had, as one auditing agency delicately phrased it, "overestimated its reserves."[33]

As the Philippine economy went into free fall, AFP salaries were too low to keep soldiers honest. In 1984, a major in the AFP earned 850 pesos a month, about $42.50, hardly sufficient to support a middle-class lifestyle. Officers engaged in smuggling and extortion, exploiting local communities for kickbacks. Enlisted men meanwhile attached themselves to larger patronage systems and gangster rackets run by their officers. Draftees, who made up an ever-larger fraction of the AFP, counted the days until the end of their service, often making off a few days early, taking their weapons with them to sell on the black market.[34]

One survival strategy for Filipinos who could afford it was migration, which accelerated after the economic crisis of 1983, with some 400,000 leaving in 1984 alone. With more than 700,000 names on the waiting list for US visas, many Filipinos headed elsewhere in Asia or to the Middle East. Marcos continued to support migration, both as a safety valve for domestic dissent and, increasingly, as a source of foreign-currency remittances to stabilize the national economy. In 1982, he went so far as to issue an executive order requiring workers on government-sponsored overseas contracts to remit at least half their salaries through Philippine government banking mechanisms. While wielding a stick against working-class emigrants, Marcos offered carrots to middle-class Filipino Americans. In 1981, a Marcos-sponsored plebiscite extended dual citizenship to Filipinos abroad, and new programs lured migrants (and their dollars) to return as tourists. Making a blessing of a curse, Marcos boasted to Filipino Americans that their dollars would go far against the recently devalued peso.[35]

Both political and economic concerns motivated visa applicants. The Refugee Act of 1980 guaranteed entry to the United States for those with a "well-founded fear" of returning to their home country. The Refugee Act of 1980 guaranteed entry to the United States for those with a "well-founded fear" of returning to their home country. The US Immigration and, Naturalization Service (INS), however, adhering to a general policy limiting refugee applications from America's anticommunist allies approved just eighteen claims in 1983. Most political migrations went unspoken. "The political situation as well as the economy in the Philippines had a lot to do with my family moving to the United States," explained Melissa Roxas, who left as a girl in 1985 to join her mother in southern California. Her family never told her why. "I had been . . . kept from the truth about . . . the real reasons why my family had to immigrate to the U.S."[36]

The Aquino assassination shifted political dynamics in the Philippines by unifying the opposition, exposing rifts within the Philippine military, and prompting US officials to reconsider their relationship with Ferdinand Marcos. As anti-regime sentiment coalesced around Aquino's widow, Corazon Aquino, previously apolitical groups joined in: the middle class; business leaders excluded from Marcos's network of crony capitalists; the Catholic Church. Aquino's assassination mobilized new political coalitions in the United States as well. Even radical left members of the KDP, who had criticized electoral politics, hesitantly supported Corazon Aquino. Ordinary Filipino Americans sent clippings on political affairs to family members in the Philippines and increasingly called on the United States to exert pressure.[37]

The assassination made visible the factions within the Philippine military. AFP officers who believed they would take charge in any power vacuum grew frustrated as Imelda Marcos prepared to take up her husband's role. "Even if I am not here," Ferdinand Marcos told *Newsweek*, "she will symbolize the cooperation of the Marcos followers with the new leadership." Worried by Marcos and Ver's attempts to personalize military control—and increasingly shut out of their patronage networks—career military officers gravitated to the Reform the Armed Forces Movement that Juan Ponce Enrile and Fidel Ramos established a few years earlier, and which slowly moved from secret meetings of small cells to a shadow network within the AFP itself.[38]

Aquino's killing forced top-level officials in the United States to question their decades-long reliance on the Philippine military. The fact that Benigno Aquino was surrounded at the Manila airport by soldiers who either abetted or carried out his assassination made the AFP's political character embarrassingly obvious. In the Reagan White House, State and Defense Department officers concluded that Marcos's armed forces could not be counted on and began to wonder whether Marcos himself was more trouble than he was worth. As Benigno Aquino had put it before his death, "the problem is not simply that [Marcos] is an authoritarian leader, but that he is an ineffective authoritarian leader."[39]

Some US officials began to make contingency plans. In March 1984, Admiral William Crowe warned that rapid NPA growth threatened US bases. Crowe's report reached the desk of Richard Armitage, the Assistant Secretary of State for International Security Affairs, who then urged Defense Secretary Caspar Weinberger to read it. Initially skeptical and then won over, the secretary in turn arranged for Crowe to brief President Reagan in April 1984. By July, officials had convened an interagency working group under Armitage's leadership. The group's secret study concluded in 1985 that the Philippines was a "kleptocracy" and Marcos an untrustworthy figure who needed to be "mousetrapped." But "who is going to replace him?" Weinberger asked. American officials did not want to work with Imelda Marcos, certain that her accession to power would further destabilize the country. They feared that the inexperienced Corazon Aquino and her democratic allies were easy prey for leftist manipulation. So they looked for "unhappy young colonels," hopeful that a military overthrow would install a clean, pliable, and US-oriented regime. Administration officials who urged change felt that American "political leaders really lacked balls." Few were willing yet to cut and run.[40]

In the meantime, aid continued to flow. On Capitol Hill, Representative Stephen Solarz, a young New York politician, led the charge against Marcos and other human rights violators. Laws from the 1970s restricted military aid for regimes that violated human rights, but the Philippines had avoided sanction by either Carter or Reagan. Senators such as Alaska's Frank Murkowski successfully argued that the United States "would be constrained, if not crippled" by tying aid to human rights improvements. Unable to cut off funds, Solarz worked behind the scenes with Filipino American lobby groups, convened hearings that gave a platform to exiled opposition leaders, and asked how Marcos, who lived on an official salary of $7,500 a year, managed to buy $350 million worth of property in New York City, including 40 Wall Street, an office tower later acquired by New York developer Donald Trump.[41]

Ronald Reagan continued to support his friend and Cold War ally. But behind Reagan's secretary of state, George Shultz, stood a rising crowd of neoconservatives with a disdain for the previous generation's *Realpolitik*. In 1983, their leader was Shultz's adviser Paul Wolfowitz, who, as one aide later recalled, was "joined at the hip" with Richard Armitage at Defense and Gaston Sigur at the National Security Council. Wolfowitz pressed Shultz to urge Reagan to stop supporting Marcos. Wolfowitz was no human rights liberal: he thought politicians like Solarz were "posturing," insisted that an aid cutoff would have "a very destabilizing effect in the armed forces," and warned the United States not to "throw away a lot of our influence." At the Pentagon, Caspar Weinberger remained loyal. "At least Marcos is ours," the defense secretary muttered, echoing another official's consoling view that "he's a hell of a lot better than any Ayatollah."[42]

The beginning of the end came on American television. On November 3, 1985, in the middle of a contentious ABC News interview with journalist George Will, Ferdinand Marcos surprised the world by announcing an election. He was following American advice. CIA director William Casey had paid a secret visit to Manila a few months earlier, on May 8, and urged Marcos to schedule an election. Initially unreceptive, Marcos changed his mind and called the snap election for February 7, 1986. Perhaps he wanted to block criticism by journalists and human rights watchdogs, or maybe he calculated that the opposition was so fragmented he would actually win. But Corazon Aquino mobilized rapidly, turning to radio, mass rallies, and the pulpits of the Catholic Church to counter the Marcos-controlled state media. Nearly every sector endorsed her except for the radical left. Despite her description of the CPP and NPA as "brothers in the hills," the communists kept their distance, urged an election boycott, and found themselves irrelevant to rapidly unfolding events.[43]

In Washington, as Filipino Navy stewards served dinner at the White House, advisers groped for analogies. Jeane Kirkpatrick warned that the "campaign against the government of the Philippines" might generate yet another of the 1980s' "tragically repressive, aggressive dictatorships." Richard Armitage compared the Philippines with Vietnam and raised the specter of a "Diem scenario." Any effort that displayed obvious American interference, or installed an unviable replacement, would discredit the United States. Regime change, Armitage insisted, was not an option.[44]

Reagan continued to warn publicly against throwing Marcos "to the wolves," which would yield "totalitarianism, pure and simple, as the alternative." In private, he was skeptical of Corazon Aquino, especially after a visit from *New York Times* editor Abe Rosenthal, who persuaded Reagan that she was weak and politically naïve. When confronted directly, Reagan dodged the issue. *Wall Street Journal* writer Robert Novak recalled that at a White House luncheon during the Philippine election, Reagan gingerly avoided addressing the topic by summoning Hollywood nostalgia: "You know, one thing I tried to do but was never successful at was to get them to make a movie about the Philippine Scouts." The president's absent-minded comment was probably a deliberate performance. Aware of division within the administration, Reagan kept his options open. Behind the scenes, he relied on Nevada senator Paul Laxalt, a distinguished Republican with years of foreign policy experience, warm relations with both Reagan and Marcos, and in-country experience as an Army medic in Leyte in 1944. In October 1985, Laxalt became the administration's key intermediary to Ferdinand Marcos.[45]

With balloting set to begin on February 7, Reagan sent a delegation, co-chaired by Senator Richard Lugar and Representative John Murtha, to observe the country's 85,000 polling sites and its twenty million voters. (Reagan also dispatched the aircraft carrier USS *Enterprise*, just in case.) Greeting the team were two competing election commissions: the official COMELEC (Commission on Elections) and NAMFREL (National Citizen Movement for Free Elections), a civil society group with perhaps as many as half a million volunteers. Four decades after independence, President Reagan observed that "at times we need to remind ourselves that this is a Philippine election, not an American election." In Manila, Paul Wolfowitz noted "an outpouring of pro-American feeling," but Murtha attributed the appeal of outside observers less to colonial loyalty than to the fact that "it was obvious that a very significant portion of the Filipino citizens did not trust the government to conduct a fair election."[46]

As the votes came in, the distortion was obvious. On February 9, three dozen computer technicians at COMELEC, unwilling to comply with election tampering, walked off the job and took shelter at a nearby church. That night, Reagan's delegation to Manila openly criticized the election. By contrast, at the White House, Reagan shocked a February 11 press conference. He acknowledged "the possibility of fraud," suggested that "it could have been that all of that was occurring on both sides," and hoped both leaders would "work together to form a viable government." Murtha, the leading Democrat on the observer team, believed Reagan had fallen for a rumor spread by Paul Manafort, the young partner in an aggressive lobbying and public relations firm that Marcos had subsidized with $1 million in funds. In fact, the idea might have reached the president from Nancy Reagan, who was in regular touch with Imelda Marcos. Or it might simply have been wishful thinking on his part. As Shultz later put it, "I was quite aware that President Reagan wanted Marcos to change, not leave. However bad the Philippine situation might be, Ronald Reagan felt that Marcos had been a friend and ally of the United States, and Reagan stood up for people when the going was tough."[47]

On February 15, COMELEC announced that Marcos had handily won the election. US Senator Dante Fascell, chair of the Foreign Relations Committee, urged Reagan "to consider immediate suspension of all military and economic assistance to the Philippines . . . in light of the inevitable damage the United States will suffer if it fails to distance itself from [the] regime." Even Kansas senator Bob Dole, a longtime Marcos supporter, recommended that the United States should explore other locations for its bases. Despite warnings from Armitage and Wolfowitz that cutting aid would prompt communist victory, a Senate resolution passed easily.[48]

In the Philippines, Corazon Aquino spoke on February 16 before a crowd of two million people, demanding Marcos's resignation. The Catholic Bishops Conference said the regime had "no moral basis" to "command the allegiance of the citizenry." The Reform the Armed Forces and its military supporters (the "RAM Boys") found their opening. On February 22, Juan Ponce Enrile and Fidel Ramos announced their defection from Marcos and support of Aquino. Ramos condemned the fact that the "military had become practically the servants of political power in our society rather than the servants of the people." Ramos, Enrile, and some three hundred soldiers hunkered down at Camp Aguinaldo on the outskirts of Manila, and begged

Cardinal Sin to protect them. On the night of February 22, Sin spoke on church-controlled radio and asked the Philippine people to defend "our two good friends at the camp." To crush Ramos and Enrile, Marcos would have to send Presidential Security Command troops and tanks through city streets and along the EDSA, a multi-lane superhighway circling the city of Manila. The world was watching.[49]

On Sunday morning, February 23, Marcos appeared on the American television program *Meet the Press* and announced his plans to "hit Enrile and Ramos," prompting US Ambassador Stephen Bosworth to warn Marcos that "you will alienate your people and make it difficult for us to help you." Unpersuaded, Marcos ordered the tanks to move on Camp Aguinaldo, but his soldiers found several million people on the EDSA highway—among them women, children, the elderly, and clergy—blocking the route to the base. Marcos commanded the tank battalion to break through, but the soldiers refused. By the end of the day, some 80 percent of the AFP had defected to Enrile and the RAM. The regime had effectively collapsed, although whether Aquino or the military would replace it was entirely unclear. And what would happen to Marcos?[50]

Finally, Reagan shifted. On Sunday February 23, dressed in "his western shirt and boots," Reagan returned from Camp David for a meeting in the White House Situation Room. Philip Habib, an American diplomat just back from the Philippines, bluntly informed a "stunned" Reagan that "the Marcos era has ended, Mr. President." Shultz echoed Habib's comments: "He's had it." Reagan, reeling from the advice of two of his most trusted advisers, asked if the US military might intervene to protect the RAM faction and convene negotiations. Secretary of Defense Caspar Weinberger informed the president there were only 625 US Marines at Subic, and National Security Adviser John Poindexter described the millions of civilians gathering on the Manila highway. Slamming his fist on the table, Reagan came to terms. "That's all we need. One of those nuns is killed and we have a Joan of Arc."[51]

Reagan gave only a few instructions, warning those assembled that "Marcos is a proud man. He must go with dignity or there will be bloodshed." At 3:00 a.m. Manila time on Tuesday February 25, Ferdinand Marcos phoned Paul Laxalt, hoping the senator would have some good news, perhaps even a promise of rescue. Laxalt carried the message to the White House, where Reagan told the Nevada senator to assure Marcos that he "would be welcome in the United States if he saw fit to come here." But two hours later, when Laxalt called Marcos back to convey that news, it offered little comfort. Marcos asked Laxalt point-blank what to do. Laxalt told him, "Cut and cut cleanly. The time has come." After a long pause on the line, Marcos responded: "I am so very, very disappointed." Five hours later, Imelda Marcos phoned the US embassy, asking for guidance on evacuation, and then placed a call to Nancy Reagan, who reiterated to Imelda what Ferdinand Marcos had not wanted to hear from Laxalt.[52]

That morning, Ferdinand and Imelda Marcos, together with some thirty other members of their family and the Presidential Security Command, boarded four American H-3 helicopters at Malacanang and took off for Clark Air Base. The Marcoses—especially Imelda—initially proposed evacuation to Ferdinand's home province (and political home base) of Ilocos Norte, from which they believed they would triumphantly return—with US military support—to Manila. But the US military never contemplated letting them stay in the country, and it quickly became clear that the Marcoses were unwelcome at Clark. In 1979, Carter's base agreement amendments handed the AFP responsibility for security at base perimeters. At the time, Marcos boasted that "American forces are no longer in contact with anyone . . . it would be Filipino meeting Filipino," a concession then thought to be merely symbolic. On the morning of February 26, with the AFP loyal to Enrile and Aquino rather than Marcos, who guarded the gates and landing strips of US bases suddenly mattered. Evacuation plans accelerated.

Joined by sixty more close allies (including Fabian Ver), the Marcoses left Clark, first for Guam, and then to Honolulu.[53]

They arrived in Hawai'i with two planeloads of cronies and suitcases filled with gold, a fraction of the estimated $5 billion to $10 billion the Marcoses likely stole over the course of their twenty-year rule. The bullion was embarrassing enough, but even worse was the paper trail, including records documenting campaign contributions to both Presidents Carter and Reagan and to California politicians Alan Cranston and Dianne Feinstein. Other documents linked Leonilo Malabed's San Francisco–based company to the killing of Seattle activists Silme Domingo and Gene Viernes. While Marcos sat at Hickam Air Force Base at Pearl Harbor, US officials attempted to find him a new home. Using his brand-new email account, National Security Council staffer Oliver North worked his connections to Panamanian strongman Manuel Noriega, who balked, fearing the plan was "something concocted at the State Dept." The Marcoses soon settled in Honolulu, personally welcomed with leis bestowed by the wife of Governor George Ariyoshi.[54]

Marcos had his defenders to the bitter end. Days after Marcos's departure, Henry Kissinger ruefully reflected that "whatever else may be said about the Marcos regime, it contributed substantially to American security and had been extolled by American presidents for nearly two decades." Officially, President Reagan "welcomed the democratic outcome" and praised Marcos for his "difficult and courageous decision" to leave office, but privately, the president was bitter that Marcos had been "treat[ed] as shabbily as our country had treated another former ally, the shah of Iran," and fumed that Shultz's State Department recognized the Aquino government less than three hours after Marcos's helicopters left Clark.[55]

Reagan believed Shultz and Wolfowitz stood on the wrong side of history. His critics, though, were emboldened. "As the authoritarian Marcos regime fell, so did the neoconservative theory," announced liberal journalist Sidney Blumenthal. In the next few years, a wave of democratization crested over Asia, Latin America, southern Africa, and eastern Europe, sweeping away much of Jeane Kirkpatrick's rhetoric. It was also clear that the jumbled coalitions of the 1980s had contributed to a new global politics, formed in part on the streets of Manila. Many, including Paul Wolfowitz himself, were mesmerized by People Power: by the sight of crowds on the streets; by Filipinos' passionate commitment to electoral democracy; by their peaceful overthrow of an unpopular dictator; by their eager pleas for American intervention. The events of 1986 lingered in his statecraft, with repercussions two decades later. People Power made regime change look easy, and foreign policy neoconservatives in Washington may have summoned memories of Manila's superhighway when they contemplated Baghdad's Firdos Square in 2003. Meanwhile, Cold War hawks tried to tamp down democratic enthusiasms. On March 13, 1986, National Security Adviser John Poindexter warned Elliott Abrams at the State Department not to "get carried away on Chile after watching how we handled the Philippines."[56]

If People Power ended with an uncertain future, it nevertheless gave Filipinos and Americans an enduring symbol of their shared Cold War history. Soon after the Marcoses departed from Manila, the AFP and Corazon Aquino opened the doors of Malacanang, welcoming massive crowds for tours of the abandoned presidential palace. Among the trappings of Ferdinand and Imelda's authoritarian rule, there were elegant bedrooms upstairs labeled "King's Room" and "Queen's Room." In the basement, visitors found 2,400 pairs of shoes.[57]

On September 18, 1986, President Corazon Aquino triumphantly arrived in Washington. She met with—and reportedly won over—President Reagan, who nevertheless declined to honor her with the official state dinner he'd hosted for Ferdinand Marcos four years before. On Capitol Hill, a joint session of Congress filled with yellow shirts and yellow ties, yellow blouses and yellow roses, a quick change from the decades of applause that Marcos had received in the same chambers. "Slum or impoverished village, they came to me with one cry, Democracy!" Aquino intoned, clearly enjoying the shouts of "Cory, Cory." She told Congress that "you have spent many lives and much treasure to bring freedom to many lands that were reluctant to receive it. And here you have a people who won it by themselves and need only help to preserve it." Hours after her September 18 address, she received that help, as Congress voted $200 million for a "mini-Marshall Plan" devised by Representative Stephen Solarz and his Republican counterpart Jack Kemp. Senator Bob Dole grimly called it "the biggest honorarium in American history," but the bill passed easily.[58]

With Fabian Ver in exile and the AFP in the hands of West Point grad Fidel Ramos, US defense officials breathed a sigh of relief. It didn't last long. Despite international popularity, Aquino had a weak hold on power at home. She never commanded the military's full loyalty and repeatedly confronted insubordination and outright rebellion. Within days of her inauguration, to neutralize the AFP threat, Aquino sought to "get rid of Enrile," and after Secretary of National Defense Juan Ponce Enrile participated in an aborted coup attempt in November 1986, she fired him. Aquino replaced Enrile with Rafael Ileto, a general who was, like Fidel Ramos, a West Point grad, well integrated into the US military and its global reach. Among the AFP top brass, Ileto and Ramos were on the side of Aquino and civilian rule, but they were practically the only ones, and many observers worried as Marcos, days after arriving in Honolulu and inspired by the Nicaraguan *contras*, began to plot an insurgent movement to restore him to power. On at least one occasion, US officials had to intervene to keep Marcos from leaving Hawai'i.[59]

Aquino faced a dilemma: she needed to cultivate military leaders and keep them from launching a coup without alienating either the liberals who had supported her or the millions of Filipinos who had grown tired of years of dictatorship and military corruption. Voters pushed in multiple directions, often leaning toward dark-horse candidates who stood apart from both Marcos and Aquino. Local elections for mayor of the southern city of Davao in 1988 saw a young upstart, Rodrigo Duterte, mobilize peasants and slum dwellers for his campaign against Corazon Aquino's favored candidate. The son of the governor of Davao Province, Duterte was hardly an outsider, but he quickly proved adept at managing political factions and their private armies.[60]

Aquino's delicate balancing act made it hard for her to respond to the challenge of the communist New People's Army. The AFP—especially while Juan Ponce Enrile was still Secretary of National Defense—wanted to seize the initiative of People Power and crush the rebels, and the military carried enough weight that Aquino had to listen. By contrast, many of the anti–martial law liberal reformers who brought Aquino to power urged her to make the most of People Power not by crushing the rebels, but negotiating with them. Aquino began by releasing imprisoned radicals, among them NPA military commander Bernabe Buscayno and CPP political leader Jose Maria Sison. She also turned to the last refuge of any Philippine politician—an amnesty offer—signing a sixty-day truce with the NPA's political representatives that took effect on December 10, 1986.[61]

But when the ceasefire expired in February 1987, so did the AFP's patience. "To heck with human rights," General Honesto Isleta told the BBC. Under pressure from the military and fearful of a coup, Aquino did an about-face. In a March 1987 speech at the Philippine Military Academy in Baguio, she announced a crackdown on the communists, telling cadets it was time "to take out the sword of war." Then she "unleashed" the AFP, informing them they were free to launch "any kind of offensive" with "absolutely no restraint." To maintain order, Aquino also tacitly allowed rural elites to rearm their private armies under the guise of the Marcos-era Civilian Home Defense Forces, while human rights investigations slowed. In the mountains of Luzon and the jungles of Mindanao, the People Power revolution evaporated. In Washington, the State Department feared Aquino's actions would destabilize the fragile republic, but the Pentagon was enthusiastic about the turn of events.[62]

Aquino did not hesitate to call for American support. In November 1986, retired Major General John Singlaub, fresh from his recent participation in America's shadowy Iran-Contra scheme, arrived in the Philippines. In a reversal that would have caught the eye of Edward Lansdale, Singlaub brought along some of his former South Vietnamese colleagues to train Filipino militias in counterinsurgency. US Special Operations teams arrived in 1987 to train the AFP and infiltrate the NPA. So did the CIA, staffed up in March 1987 with a dozen additional agents and millions of dollars of funds. Heading up the effort was Colonel James Nicholas Rowe, a Special Forces officer and Vietnam-era POW serving as commander of the 1st Special Operations Training Battalion at Fort Bragg. The NPA took credit for his assassination in Manila on April 21, 1989: "We want to let [the Americans] know that their government is making the Philippines another Vietnam." In Manila, Senator Jovito Salonga regretted that "we have to beg for American assistance every time we have a crisis."[63]

Given Aquino's lack of political experience, her gender, and her sometimes-wobbly leadership style, many US officials and journalists interpreted her policy shifts and public double-talk as indecision. But playing both sides of the debate was a time-tested maneuver of Philippine politicians, and as Aquino dodged bullets at Malacanang, she offered something the Philippine military couldn't: a hopeful vision for the nation's future at a time when people on both sides of the Pacific wanted change in Manila. Whether at the presidential palace in Manila or the mayor's office in Davao, People Power had created expectations of change that everyday politics could never meet—especially with the US-Philippine military relationship still firmly in place.

As Filipinos ratified a new constitution in February 1987, Article 18 noted, much to the dismay of US observers, that after the MBA's expiration in 1991, "foreign military bases, troops, or facilities" were barred unless approved by a treaty ratified by the Philippine Senate. Talks began in December 1989 on the renewal of the Military Bases Agreement, set to expire in 1991. Much had happened since it was last negotiated: the fall of the Berlin Wall; a unilateral Soviet withdrawal from air and naval stations in Vietnam; US departure from bases in Greece, Turkey, and Thailand; and proposed base closures at home in the United States. Talk turned to the "end of history" and, more concretely, the possibility of reduced military spending and a "peace dividend." Pentagon brass remained in a defensive Cold War position, but after the Cold War, a new US consensus emerged that the bases were, as one commentator put it, "a valuable but not vital asset." Where would the Philippines fit in a post-1989 geopolitical order?[64]

VETERANS OF WORLD WAR II ALSO FACED PEOPLE POWER AND the Cold War's end with uncertainty. The Rescission Act was still on the books in Washington and blocked naturalization and payment of benefits, but with Ferdinand Marcos gone, political efforts in the United States looked more promising than anything on offer at Malacanang. By the 1990s, veterans mobilized legislative support from both sides of the aisle, and not only from Asian American legislators. They repeated General Douglas MacArthur's wartime insistence on "equal pay for equal risk," argued that "American veterans should get American benefits," and called for the outright repeal of the Rescission Act. Opportunity and conflict emerged in the debate over the Immigration and Naturalization Act of 1990, a comprehensive immigration act adopted that year. Hawai'i senator Daniel Inouye, himself a decorated World War II veteran, introduced an amendment granting most guerrilla and Philippine Commonwealth Army veterans a two-year window of opportunity for naturalization. Senator Inouye insisted that veterans "deserve the opportunity to become citizens of the nation for which they put their lives on the line in defense of our principles of freedom and democracy." But Inouye could only get halfway there: there would be citizenship, but no benefits. The amendment left the Rescission Act firmly in place. And it divided activists. Provisions of the bill restricting immigration meant that Latino activists uniformly opposed it. Some Filipino activists urged solidarity with other members of the multiethnic coalitions fighting anti-immigrant movements in California and elsewhere. Others saw a long-delayed opening for Filipino vets and were willing to settle for half a loaf, assuring Filipino veterans (and warning Congress) that "the fight is not over yet!"[65]

In the halls of Congress and at naturalization ceremonies, there was talk of broken promises finally made right. Dionisio Ojeda, a World War II vet and retired general in the Philippine Army, observed that "we fought side by side with the Americans. And President Roosevelt promised us everything." Representative Stephen Solarz felt the law would "fulfill the promise made by the United States to these courageous fighters," and across the Pacific, US Ambassador Frank Wisner announced at a Manila ceremony that "we have formalized a right you earned on the battlefields of World War II. . . . Justice, though delayed, ultimately has been done." Aware, though, that the 1990 act only addressed naturalization and not benefits, General Ojeda wryly noted that "we are still waiting."[66]

They would have to wait a little longer, because by late 1990, the world's attention shifted to the Iraqi invasion of Kuwait. During the Gulf War that followed, Subic Bay fulfilled its strategic role as a staging area for Persian Gulf actions, and, following vigorous debates that rehearsed earlier agonies over Korea and Vietnam, the Philippines sent a token force of two hundred medical personnel. There they might have crossed paths with Filipino workers, who had been migrating to the Middle East in greater numbers since the 1970s. During the Gulf War, Corazon Aquino worried about oil supplies and the US alliance, but she also kept an eye on the safety (and remittances) of as many as 40,000 Filipino workers living in Iraq and Kuwait. With aid from the Philippine government and international groups, at least 39,000 left the two countries, albeit temporarily. Soon after the ceasefire, the Philippine Secretary of Labor began exploring job placements for Filipinos in reconstruction work.[67]

Filipino workers and AFP medics might also have met Filipino Americans serving in the US armed forces, among them Don Polintan, who joined the Army in 1989. "The biggest thing was the college money I could get from them and basically I was just interested," he later recalled. For Polintan, his service, mostly in Saudi Arabia, was uneventful. "We knew our jobs. We stayed alert. It was calm pretty much." The Gulf War made visible the racial and ethnic striations of America's all-volunteer force, implemented after the end of the military draft in 1973. For Filipino Americans, especially working-class immigrants or recent arrivals, enlistment offered job training and educational benefits that were hard to come by in other ways. Military service connected young men and women to the long history of service within their families and communities and cemented a multi-generational bond that meant Filipino Americans would continue to be numerically overrepresented in the US armed forces. In uniform, they would remake the terms of citizenship, patriotism, and military service, just as their grandfathers had before them. And they would not forget the broken promises of the Rescission Act.[68]

Debates on the US military bases were tangled in a thicket of bureaucracy and political controversy until suddenly, on June 12, 1991, Mother Nature intervened. Mount Pinatubo, a volcano just twenty miles north of Subic and ten miles west of Clark, erupted after more than six hundred years of dormancy. While Americans and Filipinos sat at the bargaining table, the decision had been made: Clark would never reopen. "The Americans," noted Filipino American Leny Mendoza Strobel, who had grown up near Clark, "were finally ejected, not by political negotiation but by the wrath of Nature. Filipinos see this as poetic justice."[69]

The official resolution of the bases debate came that September, as the Philippine Senate debated the ratification of a new treaty with the United States. Anti-base activists, many of whom had been leaders of the People Power revolution, now held center stage in national politics. Populist senator Joseph Estrada, a former movie actor who had starred in the 1989 film *In the Claws of the Eagle*, a saga about an Olongapo bus driver, insisted that "it is about time that we cut off the rope that strangles our growth as a nation." Turning to family metaphors, Senator Raul Manglapus urged Filipinos to "slay the American father image," while Senator Leticia Shahani called for "cutting the umbilical cord." The aging former senator Lorenzo Tañada, watching from the galleries, urged a "no" vote, but legislators anguished. "I cannot tear from my mind," Senator Heherson Alvarez said, "the thought that some 60,000 Filipinos will lose their job," among them Christina, a twenty-two-year-old sex worker in Olongapo, who told a reporter that she hoped the bases would stay. "If the bases are here, I still have a chance."[70]

The Senate rejected the treaty—and thereby formally ejected the bases—on September 16, 1991, by a vote of 12 to 11. Senator Rene Saguisag boasted that foreign troops "are going home after more than 400 years. They are going to return a piece of our homeland to us, the final vestige of centuries of colonialism, America's last plantation here." At the formal turnover ceremony a year later, the newly elected President Fidel Ramos announced that "what is restored to the Filipino people today is certainly more than just a piece of real estate." By the end of 1992, Subic had closed up shop, with most navy personnel and ships transferred to Guam.[71]

When the bases closed, so did opportunities for Filipino enlistment in the US Navy, a policy that had depended on Article 27 of the MBA. After December 31, 1992, the 3,400 Filipinos in the US Navy were permitted to stay in uniform, but there would be no more to follow them. By 1992, this did not mark a drastic shift. Except for a brief uptick in enlistment during the Persian Gulf War, the service pipeline had dwindled to about four hundred sailors a year, and the global boom in merchant seafaring meant that working-class Filipinos who wanted jobs at sea had options far wider than what the Navy had promised their fathers in the 1960s. Jesse Quinsaat, a San Diego lawyer, the son of a US Navy sailor, and an early activist in the Asian American Movement, observed that "many Filipinos see the end of both [enlistment and the base agreements] as also the end of a colonial era." Planners and politicians proposed ambitious reconversion plans that mingled militarism and tourism. Unemployed base workers applied for new jobs at casino resorts and export processing zones. At Subic, former soldiers signed on with the Jungle Environment and Survival Training Camp, where visiting tourists could play at counterinsurgency. Sex work persisted even after the base closures, although many women followed or were trafficked to bases elsewhere in the Pacific.[72]

Left behind were thousands of children of US servicemen who were part of what one critic called a "heritage . . . of abandonment and suffering." They would find no opportunity in the Amerasian Homecoming Act. Passed by the US Congress in 1988 to open the door for the children of US personnel in Vietnam, the law specifically excluded those from Thailand, South Korea, and the Philippines—countries where there were still plenty of Americans serving at the time. At the formal ceremony marking the turnover of Subic Bay, President Ramos insisted that "the welfare of these young Filipino-Americans remains the joint responsibility of both countries."[73]

One of the thousands that Ramos called "throwaway children" was Lorelyn Penero Miller, who decided in 1992 that she deserved an

American passport. Her father, Charles Miller, served in the US Air Force during the Vietnam War, and was stationed at Clark, where he met (but never married) Luz Penero, who gave birth to Lorelyn in June 1970. Because the couple was unmarried and only Lorelyn's father was a US citizen—and because he had not officially affirmed his paternity before his daughter turned twenty-one—Lorelyn's claim on US citizenship expired. Had the parents' nationalities been reversed, with a US citizen mother, Lorelyn would have been a US citizen at birth, but the US Supreme Court rejected Miller's claim of sex discrimination. Justice John Paul Stevens, observing that many US servicemen were stationed overseas, called the law "well supported by valid governmental interests."[74]

The Millers were just two of thousands of families created at US military bases and then torn apart by US foreign policy. The end of the Cold War and the fall of the Marcos regime left legacies that continued to trouble Pacific relations. For some, People Power offered a new beginning, and activists filed legal claims against Marcos family assets—at least $356 million, a mere fraction of them—deposited in Swiss bank accounts. An ambitious young US Attorney named Rudolph Giuliani informed the Justice Department in 1988 that "substantial evidence exists to prove that Ferdinand and Imelda Marcos obtained hundreds of millions of dollars through embezzlement and fraud," and that the Marcoses "used the United States as their 'safe haven' for this ill-gotten wealth." Others hoped to sweep the past under the rug. After Ferdinand Marcos died in 1989, Imelda Marcos, avoiding multiple criminal and civil charges, returned to Manila two years later to run for Congress. San Francisco–based Marcos supporter Emmanuel Tipon noted that year that "as far as most Filipinos are concerned, the Marcos issue is a dead one."[75]

Veteran activism, however, was more alive than ever, even after the mixed results of the 1990 immigration act. US Consul General Bruce Beardsley immediately understood the law's implications for immigration: "No quota, no waiting," he observed. INS officials balked at the poor state of the service records of many veterans, including men such as Ceferino Carino, a seventy-seven-year-old San Diego resident and the father of three sons in the US Navy, who told a reporter that he had served with Major General Jonathan Wainwright at Bataan. "I've been interviewed for citizenship, I've done everything," he complained. One official warned of paper families, child brides, and "scalawags" with counterfeit forms. "We're already getting horror stories—bogus consultants, flimflam lawyers, sale of free application forms." The antagonistic relationship between US officials and Filipino veterans persisted. It hardly felt like finished business.[76]

Indeed, it was just the beginning. After the passage of the 1990 act, Representative Tom Campbell of California, a cosponsor, assured Americans that "it's unlikely that many of these veterans will choose to move to America in the twilight of their lives. Rather, they will choose to remain in their homeland with family and friends." At the outset of the 1990s, the decade of the largest migration of Filipino Americans in US history, that prediction turned out to be wholly inaccurate. Of about 70,000 eligible veterans still alive, 28,000 were naturalized by 1998. (Many of the remaining veterans proved unable to meet paperwork requirements.) Of those, about 17,000 migrated to the United States, some borrowing as much as $3,000 to do so. Many newly naturalized veterans in turn invoked the family reunification preferences of immigration law to sponsor the migration of relatives from the Philippines.[77]

But not all of them could. Veterans who moved from the Philippines to the United States often found that being a poor, nonwhite alien with weak English skills and a dependence on the US welfare state was not a propitious political position to assume in 1990s California. Newly won migration privileges were limited by new restrictions on welfare recipients, especially a regulation that sponsors of would-be migrants must demonstrate annual earnings of at least 125 percent of the poverty line. The latest wave of Filipino veteran migrants were disproportionately elderly and poor, and some survived on little more than Supplemental Security Income, which in 1990 paid $505 per month. Full VA benefits—at $722 per month—would push them over the 125 percent line. Thus Filipino veterans and their advocates pressed for full (or, at least, equitable) financial benefits as well. "We fought side by side with the Americans. We want equal benefits too," veteran David Sarbilla insisted at a rally outside a federal office building in Los Angeles in 1994.[78]

Opponents of equity manipulated Filipino soldiers' complicated national loyalties to reject veterans' arguments. Representative Bob Stump, an Arizona Republican and a Pacific War Navy veteran, argued that Filipino claims had already been addressed through the Rescission Act, and that because "it was Philippine soil on which the U.S. and Philippine armies fought the Japanese, . . . the government of the Philippines bears responsibility for its veterans." Stump insisted that "while Filipino forces fought bravely and certainly aided the U.S. in the war effort, in the end they fought for their own, soon-to-be-independent Philippine nation."[79]

Veterans' strategies reflected a lifetime navigating two militaries, two governments, and two cultures of citizenship, but they also tapped into a new veterans politics of the 1990s. Aging World War II veterans captured attention as the "Greatest Generation," while "forgotten" Vietnam veterans earned national headlines. Funding for veterans' social service needs thus became politically popular at precisely the moment when budgets for urban and elder poverty declined. Social service agencies already at work with poor and homeless populations on the streets of West Coast cities stopped mobilizing their Filipino clients as the urban poor. Now they were forgotten veterans, claiming a place in America's expanding warfare state in order to gain leverage over its shrinking welfare state.[80]

The 1990 legislation was supposed to end veteran protest, but instead invigorated it—and diversified it in surprising ways. Multigenerational immigrant families and Filipino congregations in urban Catholic churches linked aging World War II veterans with a new generation. Born and raised in the United States, well-versed in American social movements, and educated in multicultural schools and university ethnic studies classes developed two decades earlier by the Asian American movement, younger Filipino Americans took up the charge for equity.

Veterans also advocated for themselves. After moving to the United States and naturalizing as citizens under the 1990 law, they now engaged directly with the American political system as insiders, not outsiders. Year after year, veterans petitioned Congress, testified in public forums, and pursued high-profile acts of civil disobedience. In 1997, fifteen veterans in Washington were arrested for locking themselves to the White House fence, while colleagues in California chained themselves to a statue of General Douglas MacArthur in downtown Los Angeles's MacArthur Park during a yearlong vigil in the park. The veterans persisted: "I just keep on waiting because I am hopeful," observed seventy-two-year-old Estanislao Bargas Beloy at a 1994 LA rally. "If the INS say no," he observed, "I will feel disgusted."[81]

By the 1990s, the VA itself was pressing Congress for legislative change to redress the struggles of a small cohort of Philippine Army and guerrilla veterans with service-connected disabilities. Paid at the rate of 50 cents to the dollar on the principle that US dollars went further in the Philippines, these veterans found their benefits effectively slashed in half when they took up the 1990 law's naturalization provisions and moved to the United States. Changes in immigration law and settlement patterns were remaking the bonds of Pacific politics. But the legacies of colonialism—and the assumptions about who America's "foreign" soldiers were and what rights they had under the Constitution—remained.[82]

By the time the bases had closed and the veterans marched on Washington in 1997, Aquino was gone, replaced by Fidel Ramos, a man who had spent his entire adult life embedded in the US-Philippine military relationship. Sympathetic to American prerogatives, Ramos restored military ties that People Power and Mount Pinatubo had fractured. Ramos and his US military advisers had a surprise in store. Bruised by Philippine senators' vote against the bases, Ramos did an end run around them. The MBA had expired with great fanfare at the end of 1991, but the 1951 Mutual Defense Treaty linking the two countries remained in force, and while the new Philippine constitution forbade "foreign military bases, troops, or facilities," it said nothing about the presence of "visiting" forces. Before the bases even closed, troop visits began with joint military exercises in 1991. In February 1998, the two countries finalized a Visiting Forces Agreement (VFA) that formalized the visits. US Ambassador Thomas Hubbard assured Filipinos the VFA was merely a tool "to ensure that Philippine and U.S. forces can train together" and that "the bases era is dead and gone," but progressives feared the return of the old military relationship.[83]

During the debate over the MBA in September 1991, Senator Ernesto Maceda had argued the Senate's verdict would "determine the conduct of our domestic and foreign policies and the character of our democracy for centuries to come." As the dust started to settle in the halls of the Philippine Senate, President George H. W. Bush assured Filipinos that "we remain a Pacific power" and "we will maintain a visible, credible presence in the Asia-Pacific region." Soon thereafter, as US troop visits and joint exercises expanded, President Bill Clinton explained that "the closure of our bases there has not changed the basis for continuing cooperation between our two nations." It slowly became clear that very little was actually going to change. Only six years after they left—before they were ever really gone, actually—US military forces were back in the Philippines.[84]

It was an unsatisfying end to the People Power revolution. On both sides of the Pacific, Filipinos and their allies had taken great risks in the hopes of transformation: change not only of a single regime but of an entire country and its relationship with the United States. In the wake of the Cold War, communities next to the bases struggled to make ends meet, and local politicians—more adept at maintaining order and shaking down the Americans—were ill-equipped to lead a transformation to the new world order. Instead, they simply tried to get the Americans to return, a desire expressed in national public opinion polling and shared by plenty of the ordinary residents of Olongapo and Angeles. Among them was seventy-nine-year-old Teresita Meredith, who told an interviewer in the late 1990s that "the only time it was good here was during the Vietnam war. . . . It was good while it lasted. I think it would help our country if the Americans were back." She would soon get her wish.[85]

CHAPTER TEN

TERROR MIGRATIONS

2001–2009

Marlyn Bautista generally liked to get to work early, "just to get things started." Bautista, who was born in the Philippines, lived in Iselin, New Jersey, and had recently naturalized as a US citizen. On the morning of September 11, 2001, she arrived at her job in the accounts payable department at Marsh & McLennan, a consulting company with offices in the north tower of Manhattan's World Trade Center. She never came home. Manuel Lopez, a fifty-four-year-old tax manager who lived in Jersey City's Filipino neighborhood and worked with Bautista at Marsh & McLennan, didn't come home either. Hector Tamayo left the Philippines in 1980, found work with a civil engineering firm in the World Trade Center's south tower, and set up a home in Holliswood, Queens, where he welcomed other Filipino immigrants. "As a joke we call his house the Ellis Island," his sister-in-law explained. He did not come home either. Nor did some twenty other Filipino New Yorkers who died in the terrorist attacks that day.[1]

Jose Pineda, who was twenty-four years old and had just moved back to New York after finishing college in Manila, watched their deaths on the news. "I was just basically glued to the TV," he later recalled, "because I actually wasn't working then." Soon Pineda had a new job, at $12.00 an hour, cleaning bones for medical examiners working at Ground Zero. "I was kind of hesitant to actually work on that, because it was kind of eerie," he recalled. "But, I guess I needed a job, so it was a good stepping stone."[2]

Thousands of miles from New York City, fear accompanied Filipinos' concern for loved ones on the morning of September 11. Within weeks, as a Philippine government official warned that "terror migrations" might bring al-Qaeda operatives to the Muslim regions of the southern Philippines, another group of Filipinos made their own migrations, as they started construction jobs with a subcontractor hired by the American military service firm KBR. Working around the clock, they earned just under $900 a month, good wages by Philippine standards. But work conditions and surveillance prompted them to complain. "Why are you doing this to us, keeping us like prisoners?" they asked. "You should treat us better. We were the ones who built the prisons of your enemy." Their contract site? Guantanamo Bay Naval Station.[3]

The events of September 11 appeared at first glance to turn back the clock to 1898. As the United States and the Philippines joined a global war on terror, Filipino soldiers guarding military sites in Basra recalled familiar images of Pacific partnership. But so much was different—both in the US military and in immigration patterns. Filipinos migrated in numbers greater than ever before, but more often than not they chose destinations other than the United States. Meanwhile, a high-tech revolution in military affairs, together with manpower policies that focused on outsourcing and contracting, reworked Filipinos' connections to the US armed forces.

The global war on terror brought US soldiers to the Philippines, Filipinos to Guantánamo, Filipino Americans to Iraq, and Filipino World

War II veterans to Capitol Hill, where in 2009, veterans and their advocates finally (if bittersweetly) won passage of equitable benefits for the last surviving veterans. As the Philippines welcomed US troops who battled Muslim insurgents and watched naval vessels in South China Sea, a new kind of war bound the United States and the Philippines together in new ways. "Rapport" and "interoperability" between "exercise counterparts" replaced fraternal phrases that had grown musty since the days of Matthew Batson and the Philippine Scouts. But as "third country nationals" did the same work that *cargadores* had undertaken in 1898 and US Navy stewards and messmen had performed in the Cold War, Filipinos still claimed a place for themselves within the US military. America's first and most enduring Pacific partnership continued to serve as the foundation for US power in Asia.

BY THE TWENTY-FIRST CENTURY, FILIPINOS TOOK MIGRATION for granted. At least six million Filipinos—from a population of eighty million—were working abroad in 2001, some in the United States, but most elsewhere: as construction workers in Saudi Arabia and the Gulf states; as domestics in Japan, Hong Kong, and Italy; as nurses and caregivers in Canada and Israel. Unlike in the twentieth century, most migrants were women. Most intended to—and actually did—return, and in the meantime, they sent money. In 1998, Filipinos transferred $6.5 billion in remittances from abroad; by 2005, it was close to $10 billion. "We dream of a society that will never be torn apart just for the need to survive," the advocacy group Migrante International announced, but migration accelerated the Philippine economy and empowered Filipino workers, who brought back new skills and whose remittances smoothed the economy's ups and downs.[4]

As families spread across borders and time zones, a complex network of government agencies, placement services, travel bureaus, and moneychangers structured global migrations more intensely than anything Hawaiian pineapple pickers or US Navy stewards had experienced. New inventions, too, perhaps most notably the balikbayan box, a standard-size shipping box designed for *balikbayan*, or "people coming home": a container into which Filipino migrants placed what critic E. San Juan Jr. described as "all kinds of goods, legal or contraband, genuine or spurious signs of duty or status-jockeying." Packed inside were US dollars, South Korean pop music, or Japanese electronics. Also in the balikbayan box was a political consciousness shaped by Filipinos' sense of themselves as migrants. National loyalties and identifications had become fluid, and the term "diaspora" emerged more frequently; but although the term was new, diaspora itself was not. Filipinos had moved between nations and cultures for more than a century.[5]

Migration turned overseas Filipino workers (OFWs) into what the Philippine government called "new heroes of the nation." Politicians quickly learned they were judged on how well they protected overseas Filipinos. News, protest, and gossip traveled over the internet and cell phones, and stories of migrants in trouble became the stuff of Philippine tabloids and transnational soap operas. At the turn of the twenty-first century, high-profile cases of OFWs facing prosecution in foreign legal systems captured the attention of Filipinos at home and abroad. Most dramatically, when the government of Singapore executed domestic worker Flor Contemplacion in March 1995 on a controversial murder charge, the verdict provoked political crisis in the Philippines and a temporary suspension of joint naval exercises between the two nations.[6]

Regulations laid down during martial law made the Philippine government the official labor broker for international contracts with private corporations and military contractors. Aggressive "labor diplomacy" gave the government a hold on migrants, their capital, and, in turn, their votes. Workers, though, set their own priorities: during the Contemplacion crisis, when President Fidel Ramos offered Philippine military aircraft to bring home all 70,000 OFWs in Singapore, only eighty people took advantage of his offer. Thanks to globalization and the end of the Cold War, new figures symbolized the US-Philippine relationship: where once stood the Filipino Navy steward, there was a Filipina caregiver; remittances replaced military aid; call centers now employed more people than the bases ever did. In fact, business process outsourcing could incorporate Filipinos in the US economy without migration, as thousands worked the phone lines or chat rooms for American companies without ever leaving the Philippines.[7]

Still, beneath the surface, key continuities linked migrant patterns to the Philippines' military past. First of all, there were habits and traditions. Filipinos continued moving to the United States because they had already been doing so. American popular culture and consumer goods still formed the tastes and ambitions of young migrants. "The U.S. is the ultimate," explained Rosalie Portagana, a nurse who aspired to migrate there. "If you make it to the U.S., there is no place else to go." Then, too, immigration followed legal opportunity. Migrants who entered the United States as veterans—including the 17,000 who took advantage of the World War II veteran naturalization provisions of the 1990 Immigration Act—could sponsor their relatives in turn.[8]

The 1990s marked a high-water mark of migration to the United States as the Filipino American population reached 2.6 million in the 2000 census—and 3.4 million a decade later. Historic destinations such as San Diego, Los Angeles, and Honolulu continued to draw Filipino migrants. In fact, the 2010 census reported Filipinos were the largest ethnic group in the state of Hawai'i. But increasingly, Filipino Americans lived everywhere, no longer settling in West Coast ethnic enclaves, nor even in cities, choosing like most other middle-class Americans to live in the suburbs. Van Nuys, Arleta, Northridge, and North Hills in LA's San Fernando Valley; the Bay Area's Daly City, San Bruno, and Vallejo; and

National City outside San Diego featured some of the highest concentrations of Filipinos in the mainland United States. The fastest growth rates were actually outside the Pacific coast region in states such as Texas and Florida. Naval stations were no longer reliable predictors of Filipino communities.[9]

In the United States, unskilled Filipino workers found jobs in the service sector and caregiving, with perhaps as many as 500,000 of them working in the shadows as undocumented migrants. (Several undocumented Filipinos, in fact, were left unemployed after the 9/11 attacks.) But Filipinos increasingly found high-skill jobs at firms that sponsored their H1B visas, continuing a two-tier class structure of professional elites and working-class migrants, the latter now found in service sector jobs rather than farms or canneries. Migrants' children, educated at above-average levels, moved into the middle class. Filipino Americans navigated their relationship to other Asian ethnic groups and to communities of color, particularly in majority-minority states such as Hawai'i and California. As Asian American politicians rose to higher positions in government, relatively few of them were Filipinos.[10]

Identity politics displaced the Cold War conflicts that had shaped the martial law generation. This came with an ironic twist: just as national heroism in the Philippines was taking on new meanings unrelated to military service, something different was happening in the United States. There, tight links between American patriotism and military service made Filipino veterans evocative symbols both of Filipino Americans' loyalties and the American government's broken promises. A narrative of the forgotten veteran, harvested from post-Vietnam popular culture, mixed with an older politics of heroism and valor. At the same time, Filipino Americans who came of age during the 1990s culture wars found that multiculturalism, welfare, and immigration politics also led them to take up the cause of Filipino World War II veterans. Recast from anticommunist Cold Warriors to forgotten *manongs*, the veterans came to stand for the Filipino experience in

America. Both would be put to work in the days and weeks after the September 11 attacks.

Seated in the Philippine presidential palace at Malacanang on September 11, 2001, was Gloria Macapagal Arroyo, daughter of 1960s president Diosdado Macapagal and a former classmate of US President Bill Clinton at Georgetown University. Arroyo came to power after a wave of popular disgust dislodged her predecessor, Joseph Estrada, a former movie star charged with plundering the treasury in July 2000. When impeachment proceedings against Estrada stalled, Filipinos issued their own ruling, taking to the streets in January 2001 to overthrow the president just as they had done fifteen years earlier to Ferdinand Marcos. Operating from hastily assembled headquarters just off Manila's main highway, Arroyo and her allies in one faction of the Armed Forces of the Philippines (AFP) coordinated the protests that culminated in Estrada's resignation. US officials insisted that "we've got an ally status, it never ended," but Arroyo found little support from the new administration of US President George W. Bush, which was not focused on Southeast Asia until Arroyo started using the new language of terror to describe Muslim separatist movements in the southern Philippines.[11]

Political violence was nothing new in the Philippines, but after September 11, ongoing insurgencies took on a new appearance almost overnight. Longstanding tensions over minority rights and regional autonomy in Mindanao had, by the late 1990s, degenerated into a civil war that killed at least 120,000 people, mostly civilians, with another two million displaced from their homes and ancestral communities. A 1996 ceasefire agreement brought peace between the government and the Moro National Liberation Front (MNLF). The more militantly jihadist Moro Islamic Liberation Front (MILF), formed in the

1980s, continued to resist accommodation with either the military or the MNLF, until it, too, signed a tentative ceasefire agreement with the Arroyo government in August 2001.[12]

Some insurgents, especially in the MILF, built on global networks of Islamic radicalism. Soon after Iran's 1979 revolution, leaders there hosted MNLF rebels at training camps. At some point in the 1980s, a young Afghan *mujahid* named Osama bin Laden pressed his brother-in-law Mohammed Jamal Khalifa to recruit Muslim rebels from the Philippines to join the Afghan war. Hashim Salamat, Mindanao-based leader of the jihadist-minded MILF, sent volunteers. In turn, Khalifa later supported MILF activities in the southern Philippines through the International Islamic Relief Organization (IIRO), a charity he founded in 1988, traveling to the Philippines at least through 1995 and perhaps as late as 1998. In 1999, Al Haj Murad, the MILF chief of staff, claimed that Osama bin Laden provided the financing for IIRO until bin Laden retreated to Afghanistan, after which the funds dried up. Central Asian jihadist soldiers may have trained at MILF headquarters at a remote camp in Mindanao until the AFP raided the site in July 2000, killing some Pakistani experts and leaders along with the MILF trainees.[13]

By the early 1990s, the MILF found itself challenged by a rival group with a more militant approach to its goal of Muslim autonomy in the southern Philippines. Abu Sayyaf, meaning "sword bearer" or "executioner," was founded by Abdurajak Abubakar Janjalani, born and raised in Basilan in the southern Philippines. Janjalani studied in Saudi Arabia and spent time in Libya and Afghanistan, where he interacted with the *mujahedeen*, then returned to Basilan in the late 1980s and mobilized the most radical MILF soldiers into his new army. With money from bin Laden's brother-in-law Mohammed Jamal Khalifa, the Abu Sayyaf Group (ASG) became more ambitious, launching a grenade attack in 1991, and then targeting Christian missionaries for kidnappings, which in turn yielded ransoms that swelled the organization's coffers. An April 1995 raid on the city of Ipil near Zamboanga killed more than fifty people and announced that ASG was a serious player.[14]

As homegrown radical organizations had done for decades, Abu Sayyaf tried to build connections between Philippine concerns and like-minded global movements. The closest link between Abu Sayyaf and al-Qaeda came during a brief period that Ramzi Yousef, the Pakistani radical who masterminded the February 1993 bombing of New York's World Trade Center, spent in hiding in the Philippines. In 1991, two years before the attack, Yousef traveled to the Philippines, and in early 1992, he met with ASG's Janjalani in Basilan, where the two reportedly discussed Yousef's desire to use Mindanao as "a launching pad" for a global campaign of terror. At some point a few months after the New York bombings, Yousef fled to the Philippines via Pakistan.[15]

In Manila, Yousef and his uncle Khalid Sheikh Mohammed planned Operation Bojinka, a plot to blow up twelve commercial airplanes in flight over the Pacific. Mohammed (known to US officials by his initials, KSM) left the Philippines in September 1994, leaving Yousef and his team to case airports in Manila, Seoul, and Hong Kong and test explosives at a Manila movie theater. On a December 11, 1994, training mission, they planted a bomb on a Philippine Airlines flight, killing one passenger. Yousef and Janjalani also plotted—reportedly at bin Laden's direction—to assassinate President Bill Clinton during his November 1994 visit to the Philippines and may have been targeting Pope John Paul II before his January 1995 tour. When a chemical explosion in the plotters' Manila apartment prompted a quick evacuation, Yousef ran downstairs and was spotted by a security guard. He abandoned Operation Bojinka, fled to Pakistan, and was arrested in Islamabad in February 1995. But he took with him to Pakistan an idea, hatched in the wake of the Philippine Airlines attack, which he certainly discussed with his fellow plotter, Abdul Hakim Murad, and may have discussed with KSM: instead of blowing up planes, why not use them as weapons? Perhaps, Yousef asked Murad, a hijacked plane could be flown into the CIA headquarters?[16]

As for Abu Sayyaf's Janjalani, Philippine police assassinated him in Basilan in 1998. His brother Khadafy Janjalani took over, but Abu Sayyaf never recovered and steadily declined into a criminal organization with a loosely jihadist ideology. Kidnapping still provided Abu Sayyaf a steady income, and as money poured into Basilan, recruits emerged from the ranks of the poor. In May 2001, ASG kidnapped another twenty tourists from a resort in the Palawan Islands, among them three Americans: missionaries Martin and Gracia Burnham and Guillermo Sobero. ASG beheaded Sobero in June 2001, and Martin Burnham was later killed in an AFP-led rescue attempt. Well before the 9/11 attacks, ASG's tenuous connections to Islamist ideology likely made al-Qaeda operatives skeptical of its reliability as a partner in global jihad. Nur Misuari, founder of the rival MNLF, explained in November 2001 that "knowing bin Laden, I don't think he would attach himself to such dirty people."[17]

Indeed, radical factions in Mindanao probably had no more interest in being a marginal appendage of a Middle East–dominated global Islamic insurgency network than they did in being a powerless minority in a Philippine province. Separatism and jihad were minor themes in Filipino politics, and the groups' most important connections were to local and regional networks of weapons and funding. Even during the peak of Abu Sayyaf activity in the 1990s, few of its opponents called for a massive response from the Philippine military, and none for direct US intervention. The decision after September 11 to call these groups "Islamic terrorists" was a political move determined by global politics, not domestic realities.[18]

Nevertheless, President Arroyo's response on September 12 was swift. In the immediate aftermath of the attacks on the United States, she announced that as part of Philippine support for the war in Afghanistan, she was permitting US access to its former bases at Clark and Subic, and noted that her government was investigating Khalifa's charity, the IIRO. On September 24, the US blocked banking activities by Abu Sayyaf, which was already on the US government's list of terrorist organizations. The Philippine National Security Council met days after the attacks to discuss a request for US military aid, and despite Arroyo's insistence that "there won't be a 'shopping list,'" the council in fact drew up a list. "The biggest issue," reported Representative Gerry Salapuddin, "wasn't whether military aid should be sought, but how to go about it."[19]

Within weeks, the Philippines had become the "second front" in the Global War on Terror. Speaking at an event supporting ASG captives Martin and Gracia Burnham, Kansas senator Sam Brownback noted that "it appears the Philippines is going to be the second, the next target, after Afghanistan in the war on terrorism." Deputy Secretary of Defense Paul Wolfowitz also sounded the alarm: "These guys have figured out that Southeast Asia . . . [is] an easier place to operate for them than the pretty repressive regimes in the Middle East." As news reports warned of al-Qaeda's global reach, Philippine security leaders—along with US FBI director Robert Mueller—wondered whether American raids were pushing terrorists out of Afghanistan and into more distant regions through a dynamic that Concepcion Clamor, the Assistant Director-General of the Philippine National Intelligence Coordinating Agency, called "terror migration."[20]

Opening the war on terror's second front required reestablishing the military partnership that had been partly sundered in the wake of People Power. As the Philippine government quickly folded itself into American antiterrorism policies, that did not take long. In late September 2001, the commander of the US Pacific Fleet met with Philippine officials on the presidential yacht in Subic Bay, and by late October, just six weeks after 9/11, the first US soldiers arrived in the

Philippines. Secretary of Defense Donald Rumsfeld announced that twenty-three counterterrorism experts—along with military equipment and a pack of bloodhounds—were headed to Basilan to advise and train the AFP. A Pentagon spokesman explained that "Abu Sayyaf is not just a Philippine problem," but posed "as much of a threat to the U.S. as to the Philippines." Radical leader Jose Maria Sison denounced President Arroyo's "abject servility to the US," and in Mindanao, Reverend Eliseo Mercado Jr. noted that "now you've got American troops in camouflage uniforms going into Muslim villages. In the long run, that will radicalize the Muslims."[21]

In November, Arroyo traveled to Washington, where George Bush promised a $100 million aid package, including a US Coast Guard cutter, several helicopters, 30,000 rifles, and cash earmarked for development projects in Mindanao. Behind closed doors, to Arroyo and her Secretary of National Defense Angelo Reyes, Bush suggested much more. "We are offering American forces to fight in the Philippines," Reyes recalled the president saying. Arroyo declined: "No, no. We don't need American forces because our soldiers are good." At a press conference, Bush explained that "we've got no better friend in that part of the world than the Philippines," but both presidents evaded questions about sending US ground troops to fight ASG. In December, following up on Bush's assertion that "the front against terror is not just in Afghanistan," US officials announced Operation Enduring Freedom—Philippines, denoting the Philippines as an official partner in the global war on terror. Soon thereafter followed the largest US counterterrorism deployment outside Afghanistan.[22]

It was called Balikatan ("Shoulder to Shoulder"), and it wasn't new. Joint exercises between the US and Philippine armed forces began in 1991 before the bases were even closed. The Philippine Supreme Court stopped them in 1995, but they resumed in 1999 under the Visiting Forces Agreement. After 9/11, Balikatan offered a useful umbrella under which the United States could return to the Philippines. In January

2002, some 1,300 US troops, including 150 Special Operations soldiers, 660 Marines, and 300 Navy engineers—a force that Secretary of Defense Donald Rumsfeld called "not a modest number"—joined their Filipino "exercise counterparts" on Basilan Island. The initiative, little discussed in the United States and not debated by the US Congress, nevertheless reflected US foreign policy priorities more than Philippine political realities.[23]

Balikatan ostensibly focused on "mutual counter-terrorism advising, assisting and training" in equipment use, and interoperability "relative to Philippine efforts against the Abu Sayyaf Group." This was hardly a training mission, though, as military forces don't typically hold exercises in the middle of a combat zone, and the six-month duration of the annual Balikatan exercise suggested a semi-permanent military presence for the United States. Secretary of State Colin Powell assured American audiences that "this is nothing like Vietnam." But in Manila, administration critic and former senator Francisco Tatad fumed that by using military training exercises to bring US troops into combat with Abu Sayyaf, Arroyo had succeeded, "in one deceptive and treasonous move, . . . in making the Philippines a virtual extension of Afghanistan." Balikatan did little to dislodge Abu Sayyaf. Instead, it destabilized its fragile peace process, radicalized some local Muslim Filipinos, poured unmarked bills and pilfered weapons into Mindanao, and forced the ASG deeper into thuggery and violence. From the Middle East, an al-Qaeda propagandist praised a new round of ASG attacks in June 2002 as "but a tiny part of the exchange for those killed" by Western powers. "America knows only the language of force," he wrote. "America is kept at bay by blood alone."[24]

Arroyo, for her part, embraced the language of force and the new global war on terror. In her State of the Nation Address on July 22, 2002, Arroyo called for a "total offensive" on internal security issues to "break the back of all forms of terrorism and criminality," and widened her operations beyond the jihadists of Mindanao. On August 3,

2002, Secretary of State Colin Powell visited the Philippines, and just a few days later, the US government placed the Communist Party of the Philippines (CPP) and its armed wing, the New People's Army (NPA), on America's list of foreign terrorist organizations, as Arroyo and Powell saw eye to eye on the second front of the war on terror. The NPA's Maoist-inspired rebels counted no more than a few thousand armed members, down about half from their peak in the mid-1980s, and decimated by internecine fighting in the 1990s that tore apart the CPP. Powell's move failed: a freeze on CPP assets meant it had to raise money illegally, so it turned to extortion and racketeering. Arroyo's plea backfired as well, making her look like a political opportunist and an American puppet.[25]

Tellingly, and surely at Arroyo's request, Secretary Powell's list of terrorist organizations did not include either the MNLF or the MILF, the two largest Muslim separatist groups. In 2002, Arroyo was actively negotiating with both of them and opposed labeling either a terrorist group, despite the fact that the MILF was surely far better connected to regional and global terror networks than the beleaguered ASG. Arroyo's position upset American officials, who worried that Mindanao was a terrorist "breeding ground" that needed to be shut down once and for all. There were reasons to be concerned: when an Abu Sayyaf bombing outside a karaoke bar in Zamboanga in October 2002 killed two Filipinos and an American soldier, Sergeant First Class Mark Wayne Jackson, it challenged the AFP's assertion that ASG was a "spent force."[26]

Balikatan 03, a much larger joint exercise set for February 2003 on the island of Jolo, was far more than a training mission. Plans called for US forces to engage in direct combat, to use airpower, and in fact gave no end date to the operation, its reach newly amplified by a Mutual Logistics Support Agreement that allowed the US military to use Philippine sites for landing, refueling, stockpiling, and other aspects of the war on terror. On February 21, 2003, the United States quietly announced it would send more than 1,700 troops—some 350 Special Forces soldiers and more than 1,000 marines with Cobra helicopters—to Jolo "to disrupt and destroy" Abu Sayyaf. The Bush administration announced that "the intent is for US troops to actively participate," prompting protests in the Philippines, where Secretary of Foreign Affairs Blas Ople dismissed Pentagon descriptions of Balikatan as statements of "junior officials who don't know what they are talking about." Arroyo administration officials even went so far as to deny that US troops were in country. Pentagon officials fumed, insisting that "as we have stated, the U.S. and Philippine government have agreed to conduct combined operations in the southern Philippines to disrupt and defeat the Abu Sayyaf group." Later revelations from US State Department cables documented that American military forces actively participated in combat operations and US officials denied it, sticking to the story that they were there to "advise, train, and share information with AFP forces."[27]

Widespread protests challenged Balikatan's effort to turn the southern Philippines into a theater of the global war on terror. Opposition senator Aquilino Pimentel warned that "if American troops will be deployed [to Mindanao], that would be viewed as nothing short of an invasion by foreign troops. It would be Vietnam reincarnated in Sulu." Protestors in the city of Jolo announced, "We will not let history repeat itself! Yankee back off!" while others recalled the US assault on Muslim Filipinos at Bud Dajo in 1906. "The wounds over the massacre of our forefathers by the American colonialists have not been healed," asserted Temojin Tulawie during a February 2003 radio program. Popular opinion was mixed. Some 84 percent of respondents in a Philippine poll said they approved of Balikatan. One US Special Forces officer deemed Balikatan a public relations success: "When we arrived in Basilan, Muslim kids made throat-slashing gestures at us. By the time we left, they were our friends."[28]

Inspired by the renewed US-Philippine military alliance, Gloria Arroyo increasingly flexed her muscle against opponents under the umbrella of counterterrorism. Oplan Bantay Laya (Operation Freedom Watch) targeted leftist movements, church groups, and labor unions. "The government considers as suspect and subversive anyone who helps and is on the side of the poor," claimed Melissa Roxas, a Filipino American radical abducted by a squad of AFP soldiers in May 2009. The Human Security Act of 2007, an omnibus antiterrorism bill modeled in part on the USA PATRIOT Act of 2001, criminalized groups that created a "condition of widespread and extraordinary fear and panic among the populace." Arroyo used that provision with a heavy hand against her domestic opponents. In April 2009, the United Nations Committee against Torture issued a report denouncing the "widespread use of torture" and the "climate of impunity" that surrounded the Human Security Act.[29]

At first glance, Balikatan resembled the partnership in the war on terror that the Bush and Arroyo administrations said it was. Phrases such as "capability enhancement" and "rapport and interoperability" were twenty-first-century iterations of the language of military fraternalism that had brought American and Filipino soldiers together as allies in Korea and Vietnam. But as US helicopters flew over Pershing Plaza in the southern Philippine city of Zamboanga, some very old ways of thinking persisted. In classified cables, US intelligence agencies praised "the conservative Philippine defense establishment—whose doctrine, equipment, and training are all US-based." The unequal relationship was not lost on the CPP's Jose Maria Sison, who taunted the AFP that "they are not at all ashamed that the US proclaims to the whole world that [they] do not know how to fight the Abu Sayyaf group, unless military officers and men advise, train and command them." Balikatan, designed to serve new US security interests, replicated colonial conditions.[30]

On the ground, Filipino soldiers stood shoulder to shoulder with Americans, as their fathers and grandfathers had done. Like them, the new generation of soldiers had to figure out how to reconcile their personal and national ambitions with the demands of America's wars in Asia. Filipino Muslims made difficult choices, too, as they moved opportunistically or unwillingly between the MILF and Abu Sayyaf, or navigated between the AFP and private militias. The global war on terror's rhetoric led Americans to misunderstand the situation and the Filipinos to misrepresent it. The same flexibility of language would mark the Pacific partnership as the Philippines joined the United States in its next war.

As the United States mobilized for war in Iraq, the Philippines briefly appeared in American national consciousness, first as an analogy and then as an ally. Both instances were the work of Bush administration neoconservatives, many of whom embraced imperial policies and, at times, even the political label. "We're an empire now, and when we act, we create our own reality," White House adviser Karl Rove told a reporter in 2004. Commentator Max Boot, describing the Philippine-American War as "one of the most successful counterinsurgencies waged by a Western army in modern times," thought that "America should not be afraid to fight 'the savage wars of peace' if necessary to enlarge 'the empire of liberty.' It has been done before." Many of the Iraq War's architects could also draw on their experiences in the Philippines in the decades before September 11: Donald Rumsfeld had negotiated the failed 1976 basing agreement; John Negroponte, US ambassador to the United Nations, had held the ambassador's post in Manila in the 1990s; Richard Armitage had watched out for Defense Department interests in Southeast Asia in the 1980s and handled the Military Base Agreement negotiations in the late 1980s; Paul Wolfowitz headed the East Asian and Pacific Affairs division at State during the Marcos era.[31]

Analogies came not only from pundits and past experience, but from within the US military itself. Service journals of the 2000s brimmed with articles on counterinsurgency, small wars, and the lessons of 1898. Studies published by mid-career officers detailed to military staff schools boasted of the successful pacification of the Muslim populations of Mindanao a century earlier. One study on the capture of Emilio Aguinaldo in 1901 conceded that "American leaders grossly underestimated the insurgency's strength"—a telling sentence to write May 2004 at the height of the Iraqi insurgency—but concluded that the operation nevertheless "ended in both tactical and strategic success." Lessons were not always learned: CIA Director Michael Hayden later wrote that National Security Adviser Stephen Hadley "regretted not better understanding the history of waterboarding and the association of a technique by the same [*sic*] name with Japanese war criminals and the Philippine insurrection."[32]

Meanwhile, in the Philippines, the Iraq War presented a political challenge. When polled about the possibility of war in February 2003, a mere 2 percent of respondents agreed that the Philippines should "support the US in its fight against Iraq even without UN support." Arroyo pursued the policy anyway, fearful that not doing so would alienate the United States and cut off military aid. But unlike her predecessors, Arroyo couldn't simply please America—she also had to consider her country's relationship with the Middle East. By 2003, nearly 1.4 million Filipinos lived and worked in the region. Remittances from the area contributed nearly 10 percent of the Philippines' GDP, and the country was dependent on the region's oil. Arroyo also feared that war in Iraq might radicalize the Muslim minority in the southern Philippines, many of whom had relatives working abroad. A disproportionate number of Filipino workers in the Middle East were Muslims, displaced by war in Mindanao and drawn by shared religious beliefs. As war clouds prompted calls for Filipino repatriation, economists estimated a $162 million price tag to bring OFWs home. "We are anxiously preparing for the worst," a Filipino nurse working in Baghdad reported to her relatives in New York as Arroyo paid a high-profile visit to Filipinos in Kuwait in February 2003. But the march to war was unstoppable.[33]

On March 20, 2003, just days after the war began, Arroyo announced that the Philippines would join it. "We are part of the coalition of the willing in terms of political and moral support for actions to rid Iraq of weapons of mass destruction. We are part of a long standing security alliance as well as the global coalition against terrorism. This relationship is vital to our national security." Arroyo's approval ratings plummeted to the lowest point in her presidency. She then departed in May for a state dinner in Washington, meant to reward the Philippines for joining the coalition. The visit brought the Philippines official designation as a "major non-NATO ally" and $356 million in additional military equipment, training, and foreign aid, including $95 million for AFP training and economic development in Mindanao.[34]

In return, President Bush visited the Philippines during an Asian tour in October 2003, where, dressed in a cream-colored traditional *barong* shirt, he addressed a joint session of the Philippine legislature. Bush noted the United States and the Philippines were "bound by the strongest ties that two nations can share," and pledged aid "to modernize and reform" the AFP. Then, proclaiming that "America is proud of its part in the great story of the Filipino people," Bush asserted—in an astonishing misreading of history—that "together our soldiers liberated the Philippines from colonial rule." Maybe he was thinking of the Philippine Scouts, whose military service swapped one colonial ruler for another, or maybe he had in mind the guerrilla soldiers of World War II, whose claims for veterans benefits languished unanswered on Capitol Hill. Either way, the history of the US military in the Philippines offered American policy makers evidence not of empire, but of liberation and regime change.[35]

A small contingent of Philippine troops arrived in Iraq in July 2003. They never numbered more than fifty-one soldiers, mostly military police and medics, who served under the command of the Polish-led units of Multinational Forces in the Center South Region just outside Baghdad. They served without incurring a single casualty. Filipino soldiers in Iraq were far outnumbered by Filipino American troops. At the beginning of the war, the US Defense Manpower Data Center estimated that 31,000 noncitizens wore American uniforms, about 20 percent of them Filipinos—a greater fraction than any other country, even Mexico. So many first- and second-generation Filipino Americans enlisted that Defense Department policies awarding bonus pay for service personnel fluent in foreign languages excluded Tagalog as among those languages already "dominant in the force."[36]

Recruited as volunteers, Filipino Americans served in every aspect of the Iraq War. Born in the Philippines and raised in Daly City, California, Marine Lance Corporal OJ Santa Maria was just twenty-one when the Iraq War began. Injured during the initial invasion, he was naturalized as a US citizen in a military hospital outside Washington, with President Bush looking on. "We're proud to have you as an American," Bush told the young marine, who explained that "if I could move my arm, I'd go back to Iraq, sir. I wanted to be back with my platoon, back with my brothers."[37]

Santa Maria was already eligible for US citizenship, but others had to wait until November 2003, when the Bush administration implemented so-called fast-track naturalization provisions that awarded US citizenship following just one year of military service. Among the fast-trackers were Specialists Jobert Floresca and James Garrovillas, who both joined the US Army after September 11. "My whole family was U.S. citizens, and I'm the only one who wasn't a U.S. citizen," Floresca observed at his naturalization ceremony, conducted at Camp Victory, a US Army installation set up in a former palace of Saddam Hussein. Garrovillas was thrilled. "I think it's awesome. I've waited for years to get it. It's nice having it in a palace in Iraq. It beats having it in the United States." Citizenship could even be awarded posthumously, as it was to Marine Gunnery Sergeant Joseph Menusa, who enlisted in California and was killed in the first days of the war.[38]

Uniformed military service gathered a few dozen Philippine soldiers and a few thousand Filipino Americans. The real contribution of Filipinos to the Iraq War derived from a new US military personnel policy that relied on military contractors to manage the occupation of postwar Iraq. Within weeks of the war's beginning, Roberto Romulo, the head of the Philippine Task Force for the Reconstruction of Iraq, arrived in Washington to meet military contractors and persuade US Defense Department officials that as a partner in the Coalition of the Willing, Filipinos should have "preferential treatment" in civilian labor contracts. American aid to the Philippines, finalized by Arroyo and Bush during her May 2003 Washington visit, not only funded Philippine troops but the recruitment and pay of OFWs in postwar Iraq. With so many workers already in the Persian Gulf, finding laborers would not be difficult, and in fact, around 4,000 workers had already made their way by the summer of 2004 to jobs in Iraq. US military contractors' employment of third-country nationals (TCNs) reflected a shift under way for a generation: the US military was leaner and meaner, reliant on highly trained career service members. Simultaneously, private-sector firms all across the industrialized world were increasingly outsourcing basic labor tasks to contractors, and the Defense Department learned their lessons of cost efficiency. But as the war's popularity declined in 2004, TCNs also helped the Pentagon to reduce the number of US forces on the ground. It was the same calculation Matthew Batson made when he advocated the formation of the Philippine Scouts a century earlier.[39]

Having already built a worldwide network to control flows of migrant workers, the Philippines was well placed to put its citizens to work on behalf of US foreign policy and to call them "heroes of the nation" for doing so. To manage workers' placement, the Philippine government relied on the same government-controlled labor contracting bureaucracy Ferdinand Marcos had established three decades earlier. One account reported that some 80 percent of OFWs found work with Prime Projects International, a subcontractor for US-based security firm KBR (formerly Kellogg, Brown and Root). Prime placed some OFWs at Camp Victory outside Baghdad, where they may have watched as Jobert Floresca and James Garrovillas took their naturalization oaths. Filipinos and other TCNs did mundane tasks such as cooking and hairdressing, and even filled a contract for US firm Halliburton to kill feral cats in Baghdad's Green Zone. They earned salaries tied not to the US minimum wage or Iraqi combat pay but to the prevailing wage scales in the Philippines. TCNs' work was not lost on al-Qaeda. In an open letter "to the Muslims of Iraq," al-Qaeda condemned the United States "for having drafted the dregs of humanity and gone to beg for mercenaries from east and west."[40]

One of those workers was Angelo de la Cruz. In early 2004, de la Cruz was forty-six years old, married, and the father of eight children. He left his family behind in the small city of Buenavista in the Philippine province of Pampanga—about twenty miles from Macabebe—to take a job as a truck driver with a Saudi Arabian construction firm. The Saudis generally placed drivers in booming Gulf cities such as Riyadh or Dubai, but by 2004, the firm was pursuing contracting opportunities with the US-led occupation and reconstruction of Iraq. And so at some point that year, Angelo de la Cruz started working in Iraq, drawn by the triple salary that compensated for dangerous work conditions.[41]

On July 6, 2004, while driving an oil tanker back to Saudi Arabia after a delivery to the war-torn city of Fallujah, de la Cruz was abducted by the insurgent Islamic Army in Iraq. His kidnappers called on the Philippines to withdraw the contingent of fifty-one soldiers and police officers who made up its token contribution to coalition forces in Iraq. They gave President Arroyo two weeks. In the United States, this was not headline news. De la Cruz was just one of many foreign workers—Bulgarians, Pakistanis, Turks, Jordanians, Kuwaitis, Egyptians, Lebanese, South Koreans, and Americans—who had been abducted or killed since the beginning of the war. Nor was he even the first Filipino kidnapped: insurgents killed three Filipino workers in early 2004, an event that prompted many Filipino OFWs to leave Iraq.[42]

In the Philippines, however, de la Cruz's abduction was an explosion. The war had never been popular in the Philippines, and in fact, the government had already committed to an August 20 troop withdrawal date. President Arroyo also knew she held a tenuous hold on political power in the wake of a contested (and possibly irregular) election she won in May 2004. That summer, interviews with de la Cruz's relatives played on Philippine television and the Al Jazeera network, prayer vigils convened in Manila and Pampanga, some 4,000 Catholic clergy signed petitions, and phone calls arrived from nervous American diplomats who had already lost Spain, Honduras, Nicaragua, Norway, and the Dominican Republic from the Coalition of the Willing. President Arroyo now found herself in an impossible position. On the one hand, her political standing abroad obliged her to curry favor with the United States, a role that would have required standing firm in Iraq, refusing to negotiate, and possibly sacrificing de la Cruz. On the other hand, her political survival at home depended on demonstrating that the Philippine state could protect overseas workers by intervening with diplomacy or even ransom to bring OFWs home.[43]

At first, Arroyo announced that she would not give in to the terrorists' demands. Meanwhile, popular pressure grew to meet the kidnappers' demand for a July 20 withdrawal, with administration critic Paul Quintos asserting that "Arroyo's boot-licking stains her regime with the blood-soaked boots of U.S. imperialism" and the Communist Party of the Philippines insisting that the "Arroyo regime is responsible for putting the lives of Filipino workers . . . in danger" to please the United States. Arroyo barred any further Filipino migration to Iraq, while

Secretary of Foreign Affairs Delia Albert dug in her heels: "In line with our commitment to the free people of Iraq, we reiterate our plan to return our humanitarian contingent as scheduled on August 20."[44]

Protests by peace groups and migrant advocates continued. On Tuesday July 13, as police used water cannons to break up a Manila rally, Arroyo convened an emergency cabinet meeting, at which she decided to withdraw the troops. Arroyo initially remained vague in the wake of the session. A spokesman said the troops would leave "as soon as possible" but did not confirm the earlier July 20 pullout date. The next day, July 14, the troops started to leave. "As of today, our head count is down from 51 to 43," Secretary Delia Albert announced. De la Cruz was still nowhere to be found.[45]

Then, on Thursday July 15, Arroyo announced that the Philippine contingent would be returning one month earlier than its scheduled departure, and de la Cruz finally appeared on Al Jazeera television news. In Manila, crowds cheered, but American officials were furious. "We think that withdrawal sends the wrong signal," growled Richard Boucher, a State Department spokesman. "It is important for people to stand up to terrorists and not allow them to change our behavior." General John Abizaid, commander of US forces, thought it "regrettable [that] we lose a member of the coalition and regrettable countries are . . . appeasing terrorists as opposed to standing up to them."[46]

Arroyo paid a heavy price for choosing domestic politics over Bush's global alliance. Other coalition partners and close allies criticized the Philippines; Australia's foreign minister called the decision "marshmallowlike." US Ambassador Francis Ricciardone—who admitted to the press that American officials "were quite surprised" by Arroyo's decision—affirmed that "we are allies. We are here for you." But the State Department quickly cut off military and economic aid like a parent trimming a child's allowance. When eighty-nine Filipinos held in US immigration custody were deported that week, it had nothing to do with Iraq, but Filipino Americans understood and discussed it as diplomatic retribution.[47]

Philippine Senate majority leader Francis Pangilinan remained unapologetic: "If the U.S. and Australia had a million unarmed citizens in the Middle East," he noted, "their view would be starkly different." Representative Teodoro Casiño believed the rift was only temporary. Arroyo, he thought, "will definitely make it up to the U.S." But the *New York Times* opined that "terrorists in Iraq scored a victory. Manila's retreat will only place all other foreign nationals in Iraq in greater peril." Perhaps as many as 6,000 Filipinos defied the ban on travel and entered Iraq illegally. One woman later reported torture at the hands of her Iraqi employer, who "bragged to friends that he treated her like a prisoner from the Abu Ghraib prison in Iraq."[48]

Finally, on the morning of Tuesday July 20, immediately after the Philippines withdrew its contingent, de la Cruz, dressed in a gray polo shirt, with long, shaggy hair, was delivered to the Philippine embassy in Baghdad. On television, Arroyo called the crisis "a time of trial and a time of triumph. I made a decision to bring our troops home a few days early in order to spare the life of Angelo. I do not regret that decision. Every life is important." Later, back home in Buenavista, wearing an I Am a Filipino t-shirt, de la Cruz expressed his gratitude. "The president gave value to my life and I will never forget that."[49]

Angelo de la Cruz later migrated to the United States—his uncle lived in California—but he didn't like it. "In America, when you do not have a job, it's bad," he explained. After eighteen months, he went home to the Philippines.[50]

Throughout the 2000s, Filipino World War II veterans' decades-long struggle for equitable benefits from the US government continued. Gloria Arroyo's Washington visits prompted generous military aid but didn't win anything for Filipino veterans, as Bush's desultory response at a November 2001 joint press conference revealed:

> *Q.* Did you ask the U.S. President to support the veterans equity bill?
>
> *President Bush.* The what bill?
>
> *Q.* The Filipino veterans equity bill.
>
> *President Bush.* Oh, the veterans security. She did bring up the issue. And she strongly brought it up, and she was an advocate for the Filipino veterans bill, which has been an issue around here for a long period of time.

On Capitol Hill, advocates repeatedly introduced legislation, and the VA endorsed it from the sidelines, but time and again it stalled in committee or on the floor of the House or Senate. Longstanding assumptions about the foreignness of Filipino soldiers and about the costs of granting full equity persisted. In late 2008, North Carolina senator Richard Burr objected to "aid for foreigners" and warned that equity legislation would take "money away from our veterans in this country."[51]

January 2009 brought a new constellation of forces. Along with the worst economic crisis since the Great Depression came the 111th Congress, which placed Senator Daniel Inouye in the chair's seat of the Senate Committee on Appropriations, Senator Daniel Akaka in charge of the Senate Committee on Veterans' Affairs, and across the Capitol, San Diego's Representative Bob Filner at the head of the House Committee on Veterans' Affairs. Together, they succeeded in folding longstanding proposed legislation for Filipino veterans equity into the American Recovery and Reinvestment Act. "It is about time we close this dark chapter. I love America. I love serving America," intoned Senator Inouye, himself a disabled veteran of the Second World War. "I am proud of this country, but this is a black chapter. It has to be cleansed." Arizona senator John McCain complained that equity had been slipped into an economic stimulus bill. "We are going to give millions of dollars to those who live in the Philippines. Do not label that as job stimulation." Inouye conceded the point: "It does not create jobs. But the honor of the United States is what is involved." McCain, though, remained insistent in his preference for supporting "our own veterans," despite the fact that the beneficiaries of the proposed legislation were, almost without exception, citizens of the United States or eligible for naturalization.[52]

The Recovery Act, signed on February 17, included an authorization of $198 million for a Filipino Veterans Equity Fund, which paid a one-time sum of $15,000 for eligible veterans with US citizenship and $9,000 for veterans who were Philippine citizens. Symbolically, but importantly, the act overturned the spirit (and, for the most part, the letter) of the Rescission Act by designating service in the wartime US Armed Forces in the Far East (USAFFE) as "active service" for the purpose of administering VA and other federal benefits. But there was, again, a quid pro quo. In exchange, the United States would consider all other claims closed as of September 17, 2009.[53]

In public, veterans and their advocates celebrated, but behind closed doors, the conversation was harder, even bitter. They knew the victory was imperfect, and that it would serve all too few of the USAFFE soldiers who had defended and liberated the Philippines between 1941 and 1945. Journalists and congressional researchers estimated the eligible population of Filipino World War II veterans still alive in 2009 at somewhere between 15,000 and 18,000 people (not including survivors also affected by changes in some benefit provisions). About 3,000 of them lived in the United States. Within the law's first year, the VA received 36,000 applications, but the passage of time and the challenge of documenting guerrilla service nearly seven decades after the fact meant that the VA released payments for only 12,400 veteran applicants, about equally divided between citizens and noncitizens.[54]

The achievement of lump-sum payments in the Recovery Act of 2009 came with flourishes of nostalgia and back-patting patriotism. Representative Michael Honda, the chair of the Congressional Asian

Pacific American Caucus, boasted that "after a decades-long struggle, Filipino World War II veterans have finally received the recognition and compensation they deserve for their brave service to the U.S. during World War II." It had all the markings of a happy ending, and on some level, it was. But perhaps Lillian Galedo, co-chair of the National Alliance for Filipino Veterans Equity, was more right than she realized when she described the stimulus as "yet another beginning."[55]

DURING THE ANGELO DE LA CRUZ HOSTAGE CRISIS IN 2004, UN Secretary General Kofi Annan called the Filipino truck driver an "innocent civilian," whereas in her televised address after his release, Gloria Arroyo praised him a "Filipino everyman, a symbol of the hard-working Filipino seeking hope and opportunity." To Filipinos, Angelo de la Cruz was, like Flor Contemplacion before him, a fellow overseas Filipino worker. To the United States government, de la Cruz was a third-country national, an everyman of the twenty-first-century US armed forces. His service to America took place entirely outside the United States. But Angelo de la Cruz was not in Fallujah merely because he responded to the incentives of the labor market. He was brought there by a century of history and by new demands of US foreign policy. On Capitol Hill, Filipino World War II veterans finally won their rights more than sixty years after the broken promises of the Rescission Act, and in the years after the September 11 attacks, even civilians who died that morning were deemed eligible for interment at Arlington National Cemetery. For Angelo de la Cruz, there would be no such honors and no such rights. The United States had made him no promises. The United States owed him no debt.[56]

CHAPTER ELEVEN

THE PIVOT AND AFTER

By the 2010s, the century-long Pacific partnership between the United States and the Philippines found yet another beginning. President George W. Bush left office in January 2009; in June 2010, Gloria Arroyo handed power to her successor, Benigno Aquino III, who promised to complete the reforms that his assassinated father Benigno and revered mother Corazon had initiated. Meanwhile, more than a hundred years after it actually began, the new administration in Washington launched "America's Pacific Century." In November 2011, President Barack Obama announced what he deemed a "fundamental truth": that "the United States has been, and always will be, a Pacific nation." Secretary of State Hillary Clinton declared that the administration would "pivot to new global realities" in Asia.[1]

The pivot—a plan to move American defense resources and personnel from the Middle East to the Pacific—was all about China. Chinese influence raised fears of a growing split between the two historic allies, as the new power's rapid economic growth simultaneously expanded the Philippine economy and detached it from reliance on the United States. With an eye on China's military modernization, the United States continued to assert it was the Philippines' sole means of defense. Obama insisted the Philippines was the "bedrock of security in Asia," while Secretary Clinton gently distinguished the United States from China by asserting that the United States was "the only power with a network of strong alliances in the region, no territorial ambitions, and a long record of providing for the common good." Clinton called for increased ship visits to the Philippines and support for joint special operations in Mindanao. The Enhanced Defense Cooperation Agreement (EDCA), signed by the two countries during a Manila visit by President Barack Obama in April 2014, formalized the ongoing integration of the two nations' militaries that President Fidel Ramos had shaped in the wake of the closure of US military bases. EDCA authorized frequent long-term visits by US forces, while allowing the United States to build facilities at Philippine bases "upon the invitation of the Philippine Armed Forces" and to "preposition" equipment there in anticipation of some future conflict. The terms were almost as favorable as the Military Bases Agreement the two countries signed back in 1947, although unlike the MBA, the new pact had no provisions for the recruitment of Filipinos into the US armed forces. Evan Medeiros, the US National Security Council Director for Asian Affairs, called EDCA "the most significant defense agreement that the United States has concluded with the Philippines in decades." As China watched, the Philippines opened five naval bases to US vessels, and in 2014 convened Balikatan, the annual joint exercises, in the middle of the South China Sea.[2]

The pivot also moved attention (and troops) away from the Middle East just as jihadist politics reverberated in the southern Philippines. As a young radical, Isnilon Hapilon had joined Abu Sayyaf in the 1990s and participated in the kidnapping and killing of American missionaries in Palawan in 2000. By the early 2010s, discontent over land, minority rights, and religious expression persisted throughout the region. Hapilon gathered Abu Sayyaf's remnants under his leadership, and in an internet video circulated in July 2014, the group pledged its allegiance to the Islamic State movement, or ISIS. Hapilon's faction seized control of the southern city of Marawi, and fears of terrorism's "second front" returned. In May 2017, the Philippine military—with US support—brought its full firepower to bear on the dissident group. Five months of shelling and house-to-house assaults left Hapilon dead and Abu Sayyaf scattered once again. But in Marawi tens of thousands had been displaced from their homes, and the city lay in ruins. More than a decade after experts first claimed Mindanao was the soft underbelly of global jihad, the war on terror's second front was still open. US and Philippine politicians once again folded the southern Philippines into a global crisis by viewing local problems through an American lens.[3]

Nor was all well at the presidential palace at Malacanang. More than thirty years later, People Power clearly had not been the transformation it was hailed as on the streets of Manila in February 1986. Politicians prattled on about the "unfinished revolution" but offered little explanation for why its tasks were so long left undone, opening doors for media-savvy populists who tapped everyday resentments. Ordinary Filipinos endured grinding poverty and drug gangs, while a rising middle class demanded public safety, better infrastructure, and an end to corruption. The poor wanted someone to speak for them, and the middle class wanted the government to do something.

This combination of cynicism and populism was a ticking time bomb, and the May 2016 election of Rodrigo Duterte was its explosion. The longtime mayor of the southern city of Davao ran an outsider campaign, promising peace with the communists, steady economic growth, and above all, order—bathed in the nostalgic glow of Ferdinand Marcos's 1972 declaration of martial law. After his inauguration, Duterte set out to disrupt the entrenched powers of the military, the Catholic Church, and the concentrated wealth of an oligarchy known in the

Philippines as the "forty families." Along the way, Duterte insulted the pope, the Secretary General of the United Nations, and Barack Obama; engineered the detention of his leading legislative opponent and the removal of the country's top judge; declared martial law in Mindanao; targeted press critics and unleashed internet trolls; advocated the rape of an outspoken Australian missionary; and boasted of his extrajudicial tactics. He leveraged Filipinos' hazy fondness for the law and order of the first years of President Ferdinand Marcos's martial law regime and in November 2016 even authorized the burial of his discredited predecessor at the Heroes Cemetery, a resting site of national honor on the grounds of the former Fort McKinley, just steps away from the Manila American Cemetery. But the violence continued. Human Rights Watch, an international non-governmental organization, estimated the first two years of Duterte's war on drugs had left at least 23,000 people dead. And yet, according to polls, he was the most popular president in Philippine history, notching a 79 percent approval rating in April 2019.[4]

In his relations with the United States, Duterte appeared to find a kindred spirit in President Donald Trump, also elected in 2016. The two leaders praised each other, and Duterte promised a state visit to his "friend" in Washington "soon." Duterte and Trump unwittingly overlapped when they tapped the long history of the US military in the Philippines. On the campaign trail in 2016, Donald Trump repeated false stories that Brigadier General John Pershing had used pig's blood as a weapon of counterinsurgency against Muslim rebels in the early twentieth century. Historians and military officers debunked the tale, though Trump continued to tell it, and to share what he took to be its historical lesson of war against Muslim enemies: "Some things never change, folks. Some things never change." America's grim history in Mindanao served Duterte, too. After US officials criticized the human rights violations of his war on drugs, the Philippine president displayed a photograph of the 1906 Bud Dajo massacre. "You're investigating me and the internal affairs of my country?" he asked. "I'm investigating you, and . . . I will expose it to the world what you did to the Filipinos, especially to the Moro Filipinos," he said, reminding listeners that the United States has never apologized for the killing of unarmed civilians at Bud Dajo more than a century ago.[5]

Warm relations between Trump and Duterte cooled when the Philippine president proclaimed a pivot of his own. In October 2016, during a visit to Beijing, Duterte announced that the Philippines would "realign" toward China. He then called for a "separation from the United States," and threatened to cancel the EDCA: "I want them out," Duterte fumed. Secretary of Foreign Affairs Perfecto Yasay meanwhile asserted that Filipinos must break the "invisible chains" binding them as "little brown brothers" to the United States. On the campaign trail, Duterte talked tough on China, boldly claiming he would "ride a jet ski" to defend disputed Philippine islands in the South China Sea. But by August 2019, Duterte had made his fifth state visit to China in just two years in office. In Beijing, he spoke moderately, and as president rarely implemented policies that might anger Chinese leaders or stop the flow of Chinese foreign investment. After a United Nations tribunal sided with the Philippines in its contest over disputed islands, Duterte merely noted that it was not the "appropriate time" to take up the claims.[6]

High-profile visits to Beijing aside, Duterte found pivoting away from the United States harder than he imagined. Cooperation with China stumbled over ongoing conflicts in the South China Sea and as concerns emerged about Chinese financial infiltration at Subic Bay and elsewhere. Nor did Duterte change most Filipinos' views of America. A 2014 opinion poll revealed that 85 percent of Filipinos thought positively about the United States—higher than the percentage of Americans who felt that way about their own country. By contrast, in a poll five years later, only 27 percent of Filipinos agreed that "what the Chinese government wants to happen in the Philippines is good for the Filipinos." In the twentieth century, two great statesmen of Philippine politics, the military-minded Carlos Romulo and the military opponent Lorenzo Tañada, grappled with the central question of Philippine foreign policy: was the country safer with the Americans there or without them? Both men were passionate Filipino patriots, but their commitments led them to opposite conclusions: Tañada doubted that national sovereignty could ever be achieved under the shadow of the United States, whereas Romulo believed that it could only be won and defended with the United States. In the twenty-first century, the potential threat is different. The debate is exactly the same.[7]

For its part, the United States has been equally hesitant to step away from its longtime partner—and unwilling to give up the century-long foundation of its power in Asia. With its eye on China, the US Defense Department has begun urging a "free and open Indo-Pacific," announcing in a June 2019 strategy document that "no one nation can or should dominate" the region. The basics of US-Philippine military relations remain: the Mutual Defense Treaty commits the United States to military protection, and US Secretary of State Michael Pompeo insisted that "any armed attack on Philippine forces" in the South China Sea would "trigger mutual defense obligations." With the EDCA in place, there are more joint maneuvers, training, and ship visits than ever—some 280 exercises in 2019 alone.[8]

In the twenty-first century, those visits are not only military but humanitarian. Following the devastation of Typhoon Haiyan in November 2014, more than 13,000 US troops arrived on Philippine shores—far more than ever visited during the Balikatan exercises of the 2000s. Climate change and extreme weather cast a shadow over the next Pacific Century, and humanitarian interventions—a component of something Defense Department planners call "military operations other than war"—will surely bring more American soldiers to the Philippines. Critics of US policy wonder if US military interventions that come cloaked in the garb of humanitarian rescue represent the twenty-first century's version of William McKinley's "benevolent assimilation." The two countries' shared history suggests that as the US armed forces evolve to meet the threat of climate change, American soldiers will return to the Philippines and will again call themselves protectors or liberators, not invaders.[9]

Filipinos will march alongside them. A century after Commodore George Dewey urged Emilio Aguinaldo to "come soon as possible," and seventy years since General Douglas MacArthur greeted Philippine independence by announcing "the end of empire," US armed forces continue as a permanent feature of Philippine life. The old rivals—Spain, Japan, the Soviet Union—pose no threat. Korea and Vietnam are slowly forgotten. But the wars continue. As the United States faces new challenges in Asia, Americans will rely on the Philippines as a crucial partner in Pacific power. By recruiting labor, using Philippine bases, and leveraging Filipinos' transpacific ties of nation and family, the United States will continue to build in the Philippines on the foundation that Matthew Batson laid when he established the Philippine Scouts in 1899. And like Batson's servant Jacinto, Filipinos will find ways to bend American ambitions to their own national interests.

IN DECEMBER 2018, THE TWO COUNTRIES' SHARED HISTORY brought one final Pacific crossing. In September 1901, after Filipino revolutionaries killed forty-eight American soldiers in the village of Balangiga, Brigadier General Jacob Smith turned their island of Samar into a "howling wilderness." American soldiers from the US 11th Infantry Regiment, the Wyoming Volunteers, razed Balangiga's

Church of San Lorenzo de Martir and seized the church bells that had rung on that fateful morning to summon the insurgents to battle. In the intervening decades, the bells wandered through America's military empire, with two of them making their way to Francis E. Warren Air Force Base outside Cheyenne, Wyoming, and the third to a US Army base in South Korea. For those Americans who knew anything about them, they were trophies of war and silent monuments to fallen American soldiers.

To Filipinos, they were a stolen heritage. In 1990, then serving as President Corazon Aquino's Secretary of National Defense, Fidel Ramos—West Point grad, PEFTOK hero, PHILCAG officer, loyal American ally—asked his counterpart, Defense Secretary Dick Cheney, a Wyoming man, to return the Balangiga bells. A few years later, as president, Ramos asked, insisted, and begged for their return. Wyoming's American Legion adjutant demurred that "we just don't believe in dismantling war memorials," and federal legislation blocked their transfer. A generation later, in his 2017 State of the Nation Address, Duterte again demanded their return. "Those bells are reminders of our forebears . . . who resisted the American colonizers and sacrificed their lives in the process," he explained, and called on the United States: "Return them to us, this is painful for us."[10]

The two nations reaffirmed the bonds of war in December 2018. More than a century after American soldiers shipped off from the Presidio to conquer the Philippines, decades after Filipino sailors boarded the steel ships of the Great White Fleet, years after two Filipino American enlisted men took their US citizenship oaths in Saddam Hussein's abandoned palace, US Secretary of Defense James Mattis watched as the Balangiga bells were loaded onto a US Air Force C-130 cargo plane in Wyoming. At a ceremony in Balangiga on December 11, the United States officially returned them to the Republic of the Philippines. Mattis's counterpart, Secretary of National Defense Delfin Lorenzana, observed that "it's time for healing, it is time for closure, it is time to look ahead as two nations should with a shared history as allies." That shared history is not simply an alliance, but the story of two nations bound by war. When the bells of Balangiga tolled to summon Filipinos to battle in 1901, their sounds marked the beginning of America's first Pacific Century. What followed were a hundred years of difficult choices, broken promises, and unending war. In December 2018, the bells rang again. Their sounds echoed across the silent stones of the Manila American Cemetery and the wide expanse of the Pacific Ocean. The second Pacific Century had just begun. This one can be different.[11]

Acknowledgments

I BEGIN BY THANKING THE VETERANS, FOR SACRIFICES FROM THE humble to the supreme, and for pushing America to fulfill its promises. In 1946, President Harry Truman spoke of a shared "moral obligation" to those who gave "so much for the common cause." I offer this book as partial payment of a long-overdue debt.

I have incurred debts of my own along the way. Assembling this book from a fragmentary and scattered historical record required the patience of librarians, the care of archivists, the commitment of community historians, and the generosity of people who shared their stories. I pay special thanks here to pathbreaking historians Dorothy Cordova and the late Fred Cordova, to pioneering scholar Barbara Posadas, and to the unforgettable memory of Dawn Bohulano Mabalon. Dawn supported this book from day one, and I offer it in tribute to her legacy.

In Manila, Dito Borromeo, Rofel Brion, Waldette Cueto, and Von Totanes were generous hosts and thoughtful critics. Vergilio Totanes made possible research at the National Defense College of the Philippines. In San Francisco, Donald Ungar retold courtroom stories with all the brains and passion he brought to the fight forty years earlier. Mel Orpilla introduced me to Mare Island and Vallejo, while Rudy Asercion opened his doors and allowed me to join a community of Bay Area veterans who shared with me the most memorable interviews I've ever done. On the east coast, Allan Bergano, Edwina Bergano, and Jeffrey Acosta introduced me to Hampton Roads. Dawn Mabalon and Jude Soundar connected me to Major General (ret.) Antonio Taguba, Marie Blanco, Ben de Guzman, Jon Melegrito, and an inspiring cadre of veteran advocates committed to sharing this history. Eugena Lee, Robert McGreevey, and Brian Remlinger provided research assistance. Dozens of archivists and librarians went above and beyond, but my heartiest thanks goes to Michelle Baildon, formerly of the MIT Libraries.

Financial support came from the Haynes Research Grant of the Historical Society of Southern California and the US Army Heritage and Education Center's General and Mrs. Matthew B. Ridgway Military History Research Grant. A year as a Fellow at Harvard's Charles Warren Center for Studies in American History transformed and extended the project. I am particularly thankful to the other fellows and to our faculty conveners Sven Beckert and Erez Manela. I never could have won fellowships without the labor of Beth Bailey, John Dower, Gary Gerstle, Michael Neiberg, and Daniel Rodgers. Thanks to Dean Deborah Fitzgerald and Dean Melissa Nobles of MIT's School of Humanities, Arts, and Social Sciences, to the MIT Policy Lab, and to my History chairs, Anne McCants, Jeffrey Ravel, and Craig Wilder.

It takes an army to finish a book, and this one took a navy and an air force too. For insightful readings, research leads, and providing venues for presenting this work, I thank Leia Castañeda Anastacio, Noelani Arista, Clara Altman, Catherine Choy, David Ciarlo, Genevieve Clutario, Adrian De Leon, Mary Dudziak, David Ekbladh, Yasuo Endo, Zach Fredman, Ann-Marie Gleeson, Vernadette Gonzalez, Michael Hames-Garcia, Daniel Immerwahr, Ryan Irwin, Junko Isono Kato,

Justin Jackson, Martha Jones, Lili Kim, katrina quisumbing king, Paul Kramer, Antonio Lanuza, Vina Lanzona, Alison Laporte-Oshiro, Simeon Man, Joven Maranan, Daniel Margolies, Diana Martinez, Reo Matsuzaki, Hiromu Nagahara, Christopher Nichols, Kristin Oberiano, Mary Anne Ocampo, Harriet Ritvo, Andrew Sandoval-Strausz, Zachary Schrag, Sayuri Shimizu, James Sparrow, Ellen Stroud, Anna Su, Nicola Tan, Emma Teng, Astrid Tuminez, Theresa Ventura, Chuong-Dai Vo, Jessica Wang, Barbara Welke, Mark Wilson, Tessa Ong Winkelmann, Colleen Woods, and Susan Zeiger. Alan Brinkley and Pauline Maier read my work early on, and I still miss their guidance. Alfred McCoy, Francisco Scarano, Robert Gerwarth, Erez Manela, Daniel Bender, Jana Lipman, Beth Bailey, and David Farber gave me space to try out my ideas in print. Special thanks to Brooke Blower, David Engerman, Lynn Johnson, and Bruce Schulman for writing with me in Boston, to John Dower and Ellen Sebring for teaching me how to look carefully at images, and to Megan Kate Nelson, Daniel Sharfstein, and Michael Willrich for publication advice. Friends, family, and colleagues in Boston and beyond have sustained the author.

At Basic Books, Brian Distelberg was an early and thoughtful champion of this book. He had an impeccable ability to figure out where I needed to go, point me in the right direction, and let me get there in my own way. He is hands down the best reader I have ever encountered. Alex Colston sharpened the prose and clarified the message, Michael McConnell put the book in shape, and Melissa Veronesi kept it on track.

Finally, the dedication says it all.

Abbreviations Used in Notes

BG	*Boston Globe*
CSM	*Christian Science Monitor*
CT	*Chicago Tribune*
DoSB	*Department of State Bulletin*
FEER	*Far Eastern Economic Review*
GPO	Government Printing Office
LAT	*Los Angeles Times*
NYT	*New York Times*
PPP	*Public Papers of the Presidents*
TIAS	Treaties and Other International Acts Series
USNWR	*U.S. News and World Report*
WP	*Washington Post*
WSJ	*Wall Street Journal*

Notes

Additional references and a full bibliography can be found on the author's website at at the MIT Libraries storage site at https://dspace.mit.edu/handle/1721.1/123446.

INTRODUCTION

1. Iris Yokoi, "Filipino Veterans Shelter in Jeopardy," *LAT*, October 4, 1992; death record, October 21, 2003, Riverside National Cemetery, Riverside, CA.

2. Hillary Clinton, "America's Pacific Century," *Foreign Policy* no. 189 (November 2011): 63; A. T. Mahan, "The United States Looking Outward," *Atlantic Monthly* 66 (December 1890): 822.

3. "Life of Filipino in Navy," *Philippines Free Press*, April 14, 1917; Rudyard Kipling, "The White Man's Burden," *McClure's* 12 (February 1899): 290–291.

4. Joseph Evans to Brother Will, May 5, 1898, Papers of Joseph G. Evans (Coll 2449), and Mark Bocek Oral History (SR 0813), Oregon Historical Society, Portland.

5. "New Census Data Show US Filipino Population Grew to Nearly 4.1 Million in 2018," *FilAm Star*, November 21–27, 2019.

6. D. L. England, "Summary History and Highlights of Jeep in the Philippines," November 6, 1973, Box 10, Roy Dikeman Chapin Papers, Bentley Historical Library, Ann Arbor, MI.

7. Thomas S. Jones, "Operations of Troop C, Philippine Scouts, Northern Luzon: The First Two Years," typescript (1946), 32, Box 52, Papers of William Bowen, Douglas MacArthur Memorial Archives, Norfolk, VA.

8. Ibid., 65–66.

CHAPTER ONE: BIND YOUR SONS, 1898–1901

1. "Capt. M. A. Batson Retired," *NYT*, February 8, 1902; Edward M. Coffman, "Batson of the Philippine Scouts," *Parameters* 7 no. 3 (1977): 68–72.

2. Coffman, "Batson of the Philippine Scouts," 69, 70.

3. John A. Larkin, *The Pampangans: Colonial Society in a Philippine Province* (Berkeley: University of California Press, 1972), 119–128.

4. "Gunboats Chase Filipinos," *NYT*, May 11, 1899; Antonio Tabaniag, "The Pre-War Philippine Scouts," *University of Manila Journal of East Asiatic Studies* 9 (October 1960): 8–9.

5. Coffman, "Batson of the Philippine Scouts," 69; "Seek Release of Americans," *CT*, May 2, 1899.

6. Edward M. Coffman, "The Philippine Scouts, 1899–1942: A Historical Vignette," in *The Embattled Past: Reflections on Military History* (Lexington: University Press of Kentucky, 2014), 71.

7. Larkin, *Pampangans*, 128.

8. Robby Tantingco, "Preface," in Dennis Edward Flake, *Loyal Macabebes: How the Americans Used the Macabebe Scouts in the Annexation of the Philippines* (Angeles City, Philippines: Holy Angel University Press, 2009), n.p.

9. Bernardita Reyes Churchill, "Life in a War of Independence: The Philippine Revolution, 1896–1902," in *Daily Lives of Civilians in Wartime Asia: From the Taiping Rebellion to the Vietnam War*, ed. Stewart Lone (Westport, CT: Greenwood Press, 2007), 35; Carlos Quirino, "The Spanish Colonial Army: 1878–98," *Philippine Studies* 36 (Third Quarter 1988): 381–386.

10. John N. Schumacher, "The Cavite Mutiny: Toward a Definitive History," *Philippine Studies* 59 (March 2011): 55–81.

11. Aguinaldo, quoted in William Henry Scott, "A Minority Reaction to American Imperialism: Isabelo de los Reyes," *Philippine Quarterly of Culture and Society* 10 (March–June 1982): 3.

12. Churchill, "Life in a War of Independence," 41; Ricardo Trota Jose, *The Philippine Army, 1935–1942* (Quezon City, Philippines: Ateneo de Manila University Press, 1992), 7–8; Quirino, "Spanish Colonial Army," 383, 385.

13. Walter A. Williams, "United States Policy and the Debate over Philippine Annexation: Implications for the Origins of American Imperialism," *Journal of American History* 66 (March 1980): 828.

14. Churchill, "Life in a War of Independence," 51; Quirino, "Spanish Colonial Army," 386.

15. "The Aguinaldo-Pratt Secret Talks in Singapore," and "Filipino Manifesto to Help the Americans," May 16, 1898, in *Documentary Sources of Philippine*

History, ed. Gregorio F. Zaide (Metro Manila: National Book Store, 1990), vol. 9, pp. 113–116, 154–155; H. W. Brands, *Bound to Empire: The United States and the Philippines* (New York: Oxford University Press, 1992), 45–46.

16. Brands, *Bound to Empire*, 46; Fred C. Chamberlin, *The Blow from Behind, or, Some Features of the Anti-Imperialist Movement Attending the War with Spain* (Boston: Lee and Shepard, 1903), 2.

17. Aguinaldo, in James H. Blount, *The American Occupation of the Philippines, 1898–1912* (New York: G. P. Putnam's Sons, 1912), 7, 9, 13, 33; George Dewey, *Autobiography of George Dewey, Admiral of the Navy* (Annapolis, MD: Naval Institute Press, 1987 [1913]), 215–217, 275–278.

18. Blount, *American Occupation*, 23, 32; "The Marines at Cavite," *NYT*, August 6, 1899.

19. "Aguinaldo's Decree on the Laws of War," May 24, 1898, in Zaide, *Documentary Sources*, vol. 9, p. 172; Gabriel F. Fabella, "Don Adriano N. Rios: Romblon's Patriarch," *Historical Bulletin* 4 (September 1960): 64–65.

20. Brands, *Bound to Empire*, 46–47; Jose, *Philippine Army*, 10–13; Ronald Spector, *Admiral of the New Empire: The Life and Career of George Dewey* (Baton Rouge: Louisiana State University Press, 1974), 92.

21. Churchill, "Life in a War of Independence," 52; "The Declaration of Philippine Independence," June 12, 1898, in Zaide, *Documentary Sources*, vol. 9, pp. 235–241.

22. Diary entry, August 13, 1898, Zeno Lucas Diary (Coll 173), Oregon Historical Society, Portland [hereafter OHS]; Spector, *Admiral of the New Empire*, 96–97.

23. Brands, *Bound to Empire*, 47; Edward M. Coffman, *The Hilt of the Sword: The Career of Peyton C. March* (Madison: University of Wisconsin Press, 1966), 14; W. Cameron Forbes, *The Philippine Islands* (Boston: Houghton Mifflin, 1928), vol. 2, p. 429; D. Clayton James, *The Years of MacArthur* (Boston: Houghton Mifflin, 1975), vol. 1, p. 31.

24. Diary entry, May 3, 1898, Zeno Lucas Diary (Coll 173), OHS; Joseph Evans to Brother Will, May 5, 1898, Papers of Joseph G. Evans (Coll 2449), OHS; Kelly, quoted in Sean McEnroe, "Painting the Philippines with an American Brush: Visions of Race and National Mission among the Oregon Volunteers in the Philippine Wars of 1898 and 1899," *Oregon Historical Quarterly* 104 (Spring 2003): 53; de los Reyes, quoted in Scott, "Minority Reaction," 3; H. C. Thompson, "Oregon Volunteer Reminiscences of the War with Spain," *Oregon Historical Quarterly* 49 (September 1948): 192–204.

25. "McKinley's Benevolent Assimilation Proclamation," December 21, 1898, in Zaide, *Documentary Sources*, vol. 9, pp. 408–411.

26. Teodoro A. Agoncillo, *Malolos: The Crisis of the Republic* (Quezon City: University of the Philippines Press, 1960), 767; "Aguinaldo's Version of the Philippine Troubles," *Literary Digest* 20 (February 3, 1900): 140–141; Churchill, "Life in a War of Independence," 54–55; Mabini, quoted in Leon Wolff, *Little Brown Brother: How the United States Purchased and Pacified the Philippine Islands at the Century's Turn* (Garden City, NY: Doubleday, 1961), 256.

27. "President Aguinaldo's Appeal," February 5, 1899, in Zaide, *Documentary Sources*, vol. 10, p. 80; "Fight at Manila with Filipinos," *NYT*, February 6, 1899.

28. "Anxiety in Washington," *NYT*, February 7, 1899; A. A. Berle, *Some Popular American Fallacies Refuted* (n.p., [1900]), 5; Lewis L. Gould, *The Spanish-American War and President McKinley* (Lawrence: University Press of Kansas, 1982), 117; Margaret Leech, *In the Days of McKinley* (New York: Harper, 1959), 357–358; William A. Robinson, *Thomas B. Reed: Parliamentarian* (New York: Dodd, Mead, 1930), 369–370; Henry Cabot Lodge to Theodore Roosevelt, February 9, 1899, in *Selections from the Correspondence of Theodore Roosevelt and Henry Cabot Lodge, 1884–1918* (New York: Scribner's, 1925), vol. 1, p. 391; "Senate Ratifies the Treaty," *NYT*, February 7, 1899.

29. 30 Stat. 981 (March 2, 1899); Churchill, "Life in a War of Independence," 55, 56; Forbes, *Philippine Islands*, vol. 1, p. 192; Heath Twichell Jr., *Allen: The Biography of an Army Officer, 1859–1930* (New Brunswick, NJ: Rutgers University Press, 1974), 95–96.

30. Adna Chaffee, quoted in Timothy K. Nenninger, *The Leavenworth Schools and the Old Army: Education, Professionalism, and the Officer Corps of the United States Army, 1881–1918* (Westport, CT: Greenwood Press, 1978), 55; Thompson, "Oregon Volunteer Reminiscences," 202.

31. Flake, *Loyal Macabebes*, 9; diary entry, July 2, 1898, Zeno Lucas Diary (Coll 173), OHS; Charles Maccubbin, "Recollections: The U.S. Army Service Memoirs of Charles Maccubbin: Private to Major, 1886–1919," typescript (1988), 50–51, Box 1, Papers of Charles Maccubbin, Library of Congress Manuscript Division, Washington, DC [hereafter LCMD].

32. John Willis Greenslade to My Dear Sister, April 21, 1900, Box 1, Papers of John Willis Greenslade, LCMD; F. F. Hilder, "The Philippine Islands," *National Geographic Magazine* 9 (June 1898): 280; diary entry, July 7, 1898, Zeno Lucas Diary (Coll 173), OHS; Telfer, quoted in McEnroe, "Painting the Philippines," 40.

33. Paul A. Kramer, *The Blood of Government: Race, Empire, the United States, and the Philippines* (Chapel Hill: University of North Carolina Press, 2006), 130–132; Alfredo S. Veloso, ed., *Testament and Letters of Apolinario*

Mabini (Quezon City, Philippines: Asvel, 1964), 305–306; Apolinario Mabini, "La instranigencia," *La Revolucion Filipina* 2 (November 6, 1899): 111.

34. Fred R. Brown, *History of the Ninth U.S. Infantry, 1799–1909* (Chicago: Donnelly, 1909), 543; Augustus C. Buell, "Kipling's Poem," *NYT*, January 25, 1902; "Filipino Crimes," *Army and Navy Journal*, November 2, 1901, p. 202; "Filipino Crimes," *Army and Navy Journal*, December 28, 1901, p. 423; Clayton D. Laurie, "The Philippine Scouts: America's Colonial Army, 1899–1913," *Philippine Studies* 37 (Second Quarter 1989): 177; US Department of War, *The People of the Philippines* (Washington, DC: GPO, 1901), 36.

35. "A Black Soldier in the Philippine Islands," in *These Truly Are the Brave: An Anthology of African American Writings on War and Citizenship*, ed. A. Yemisi Jimoh and Françoise N. Hamlin (Gainesville: University Press of Florida, 2015), 220–221; Robinson, quoted in Willard B. Gatewood Jr., *"Smoked Yankees" and the Struggle for Empire: Letters from Negro Soldiers, 1898–1902* (Urbana: University of Illinois Press, 1971), 268; Kramer, *Blood of Government*, 128; David J. Silbey, *A War of Frontier and Empire: The Philippine-American War, 1899–1902* (New York: Hill and Wang, 2007), 111; officer quoted in Wolff, *Little Brown Brother*, 100.

36. Brands, *Bound to Empire*, 54; Spector, *Admiral of the New Empire*, 98–100.

37. David H. Burton, *Taft, Wilson, and World Order* (Madison, NJ: Farleigh Dickinson Press, 2003), 33; Taft, quoted in Ralph Eldin Minger, *William Howard Taft and United States Foreign Policy: The Apprenticeship Years, 1900–1908* (Urbana: University of Illinois Press, 1975), 31.

38. Rowland W. Berthoff, "Taft and MacArthur, 1900–1901: A Study in Civil-Military Relations," *World Politics* 5 (January 1953): 196–213; Minger, *Taft and United States Foreign Policy*, 30–54; Kenneth Ray Young, *The General's General: The Life and Times of Arthur MacArthur* (Boulder, CO: Westview Press, 1994), esp. 272.

39. Agoncillo, *Malolos*, 562; "Amnesty Offered to Filipino Rebels," *NYT*, June 21, 1900; "In the Philippines," 563; William Harding Carter, *The Life of Lieutenant General Chaffee* (Chicago: University of Chicago Press, 1917), 241; Maria Serena I. Diokno, "Perspectives on Peace during the Philippine-American War of 1899–1902," *South East Asia Research* 5 (March 1997): 15–16; Stuart Creighton Miller, *"Benevolent Assimilation": The American Conquest of the Philippines, 1899–1903* (New Haven, CT: Yale University Press, 1982), 134–135; "Philippine Amnesty Proclamation," *Literary Digest*, June 23, 1900, pp. 779–780; "Terms of the Proclamation," *NYT*, June 22, 1900; Wolff, *Little Brown Brother*, 322–323.

40. Thomas A. Bailey, "Was the Presidential Election of 1900 a Mandate on Imperialism?" *Mississippi Valley Historical Review* 24 (June 1937): 45; "Did Senator Hoar Cause the Philippine Rebellion?" *Literary Digest*, January 27, 1900, 105–106; John M. Gates, "Philippine Guerrillas, American Anti-Imperialists, and the Election of 1900," *Pacific Historical Review* 46 (February 1977): 57; James R. Parker, "Senator John C. Spooner: Advocate of the American Empire, 1899–1906," *Maryland Historian* 5 (Fall 1974): 117; Arthur M. Schlesinger Jr. and Fred L. Israel, eds., *History of American Presidential Elections, 1789–1968* (New York: Chelsea House, 1985), vol. 5, p. 1920.

41. Aguinaldo, quoted in Kramer, *Blood of Government*, 133; Andrew J. Birtle, "The U.S. Army's Pacification of Marinduque, Philippine Islands, April 1900–April 1901," *Journal of Military History* 61 (April 1997): 263; Brands, *Bound to Empire*, 54; Gates, "Philippine Guerrillas," 64; Apolinario Mabini, "A Filipino Appeal to the People of the United States," *North American Review* 170 (January 1900): 60.

42. Gates, "Philippine Guerrillas," 62; diary entry, January 8, 1901, Simeon Villa Diary, Manuscripts and Archives, New York Public Library, New York [hereafter NYPL].

43. Flake, *Loyal Macabebes*, 7; Victor Holman, "Seminole Negro Indians, Macabebes, and Civilian Irregulars: Models for Future Employment of Indigenous Forces" (M.A. thesis, US Army Command and General Staff College, 1995), 29–30; diary entry, March 4, 1899, Zeno Lucas Diary (Coll 173), OHS; Allan D. Marple, "The Philippine Scouts: A Case Study in the Use of Indigenous Soldiers, Northern Luzon, the Philippine Islands, 1899" (M.A. thesis, US Army Command and General Staff College, 1983), 72; Miller, *"Benevolent Assimilation,"* 80–82; Philippine Scouts Heritage Society, *Heritage of Valor: A History of the Philippine Scouts, 100th Anniversary* (Fort Sam Houston, TX: Fort Sam Houston Museum, 2001), 3.

44. Coffman, "Batson of the Philippine Scouts," 68; Holman, "Macabebes," 30–31; Laurie, "Philippine Scouts," 179; "Macabebe Scouts Organize," *Atlanta Constitution*, September 6, 1899, p. 1; Marple, "Philippine Scouts," 73; "Two More Companies of Macabebes," *NYT*, December 2, 1899; Henry Parker Willis, *Our Philippine Problem: A Study of American Colonial Policy* (New York: Henry Holt, 1905), 120.

45. "Capt. Batson Arrives," *BG*, March 24, 1900; Coffman, "Batson of the Philippine Scouts," 71; "Did Good Work," *BG*, April 7, 1900; "Lawton Plan May Be Adopted," *LAT*, February 25, 1900; Miller, *"Benevolent Assimilation,"* 183; Willis, *Our Philippine Problem*, 120.

46. William H. Johnston, "Employment of Philippine Scouts in War," *Journal of the Military Service Institution of the United States* 38 (March–April 1906): 297; William Howard Taft to Elihu Root, July 30, 1900, Reel 463, Papers of William Howard Taft, LCMD.

47. Donald Chaput, "Founding of the Leyte Scouts," *Leyte-Samar Studies* 9 no. 2 (1975): 6; Johnston, "Employment of Philippine Scouts in War," 76–77; James W. Powell, "The Utilization of Native Troops in Our Foreign Possessions," *Journal of the Military Service Institution of the United States* 30 (January 1902): 35; Maxwell S. Simpson, Letter to Editor, *United Service Magazine* 2 (September 1902): 333; Tabaniag, "Pre-War Philippine Scouts," 9–10.

48. Charles D. Rhodes, "The Utilization of Native Troops in Our Foreign Possessions," *Journal of the Military Service Institution of the United States* 30 (January 1902): 11; Scott, "Minority Reaction," 3.

49. "Exploits of the Macabebes," *WP*, April 7, 1900; John W. Ward, "The Use of Native Troops in Our New Possessions," *Journal of the Military Service Institution of the United States* 31 (November 1902): 797.

50. Wilson, quoted in Chaput, "Founding of the Leyte Scouts," 7, 8; Jose, *Philippine Army*, 15; Clayton D. Laurie, "An Oddity of Empire: The Philippine Scouts and the 1904 World's Fair," *Gateway Heritage* 15 (Winter 1994–95): 48–50; Laurie, "Philippine Scouts," 182.

51. Davis, quoted in Coffman, "Philippine Scouts," 73; Rhodes, "Utilization of Native Troops," 7, 17.

52. Coffman, "Philippine Scouts," 73; John Gordon IV, "Among the Best: The Philippine Scouts," *Military Review* 67 (September 1987): 70; Johnston, "Employment of Philippine Scouts in War," 74, 294.

53. Chaput, "Founding of the Leyte Scouts," 5, 9; Johnston, "Employment of Philippine Scouts," 291; Laurie, "Oddity of Empire," 49; Marple, "Philippine Scouts," 90; Rhodes, "Utilization of Native Troops," 17; H. C. Thompson, "War without Medals," *Oregon Historical Quarterly* 59 (December 1958): 317.

54. Johnston, "Employment of Philippine Scouts," 71; Tabaniag, "Pre-War Philippine Scouts," 9, 10.

55. Lawton, quoted in Marple, "Philippine Scouts," 87.

56. 31 Stat. 748 (February 2, 1901), sec. 36, at 757; Twain, "The Stupendous Procession," in *Mark Twain's Weapons of Satire: Anti-Imperialist Writings on the Philippine-American War*, ed. Jim Zwick (Syracuse: Syracuse University Press, 1992), 46–47.

57. "Frederick Funston at the Dinner in His Honor, March 8, 1902," in *Speeches at the Lotos Club*, ed. John Elderkind et al. (New York: Lotos Club,

1911), 67–80; Frederick Funston, *Memories of Two Wars: Cuban and Philippine Experiences* (Lincoln: University of Nebraska Press, 2009 [1911]), vii, 385–389.

58. Emilio Aguinaldo, with Vicente Albano Pacis, *A Second Look at America* (New York: R. Speller, 1957), 113–129; diary entries, January 1, 1900, January 6, 1900, February 16, 1900, in Simeon Villa Diary, NYPL.

59. Aguinaldo, *Second Look*, 124; Funston, *Memories of Two Wars*, 391–399 (Bustos quote on 399).

60. Emilio Aguinaldo, "The Story of My Capture," in Zaide, *Documentary Sources*, vol. 10, pp. 364–371; Blount, *American Occupation*, 338–339; "Frederick Funston," 77–78; Funston, *Memories of Two Wars*, 420, 422, 426; Brian McAllister Linn, *The Philippine War, 1899–1902* (Lawrence: University Press of Kansas, 2000), 274–276; Wolff, *Little Brown Brother*, 340–342.

61. "Deceit in War," *The Outlook*, April 6, 1901, p. 744; Funston, *Memories of Two Wars*, 422.

62. "Aguinaldo's Manifesto," *The Outlook*, April 27, 1901, pp. 931–932; "Aguinaldo Takes the Oath of Allegiance to the United States," April 1, 1901, in Zaide, *Documentary Sources*, vol. 10, p. 372; Donald Chaput, "Leyte Leadership in the Revolution: The Moxica-Lukban Issue," *Leyte-Samar Studies* 9 no. 1 (1975): 8; Robert W. Hart, *The Philippines Today* (New York: Dodd, Mead, 1928), 24; "Insurgents Disheartened," *NYT*, March 30, 1901; Henry F. Pringle, *The Life and Times of William Howard Taft* (New York: Farrar and Rinehart, 1939), vol. 1, p. 196; Juan Villamor, *Unpublished Chronicle of the Filipino-American War in Northern Luzon, 1899–1901* (Manila: Imprenta Juan Fajardo, 1926), 16; Young, *The General's General*, 286–288.

63. Marcelo Canania Oral History transcript (1968), 6, Center for Oral and Public History, California State University, Fullerton; "General Juan Climaco of Cebu Exhorts Filipinos after Aguinaldo's Capture," April 1, 1901, in Zaide, *Documentary Sources*, vol. 10, p. 373.

64. de los Reyes, quoted in Scott, "Minority Reaction," 11.

65. Diary entry, February 5, 1900, Simeon Villa Diary, NYPL.

CHAPTER TWO: DEFENDING THE PACIFIC, 1901–1914

1. Jordan, quoted in Andrew J. Birtle, "The U.S. Army's Pacification of Marinduque, Philippine Islands, April 1900–April 1901," *Journal of Military History* 61 (April 1997): 260; Fred R. Brown, *History of the Ninth U.S. Infantry, 1799–1909* (Chicago: R. R. Donnelly and Sons, 1909), 602–603; Edward M. Coffman, *The Hilt of the Sword: The Career of Peyton C. March* (Madison: University of Wisconsin Press, 1966), 22; John M. Gates, "The Pacification of the Philippines, 1898–1902," in *The American Military and the Far East*, ed. Joe C.

Dixon (Colorado Springs: United States Air Force Academy and Office of Air Force History, 1980), 84; Paul A. Kramer, *The Blood of Government: Race, Empire, the United States, and the Philippines* (Chapel Hill: University of North Carolina Press, 2006), 136–137; Brian McAllister Linn, *The Philippine War, 1899–1902* (Lawrence: University Press of Kansas, 2000), 212–214; William Howard Taft to Elihu Root, November 14, 1900, and December 27, 1900, Reel 463, Papers of William Howard Taft, Library of Congress Manuscript Division, Washington, DC [hereafter LCMD]; Heath Twichell Jr., *Allen: The Biography of an Army Officer, 1859–1930* (New Brunswick, NJ: Rutgers University Press, 1974), 102.

2. Root, quoted in Rowland W. Berthoff, "Taft and MacArthur, 1900–1901: A Study in Civil-Military Relations," *World Politics* 5 (January 1953): 209; Chaffee, quoted in William Harding Carter, *The Life of Lieutenant General Chaffee* (Chicago: University of Chicago Press, 1917), 239; and George Yarrington Coats, "The Philippine Constabulary, 1901–1917" (Ph.D. dissertation, Ohio State University, 1968), 25.

3. "An American St. Helena," *NYT*, January 10, 1901; Margarita R. Cojuangco, "Islands in Turmoil," in Margarita R. Cojuangco et al., *Konstable: The Story of the Philippine Constabulary, 1901–1991* (Manila: AboCan, 1991), 5; "Deportation of Mabini and Other Patriots to Guam," January 13, 1901, in *Documentary Sources of Philippine History*, ed. Gregorio F. Zaide (Metro Manila: National Book Store, 1990), vol. 10, pp. 326–329; "Filipinos to Be Exiled," *NYT*, January 8, 1901.

4. Phil. Comm. Act no. 175 (July 18, 1901); Berthoff, "Taft and MacArthur," 198, 200; Coats, "Philippine Constabulary," 4; Cojuangco, "Islands in Turmoil," 7, 12; Ralph Eldin Minger, *William Howard Taft and United States Foreign Policy: The Apprenticeship Years, 1900–1908* (Urbana: University of Illinois Press, 1975), 44; Kenneth Ray Young, *The General's General: The Life and Times of Arthur MacArthur* (Boulder, CO: Westview Press, 1994), 277–278.

5. Henry T. Allen to Col. John A. Johnston, January 21, 1902, Box 7, Papers of Henry T. Allen, LCMD; Donald Chaput, "Founding of the Leyte Scouts," *Leyte-Samar Studies* 9 no. 2 (1975): 8; Twichell, *Allen*, 89–93, 96, 105, 111.

6. Henry T. Allen to Caspar Whitney, January 15, 1902, and Henry T. Allen to Col. Charles G. Treat, January 14, 1902, Box 7, Papers of Henry T. Allen, LCMD.

7. Coats, "Philippine Constabulary," 14, 15, 19; Cojuangco, "Islands in Turmoil," 13, 14 17; Rene R. Cruz, "The Colonial Experience," in Cojuangco et al., *Konstable*, 32; Henry Parker Willis, *Our Philippine Problem: A Study of American Colonial Policy* (New York: Henry Holt, 1905), 148.

8. Coats, "Philippine Constabulary," 22; Cojuangco, "Islands in Turmoil," 15, 16; Carl Stone to Mother, September 20, 1903, and October 11, 1903, Papers of Carl L. Stone, Minnesota History Center, St. Paul [hereafter MHC].

9. Cojuangco, "Islands in Turmoil," 16.

10. Coats, "Philippine Constabulary," 53; Allen, quoted in Cojuangco, "Islands in Turmoil," 11; Cruz, "Colonial Experience," 27; Harbord, quoted in George A. Malcolm, *American Colonial Careerist: Half a Century of Official Life and Personal Experience in the Philippines and Puerto Rico* (Boston: Christopher Pub., 1957), 62; "The Philippine Constabulary," *Infantry Journal* 30 (April 1927): 422.

11. Henry T. Allen to Henry C. Corbin, February 1, 1902, Box 7, Papers of Henry T. Allen, LCMD; Cruz, "Colonial Experience," 30; Jeremiah W. Jenks, "The Philippine Constabulary and Its Chief," *Review of Reviews* 26 (October 1902): 436–438; Alfred W. McCoy, *Policing America's Empire: The United States, the Philippines, and the Rise of the Surveillance State* (Madison: University of Wisconsin Press, 2009), 59–205; Twichell, *Allen*, 105; Willis, *Our Philippine Problem*, 145–146.

12. Coats, "Philippine Constabulary," 7; Cruz, "Colonial Experience," 27, 29, 36; Ricardo Trota Jose, *The Philippine Army, 1935–1942* (Quezon City, Philippines: Ateneo de Manila University Press, 1992), 18; "The Philippine Constabulary," *Army and Navy Journal*, March 1, 1902, p. 639.

13. Birtle, "Pacification of Marinduque," 277; "Memorandum of Work Accomplished," 23–25, Box 4, Papers of Charles Burke Elliott, LCMD; James Alexander Robertson, "The Philippines since the Inauguration of the Philippine Assembly," *American Historical Review* 22 (July 1917): 818; W. S. Scott to Henry T. Allen, Box 3, Papers of Clarence Edwards, Massachusetts Historical Society, Boston; Peter W. Stanley, *A Nation in the Making: The Philippines and the United States, 1899–1921* (Cambridge: Harvard University Press, 1974), 123; Willis, *Our Philippine Problem*, 122, 123, 143.

14. Anti-Imperialist League, *Soldiers' Letters: Being Materials for a History of a War of Criminal Aggression* (Boston: Anti-Imperialist League, 1899); Susan A. Brewer, *Why America Fights: Patriotism and War Propaganda from the Philippines to Iraq* (New York: Oxford University Press, 2009), 14–45.

15. Marcelo Canania Oral History transcript (1968), 11, Center for Oral and Public History, California State University, Fullerton [hereafter CSUF]; Frank T. Reuter, *Catholic Influence on American Colonial Policies, 1898–1904* (Austin: University of Texas Press, 1967), 72–73; "Statement of Fred F. Newell," typescript, Box 84, Papers of Herbert Welsh, Historical Society of Pennsylvania, Philadelphia [hereafter HSP]; Moorfield Storey and Julian Codman, *Secretary Root's Record: "Marked Severity" in Philippine Warfare* (Boston: Geo. H. Ellis, 1902), 11.

16. Two rich but conflicting accounts of events in Balangiga appear in Zaide, *Documentary Sources*, vol. 10, pp. 397–406.

17. Brown, *History of the Ninth U.S. Infantry*, 576–583; "Filipinos Kill 48 Americans," *NYT*, September 30, 1901; "Gen. Chaffee's Report," *NYT*, January 20, 1902; Linn, *Philippine War*, 310–313; "Oppose Civic Rule," *WP*, January 20, 1902; Twichell, *Allen*, 103.

18. "Filipinos Burned Bodies of Soldiers at Balangiga," *NYT*, October 3, 1901; David L. Fritz, "Before the 'Howling Wilderness': The Military Career of Jacob Hurd Smith," *Military Affairs* 43 (December 1979): 186–187, 189; Linn, *Philippine War*, 313, 315.

19. William E. Birkhimer, *Military Government and Martial Law*, 3d ed. (Kansas City, MO: Franklin Hudson, 1914), 123–124; Birtle, "Pacification of Marinduque," 271; Bernardita Reyes Churchill, "Life in a War of Independence: The Philippine Revolution, 1896–1902," in *Daily Lives of Civilians in Wartime Asia: From the Taiping Rebellion to the Vietnam War*, ed. Stewart Lone (Westport, CT: Greenwood Press, 2007), 58; "Filipinos Being Hard Pressed by Gen. Bell," *NYT*, January 6, 1902; "How the Concentration Policy Works," *Army and Navy Journal*, April 26, 1902, p. 856; Glenn Anthony May, *Battle for Batangas: A Philippine Province at War* (New Haven, CT: Yale University Press, 1991), 242–269; Stuart Creighton Miller, *"Benevolent Assimilation": The American Conquest of the Philippines, 1899–1903* (New Haven, CT: Yale University Press, 1982), 207–208; Richard E. Welch Jr., *Response to Imperialism: The United States and the Philippine-American War, 1899–1902* (Chapel Hill: University of North Carolina Press, 1979), 138–139.

20. George Kennan, "The Philippines: Present Conditions and Possible Courses of Action," *The Outlook*, March 9, 1901, pp. 582–583; Kramer, *Blood of Government*, 137–151.

21. "The Charges of Torture," *The Outlook*, February 1, 1902, p. 254; Edmund Morris, *Theodore Rex* (New York: Random House, 2001), 97–99; Theodore Roosevelt to Elihu Root, February 18, 1902, and March 19, 1902, in *The Letters of Theodore Roosevelt*, ed. Elting E. Morison (Cambridge: Harvard University Press, 1951–54), vol. 3, pp. 232–233, 244–247; Welch, *Response to Imperialism*, 136–137.

22. "Frederick Funston at the Dinner in His Honor, March 8, 1902," in *Speeches at the Lotos Club*, ed. John Elderkind et al. (New York: Lotos Club, 1911), 65; Root, quoted in Judith Icke Anderson, *William Howard Taft: An Intimate History* (New York: Norton, 1981), 74; "Reply for the Army," *WP*, August 7, 1902; Luke E. Wright, "Gen. Wright's Speech," in *Banquet in Honor of Gen. Luke E. Wright* (n.p., [1902]), 19.

23. Henry T. Allen to Arthur Murray, February 1, 1902, Box 7, Papers of Henry T. Allen, LCMD; *Army and Navy Journal*, October 26, 1901, p. 195;

John Bancroft Devins, *An Observer in the Philippines, or, Life in Our New Possessions* (New York: American Tract Society, 1905), 153–154.

24. Samuel Forbes Adam, "The War in the Philippines," *NYT*, May 18, 1902; H. W. Brands, *Bound to Empire: The United States and the Philippines* (New York: Oxford University Press, 1992), 56; "Cruelty Charge Denied," *NYT*, February 20, 1902; "Gen. Chaffee's Report," *NYT*, January 20, 1902; "Governor Taft and Secretary Root on the Philippines," *The Outlook*, March 1, 1902, p. 497; "Oppose Civic Rule," *WP*, January 20, 1902; "The Proceedings," *NYT*, February 23, 1902.

25. Theodore Roosevelt to William Austin Wadsworth, May 7, 1902, in *Letters of Theodore Roosevelt*, vol. 3, p. 259; US Department of War, *The People of the Philippines* (Washington, DC: GPO, 1901), 12.

26. Brands, *Bound to Empire*, 56; "Charges of Torture," 254; "Gen. Hughes's Testimony," *NYT*, March 12, 1902; G. K. [George Kennan], "The Charges of Cruelty in the Philippines," *The Outlook*, March 22, 1901, p. 711; Kennan, "Philippines," 583; Brian McAllister Linn, *The U.S. Army and Counterinsurgency in the Philippine War, 1899–1902* (Chapel Hill: University of North Carolina Press, 1989), 144–146; "'Water Cure' and Wine," *NYT*, May 16, 1902.

27. Donald Chaput, "Atrocities and War Crimes: The Cases of Major Waller and General Smith," *Leyte-Samar Studies* 12 (1978): 64–77; Morris, *Theodore Rex*, 100–101.

28. "The Charges of Cruelty in the Philippines," *The Outlook*, April 19, 1902, pp. 936–937; Brian M. Linn, "The Struggle for Samar," in *Crucible of Empire: The Spanish-American War and Its Aftermath*, ed. James C. Bradford (Annapolis, MD: Naval Institute Press, 1993), 172; Miller, *"Benevolent Assimilation,"* 236–238; "Philippine Affairs," *The Outlook*, May 31, 1902, p. 290; Twichell, *Allen*, 102–103; Welch, *Response to Imperialism*, 139–140.

29. Fritz, "Before the 'Howling Wilderness,'" 187, 189; "General Smith Punished," *The Outlook*, July 26, 1902, p. 754; "The Investigations of Charges of Misconduct," *The Outlook*, May 10, 1902, p. 96; Linn, "Struggle for Samar," 171–172; Morris, *Theodore Rex*, 603; Twichell, *Allen*, 104.

30. "President Roosevelt's Speech," *The Outlook*, June 7, 1902, p. 337; "At Arlington, Memorial Day, May 30, 1902," in Theodore Roosevelt, *Presidential Addresses and State Papers* (New York: Review of Reviews, 1910), vol. 1, pp. 56–67.

31. 32 Stat. 691 (July 1, 1902).

32. Phil. Comm. Act no. 781 (June 1, 1903); Birtle, "Pacification of Marinduque," 280; James H. Blount, *The American Occupation of the Philippines, 1898–1912* (New York: G. P. Putnam's Sons, 1912), 417–418; Coats, "Philippine Constabulary," 48; Brian McAllister Linn, *Guardians of Empire: The U.S. Army*

and the Pacific, 1902–1940 (Chapel Hill: University of North Carolina Press, 1997), 23, 253; "The Philippine Native Soldiery," *LAT*, July 9, 1904; Willis, *Our Philippine Problem*, 131–132; Dean C. Worcester, *The Philippines Past and Present* (New York: Macmillan, 1930), 315, 319.

33. Jose, *Philippine Army*, 19; George A. Malcolm, *The Government of the Philippine Islands: Its Development and Fundamentals* (Rochester, NY: Lawyers Co-Operative, 1916), 444–445, 578–580, 600–603, 626–635; May, *Battle for Batangas*, 290–291; "On the Trail of Filipinos," *WP*, February 13, 1904.

34. Mary C. Brooke, *Memories of Eighty Years* (New York: Knickerbocker Press, 1916), 104. Figures on Filipino casualties are the subject of substantial debate among historians. Two of the most contentious interpretations include John M. Gates, "War-Related Deaths in the Philippines, 1898–1902," *Pacific Historical Review* 53 (August 1984): 367–378; Glenn May, "150,000 Missing Filipinos: A Demographic Crisis in Batangas, 1887–1903," *Annales de Demographie Historique* (1985): 215–243.

35. Kramer, *Blood of Government*, 229–284; Clayton D. Laurie, "An Oddity of Empire: The Philippine Scouts and the 1904 World's Fair," *Gateway Heritage* 15 (Winter 1994–95): 50.

36. Charles B. Elliott to Edwin A. Jaggard, December 28, 1909, Box 1, Papers of Charles Burke Elliott, MHC; Bertha Lum, *Gangplanks to the East* (New York: Henkle-Yewdale House, 1936), 286, 288–291; Stirling, quoted in Vernon L. Williams, "Naval Service in the Age of Empire," in *Crucible of Empire*, ed. Bradford, 184.

37. "Economic Conditions of Samar," typescript (1912), 17, 27, Box 11, Papers of William M. Connor, Special Collections Library, University of Virginia, Charlottesville; *Navy Guide to Cavite and Manila: For the Battle Ship Fleet* (Manila: n.p., 1908), 77.

38. "New England Welcomes President Roosevelt," *NYT*, August 23, 1902; Andrew J. Bacevich Jr., "Disagreeable Work: Pacifying the Moros, 1903–1906," *Military Review* 62 (June 1982): 49–61.

39. Mark Bocek Oral History (SR 0813), Oregon Historical Society, Portland; Bertha Davidson, "Arkansas in the Spanish-American War," *Arkansas Historical Quarterly* 5 (Autumn 1946): 218.

40. Charles Byler, "Pacifying the Moros: American Military Government in the Southern Philippines, 1899–1913," *Military Review* 85 (May–June 2005): 43; Moorfield Storey, *The Moro Massacre* (Boston: Anti-Imperialist League, [1906]), n.p.

41. J. G. Harbord, "Our Mohammedan Constabulary in Mindanao and Sulu," *The World To-Day* 15 (September 1908): 957, 961.

42. J. A. S. Grenville, "Diplomacy and War Plans in the United States, 1890–1917," *Transactions of the Royal Historical Society*, 5th ser., vol. 11 (1961): 9; Nelson A. Miles, *Serving the Republic: Memoirs of the Civil and Military Life of Nelson A. Miles, Lieutenant-General, United States Army* (New York: Harper and Bros., 1911), 306–313; Twichell, *Allen*, 102; Robert Wooster, *Nelson A. Miles and the Twilight of the Frontier Army* (Lincoln: University of Nebraska Press, 1993), 232–248.

43. Richard D. Challener, *Admirals, Generals, and American Foreign Policy, 1898–1914* (Princeton: Princeton University Press, 1973), 235.

44. Wood, quoted in Challener, *Admirals, Generals*, 238.

45. William Reynolds Braisted, *The United States Navy in the Pacific, 1897–1909* (Austin: University of Texas Press, 1958), 218; Seward W. Livermore, "American Naval-Base Policy in the Far East, 1850–1914," *Pacific Historical Review* 13 (June 1944): 131.

46. Braisted, *Navy in the Pacific*, 123, 221; "Forts Stir House," *WP*, February 15, 1906; Theodore Roosevelt to Theodore Elijah Burton, February 23, 1904, in *Letters of Theodore Roosevelt*, vol. 4, pp. 735–737; "Want to Fortify Colonies," *NYT*, December 4, 1906.

47. "Filipinos Look to Japan," *WP*, July 12, 1907; Wood, quoted in Jack Edward McCallum, *Leonard Wood: Rough Rider, Surgeon, Architect of American Imperialism* (New York: New York University Press, 2006), 233.

48. Challener, *Admirals, Generals*, 236; Livermore, "American Naval-Base Policy," 130; "Manila Defenses Rushed," *WP*, July 10, 1907; Louis Morton, "Military and Naval Preparations for the Defense of the Philippines during the War Scare of 1907," *Military Affairs* 13 (Summer 1949): 97; "Philippine Guns in Place," *CT*, October 8, 1907; "Taft Bound for Subig Bay to Inspect Coast Defenses," *CT*, October 24, 1907.

49. Braisted, *Navy in the Pacific*, 175–180; Neil Bradley Hall, "Planning in the Periphery: The Case of Olongapo City in the Philippines" (Ph.D. dissertation, University of New Orleans, 1993), 124; Charles M. Hubbard and Collis H. Davis Jr., *Corregidor in Peace and War* (Columbia: University of Missouri Press, 2006), 51; Livermore, "American Naval-Base Policy," 131; Morton, "Military and Naval Preparations," 96–97, 102.

50. Theodore Roosevelt to William Howard Taft, August 21, 1907, in *Letters of Theodore Roosevelt*, vol. 5, pp. 761–762; Theodore Roosevelt to Charles Warren Fairbanks, February 21, 1908, in ibid., vol. 6, p. 951; Theodore Roosevelt, *An Autobiography* (New York: Scribner's, 1926 [1913]), 492.

51. Grenville, "Diplomacy and War Plans," 16; Linn, *Guardians of Empire*, 85–86.

52. Braisted, *Navy in the Pacific*, 223–230; Challener, *Admirals, Generals*, 233; Martin Meadows, "Eugene Hale and the American Navy," *American Neptune* 22 (July 1962): 192; Morton, "Military and Naval Preparations," 96.

53. Williams, "Naval Service in the Age of Empire," 193.

54. Frederick S. Harrod, *Manning the New Navy: The Development of a Modern Naval Enlisted Force, 1899–1940* (Westport, CT: Greenwood Press, 1978), 55–60; "Men of Navy Are Citizens," *WP*, January 8, 1916; Matthew Radom, "The 'Americanization' of the U.S. Navy," *US Naval Institute Proceedings* 63 (February 1937): 231; Ronald H. Spector, "Josephus Daniels, Franklin Roosevelt, and the Reinvention of the Enlisted Man," in *FDR and the U.S. Navy*, ed. Edward J. Marolda (New York: St. Martin's Press, 1998), 23.

55. George Melling, comp., *Laws Relating to the Navy, Annotated* (Washington, DC: GPO, 1922), 554; James R. Reckner, "'The Men Behind the Guns': The Impact of the War with Spain on the Navy Enlisted Force," in *Theodore Roosevelt, the U.S. Navy, and the Spanish-American War*, ed. Edward J. Marolda (New York: Palgrave, 2001), 96–97; US Department of the Navy, *Annual Reports of the Navy Department for the Fiscal Year 1907* (Washington, DC: GPO, 1908), 22–23, 384–385.

56. "Announcement for the Philippine Nautical School for 1905–06," *Philippine Teacher* 1 (March 15, 1905): 20–22; George Matthew Dutcher, *The Political Awakening of the East: Studies of Political Progress in Egypt, India, China, Japan, and the Philippines* (New York: Abingdon Press, 1925), 265; Melling, *Laws Relating to the Navy*, 1443; Manuel I. Tibayan, "The Maritime History of the Philippines" (M.A. thesis, Lyceum of the Philippines, 1965), 47–48, 56–57, 63–64, Filipinas Heritage Library, Makati, Philippines; US Navy Bureau of Naval Personnel, *Officers and Enlisted Men of the United States Navy Who Lost Their Lives during the World War, from April 6, 1917 to November 11, 1918* (Washington, DC: GPO, 1920), 311.

57. Marcelo Canania Oral History, transcript (1968), 14, 18–19, CSUF; Churchill, "Life in a War of Independence," 35; "Interview with Maria Garcia Cardoz," and "Interview with Johnny Garcia," Box 142, Federal Writers Project Racial Minorities Survey, Young Research Library, UCLA, Los Angeles.

58. *Navy Guide to Cavite and Manila*, 76–77; Theobald Otjen, "The Philippine Problem," *Filipino Students' Magazine* 2 (December 1906): 8; Radom, "Americanization of the Navy," 234; US Navy, *Annual Reports, 1907*, 1231–1233.

59. Michael Lee Lanning, *The African-American Soldier: From Crispus Attucks to Colin Powell* (Secaucus, NJ: Carol, 1997), 112–113; Bernard C. Nalty, *Strength for the Fight: A History of Black Americans in the Military* (New York:

Free Press, 1986), 78–86; Reckner, "The Men Behind the Guns," 103; John Darrell Sherwood, *Black Sailor, White Navy: Racial Unrest in the Fleet during the Vietnam War Era* (New York: New York University Press, 2007), 4.

60. Harrod, *Manning the New Navy*, 55; Lanning, *African-American Soldier*, 114–115; "Life of Filipino in Navy," *Philippines Free Press*, April 14, 1917; "No Japanese in U.S. Navy," *WP*, September 19, 1915.

61. Lanning, *African-American Soldier*, 114; "Training of Our Youthful Bluejackets," *NYT*, July 21, 1912; US Navy, *Annual Reports, 1907*, 385–386.

62. Richard Wainwright, "The United States and the Far East: An Economic and Military Program," *Annals of the American Academy of Political and Social Science* 54 (July 1914): 252–253.

63. Judith Hicks Stiehm, *The U.S. Army War College: Military Education in a Democracy* (Philadelphia: Temple University Press, 2002), 30.

CHAPTER THREE: PACIFIC OUTPOST, 1914–1934

1. "A Boy's a Boy for A' That," *The Outlook*, May 5, 1915, p. 5; "Boy Scouts around the World," *Boys' Life* 5 (August 1915): 21.

2. Roy Watson Curry, *Woodrow Wilson and Far Eastern Policy, 1913–1921* (New York: Bookman Associates, 1957), 73.

3. "Aguinaldo Aids the Loan," *NYT*, June 14, 1917; Francis Burton Harrison to Lindley Garrison, March 28, 1915, and July 8, 1915, Box 42, Papers of Francis Burton Harrison, Library of Congress Manuscript Division, Washington, DC [hereafter LCMD]; "Harrison Admits Filipino Outbreaks," *NYT*, December 28, 1914; L. H. Thibault, "The War Affects the Philippines: Special Correspondence," *Asia* 17 (September 1917): 558; "Washington in Dark as to Filipino Plot," *NYT*, December 26, 1914.

4. "An Address at a Birthday Banquet in Staunton," December 28, 1912, in *The Papers of Woodrow Wilson*, ed. Arthur S. Link et al. (Princeton: Princeton University Press, 1966–94), vol. 25, p. 635 [hereafter *PWW*].

5. Onofre D. Corpuz, *The Bureaucracy in the Philippines* (Quezon City: University of the Philippines Institute of Public Administration, 1957), 195–204; "Inaugural Address of Francis Burton Harrison," in *At the Helm of the Nation: Inaugural Addresses of the Presidents of the Philippine Republic and the Commonwealth*, comp. Consuelo V. Fornacier (Manila: National Media Production Center, 1973), 217–220.

6. Gene Smith, *Until the Last Trumpet Sounds: The Life of General of the Armies John J. Pershing* (New York: John Wiley and Sons, 1998), 92–93.

7. Phil. Act, no. 221 (September 8, 1911); Peter Gordon Gowing, *Mandate in Moroland: The American Government of Muslim Filipinos, 1899–1920*

(Quezon City: Philippine Center for Advanced Studies, 1977), 235. Traveler Harry L. Foster claimed in his 1924 account that "the American authorities have discovered that by burying a pig with the body of a man who had run amok they could inflict a most humiliating punishment upon the pig-loathing Mohammedan." Harry L. Foster, *A Beachcomber in the Orient* (New York: Dodd, Mead, 1924), 254.

8. "Americans Take Moro Fort," *NYT*, June 13, 1913; Charles Byler, "Pacifying the Moros: American Military Government in the Southern Philippines, 1899–1913," *Military Review* 85 (May–June 2005): 44; Gowing, *Mandate in Moroland*, 238–242; "Inquiry into Moro Battle," *CT*, June 25, 1913; Samuel K. Tan, "Sulu Under American Military Rule, 1899–1913," *Philippine Social Science and Humanities Review* 32 (March 1967): 80–82.

9. Pershing, quoted in Donald Smythe, "Pershing and Counterinsurgency," *Military Review* 46 (September 1966): 91.

10. Quezon, quoted in Claude Buss Oral History, transcript (1984), 6, Center for Oral and Public History, California State University, Fullerton [hereafter CSUF]; Rene R. Cruz, "The Colonial Experience," in Margarita R. Cojuangco et al., *Konstable: The Story of the Philippine Constabulary, 1901–1991* (Manila: AboCan, 1991), 50; Jim Marshall, "Spearhead of Our Defense," *Collier's*, September 8, 1936, p. 38.

11. Burgess, quoted in Curry, *Woodrow Wilson and Far Eastern Policy*, 84; Quezon, quoted in ibid., 80.

12. Wilson, quoted in Curry, *Woodrow Wilson and Far Eastern Policy*, 86; Warren G. Harding, "The Philippine Islands," in Frederick E. Schortemeier, *Rededicating America: Life and Recent Speeches of Warren G. Harding* (Indianapolis: Bobbs-Merrill, 1920), 236–237; Root, quoted in Whitney T. Perkins, "The New Dependencies under McKinley," in *Threshold to American Internationalism: Essays on the Foreign Policies of William McKinley*, ed. Paolo E. Coletta (New York: Exposition Press, 1970), 276.

13. 39 Stat. 545 (August 29, 1916).

14. 39 Stat. 166 (June 3, 1916); John Whiteclay Chambers II, *To Raise an Army: The Draft Comes to Modern America* (New York: Free Press, 1987), 113–117; Edward M. Coffman, "The Philippine Scouts, 1899–1942: A Historical Vignette," in *The Embattled Past: Reflections on Military History* (Lexington: University Press of Kentucky, 2014), 74; Brian McAllister Linn, *Guardians of Empire: The U.S. Army and the Pacific, 1902–1940* (Chapel Hill: University of North Carolina Press, 1997), 253; Philippine Scouts Heritage Society, *Heritage of Valor: A History of the Philippine Scouts, 100th Anniversary* (Fort Sam Houston, TX: Fort Sam Houston Museum, 2001), 5.

15. Alfred W. McCoy, *Policing America's Empire: The United States, the Philippines, and the Rise of the Surveillance State* (Madison: University of Wisconsin Press, 2009), 293–346.

16. George Yarrington Coats, "The Philippine Constabulary, 1908–1917" (Ph.D. dissertation, Ohio State University, 1968), 26–27; Cruz, "Colonial Experience," 50, 53, 55; George A. Malcolm, *American Colonial Careerist: Half a Century of Official Life and Personal Experience in the Philippines and Puerto Rico* (Boston: Christopher Pub., 1957), 63; "News of the Week," *Philippines Free Press*, May 5, 1917.

17. "The Fourth Liberty Loan Drive in the Islands," *Philippine Review* 3 (November 1918): 886.

18. "110,000 to March in Today's Great Patriotic Parade," *NYT*, July 4, 1918; "Day-Long Pageant Pictures America United for War," *NYT*, July 5, 1918; "Filipino's Gift Touches Wilson," *WP*, May 11, 1918; Ramona S. Tirona, "A Social Survey of the Filipinos in Brooklyn," *Philippine Herald* 2 (December 1921): 7–10; Woodrow Wilson to Joseph Patrick Tumulty, May 9, 1918, *PWW*, vol. 47, pp. 578–579.

19. "California's Labor Situation in a Nutshell," *LAT*, May 27, 1917; "Draft Tangle Is Now Before Army Department Head," *Hawaiian Gazette*, August 16, 1918; "Growers' Convention Votes to Import Filipino Labor," *LAT*, May 17, 1917; "May Solve Labor Problem in Valley," *LAT*, March 15, 1918; Thomas G. Thrum, comp., *Hawaiian Almanac and Annual for 1923: The Reference Book of Information and Statistics Relating to the Territory of Hawaii* (Honolulu: Thos. G. Thrum, 1923), 12–13.

20. Chambers, *To Raise an Army*, 229; Enoch H. Crowder, *Second Report of the Provost Marshal General to the Secretary of War on the Operations of the Selective Service System to December 20, 1918* (Washington, DC: GPO, 1919), 320; Manuel H. David, *Our National Guard* (Manila: n.p., 1921), 16; "Filipino Shows His Loyalty," *BG*, June 1, 1917; "Hawaiians Pledge Fealty of Islands to United States in War and Peace," *WP*, July 14, 1918; Maximo M. Kalaw, *Self-Government in the Philippines* (New York: Century, 1919), 61; "Senate Passes Resolution Opening New Army to Aliens," *Honolulu Star-Bulletin*, September 12, 1917; "Uncle Sam's Adopted Sons Are Eager to Fight," *WP*, July 29, 1917.

21. "Filipinos Entering Navy," *LAT*, April 1, 1917; Frederick S. Harrod, *Manning the New Navy: The Development of a Modern Naval Enlisted Force, 1899–1940* (Westport, CT: Greenwood Press, 1978), 60; Ronald H. Spector, "Josephus Daniels, Franklin Roosevelt, and the Reinvention of the Naval Enlisted Man," in *FDR and the U.S. Navy*, ed. Edward J. Marolda (New York: St.

Martin's Press, 1998), 24–26; Ruth Danenhower Wilson, *Jim Crow Joins Up: A Study of Negroes in the Armed Forces of the United States*, rev. ed. (New York: Press of William J. Clark, 1944), 46.

22. David, *Our National Guard*, 16; "Filipino Offers His Services to Defend 'Noble American Nation,'" *Philippines Free Press*, April 14, 1917; "Filipinos Are Enlisting," *WP*, April 1, 1917; "One Hundred Seek to Join U.S. Navy," *Hawaiian Gazette*, June 12, 1917; Tirona, "Social Survey of the Filipinos in Brooklyn."

23. Helen Starr Henifin, "Life on a Navy Transport," *LAT*, January 3, 1932; "Interview with Johnny Garcia," Box 142, Federal Writers Project Racial Minorities Survey, Young Research Library, UCLA, Los Angeles [hereafter UCLA]; Richard E. Miller, *The Messman Chronicles: African Americans in the U.S. Navy, 1932–1943* (Annapolis, MD: Naval Institute Press, 2004), 12; Tirona, "Social Survey of the Filipinos in Brooklyn," 7.

24. K. C. McIntosh, "Some Notes on Training Men for Clerical and Commissary Rates," *US Naval Institute Proceedings* 45 (February 1919): 230, 231–232.

25. "Filipino Chief Trundles Pies," *LAT*, July 20, 1919; "Interview with Immanuel Tardez," Box 142, Federal Writers Project Racial Minorities Survey, UCLA; McIntosh, "Some Notes on Training Men," 226.

26. 39 Stat. 576 (August 29, 1916), ch. 417; Vicente G. Bunuan, "The Philippines: Attitude of the Filipinos," in *Report of the Sixth Conference on the Cause and Cure of War Held in Washington, D.C., January 19–22, 1931* (n.p., n.d.), 6, Vicente Bunuan Collection, Historical Society of Pennsylvania, Philadelphia; Vicente G. Bunuan, "Justice to Filipinos," *The Nation*, January 23, 1929, pp. 116–117; Yen Le Espiritu, *Home Bound: Filipino American Lives across Cultures, Communities, and Countries* (Berkeley: University of California Press, 2003), 98–105; C. W. Franks to Bureau of Insular Affairs, February 19, 1931, Box 880, General Classified Files, Record Group 350: Records of the Bureau of Insular Affairs, National Archives and Records Administration, College Park, MD [hereafter NARA]; Miller, *Messman Chronicles*, 6; Geronimo Suva, "Physical Education in the Philippines," in *The Social Integration of the Philippines* (Manila: Philippine Commission of Independence, 1924), 66; US Navy, *Annual Register of the United States Naval Academy, Annapolis, Md., October 1, 1923* (Washington, DC: GPO, 1923), 48; US Navy, *Regulations Governing the Admission of Candidates into the U.S. Naval Academy as Midshipmen, May 1923* (Washington, DC: GPO, 1923), 3; Wilson, *Jim Crow Joins Up*, 46.

27. "Interview with Johnny Garcia," and "Interview with Immanuel Tardez," Box 142, Federal Writers Project Racial Minorities Survey, UCLA.

28. 16 Stat. 254 (July 14, 1870), at 256.

29. 40 Stat. 542 (May 9, 1918); *Toyota v. United States*, 268 U.S. 402 (1925); Chambers, *To Raise an Army*, 230–231.

30. 40 Stat. 542 (May 9, 1918), ch. 69; Petition no. 179-M: Carlos Pausa Treas, January 17, 1919, Petition no. 180-M: Ramon Claro Mores, January 17, 1919, Petition no. 181-M: Juan Luan Llorente, January 23, 1919, Petition no. 184-M: Jose Ricafrente, February 14, 1919, Box 1, Volume B, and Petition no. 337-M: Juaquin [*sic*] Ramirez Baltazar, December 29, 1919, Box 2, Volume D, Military Petitions for Naturalization, RG 21: Records of District Courts of the United States, National Archives and Records Administration, Pacific Region, Laguna Niguel [now Riverside]; US Department of the Navy, *Naval Digest 1921* (Washington, DC: GPO, 1923), 26–27.

31. Phil. Act no. 2715 (March 17, 1917); Ricardo Trota Jose, *The Philippine Army, 1935–1942* (Quezon City, Philippines: Ateneo de Manila University Press, 1992), 20.

32. "Calls upon Young Filipinos to Rally," *Philippines Free Press*, April 21, 1917; David, *Our National Guard*, 1.

33. Francisco M. Africa, "The Filipino Soldier," *Philippine Review* 3 (March 1918): 192 (italics in original); "Congress Will Accept the Offer of 25,000 Filipino Soldiers—Quezon," translated clipping from *El Ideal*, September 17, 1917, Box 403, General Classified Files, RG 350, NARA; Ricardo Trota Jose, "The Philippine National Guard in World War I," *Philippine Studies* 36 (Third Quarter 1988): 277, 278; Quezon, quoted in "Filipinos Anxious to Aid in the War," *NYT*, December 10, 1917; Thibault, "War Affects the Philippines," 557–558.

34. "Army of Filipinos May Guard Mexican Border," *LAT*, July 6, 1918; Newton D. Baker to Woodrow Wilson, July 2, 1918, *PWW*, vol. 48, pp. 483–484; Brent, quoted in in "Filipinos Make Active War Preparations," clipping from *Oriental News and Comment*, n.d., Box 403, General Classified Files, RG 350, NARA; "Filipinos in Active Service," *Maui News*, January 11, 1918; "Old Enemies Who Are Now Friends," *NYT*, June 17, 1918; Antonio Tabaniag, "The Pre-War Philippine Scouts," *University of Manila Journal of East Asiatic Studies* 9 (October 1960): 12.

35. Jose, "Philippine National Guard," 285.

36. 40 Stat. 432 (January 26, 1918); Suzanne Gronemeyer Carpenter, "Toward the Development of Philippine National Security Capability, 1920–1940" (Ph.D. dissertation, New York University, 1976), 24; Jose, "Philippine National Guard," 282; US Department of War, *War Department Annual Reports, 1918* (Washington, DC: GPO, 1918), vol. 3, pp. 1–2.

37. 40 Stat. 1890 (November 18, 1918); Francis A. Gealogo, "The Philippines in the World of the Influenza Pandemic of 1918–1919," *Philippine Studies* 57 no. 2 (2009): 282–283; "It's Brigadier General Quinlan," *Manila Cablenews-American*, November 16, 1918; "More Guardsmen Come," *Manila Cablenews-American*, November 9, 1918; "First Parade of Guard Is Today," *Manila Cablenews-American*, November 14, 1918; Jose, *Philippine Army*, 20; Jose, "Philippine National Guard," 286, 294–299; Kalaw, *Self-Government in the Philippines*, 63–64; Young Men's Christian Association, *Service with Fighting Men: An Account of the American Young Men's Christian Associations in the World War* (New York: Association Press, 1922), vol. 1, pp. 421–422.

38. Leandro H. Fernández, *A Brief History of the Philippines*, rev. ed. (Boston: Ginn, 1932), 310; Jose, "Philippine National Guard," 296–297; Kalaw, *Self-Government in the Philippines*, 63; "Report of the Governor General of the Philippine Islands," in *War Department Annual Reports, 1919*, vol. 3, p. 6.

39. Josephus Daniels to Newton D. Baker, November 22, 1917, and August 9, 1918, Box 1220, General Classified Files, RG 350, NARA; Harrod, *Manning the New Navy*, 62; Kalaw, *Self-Government in the Philippines*, 60; Florante G. Pascual, "Remember the National Guard?" *Philippines Free Press*, May 21, 1966; "Joint Resolution of the Philippine Legislature," November 28, 1917, and Francis Burton Harrison to Bureau of Insular Affairs, November 14, 1917, Box 1220, General Classified Files, RG 350, NARA; Woodrow Wilson to Newton D. Baker, November 19, 1917, *PWW*, vol. 45, p. 75.

40. "Filipinos Will Man U.S. Boats," clipping from *Newark Star-Eagle*, May 12, 1919, Box 1220, General Classified Files, RG 350, NARA; "Launching of the Rizal," *Philippines Free Press*, February 1, 1919; "Launch Warship for Philippines," *Manila Cablenews-American*, November 15, 1918; Juan F. Salazar, "When Mrs. De Veyra Cracked the Champagne Bottle," *Philippines Free Press*, February 8, 1919; "Two U.S. Warships with Filipino Crews," *Atlanta Constitution*, May 19, 1919.

41. "Filipino Sailors to Man Gift Ships," *LAT*, May 30, 1919; Francis Burton Harrison, *The Corner-Stone of Philippine Independence* (New York: Century, 1922), 185–186; Francis Burton Harrison to Bureau of Insular Affairs, October 6, 1919, Box 1220, General Classified Files, RG 350, NARA; "Chronicle Answers Army Queries," *San Francisco Chronicle*, August 28, 1919.

42. "Filipinos Rally to Flag," *NYT*, May 8, 1917; "An Address to a Joint Session of Congress," April 2, 1917, *PWW*, vol. 41, p. 525.

43. Conrado Benitez, "The Political Desires of the Filipino People," *Journal of International Relations* 10 (October 1919): 152; George Matthew Dutcher,

The Political Awakening of the East: Studies of Political Progress in Egypt, India, China, Japan, and the Philippines (New York: Abingdon Press, 1925), 276; Patrick Gallagher, "Filipinos' Future Is Problem Ahead When Peace Comes," *Atlanta Constitution*, April 6, 1919; Vladimir Lenin, "Fourth Letter from Afar," March 25, 1917, in *Letters from Afar* (Moscow: Progress Publishers, 1971), 46; "News of the Week," *Philippines Free Press*, February 8, 1919; "The Philippines and the League," *Philippines Free Press*, February 8, 1919; "An Address to a Joint Session of Congress," January 8, 1918, *PWW*, vol. 45, pp. 534–539.

44. "An Address in Kansas City," September 6, 1919, *PWW*, vol. 63, p. 74.

45. Kojiro Sato, *If Japan and America Fight*, trans. Jihei Hashiguchi (Tokyo: Meguro Buren, 1921); Hector C. Bywater, *The Great Pacific War: A History of the American-Japanese Campaign of 1931–33* (Boston: Houghton Mifflin, 1925).

46. Vicente G. Bunuan, "Democracy in the Philippines," *Annals of the American Academy of Political and Social Science* 131 (May 1927): 26; "Gilding the Cage for the Filipinos," *New Republic*, January 5, 1927, p. 180; Sylvia Jukes Morris, *Rage for Fame: The Ascent of Clare Boothe Luce* (New York: Random House, 1997), 426.

47. Phil. Act no. 2715 (March 17, 1917); Carpenter, "Philippine National Security Policy," 26–27; David, *Our National Guard*, 31, 34; Teofilo G. Guillermo, "Military Training, a Curse," *Philippine Observer* 29 (June 1932): 18; [Carlos P. Romulo], "Eventually—Why Not Now?" *Philippine Herald* 1 (February 1921): 15–16.

48. Bunuan, "Philippines: Attitude of the Filipinos," 7; Quezon, quoted in Frazier Hunt, *The Rising Temper of the East: Sounding the Human Note in the World-Wide Cry for Land and Liberty* (Indianapolis: Bobbs-Merrill, 1922), 185.

49. Duran, quoted in Teodoro A. Agoncillo, *The Fateful Years: Japan's Adventure in the Philippines, 1941–45* (Quezon City, Philippines: Garcia, 1965), vol. 2, p. 912; Pio Duran, *Philippine Independence and the Far Eastern Question* (Manila: Community Pub., 1935), 103, 132, 152.

50. Bunuan, "Democracy in the Philippines," 26; Jose P. Melencio, *Arguments against Philippine Independence and Their Answers* (Washington, DC: Philippine Press Bureau, 1919), 22.

51. Gabaldon, quoted in Carpenter, "Philippine National Security Policy," 18; K. K. Kawakami, *Japan's Pacific Policy: Especially in Relation to China, the Far East, and the Washington Conference* (New York: Dutton, 1922), 26.

52. Frank H. Schofield, "Incidents and Present Day Aspects of Naval Strategy," *US Naval Institute Proceedings* 49 (May 1923): 782.

53. W. M. Belote, "The Rock in the 'Tween War Years," *Bulletin of the American Historical Collection* 19 (January–March 1991): 27; Commonwealth

of the Philippines, Department of Public Instruction, Bureau of Public Welfare, *Annual Report of the Director of Public Welfare for the Calendar Year January 1 to December 31, 1938* (Manila: Bureau of Printing, 1939), 55–56; Neil Bradley Hall, "Planning in the Periphery: The Case of Olongapo City in the Philippines" (Ph.D. dissertation, University of New Orleans, 1993), 125–126.

54. "Arming and Disarming," *North American Review* 224 (June–July–August 1927): 181–182; Greg Kennedy, "Depression and Security: Aspects Influencing the United States Navy during the Hoover Administration," *Diplomacy and Statecraft* 6 (July 1995): 344, 356; Gerald E. Wheeler, "Republican Philippine Policy, 1921–1933," *Pacific Historical Review* 28 (November 1959): 387–388.

55. "Asiatic Fleet Size to Be Cut," *LAT*, November 12, 1931; Kendall Banning, *The Fleet Today* (New York: Funk and Wagnalls, 1941), 319, 324; Waldo Drake, "There Are Halls of Fame—At Sea!" *LAT*, January 6, 1935.

56. Harry Bernardino, "Hero of War for Democracy," in Timoteo J. Pascual and Liwayway P. Guillermo, *Morong's 400 Years* (Morong: Morong's 400 Years Publication Committee, 1978), 198–202; Tomas M. Claudio, World War I Draft Registration Card, June 3, 1917; Nevada Adjutant General's Office, *Nevada's Golden Stars: A Memorial Volume* (Reno: A. Carlisle, [1924]), 62–63; David, *Our National Guard*, 25.

57. Jose, "Philippine National Guard," 298; "Navy Recruiting Increases," *WP*, March 23, 1919.

CHAPTER FOUR: DEFENDING THEMSELVES, 1934–1941

1. "Jobless Veterans Feast in Solitude," *NYT*, December 26, 1933.

2. Ibid.; Ruth Hampton to Veterans Administration, July 23, 1941, Box 757, Record Group 126: Records of the Office of the Territories, National Archives and Records Administration, College Park, MD [hereafter NARA].

3. Dwight D. Eisenhower, *At Ease: Stories I Tell to Friends* (Garden City, NY: Doubleday, 1967), 216.

4. *Manila Times*, November 26, 1929, quoted in Quintard Taylor, *The Forging of a Black Community: Seattle's Central District from 1870 through the Civil Rights Era* (Seattle: University of Washington Press, 1994), 122.

5. "Interview with Anonymous Filipino," February 2, 1937, Box 142, Federal Writers Project Racial Minorities Survey, Young Research Library, UCLA, Los Angeles [hereafter UCLA].

6. Mariano Angeles Oral History, November 6, 1975, Washington State Oral/Aural History Program (Olympia: Washington State Archives, 1974–1977), 8 [hereafter WSOAHP].

7. Emory S. Bogardus, "The Filipino Immigrant Problem," *Sociology and Social Research* 13 (May–June 1929): 474; "Labor on Hawaiian Sugar Plantations," *Monthly Labor Review* 30 (March 1930): 33; Paul Scharrenberg, "The Philippine Problem: Attitude of American Labor toward Filipino Immigration and Philippine Independence," *Pacific Affairs* 2 (February 1929): 50; Lydia N. Yu-Jose, "Turn of the Century Emigration: Filipinos to Hawaii, Japanese to the Philippines," *Philippine Studies* 46 (First Quarter 1998): 92–94, 100.

8. E. V. "Vic" Bacho, *The Long Road: Memoirs of a Filipino Pioneer* (Seattle: n.p., [1992?]), 10, 11; Yasonia, quoted in Roberto V. Vallangca, ed. and comp., *Pinoy: The First Wave (1898–1941)* (San Francisco: Strawberry Hill Press, 1977), 75.

9. Fabian Bergano OH, WSOAHP, 7; Benicio Catapusan, "The Filipino Labor Cycle in the United States," *Sociology and Social Research* 19 (September–October 1934): 61–63; Edward K. Strong Jr., *Japanese in California* (Stanford: Stanford University Press, 1933), 15, 105.

10. J. B. Baldovino, "Pros and Cons of Law Institutions," *Philippines Star Press*, August 28, 1937; "Interview with Eddie Manzoa," February 10, 1937, Box 142, Federal Writers Project Racial Minorities Survey, UCLA.

11. Bogardus, "Filipino Immigrant Problem," 473; Herman Feldman, *Racial Factors in American Industry* (New York: Harper and Bros., 1931), 98; "The Filipino Problem in California," *Monthly Labor Review* 30 (June 1930): 72–73; "Fruit Growers Discuss Labor," *LAT*, November 18, 1927.

12. Feldman, *Racial Factors in American Industry*, 97–99; "Filipino Problem in California," 74; Paul A. Kramer, *The Blood of Government: Race, Empire, the United States, and the Philippines* (Chapel Hill: University of North Carolina Press, 2006), 407–413, 428–431; "Manila Protests California Rioting," *NYT*, January 26, 1930; Glenna Matthews, *Silicon Valley, Women, and the California Dream: Gender, Class, and Opportunity in the Twentieth Century* (Stanford: Stanford University Press, 2003), 32; "Mob Kills Filipino; 7 Californians Held," *NYT*, January 24, 1930, p. 5; "Riot Death of Filipino Protested," *LAT*, January 28, 1930; Scharrenberg, "Philippine Problem," 50; Ronald Takaki, *Strangers from a Different Shore: A History of Asian Americans* (New York: Penguin, 1989), 327–328.

13. Emory S. Bogardus, "Filipino Immigrant Attitudes," *Sociology and Social Research* 14 (May–June 1930): 479; Theodore Roosevelt Jr., *Colonial Policies of the United States* (Garden City, NY: Doubleday, Doran, 1937), 172.

14. Foster R. Dulles, "The Philippines and the Hare-Hawes-Cutting Act," *Foreign Policy Reports* 9 (January 3, 1934): 246–256; "Hawes Act Fought by Most Filipinos," *NYT*, March 19, 1933; Richard Lowitt, *Bronson M. Cutting: Progressive Politician* (Albuquerque: University of New Mexico Press,

1992), 168–169, 207–208, 229–232; Vicente Villamin, "The Philippines Question Again," typescript, n.d. [after 1933], Box 12, Papers of Douglas Southall Freeman, Special Collections Library, University of Virginia, Charlottesville [hereafter UVA].

15. Grant K. Goodman, "Consistency Is the Hobgoblin: Manuel L. Quezon and Japan, 1899–1934," *Journal of Southeast Asian Studies* 14 (March 1983): 89–92; Manuel Luis Quezon, *The Good Fight* (New York: D. Appleton–Century, 1946), 149, 151.

16. Roosevelt, quoted in "Philippines Bill Near," *LAT*, March 3, 1934; Tydings, quoted in Takaki, *Strangers from a Different Shore*, 331–332; McDuffie, quoted in "Roosevelt Acts for Filipino Independence," *WP*, March 3, 1934.

17. "Manila Apathetic to M'Duffie Bill," *NYT*, March 21, 1934.

18. 48 Stat. 456 (March 24, 1934), at 462–463.

19. Kendall Banning, *The Fleet Today* (New York: Funk and Wagnalls, 1941), 91; Frederick S. Harrod, *Manning the New Navy: The Development of a Modern Naval Enlisted Force, 1899–1940* (Westport, CT: Greenwood Press, 1978), 60–61.

20. Banning, *The Fleet Today*, 119; Richard E. Miller, *The Messman Chronicles: African Americans in the U.S. Navy, 1932–1943* (Annapolis, MD: Naval Institute Press, 2004), 15, 17; "Navy Weeds Filipino Gobs from Service," *CT*, November 12, 1934.

21. "Filipinos Arrive at Naval Academy," *WP*, December 29, 1934; "Navy Weeds Filipino Gobs from Service"; "Nip Plot to Oust Race Employes [*sic*] at Naval Academy," *Chicago Defender*, November 17, 1934.

22. Manuel Quezon to Claude A. Swanson, August 29, 1935, and Claude A. Swanson to Harry H. Woodring, March 30, 1938, Box 691, General Classified Files, Record Group 350: Records of the Bureau of Insular Affairs, NARA.

23. Berkeley Walker, "Racial Minorities Survey—Filipino," typescript, June 2, 1937, Box 142, Federal Writers Project Racial Minorities Survey, UCLA.

24. D. F. Gonzalo, "Social Adjustments of Filipinos in America," *Sociology and Social Research* 14 (November–December 1929): 169.

25. Emory S. Bogardus, "American Attitudes towards Filipinos," *Sociology and Social Research* 14 (September–October 1929): 68; Bogardus, "Filipino Immigrant Attitudes," 473, 475; Bogardus, "Filipino Immigrant Problem," 478; "Causes of California Race Riots," *Literary Digest*, February 15, 1930, p. 12; Carol Hemminger, "Little Manila: The Filipino in Stockton Prior to World War II," *Pacific Historian* 24 (Spring 1980): 28; Albert W. Palmer, *Orientals in American Life* (New York: Friendship Press, 1934), 89.

26. Bogardus, "Filipino Immigrant Problem," 477; Gonzalo, "Social Adjustments of Filipinos," 169, 170, 172 n. 11.

27. "Annapolis Opposes Filipino Mess Boys," *WP*, November 2, 1934; Bogardus, "Filipino Immigrant Problem," 477; Henry Empeno, "Anti-Miscegenation Laws and the Pilipino," in *Letters in Exile: An Introductory Reader on the History of Pilipinos in America* (Los Angeles: UCLA Asian American Studies Center, 1976), 63–71; Marina E. Espina, "Seven Generations of a New Orleans Filipino Family," in *Perspectives on Ethnicity in New Orleans*, ed. John Cooke (n.p.: Committee on Ethnicity in New Orleans, 1979), 34; Stephanie Hinnershitz, *Race, Religion, and Civil Rights: Asian Students on the West Coast, 1900–1968* (New Brunswick, NJ: Rutgers University Press, 2015), 96–97; W. A. Plecker to Grace Davidson, October 4, 1935, Box 41, Papers of John Powell, UVA.

28. *De Cano v. State*, 110 P. 2d 627 (1941); "Filipino Right to Own Land Here Upheld," *Philippine Journal*, April 22, 1940; Hinnershitz, *Race, Religion, and Civil Rights*, 91.

29. Beth Tompkins Bates, *Pullman Porters and the Rise of Protest Politics in Black America, 1925–1945* (Chapel Hill: University of North Carolina Press, 2001), 21; Benicio Catapusan, "The Filipinos and the Labor Unions," *American Federationist* 47 (February 1940): 173–176; Hemminger, "Little Manila," 29, 211; Hinnershitz, *Race, Religion, and Civil Rights*, 90; Bruno Lasker, *Filipino Immigration to Continental United States and to Hawaii* (Chicago: University of Chicago Press, 1931), 174–176; Carey McWilliams, "Exit the Filipino," *The Nation*, September 4, 1935, p. 265; Barbara M. Posadas, "The Hierarchy of Color and Psychological Adjustment in an Industrial Environment: Filipinos, the Pullman Company, and the Brotherhood of Sleeping Car Porters," *Labor History* 23 (Summer 1982): 355, 362, 369; Larry R. Salomon, *Roots of Justice: Stories of Organizing in Communities of Color* (Berkeley, CA: Chardon Press, 1998), 16–18, 19.

30. Walker, "Racial Minorities Survey—Filipino," Federal Writers Project Racial Minorities Survey, UCLA.

31. James O'Donnell Bennett, "Be Vigilant! Is Pershing Word on Defense Day," *CT*, September 13, 1924; "Defense Day Flight over City Mapped for World Airmen," *WP*, September 11, 1924; Filipino Federation of America, *Anniversary Program* (1938), in Filipino Federation of America Records, Historical Society of Pennsylvania, Philadelphia; "Legion Post Commander Shot and Killed by Bandit," *CT*, April 8, 1932; Palmer, *Orientals in American Life*, 97; Barbara M. Posadas, "At a Crossroad: Filipino American History

and the Old-Timers' Generation," *Amerasia Journal* 13 no. 1 (1986–87): 90–92; Luis S. Quianio, "Who's Who in 'Little Manila,'" *Philippines Star Press*, August 28, 1937.

32. *Miguel v. McCarl*, 291 U.S. 442 (1935), at 449, 453; Antonio Tabaniag, "The Pre-War Philippine Scouts," *University of Manila Journal of East Asiatic Studies* 9 (October 1960): 17.

33. 49 Stat. 478 (July 10, 1935); Welch, quoted in Casiano Pagdilao Coloma, *A Study of the Filipino Repatriation Movement* (San Francisco: R and E Research Associates, 1974 [1939]), 37; McWilliams, "Exit the Filipino," 265; Mae M. Ngai, *Impossible Subjects: Illegal Aliens and the Making of Modern America* (Princeton: Princeton University Press, 2004), 120–125, 129–138.

34. Emory S. Bogardus, "Filipino Repatriation," *Sociology and Social Research* 21 (September–October 1936): 70; Coloma, *Filipino Repatriation Movement*, 26; Arleen Garcia De Vera, "Constituting Community: A Study of Nationalism, Colonialism, Gender, and Identity among Filipinos in California, 1919–1946" (Ph.D. dissertation, University of California Los Angeles, 2002), 224; Walker, "Racial Minorities Survey—Filipino," Federal Writers Project Racial Minorities Survey, UCLA.

35. Lewis E. Gleeck Jr., "The Putsch that Failed," *Bulletin of the American Historical Collection* 26 (July–September 1998): 35–45; Joseph Ralston Hayden, *The Philippines: A Study in National Development* (New York: Macmillan, 1942), 428–432; Michael Schaller, *Douglas MacArthur: The Far Eastern General* (New York: Oxford University Press, 1989), 31–32; Robert Aura Smith, *Philippine Freedom, 1946–1958* (New York: Columbia University Press, 1958), 94–95, 97.

36. Stephen E. Ambrose, *Eisenhower* (New York: Simon and Schuster, 1983), vol. 1, p. 105; George A. Malcolm, *American Colonial Careerist: Half a Century of Official Life and Personal Experience in the Philippines and Puerto Rico* (Boston: Christopher Pub., 1957), 68.

37. Ambrose, *Eisenhower*, 113; Kenneth S. Davis, *Soldier of Democracy: A Biography of Dwight D. Eisenhower* (Garden City, NY: Doubleday, Doran, 1945), 250; Eisenhower, *At Ease*, 219, 225; Daniel D. Holt, "An Unlikely Partnership and Service: Dwight Eisenhower, Mark Clark, and the Philippines," *Kansas History* 13 (Autumn 1990): 156; Marilyn Irvin Holt, *Mamie Doud Eisenhower: The General's First Lady* (Lawrence: University Press of Kansas, 2007), 25–27.

38. Ricardo Trota Jose, *The Philippine Army, 1935–1942* (Quezon City, Philippines: Ateneo de Manila University Press, 1992), 30–59; Louis Morton, *The Fall of the Philippines* (Washington, DC: Office of the Chief of Military History, Department of the Army, 1953), 8–13.

39. Maximo M. Kalaw, "Why I Favor the Defense Bill," *Philippine Forum* 1 (February 1936): 73, 74; Camilo Osias, "My Opposition to the National Defense Bill," *Philippine Forum* 1 (January 1936): 30, 32.

40. Schaller, *Douglas MacArthur*, 33–34.

41. Ambrose, *Eisenhower*, 106; Davis, *Soldier of Democracy*, 247–248; Eisenhower, *At Ease*, 221; MacArthur, quoted in Jim Marshall, "Spearhead of Our Defense," *Collier's*, September 8, 1936, p. 12; Schaller, *Douglas MacArthur*, 33.

42. Coloma, *Filipino Repatriation Movement*, 45; Harold E. Fey, "Militarizing the Philippines," *The Nation*, June 10, 1936, pp. 736–737; Jose, *Philippine Army*, 53–55.

43. Ambrose, *Eisenhower*, 106, 109; Bureau of Public Welfare, *Annual Report, 1937*, 12–13; Davis, *Soldier of Democracy*, 248–249; "The March of Events," *Philippine Forum* 1 (September 1936): 19–20; Schaller, *MacArthur*, 35–36; *Second Annual Report of the President of the Philippines to the President and the Congress of the United States Covering the Calendar Year Ended December 31, 1937* (Washington, DC: GPO, 1939), 8–10.

44. "Army of Producers Wanted," *Philippine Forum* 2 (December 1936): 17; Delbert Ausmus Oral History, typescript (1965), 1285–1287, 1303, Papers of Delbert Ausmus, UCLA; Jose, *Philippine Army*, 74–79; Philippine Army, *Semi-Annual Report of the Chief of Staff of the Philippine Army for the Period January 1 to June 30, 1939* (Manila: Bureau of Printing, 1940), 6; Catherine Porter, *Crisis in the Philippines* (New York: Knopf, 1942), 115; *Third Annual Report of the President of the Philippines to the President and the Congress of the United States Covering the Calendar Year Ended December 31, 1938* (Washington, DC: GPO, 1940), 11.

45. Hayden, *Philippines*, 741, 743; Alfred W. McCoy, *Closer than Brothers: Manhood at the Philippine Military Academy* (New Haven, CT: Yale University Press, 1999), 49–51; *Third Annual Report*, 11–12.

46. Ambrose, *Eisenhower*, 113; Davis, *Soldier of Democracy*, 250–251; Eisenhower, *At Ease*, 226–227; "Reminiscences of William L. Lee," Oral History Research Office, Columbia University, New York; Porter, *Crisis in the Philippines*, 116; *Third Annual Report*, 10; H. Ford Wilkins, "Wings for the Filipino," *NYT*, April 24, 1938.

47. Eisenhower, quoted in Holt, "Unlikely Partnership," 156; diary entry, January 30, 1937, in Harold Ickes, *The Secret Diary of Harold L. Ickes* (New York: Simon and Schuster, 1953–54), vol. 2, p. 62; Richard Meixsel, "A Uniform Story," *Journal of Military History* 69 (July 2005): 791–800; Schaller, *MacArthur*, 34–38.

48. Ambrose, *Eisenhower*, 117–118; Eisenhower, *At Ease*, 231, 246–247; Holt, *Mamie Doud Eisenhower*, 28; Malcolm, *American Colonial Careerist*, 70; Carol

Morris Petillo, *Douglas MacArthur: The Philippine Years* (Bloomington: Indiana University Press, 1981), 93; Schaller, *MacArthur*, 40.

49. Emilio Aguinaldo and Jose Alejandrino, *Economic Aspects of National Defense* (n.p.: Pagkakaisa ng Bayan, [1936]), 9.

50. James S. Allen, "Manuel Quezon—Philippine Dictator," *The Nation*, March 20, 1937, p. 321; Delbert Ausmus OH, 1295, UCLA; C. C. Bartolome, "The Need for a National Physical Education Movement in the Philippines Today," *Philippine Social Science Review* 7 (October 1935): 280–281; "Defense Program Upheld by Quezon," *NYT*, April 4, 1937; E. K. Higdon, "Enroll Girls in Philippine Army," *Christian Century*, January 8, 1936, pp. 58–59; E. K. Higdon, "Filipinos Back Military Regime," *Christian Century*, January 13, 1937, p. 54; Serafin E. Macaraig, *Community Problems: An Elementary Study of Philippine Social Conditions* (Manila: Educational Supply, 1933), 75, 82; "President Quezon's Citizenship Code," in Filipino Agricultural Laborers' Association, *FALA Year Book, 1940* (Stockton, CA: FALA, 1940), Box 15, Papers of Carey McWilliams, UCLA.

51. James S. Allen, "Who Owns the Philippines?" *The Nation*, April 24, 1937, pp. 463–465; David Bernstein, *The Philippine Story* (New York: Farrar, Straus, 1947), 240; Keith Thor Carlson, *The Twisted Road to Freedom: America's Granting of Independence to the Philippines* (Quezon City: University of the Philippines Press, 1995), 46; De Vera, "Constituting Community," 230–231.

52. Allen, "Manuel Quezon—Philippine Dictator," 322; Porter, *Crisis in the Philippines*, 92; Florentino Rodao, "Spanish Falange in the Philippines, 1936–1945," *Philippine Studies* 43 (First Quarter 1995): 3, 12, 15; Rodao, *Franquistas sin Franco: una historia alternativa de la Guerra Civil española desde Filipinas* (Granada: Comares, 2012), 78–85.

53. Quezon, quoted in Allen, "Manuel Quezon," 322.

54. Hayden, *Philippines*, 361–389; "Philippine Rebels Are Held in Check," *NYT*, May 4, 1935; Motoe Terami-Wada, "The Sakdal Movement, 1930–34," *Philippine Studies* 36 (Second Quarter 1988): 132, 138, 149.

55. Benjamin Gitlow, *I Confess: The Truth about American Communism* (New York: Dutton, 1940), 475, 486; Salomon, *Roots of Justice*, 16; "Second U.S. Congress against War and Fascism," *China Today* 1 (November 1934): 23; "1300 at Anti-War Meeting Cheer Unity," clipping from *Western Worker*, May 2, 1935, Box 2, Papers of Karl Yoneda, UCLA.

56. 54 Stat. 230 (June 14, 1940).

57. John E. Haynes, *Red Scare or Red Menace?: American Communism and Anticommunism in the Cold War Era* (Chicago: Ivan R. Dee, 1996), 33; "Roosevelt Signs Bill to List Aliens," *NYT*, June 30, 1940; John W. Sherman, *A*

Communist Front at Mid-Century: The American Committee for Protection of the Foreign Born, 1933–1959 (Westport, CT: Praeger, 2001), 54–55.

58. 48 Stat. 456 (March 24, 1934); "Commissioner's Message Regarding Registration," *Philippine Journal*, August 31, 1940; "Filipinos Should Withhold Registration Pending Decision by State Department," *Commonwealth Journal*, September 5, 1940.

59. "Mass Registration Stockton Pinoys at FALA Office," *Philippine Journal*, August 31, 1940; "Washington Filipinos Defies Alien Status," *Commonwealth Journal*, September 5, 1940; "You Should Register Now," *Philippine Journal*, August 31, 1940.

60. Committee for the Protection of Filipino Rights, *An Appeal to Reason* (San Francisco, n.d. [1940?]), Box 15, Papers of Carey McWilliams, UCLA; "Interest on Citizenship Fight Is Merged," *Commonwealth Journal*, September 5, 1940; "Picket Demonstration against Japan's War Moves in China," *China Today* 1 (July 1935): 199.

61. Hugh S. Johnson, "Anchors Away," *Saturday Evening Post*, October 5, 1940, pp. 77, 80; Pacis, quoted in Porter, *Crisis in the Philippines*, 6; Nicholas Roosevelt, *A Front Row Seat* (Norman: University of Oklahoma Press, 1953), 161.

62. "The Philippines: Prelude to Dictatorship?" *Time*, September 2, 1940, pp. 16–17; Porter, *Crisis in the Philippines*, 91, 98–105; Hirosi Saito, "My Impressions in the Far East and Japanese-American Relations," *Annals of the American Academy of Political and Social Science* 177 (January 1935): 246, 247; "U.S. to Face Issue on Philippine Land," *NYT*, March 28, 1935; Yu-Jose, "Turn of the Century Emigration," 90, 97, 100; "Yulo Praises New Immigration Law," *Philippine Journal*, May 13, 1940.

63. Hernando J. Abaya, *The CLU Story: 50 Years of Struggle for Civil Liberties* (Quezon City, Philippines: New Day, 1987), 4; Claude Buss Oral History (1984), 8, Center for Oral and Public History, California State University, Fullerton [hereafter CSUF]; Malcolm, *American Colonial Careerist*, 71; Smith, *Philippine Freedom*, 101, 105.

64. Commonwealth Act no. 600 (August 21, 1940); Abaya, *CLU Story*, 1–3, 9–23; diary entry, February 27, 1937, in Ickes, *Secret Diary of Harold Ickes*, vol. 2, p. 83; Philippine Army, *Semi-Annual Report (1939)*, 7–8; Schaller, *MacArthur*, 39–40.

65. Hayden, *Philippines*, 731; Porter, *Crisis in the Philippines*, 111–112; "Quezon's Food Plan Supplies Philippines with War Larder," *WP*, December 21, 1941; Schaller, *MacArthur*, 40.

66. Buss OH, CSUF, 7; Civilian Emergency Administration, *Rules and Regulations for the Organization and Training of Volunteer Guards and the Air Raid Wardens Service and Air Raid Precautions* (Manila: Bureau of Printing,

1941), 55; Manuel Quezon to Francis Bowes Sayre, April 3, 1941, and Francis Bowes Sayre to Harold Ickes, April 9, 1941, Box 5, Papers of Francis Bowes Sayre, Library of Congress Manuscript Division, Washington, DC [hereafter LCMD].

67. Executive Order 8832 (July 26, 1941); Buss OH, CSUF, 4, 9; "M'Arthur Made Chief in Far East," *NYT*, July 27, 1941; Roosevelt, quoted in Jean Edward Smith, *FDR* (New York: Random House, 2007), 517; "U.S. Moves to Weld Strong Island Army," *LAT*, July 27, 1941.

68. "Roosevelt Order on Army," *NYT*, July 27, 1941.

69. Delbert Ausmus OH, 1307, UCLA; Jose, *Philippine Army*, 196; Christopher L. Kolakowski, *Last Stand on Bataan: The Defense of the Philippines, December 1941–May 1942* (Jefferson, NC: McFarland, 2016), 3; Edward S. Miller, *War Plan Orange: The U.S. Strategy to Defeat Japan, 1897–1945* (Annapolis, MD: Naval Institute Press, 1991), 61–62; Morton, *Fall of the Philippines*, 27–28.

70. John Gordon IV, "Among the Best: The Philippine Scouts," *Military Review* 67 (September 1987): 70–71; Philippine Scouts Heritage Society, *Heritage of Valor: A History of the Philippine Scouts, 100th Anniversary* (Fort Sam Houston, TX: Fort Sam Houston Museum, 2001), 15; Porter, *Crisis in the Philippines*, 110, 112–113; Schaller, *MacArthur*, 40.

71. Douglas MacArthur to Francis Bowes Sayre, October 10, 1941, Box 5, Papers of Francis Bowes Sayre, LCMD; Porter, *Crisis in the Philippines*, 119; Bessie Hackett Wilson OH, CSUF, 9.

72. A. A. Hoehling, *The Week before Pearl Harbor* (New York: Norton, 1963), 102, 105, 142–146; Hull, quoted in Page Smith, *Redeeming the Time: A People's History of the 1920s and the New Deal* (New York: McGraw-Hill, 1987), 1086.

CHAPTER FIVE: DEFEATS, 1941–1944

1. Virgilio Menor Felipe, *Hawai'i: A Pilipino Dream* (Honolulu: Mutual Pub., 2002), 159; Lawrence H. Fuchs, *Hawaii Pono: An Ethnic and Political History* (New York: Harcourt, Brace and World, 1961), 299; Knox, quoted in Louis Morton, *Fall of the Philippines* (Washington, DC: Office of the Chief of Military History, Department of the Army, 1953), 78.

2. Morton, *Fall of the Philippines*, 79.

3. Richard B. Meixsel, *Clark Field and the U.S. Army Air Corps in the Philippines, 1919–1942* (Quezon City, Philippines: New Day, 2002), 106.

4. Morton, *Fall of the Philippines*, 86–90.

5. Gregoria I. Espinosa, "Filipino Nurses in Bataan and Corregidor," *American Journal of Nursing* 46 (February 1946): 97–98; Mallonée, quoted in Morton, *Fall of the Philippines*, 80.

6. Michaelangelo Ebro-Dakudao, "A Davao Wartime Diary," *Philippine Quarterly of Culture and Society* 22 (March 1994): 69; Carlos Quirino, *Chick Parsons: America's Master Spy in the Philippines* (Quezon City, Philippines: New Day, 1984), 9.

7. Gwenfread Allen, *Hawaii's War Years, 1941–1945* (Honolulu: University of Hawaii Press, 1950), 350; Lawrence E. Davies, "Japanese End California Leases, Fearing Labor Lack and a Boycott," *NYT*, February 22, 1942; Arleen Garcia De Vera, "Constituting Community: A Study of Nationalism, Colonialism, Gender, and Identity among Filipinos in California, 1919–1946" (Ph.D. dissertation, University of California Los Angeles, 2002), 227; "How to Tell Japs from Chinese," *Life*, December 22, 1941, pp. 81–82.

8. Espinosa, "Filipino Nurses," 97; Alfredo T. Marquez, *War Memoirs of the Alcala Veterans* (Quezon City, Philippines: New Day, 1992), 53, 61; Morton, *Fall of the Philippines*, 100–108, 123–144; Kemp Tolley, "Army Snubs Navy in the Philippines," in *The Pacific War Remembered: An Oral History Collection*, ed. John T. Mason Jr. (Annapolis, MD: Naval Institute Press, 1986), 27.

9. Robert Lee Dennison, "The Philippines: Prelude to Departure," in *Pacific War Remembered*, ed. Mason, 35.

10. Maximo M. Kalaw, "Filipino Opposition to the Japanese," *Pacific Affairs* 18 (December 1945): 341; "Messages on Philippines," *NYT*, December 29, 1941.

11. Bob Seals, "Lieutenant Colonel Edwin P. Ramsey, USA-Ret.," *On Point* 17 (Summer 2011): 19.

12. D. Clayton James, *The Years of MacArthur* (Boston: Houghton Mifflin, 1975), vol. 2, p. 109; Carol Morris Petillo, *Douglas MacArthur: The Philippine Years* (Bloomington: Indiana University Press, 1981), 213.

13. Morton, *Fall of the Philippines*, 454–467.

14. Stanley L. Falk, *Bataan: The March of Death* (New York: Norton, 1962), 194-200; James, *Years of MacArthur*, vol. 1, p. 150.

15. Kevin C. Murphy, *Inside the Bataan Death March: Defeat, Travail and Memory* (Jefferson, NC: McFarland, 2014), 234.

16. Morton, *Fall of the Philippines*, 385; Jiro Saito, *The Greater East Asia War: A Historical Analysis of Its Background, Causes, Strategy and Significance* (Manila: n.p., n.d.), 31, American Historical Collection, Ateneo de Manila University, Quezon City, Philippines [hereafter AHC].

17. Thomas S. Jones, "Operations of Troop C, Philippine Scouts, Northern Luzon: The First Two Years," typescript (1946), 4, Box 52, Papers of William Bowen, Douglas MacArthur Memorial Archives, Norfolk, VA; Marquez, *Alcala Veterans*, 55.

18. Executive Order no. 8802 (June 25, 1941); John J. Corson, *Manpower for Victory: Total Mobilization for Total War* (New York: Farrar and Rinehart, 1943), 140–142; Ramon A. de la Peña to War Department, February 3, 1944, M. de Ocampo to Jack B. Fahy, June 16, 1945, and R. A. Kleindienst to L. M. Escalante, September 20, 1941, Box 757, Record Group 126: Records of the Office of the Territories, National Archives and Records Administration, College Park, MD; Louis Ruchames, *Race, Jobs, and Politics: The Story of FEPC* (New York: Columbia University Press, 1953), 92.

19. Cardenas, quoted in Melina Tria Kervkliet, *Unbending Cane: Pablo Manlapit: A Filipino Labor Leader in Hawai'i* (Honolulu: University of Hawai'i at Manoa Office of Multicultural Student Services, 2002), 95; "Filipinos' Leader Wants More Hired in War Jobs," *LAT*, October 30, 1942; Bienvenido Santos, "Filipinos at War," in *Letters in Exile: An Introductory Reader on the History of Pilipinos in America* (Los Angeles: UCLA Asian American Studies Center, 1976), 93.

20. Marcelo Canania Oral History transcript (1968), 24, Center for Oral and Public History, California State University, Fullerton [hereafter CSUF]; Genevieve Ordona Laigo Oral History, Washington State Oral/Aural History Program (Olympia: Washington State Archives, 1974–1977), 10–11 [hereafter WSOAHP]; Toribio M. Martin OH, WSOAHP, 16; F. A. Respicio, comp., *Hawaii's Filipinos and Their Part in the War: A Pictorial Record of Their Work for Victory and Freedom* (n.p.: F. A. Respicio, n.d. [1945]), Hawaiian Historical Society, Honolulu; Linda A. Revilla, "'Pineapples,' 'Hawayanos,' and 'Loyal Americans': Local Boys in the First Filipino Infantry Regiment, US Army," *Social Process in Hawaii* 37 (1996): 66–67.

21. 54 Stat. 885 (September 16, 1940); "Conscription Law Exempts Filipinos," *Philippine Journal*, August 31, 1940; "Poor and Rich, the Halt and Fit Register," *WP*, October 17, 1940.

22. "Filipinos in U.S. May Enlist in Army," *NYT*, January 3, 1942; "Poletti, Morris and McGoldrick Among Draft Registrants in City," *NYT*, February 16, 1942.

23. "Capt. Sulit Faces Deportation Soon," *Philippine Journal*, January 23, 1940; "Coast Filipinos Plan Own A.E.F.," *NYT*, January 13, 1942; Ernesto D. Ilustre, "Filipino Fighting Men," *WP*, July 28, 1942.

24. "Coast Filipinos Plan Own A.E.F."; Ilustre, "Filipino Fighting Men"; Stimson, quoted in Santos, "Filipinos at War," 93.

25. Ilustre, "Filipino Fighting Men"; Sebastian N. Inosanto, *The Story of Trinity Presbyterian Church of Stockton, California* (n.p., October 1974), 11,

Filipinos in Stockton Vertical File, Holt-Atherton Special Collections Library, University of the Pacific, Stockton, CA.

26. Ilustre, "Filipino Fighting Men"; Franc Shor, "See You in Manila!" *Reader's Digest* 42 (March 1943): 120.

27. Alex Fabros, "The Boogie Woogie Boys," *Filipinas* 1 (September 1993): 38–39; Augustin L. Santos, "The First Filipino Infantry," and "The 2nd Filipino Infantry Regiment," undated typescripts, First and Second Filipino Infantry Files, Filipino American National Historical Society, Seattle [hereafter FANHS]; Craig Scharlin and Lilia V. Villanueva, *Philip Vera Cruz: A Personal History of the Filipino Immigrants and the Farmworkers Movement*, 3d ed. (Seattle: University of Washington Press, 2000), 7.

28. Arleen De Vera, "The Tapia-Saiki Incident: Interethnic Conflict and Filipino Responses to the Anti-Filipino Exclusion Movement," in *Over the Edge: Remapping the American West*, ed. Valerie J. Matsumoto and Blake Allmendinger (Berkeley: University of California Press, 1999), 201–214; John Modell, *The Economics and Politics of Racial Accommodation: The Japanese of Los Angeles, 1900–1942* (Urbana: University of Illinois Press, 1977), 71; Edward K. Strong Jr., *Japanese in California* (Stanford: Stanford University Press, 1933), 13.

29. Lawrence E. Davies, "Evacuation Stay Denied to Japanese," *NYT*, April 23, 1942; *Ex parte Ventura*, 44 F. Supp. 520 (1942), at 520, 521; Mary Asaba Ventura and Husband, Petition for Writ of Habeas Corpus, April 13, 1942, and Oral Opinion, In the Matter of the Petition of Mary Asaba and Husband, for a Writ of Habeas Corpus, April 15, 1942, Box 83, Civil Case Files, Western District, Washington, Record Group 21: Records of District Courts of the United States, National Archives and Records Administration, Pacific-Alaska Region, Seattle.

30. *Hirabayashi v. U.S.*, 320 U.S. 81 (1943), at 111; Roger Daniels, "The Exile and Return of Seattle's Japanese," *Pacific Northwest Quarterly* 88 (Fall 1997): 170; Audrie Girdner and Anne Loftis, *The Great Betrayal: The Evacuation of the Japanese-Americans during World War II* (New York: Macmillan, 1969), 202–207; Swaine Thomas and Richard S. Nishimoto, *Japanese American Evacuation and Resettlement: The Spoilage* (Berkeley: University of California Press, 1946), 53.

31. Timothy J. Lukes and Gary Y. Okihiro, *Japanese Legacy: Farming and Community Life in California's Santa Clara Valley* (Cupertino: California History Center, 1985), 119; Brian Roberts, ed., *They Cast a Long Shadow: A History of the Nonwhite Races on Bainbridge Island* (Bainbridge Island, WA: Minority History Committee of Bainbridge Island School District, 1975), 87.

32. "California to Aid Non-Enemy Aliens," *NYT*, April 11, 1942; Lukes and Okihiro, *Japanese Legacy*, 118.

33. Velasco, quoted in De Vera, "Constituting Community," 228 (italics in original); "Filipino Labor Plan Pushed," *LAT*, August 31, 1942.

34. Felipe, *Hawai'i: A Pilipino Dream*, 163–164; Fuchs, *Hawaii Pono*, 300–301; Jonathan Y. Okamura, "Race Relations in' Hawai'i during World War II: The Non-Internment of Japanese Americans," *Amerasia Journal* 26 no. 2 (2000): 127.

35. "AMA Will Buy All U.S. Requirements of Canned Fish," *WSJ*, June 5, 1942.

36. Benicio T. Catapusan, "The Filipinos and the Labor Unions," *American Federationist* 47 (February 1940): 173–176; Doug Chin, *Seattle's International District: The Making of a Pan-Asian Community* (Seattle: International Examiner Press, 2001), 49; Chris Friday, *Organizing Asian American Labor: The Pacific Coast Canned-Salmon Industry, 1870–1942* (Philadelphia: Temple University Press, 1992), 128–132; Forrest E. LaViolette, *Americans of Japanese Ancestry: A Study of Assimilation in the American Community* (Toronto: Canadian Institute of International Affairs, 1945), 93–94.

37. Friday, *Organizing Asian American Labor*, 125, 127.

38. Ibid., 188; Ignacio I. Josue to Local Draft Board no. 223, March 2, 1942, Conrad Espe to Local Board no. 10, April 8, 1942, Prudencio P. Mori to Selective Service Local Board no. 120, May 18, 1944, and Trinidad Rojo to Rationing Division, OPA, April 14, 1944, Box 14, Cannery Workers' and Farm Laborers' Union Local 7 Records, Special Collections Library, University Washington, Seattle [hereafter CWFLU Records, UW]; Trinidad Rojo OH, WSOAHP, 44.

39. Prudencio Mori to OPA, December 8, 1943, Box 14, CWFLU Records, UW.

40. Carlos P. Romulo, *I Saw the Fall of the Philippines* (Garden City, NY: Doubleday, Doran, 1942).

41. Carlos P. Romulo, *My Brother Americans* (Garden City, NY: Doubleday, Doran, 1945), 15.

42. *Philippines Mail*, December 4, 1942, quoted in De Vera, "Constituting Community," 226.

43. Vargas, quoted in Layton Horner, "Japanese Military Administration in Malaya and the Philippines" (Ph.D. dissertation, University of Arizona, 1973), 83.

44. Teodoro A. Agoncillo, *The Fateful Years: Japan's Adventure in the Philippines, 1941–1945* (Quezon City, Philippines: Garcia, 1965), vol. 2, pp. 909, 918.

45. Tamechi Hara et al., *Japanese Destroyer Captain* (New York: Ballantine, 1961), 66–67; Ricardo T. Jose, "Labor Usage and Mobilization during the Japanese Occupation of the Philippines, 1942–45," in *Asian Labor in the Wartime Japanese Empire: Unknown Histories*, ed. Paul H. Kratoska (Armonk, NY: M. E. Sharpe, 2005), 271, 274, 281, 402 n. 24; Rokuro Tomibe, "The Secret Story of the War's End," *Bulletin of the American Historical Collection* 7 (October–December 1977): 40, 42; James Mace Ward, "Legitimate Collaboration: The Administration of Santo Tomás Internment Camp and Its Histories, 1942–2003," *Pacific Historical Review* 77 (May 2008): 192.

46. *Executive Order no. 109: Establishing a National Service Association* (n.p., n.d. [1942]), AHC; Aquino, quoted in Lewis E. Gleeck, *Laguna in American Times: Coconuts and Revolucionarios* (Manila: Historical Conservation Society, 1981), 139; Jose, "Labor Usage," 272; Joyce C. Lebra, *Japanese-Trained Armies in Southeast Asia: Independence and Volunteer Forces in World War II* (New York: Columbia University Press, 1977), 140–141.

47. Gleeck, *Laguna in American Times*, 141; Grant K. Goodman, "'As the Days Go By: Throbs of Grateful Hearts': Reeducation under the Japanese of Filipino POWs at Camp Del Pilar, Dau, Pampanga, 1942," *Philippine Studies* 62 no. 2 (2014): 270; Ray C. Hunt and Bernard Norling, *Behind Japanese Lines: An American Guerrilla in the Philippines* (Lexington: University Press of Kentucky, 1986), 107–108; Lebra, *Japanese-Trained Armies*, 141–142; Cesar P. Pobre, *History of the Armed Forces of the Filipino People* (Quezon City, Philippines: New Day, 2000), 325–336.

48. Theodore Friend, *Between Two Empires: The Ordeal of the Philippines, 1929–1946* (New Haven, CT: Yale University Press, 1965), 211–228.

49. Victor Gosiengfiao, "The Japanese Occupation: 'The Cultural Campaign,'" *Philippine Studies* 14 (April 1966): 229, 230, 231; Murphy, *Inside the Bataan Death March*, 215; Tomibe, "Secret Story of the War's End," 40.

50. Espinosa, "Filipino Nurses," 98; Goodman, "'As the Days Go By,'" 265; Gosiengfiao, "Japanese Occupation," 236; Jose, "Labor Usage," 272; Major-General K. Sato, *Address to Constabulary Trainees* (n.p., n.d. [1942]), 1, AHC.

51. Gosiengfiao, "Japanese Occupation," 229; Hara, *Japanese Destroyer Captain*, 67.

52. Utsumi Aiko, "Japan's Korean Soldiers in the Pacific War," in *Asian Labor in the Wartime Japanese Empire*, ed. Kratoska, 81–89; T. Fujitani, *Race for Empire: Koreans as Japanese, Japanese as Americans during World War II* (Berkeley: University of California Press, 2011); Brandon Palmer, *Fighting for the Enemy: Koreans in Japan's War, 1937–1945* (Seattle: University of Washington Press, 2013), 125–135; Lydia N. Yu-Jose, "The Koreans in Second World War

Philippines: Rumour and History," *Journal of Southeast Asian Studies* 43 (June 2012): 335 n. 42.

53. Elmer N. Lear, "The Western Leyte Guerrilla Warfare Forces: A Case Study in the Non-Legitimation of a Guerrilla Organization," *Journal of Southeast Asian History* 9 (March 1968): 72–75; "Leyte's Hidden Army," *Newsweek*, November 6, 1944, p. 33; Marquez, *Alcala Veterans*, 56.

54. David Bernstein, "Lesson from Luzon," *Yale Review* 38 (Spring 1949): 510; Hunt and Norling, *Behind Japanese Lines*, 103; Benedict J. Kerkvliet, *The Huk Rebellion: A Study of Peasant Revolt in the Philippines* (Berkeley: University of California Press, 1977), 61–109; Luis Taruc, *Born of the People: An Autobiography* (New York: International Publishers, 1953), 67–70, 116–127.

55. Agoncillo, *Fateful Years*, vol. 2, pp. 668, 672; Josefina Dalupan Hofileña, "Life in the Occupied Zone: One Negros Planter's Experience of War," *Journal of Southeast Asian Studies* 27 (March 1996): 83–84; Hunt and Norling, *Behind Japanese Lines*, 105.

56. Donald Chaput, "Samar in World War II," *Leyte-Samar Studies* 12 no. 1 (1978): 21; David W. Hogan Jr., "MacArthur, Stilwell, and Special Operations in the War against Japan," *Parameters* 25 (Spring 1995): 113; Hunt and Norling, *Behind Japanese Lines*, 105–106.

57. J. M. Elizalde, *The Filipino Fighting Spirit* (Washington, DC: Division of Information, Office of the Resident Commissioner, 1942), 1, 3.

58. Romulo, *My Brother Americans*, 17–18.

59. Manuel Buaken, "Life in the Armed Forces," *New Republic*, August 30, 1943, p. 279; Alex S. Fabros Jr., "When Hilario Met Sally: The Fight against Anti-Miscegenation Laws," *Filipinas* (February 1995), clipping in First and Second Filipino Infantry Files, FANHS.

60. Buaken, "Life in the Armed Forces," 280.

61. Mariano Angeles OH, WSOAHP, 25–26.

62. Buaken, "Life in the Armed Forces," 280; Fabros, "Boogie-Woogie Boys," 40.

63. "It's Their Fight, Too," *CT*, April 20, 1942.

64. Joaquin G. Chung Jr., "Ruperto Kangleon: 'An Exemplary Filipino Soldier,'" in *50th Anniversary: Leyte Gulf Landings*, ed. The National Committee (Manila: National Committee, 1994), 56; Jones, "Operations of Troop C," 97; Kalaw, "Filipino Opposition," 343; "Leyte's Hidden Army," 33.

65. Willard H. Elsbree, *Japan's Role in Southeast Asian Nationalist Movements, 1940–1945* (Cambridge: Harvard University Press, 1953), 21, 42; Catherine Porter, "Japan's Blue-Print for the Philippines," *Far Eastern Survey* 12 (May 31, 1943): 109.

66. Aguinaldo, quoted in Elsbree, *Japan's Role*, 6; Marshall Andrews, "Aguinaldo Plea for Surrender Amuses MacArthur's Forces," *WP*, February 7, 1942; Reynaldo C. Ileto, "Philippine Wars and the Politics of Memory," *positions*, 13 (Spring 2005): 226; "New Philippine Regime Off to Fidgety Start," *CT*, October 18, 1943; "Philippines Now 'Free,'" *NYT*, October 14, 1943.

67. James B. Reuter Oral History, transcript, 12, CSUF; Walter Lippmann, "Mr. Jose P. Laurel," *WP*, October 16, 1943.

68. David Bernstein, "America and Dr. Laurel," *Harper's Magazine* 197 (October 1948): 84; David Steinberg, "Jose P. Laurel: A 'Collaborator' Misunderstood," *Journal of Asian Studies* 24 (August 1965): 657.

69. José P. Laurel, *War Memoirs of Dr. José P. Laurel* (Manila: José P. Laurel Memorial Foundation, 1962), 58.

70. Jose, "Labor Usage," 277.

71. Japanese Military Administration, "Open Letter to Our Countrymen," December 25, 1942, typescript, Harvard Law Library, Cambridge, MA.

72. Hofileña, "Life in the Occupied Zone," 93; Jose, "Labor Usage," 276, Tomibe, "Secret Story of the War's End," 40.

73. Chaput, "Samar in World War II," 17; Hogan, "MacArthur, Stilwell, and Special Operations," 104, 108, 110.

74. Chaput, "Samar in World War II," 16; Chung, "Ruperto Kangleon," 55–56; Hogan, "MacArthur, Stilwell, and Special Operations," 110; Lear, "Western Leyte."

75. Dennison, "Philippines: Prelude to Departure," 36.

76. Tomibe, "Secret Story of the War's End," 43.

CHAPTER SIX: LIBERATIONS, 1944–1946

1. Proclamation no. 30 (September 22, 1944); Theodore Friend, *The Blue-Eyed Enemy: Japan against the West in Java and Luzon, 1942–1945* (Princeton: Princeton University Press, 1988), 128, 130 n. 32.

2. D. Clayton James, *The Years of MacArthur* (Boston: Houghton Mifflin, 1975), vol. 2, pp. 555–557; Samuel Eliot Morison, *The Two Ocean War: A Short History of the United States Navy in the Second World War* (Boston: Little, Brown, 1963), 475.

3. Donald Chaput, "Ruperto K. Kangleon," *Leyte-Samar Studies* 11 no. 1 (1977): 17; Ricardo T. Jose, "Labor Usage and Mobilization during the Japanese Occupation of the Philippines, 1942–45," in *Asian Labor in the Wartime Japanese Empire: Unknown Histories*, ed. Paul H. Kratoska (Armonk, NY: M.E. Sharpe, 2005), 274; Carlos P. Romulo, *I See the Philippines Rise* (New York: Doubleday, 1946), 95–97.

4. Augustin L. Santos, "The First Filipino Infantry" and "The 2nd Filipino Infantry Regiment," undated typescripts, Filipino American National Historical Society, Seattle [hereafter FANHS]; Linda A. Revilla, "'Pineapples,' 'Hawayanos,' and 'Loyal Americans': Local Boys in the First Filipino Infantry Regiment, US Army," *Social Process in Hawaii* 37 (1996): 67.

5. Susan Evangelista, "Aurelio Bulosan's Wartime Diary: An Initial Look at a Newly-Discovered Document," *Philippine Studies* 37 (Fourth Quarter 1989): 474; Santos, "First Filipino Infantry," FANHS; Robert Aura Smith, *Philippine Freedom, 1946–1958* (New York: Columbia University Press, 1958), 111.

6. Executive Order no. 21 (October 28, 1944); Satoshi Nakano, "The Filipino World War II Veterans Equity Movement and the Filipino American Community," *Pacific and American Studies* 6 (March 2006): 135.

7. Elmer N. Lear, "Leyte's Civilians in a Time of Transition," *Leyte-Samar Studies* 13 no. 1 (1979): 57–61; Romulo, *I See the Philippines Rise*, 151–152.

8. Jose, "Labor Usage," 278, 282–283; José P. Laurel, *War Memoirs of Dr. José P. Laurel* (Manila: José P. Laurel Memorial Foundation, 1962), 24, 60; David Steinberg, "Jose P. Laurel: A 'Collaborator' Misunderstood," *Journal of Asian Studies* 24 (August 1965): 659.

9. Joyce C. Lebra, *Japanese-Trained Armies in Southeast Asia: Independence and Volunteer Forces in World War II* (New York: Columbia University Press, 1977), 142–143; *Manila Tribune*, December 9, 1944; Catherine Porter, "Japan's Blue-Print for the Philippines," *Far Eastern Survey* 12 (May 31, 1943): 110.

10. Richard B. Frank, "Ketsu Gö: Japanese Political and Military Strategy in 1945," in *The End of the Pacific War: Reappraisals*, ed. Tsuyoshi Hasegawa (Stanford: Stanford University Press, 2007), 76; Lebra, *Japanese-Trained Armies*, 144; Robert Ross Smith, *Triumph in the Philippines* (Washington, DC: Office of the Chief of Military History, Department of the Army, 1963), 694.

11. James, *Years of MacArthur*, vol. 2, p. 548.

12. Smith, *Triumph in the Philippines*, 293–294; Jose Victor Z. Torres, "Victims of a Tragic War: The Poor Clare Nuns in World War II (1941–1945)," *Philippine Quarterly of Culture and Society* 25 (September–December 1997): 214–215.

13. John W. Dower, *War without Mercy: Race and Power in the Pacific War* (New York: Pantheon, 1986), 44–45; Carol Morris Petillo, *Douglas MacArthur: The Philippine Years* (Bloomington: Indiana University Press, 1981), 243.

14. Douglas MacArthur, *Reminiscences* (New York: McGraw-Hill, 1964), 247; Petillo, *Douglas MacArthur*, 224.

15. James, *Years of MacArthur*, vol. 2, pp. 646, 648; MacArthur, *Reminiscences*, 252; "Return to Manila," *NYT*, February 28, 1945.

16. Executive Order no. 34 (March 10, 1945); D. L. England, "Summary History and Highlights of Jeep in the Philippines," November 6, 1973, Box 10, Roy Dikeman Chapin Papers, Bentley Historical Library, Ann Arbor, MI.

17. US House, Committee on Foreign Affairs, *Seventh and Final Report of the High Commissioner to the Philippines, July 8, 1947* (Washington, DC: GPO, 1947), 58; William Blum, *Killing Hope: U.S. Military and CIA Interventions since World War II* (Monroe, ME: Common Courage Press, 1995), 40; Nick Cullather, *Illusions of Influence: The Political Economy of United States-Philippines Relations, 1942–1960* (Stanford: Stanford University Press, 1994), 49; James, *Years of MacArthur*, vol. 2, p. 803.

18. Roosevelt, quoted in "Signs Legislation to Free Philippines," *NYT*, July 1, 1944; MacArthur, quoted in David Bernstein, *The Philippine Story* (New York: Farrar, Straus, 1947), 202; Porter, "Japan's Blue-Print," 110.

19. Teodoro A. Agoncillo, *The Burden of Proof: The Vargas-Laurel Collaboration Case* (Mandaluyong: University of the Philippines Press, 1984), 125; Bernstein, *Philippine Story*, 206.

20. Bernstein, *Philippine Story*, 209; Ernest Lachica, *Huk: Philippine Agrarian Society in Revolt* (Manila: Solidaridad, 1971), 116–117; Luis Taruc, *Born of the People: An Autobiography* (New York: International Publishers, 1953), 189, 194.

21. Agnes G. Bailen, *The Odyssey of Lorenzo M. Tañada* (Quezon City: University of the Philippines Press, 1998), 61; Bernstein, *Philippine Story*, 203–204; Keith Thor Carlson, *The Twisted Road to Freedom: America's Granting of Independence to the Philippines* (Quezon City: University of the Philippines Press, 1995), 28–53.

22. Bailen, *Odyssey*, 55.

23. Hernando J. Abaya to Bernard B. Perry, July 16, 1946, Box 78, Papers of Harold I. Ickes, Library of Congress Manuscript Division, Washington, DC; Bailen, *Odyssey*, 53; Bernstein, "America and Dr. Laurel," 85; "Filipino Cases Speeded," *NYT*, February 23, 1946.

24. Abraham Chapman, "Note on the Philippine Elections," *Pacific Affairs* 19 (June 1946): 193–198.

25. Benedict J. Kerkvliet, *The Huk Rebellion: A Study of Peasant Revolt in the Philippines* (Berkeley: University of California Press, 1977), 143–144; Taruc, *Born of the People*, 217, 225, 242.

26. James J. Halsema, "Huks, Filipino Resistance Fighters, March by Night," *WP*, March 2, 1947; Weldon Jones, "Jungle Fever," *Collier's*, October 5, 1946, p. 30.

27. Bailen, *Odyssey*, 66; Bernstein, *Philippine Story*, 241, 243–244.

28. 60 Stat. 416 (July 2, 1946); "Effect of Philippine Independence on Filipinos Residing in the United States," *Columbia Law Review* 50 (March 1950): 371–375; "Filipino Naturalization," *WP*, June 5, 1946; Grayson Kirk, "The Filipinos," *Annals of the American Academy of Political and Social Science* 223 (September 1942): 45.

29. Benicio T. Catapusan, "Filipino Attitudes toward G.I. Joe," *Sociology and Social Research* 30 (July–August 1946): 466–475; Donald Chaput, "Samar in World War II," *Leyte-Samar Studies* 12 no. 1 (1978): 18, 25–26; Alex Fabros, "The Boogie Woogie Boys," *Filipinas* 1 (September 1993): 43; Revilla, "Pineapples," 69–70; Santos, "First Filipino Infantry," and "2nd Filipino Infantry Regiment," FANHS.

30. 59 Stat. 659 (December 28, 1945); 60 Stat. 339 (June 29, 1946); Mariano Angeles Oral History, Washington State Oral/Aural History Program (Olympia: Washington State Archives, 1974–1977), 24, 27, 35 [hereafter WSOAHP]; "Guerrilla Hero's Wife, Children Face Deportation," *LAT*, August 12, 1946; Vinluan, quoted in Vince Reyes, "The War Brides," in *Filipinos in America: A Journey of Faith* (South San Francisco: Filipinas Pub., 2003), 54; Brian Roberts, ed., *They Cast a Long Shadow: A History of the Nonwhite Races on Bainbridge Island* (Bainbridge Island, WA: Minority History Committee of Bainbridge Island School District, 1975), 114–115.

31. 56 Stat. 176 (March 27, 1942).

32. Clark, quoted in Loida Nicolas Lewis, *How the Filipino Veteran of World War II Can Become a U.S. Citizen (According to the Immigration Act of 1990)* (New York: FR Publications, 1991), 4–6.

33. Ugo Carusi to Tom C. Clark, quoted in *Matter of Naturalization of 68 Filipino War Veterans*, 406 F. Supp. 931 (N.D. Cal. 1975), at 936 n. 5.

34. Hayden, quoted in US Senate, *Hearings before the Subcommittee of the Committee on Appropriations*, 79 Cong., 2 Sess. (March 26, 1946), 60.

35. Hayden, quoted in Senate, *Hearings*, 79 Cong., 2 Sess. (March 26, 1946), 58.

36. 60 Stat. 6 (February 18, 1946); *Seventh and Final Report*, 66.

37. "Statement by the President Concerning Provisions in Bill Affecting Philippine Army Veterans," February 20, 1946, *PPP: Truman, 1946*, p. 124; "Statement by the President Concerning Benefits for Philippine Army Veterans," April 4, 1946, *PPP: Truman, 1946*, p. 180; Rick Baldoz, *The Third Asiatic Invasion: Empire and Migration in Filipino America, 1898-1946* (New York: New York University Press, 2011), 231–236.

38. "News Review," *Filipino Veteran* 1 (April 1946); 24, 29, American Historical Collection, Ateneo de Manila University, Quezon City, Philippines

[hereafter AHC]; Frank H. Golay, *Face of Empire: United States-Philippines Relations, 1898–1946* (Quezon City, Philippines: Ateneo de Manila University Press, 1997), 469; Carlos Romulo to Manuel Roxas, May 23, 1946, Box 1.2, Papers of Carlos Romulo, University of the Philippines, Diliman.

39. *Seventh and Final Report*, 68, 69; Hayden, quoted in Senate, *Hearings*, 79 Cong., 2 Sess. (March 26, 1946), 61; "Editorial," *Filipino Veteran* 1 (April 1946): 8–9, AHC.

40. Lorraine Libadia OH, WSOAHP, 6, 20.

41. Mariano Angeles OH, WSOAHP, 32; Fabian Bergano OH, WSOAHP, 8; Camila Carido Notes, Box 8, Miller Interviews with Stockton Immigrant Women, Holt-Atherton Special Collections Library, University of the Pacific, Stockton, CA; Genevieve Ordona Laigo OH, WSOAHP, 12–13; Revilla, "Pineapples," 71; Sylvestre Tangalan OH, WSOAHP, 11.

42. 59 Stat. 538 (October 6, 1945), at 543; *Congressional Record*, September 26, 1945, pp. 9016–9017.

43. Hal M. Friedman, *Creating an American Lake: United States Imperialism and Strategic Security in the Pacific Basin, 1945–1947* (Westport, CT: Greenwood Press, 2001), 124, 125, 130; Colleen Woods, "Building Empire's Archipelago: The Imperial Politics of Filipino Labor in the Pacific," *Labor* 13 nos. 3–4 (2016): 131, 135.

44. Economic Survey Mission to the Philippines, *Report to the President of the United States* (Washington, DC: GPO, 1950), 13; Krug, quoted in "Truman Declares Philippines Free," *NYT*, July 5, 1946; "Recorded Message to the People of the Philippines upon the Occasion of Their Independence," July 3, 1946, *PPP: Truman, 1946*, p. 338.

45. MacArthur, quoted in H. Ford Wilkins, "Philippine Republic Is Born as U.S. Rule Ends in Glory," *NYT*, July 4, 1946.

CHAPTER SEVEN: ALLIES, 1946–1965

1. "The Position of the United States with Respect to Asia," December 30, 1949, in US Department of State, *Foreign Relations of the United States, 1949: The Far East and Australasia* (Washington, DC: GPO, 1976), vol. 2, p. 1216.

2. Ramon E. Montaño, "The Republican Years," in Margarita R. Cojuangco et al., *Konstable: The Story of the Philippine Constabulary, 1901–1991* (Manila: ABoCan, 1991) 113; "Regular Army of 40,000 Planned by Philippines," *CT*, January 27, 1946.

3. David Boguslav, "U.S. to Receive 16 Philippine Bases at Once," *CT*, March 14, 1947; "Our Philippine Bases," *NYT*, March 16, 1947; Military Bases Agreement, TIAS 1775 (March 14, 1947).

4. Osmeña, quoted in Abraham Chapman, "American Policy in the Philippines," *Far Eastern Survey* 15 (June 5, 1946): 168; Amado V. Hernandez, *Progressive Philippines: Complete Answers to Eleven Questions of "Trends" Magazine about National and International Problems* (Manila: Pilipino, 1949), 13.

5. "Our Philippine Bases."

6. William Adams Brown Jr. and Redvers Opie, *American Foreign Assistance* (Washington, DC: Brookings Institution, 1953), 406–408, 412–414, 440; James J. Dalton, "Ins and Outs in the Philippines," *Far Eastern Survey* 21 (July 30, 1952): 120; "Military Accord between U.S. and Philippines Rushed," *LAT*, March 15, 1947; Cesar P. Pobre, *History of the Armed Forces of the Filipino People* (Quezon City, Philippines: New Day, 2000), 370–371; "U.S., Philippines Sign Defense Aid Accord," *NYT*, March 22, 1947; "U.S. Relief in Philippines Assailed as 'Misdirected,'" *CT*, March 1, 1947; H. Lawrence Wilsey, "Philippine Progress and American Assistance," *World Affairs* 119 (Fall 1956): 67.

7. 62 Stat. 583 (June 24, 1948); M. Azurin, "Plan for Philippine Army Armored Units," *Armored Cavalry Journal* 56 (July–August 1947): 25; Alfred W. McCoy, *Closer than Brothers: Manhood at the Philippine Military Academy* (New Haven, CT: Yale University Press, 1999), 26–28.

8. Knox, quoted in Kenneth B. Clark, "Desegregation: An Appraisal of the Evidence," *Journal of Social Issues* 9 no. 4 (1953): 41–42; Lee Nichols, *Breakthrough on the Color Front* (New York: Random House, 1954), 55; Herbert R. Northrup et al., *Black and Other Minority Participation in the All-Volunteer Navy and Marine Corps* (Philadelphia: Industrial Research Unit, Wharton School, University of Pennsylvania, 1979), 11–12; John Darrell Sherwood, *Black Sailor, White Navy: Racial Unrest in the Fleet during the Vietnam War Era* (New York: New York University Press, 2007), 7–9.

9. Executive Order no. 9981 (July 26, 1948); President's Committee on Equality of Treatment and Opportunity in the Armed Services, *Freedom to Serve: Equality of Treatment and Opportunity in the Armed Services* (Washington, DC: GPO, 1950), 4–5.

10. "Fort M'Kinley," *NYT*, August 10, 1949; Military Bases Agreement, TIAS 1775 (March 14, 1947), sec. 27; "Philippines Acquires Manila U.S. Army Post," *NYT*, August 4, 1949; "U.S. Army to Disband Its Philippine Scouts," *NYT*, November 1, 1948.

11. Emily Porcincula Lawsin, "Beyond 'Hanggang Pier Only': Filipino American War Brides of Seattle, 1945–1965," *Filipino American National Historical Society Journal* 4 (1996): 50–50G.

12. Juanita Tamayo Lott, *Common Destiny: Filipino American Generations* (Lanham, MD: Rowman & Littlefield, 2006), 39, 45, 46; Dawn Bohulano

Mabalon, *Little Manila Is in the Heart: The Making of the Filipino/a American Community in Stockton, California* (Durham, NC: Duke University Press, 2013), 273; Benito M. Vergara Jr., *Pinoy Capital: The Filipino Nation in Daly City* (Philadelphia: Temple University Press, 2008), 23–45.

13. Norma H. Goodhue, "New Auxiliary to Legion's Manila Post Picks Officers," *LAT*, December 23, 1949; Hyung-chan Kim and Cynthia C. Mejia, comps., *The Filipinos in America, 1898–1974: A Chronology and Fact Book* (Dobbs Ferry, NY: Oceana, 1976), 46, 56, 58; "New Philippine President Stanch [*sic*] Friend of U.S.," *LAT*, April 17, 1948.

14. Valentin R. Aquino, *The Filipino Community in Los Angeles* (San Francisco: R and E Research Associates, 1974 [1952]), 32, 58, 60.

15. Chris Friday, *Organizing Asian American Labor: The Pacific Coast Canned-Salmon Industry, 1870–1942* (Philadelphia: Temple University Press, 1992), 188; Kim and Mejia, *Filipinos in America*, 55, 57.

16. David Bernstein, "Lesson from Luzon," *Yale Review* 38 (Spring 1949): 512–514; J. F., "Filipinos' Postwar War Quiets Down as Guerrillas Agree to Try Farming," *USNWR*, July 30, 1948, p. 62; Cowen, quoted in Douglas J. Macdonald, *Adventures in Chaos: American Intervention for Reform in the Third World* (Cambridge: Harvard University Press, 1992), 139; "New Philippine President"; Luis Taruc, *Born of the People* (New York: International Publishers, 1953), 233.

17. Bernstein, "Lesson from Luzon," 519; James J. Halsema, "Huks, Filipino Resistance Fighters, March by Night," *WP*, March 2, 1947; Gordon L. Harris, "The Huk Guerrillas," *Commonweal*, October 15, 1948, p. 7; Taruc, *Born of the People*, 263.

18. Russell H. Fifield, "The Hukbalahap Today," *Far Eastern Survey* 20 (January 24, 1951), 17; Carl Mydans and Shelley Mydans, *The Violent Peace* (New York: Atheneum, 1968), 395; "Fundamental Spirit," quoted in Taruc, *Born of the People*, 69; William J. Pomeroy, *The Forest: A Personal Record of the Huk Guerrilla Struggle in the Philippines* (New York: International Publishers, 1963), 12; Tomás C. Tirona, "The Philippine Anti-Communist Campaign: A Study of Democracy in Action," *Air University Quarterly Review* 7 (Summer 1954): 44.

19. State Department, quoted in Walter C. Ladwig III, "When the Police Are the Problem: The Philippine Constabulary and the Hukbalahap Rebellion," in *Policing Insurgencies: Cops as Counterinsurgents*, ed. C. Christine Fair and Sumit Ganguly (New York: Oxford University Press, 2014), 31; Franco, quoted in "Our Friends Outside," *Time*, July 3, 1950, p. 17; William J. Thorpe, "Huk Hunting in the Philippines, 1946–1953," *Airpower Historian* 9 (April 1962): 98.

20. Halsema, "Huks"; Benedict J. Kerkvliet, *The Huk Rebellion: A Study of Peasant Revolt in the Philippines* (Berkeley: University of California Press, 1977), 164; Albert Ravenholt, "The Philippines: Where Did We Fail?" *Foreign Affairs* 29 (April 1951): 407.

21. Benjamin Appel, "William Pomeroy—American Huk," *The Nation*, July 26, 1952, pp. 72–73; William J. Pomeroy, "Why I Have Joined the Huks," *Philippines Free Press*, April 14, 1951; Paul Robeson, Foreword, in Taruc, *Born of the People*, 9.

22. "Extended Anniversary," *Time*, April 10, 1950, p. 25; "Filipino 'Huk' Chief Loses Seat," *NYT*, January 14, 1949; "4 Huk Raids Kill 14; Manila Is Alerted," *NYT*, March 30, 1950; Eva-Lotta E. Hedman and John T. Sidel, *Philippine Politics and Society in the Twentieth Century: Colonial Legacies, Post-Colonial Trajectories* (New York: Routledge, 2000), 20; Jorge Maravilla, "The Postwar Huk in the Philippines," in *Guerrilla Warfare and Marxism*, ed. William J. Pomeroy (New York: International Publishers, 1968), 239; William J. Pomeroy, *Guerrilla and Counter-Guerilla Warfare: Liberation and Repression in the Present Period* (New York: International Publishers, 1964), 67.

23. Dalton, "Ins and Outs in the Philippines," 122; "Extended Anniversary"; Ladwig, "When the Police Are the Problem," 27, 28; Macdonald, *Adventures in Chaos*, 138; Robert M. Neer, *Napalm: An American Biography* (Cambridge: Harvard University Press, 2013), 104.

24. Tirona, "Philippine Anti-Communist Campaign," 48.

25. Kangleon, quoted in "Internal Dangers Avowed by Manila," *NYT*, June 27, 1950; Quirino, quoted in Tillman Durdin, "Truman's Actions Hearten Filipinos," *NYT*, June 29, 1950.

26. Macapagal, quoted in Ponciano Gabriel Mathay, "The Power of the President to Send Troops to Fight Abroad without Declaration of War," *Philippine Law Journal* 27 (1952): 412 n. 22; Camilo Osias, *Philippine Support of United Nations Forces against Communist Aggression* (Manila: Bureau of Printing, 1950), 7; "Philippines Alert for New Huk Raids," *NYT*, August 28, 1950; Republic of Korea Ministry of National Defense, *The History of the United Nations Forces in the Korean War* (Seoul: Ministry of National Defense, 1972), vol. 1, p. 735; Romulo, quoted in United States Information Service, "The Facts about Korea," typescript, n.d. [1953], American Historical Collection, Ateneo de Manila University, Quezon City, Philippines; Romulo, quoted in Lily Ann Polo, "Philippine Involvement in the Korean War: A Footnote to R.P.-U.S. Relations," *Asian Studies Journal* 20 (1982): 87–88, 90.

27. Republic Act no. 573, September 7, 1950; Quirino, quoted in Russell H. Fifield, "Philippine Foreign Policy," *Far Eastern Survey* 20 (February 21, 1951):

36, and Mathay, "Power of the President," 412 n. 21, 413 n. 26; "The President's News Conference of August 24, 1950," *PPP: Truman, 1950*, p. 594.

28. Quirino, quoted in ROK Ministry of National Defense, *United Nations Forces in the Korean War*, vol. 1, p. 303; Polo, "Philippine Involvement," 91.

29. Brian Catchpole, *The Korean War, 1950–53* (New York: Carroll and Graf, 2000), 124, 273; Bradley Lynn Coleman, *Colombia and the United States: The Making of an Inter-American Alliance, 1939–1960* (Kent, Ohio: Kent State University Press, 2008), 107, 120; "Filipino Korean Battalion Asks to Quit Fighting," *CT*, November 21, 1950; S. P. Mackenzie, *The Imjin and Kapyong Battles: Korea, 1951* (Bloomington: Indiana University Press, 2013), 80–81; ROK Ministry of National Defense, *United Nations Forces in the Korean War*, vol. 6, pp. 310–311, 314–315; "U.N. Troops' Diets Korean Headache," *NYT*, October 11, 1950.

30. Raymond Bonner, *Waltzing with a Dictator: The Marcoses and the Making of American Policy* (New York: Times Books, 1987), 101; "Filipinos Rout Enemy," *NYT*, May 19, 1952; Mita Q. Sison-Duque, *In the Beginning . . . A Nation, A President* (Manila: M.Q.S. Duque, 1994), 229–233.

31. "Ex-U.S. Navy Employees Offer to Serve Anew," *Manila Times*, August 7, 1950; "Filipinos in States Ready to Join USA," *Manila Times*, July 6, 1950; "M'Arthur Invited to Visit in Manila," *NYT*, April 12, 1951; "Philippine Scouts Offer Aid," *NYT*, July 7, 1950.

32. John G. Westover, *Combat Support in Korea: The United States Army in the Korean Conflict* (Washington, DC: Combat Forces Press, 1955), 184–185, 208–209.

33. Clark, quoted in David Curtis Skaggs, "The KATUSA Experiment: The Integration of Korean Nationals into the U.S. Army, 1950–1965," *Military Affairs* 38 (April 1974): 55.

34. Montano, quoted in Allan Lagasca Bergano et al., *In Our Uncles' Words: We Fought for Freedom* (San Francisco: T'Boli Publishing, 2006), 47; Sarmiento, quoted in Ray L. Burdeos, *Filipinos in the U.S. Navy and Coast Guard during the Vietnam War* (Bloomington, IN: AuthorHouse, 2008), 38; Luisito G. Maligat, "Study of the U.S. Navy's Philippines Enlistment Program, 1981–1991" (M.A. thesis, Naval Postgraduate School, 2000), 40–45.

35. Anderson, quoted in "Navy Racial Set-Up of Stewards to Go," *NYT*, September 29, 1953; "Navy Moves to End Steward Color Line," *NYT*, March 2, 1954; "Navy Presses Drive on Racial Barriers," *NYT*, February 8, 1954; "Navy Seen Urging Whites to Join Stewards Branch," *Navy Times*, February 13, 1954; John G. Norris, "Negroes Can Pick Branches in New Navy Enlistment Plan," *WP*, March 2, 1954.

36. Hernandez, *Progressive Philippines*, 12; Pobre, *Armed Forces of the Filipino People*, 371; Elpidio Quirino, "Huge Tasks Ahead," June 18, 1951, in *The Quirino Way: Collection of Speeches and Addresses* (n.p., 1955), 287, 284.

37. ROK Ministry of National Defense, *United Nations Forces in the Korean War*, vol. 6, pp. 319–320, 326–328.

38. US Department of Defense, *A Pocket Guide to the Philippines* (Washington, DC: GPO, [1961]), 56.

39. Leny Mendoza Strobel, "A Personal Story: Becoming a Split Filipina Subject," *Amerasia Journal* 19 no. 3 (1993): 118, 119; United States Air Force, *Welcome to Clark Air Base* (n.p., n.d.), Lopez Memorial Museum, Manila.

40. "Clark Field Civilian Housing Area: A Home Away from Home," *Manila Times*, November 20, 1959, Manila Times Clippings Collection, Lopez Memorial Museum, Manila [hereafter Manila Times Clippings Collection].

41. "Subic Bay Naval Base," *Tidewater Oil Company News* 4 (Third Quarter 1959): 5; *Welcome to US Naval Base Subic Bay* (n.p., n.d.), Lopez Memorial Museum, Manila.

42. Ferguson and Radford, quoted in US Department of State, *Foreign Relations of the United States, 1955–1957: Southeast Asia* (Washington, DC: GPO, 1989), 616, 620; "The Philippines: Battle of Subic Bay," *Newsweek*, July 25, 1955, p. 38; Harry A. Jacobs, "Native Labor—The Army's Ally Abroad," *Army Information Digest* 8 (January 1953): 27; "The Philippines: Dangerous Fief," *Time*, July 20, 1959, p. 34; Frank G. Rivera, "Olongapo (Mis) Adventures," *Examiner* (Manila), June 25, 1967, Manila Times Clippings Collection.

43. Charles T. R. Bohannan, "Antiguerrilla Operations," *Annals of the American Academy of Political and Social Science* 341 (May 1962): 20, 21, 23.

44. Donn V. Hart, "Magsaysay: Philippine Candidate," *Far Eastern Survey* 22 (May 1953): 67–70.

45. "Army with Bloodhounds," *Time*, September 18, 1950, p. 35; Ladwig, "When the Police Are the Problem," 35; Edward Lansdale, *In the Midst of Wars: An American's Mission to Southeast Asia* (New York: Harper and Row, 1972), 69–84; "The Philippines: Hope against the Huks," *Time*, April 9, 1951, p. 28.

46. Roger Daniels, *Guarding the Golden Door: American Immigration Policy and Immigrants since 1882* (New York: Hill and Wang, 2004), 118–122; Arleen De Vera, "Without Parallel: The Local 7 Deportation Cases, 1949–1955," *Amerasia Journal* 20 no. 2 (1994): 1–25; Melinda Tria Kerkvliet, *Manila Workers' Unions, 1900–1950* (Quezon City, Philippines: New Day, 1992), 97, 101–102.

47. *Izvestia*, quoted in Russell H. Fifield, "The Challenge to Magsaysay," *Foreign Affairs* 33 (October 1954): 151; Magsaysay, quoted in Simeon del

Rosario, "The Huks after Two Months of Magsaysay," *Philippine Armed Forces Journal* 7 (March 1954): 6; "Democracy in Hukland," *Time*, July 2, 1951, p. 33; Hart, "Magsaysay: Philippine Candidate," 68; "Ice Cream Every Day," *Time*, March 19, 1951, p. 40; Lansdale, *In the Midst of Wars*, 47–59; "New Guy," *Time*, January 11, 1954, pp. 20–21; "Population Shift Aiding Philippines," *NYT*, March 31, 1952; Evan Thomas, *The Very Best Men: Four Who Dared: The Early Years of the CIA* (New York: Simon and Schuster, 1995), 58.

48. "'We Smashed the Communists': Philippine Leader Tells How Guns and Food Won War on Huks," *USNWR*, February 13, 1953, p. 35.

49. "Democracy in Hukland"; "We Smashed the Communists," 32.

50. Simeon Man, *Soldiering through Empire: Race and the Making of the Decolonizing Pacific* (Oakland: University of California Press, 2018), 66; "PS to Stage Palace March Tomorrow," *Manila Times*, June 12, 1948, Manila Times Clippings Collection; Hartzell Spence, *Marcos of the Philippines* (New York: World, 1969), 204.

51. Memo from Chief Benefits Director to General Counsel, January 19, 1960, Box 6, Files Relating to Veterans Residing Abroad, Record Group 15: Records of the Veterans Administration, National Archives and Records Administration, Washington, DC [hereafter NARA].

52. Memorandum to JJW, December 9, 1957, Legislative Staff/Office Files: V.A.: Blackmarket—Philippines—1957, Box 11, Papers of John J. Williams, Special Collections Library, University of Delaware, Newark; L. O. Ty, "Million-Peso Back Pay Racket," *Philippines Free Press*, May 12, 1956.

53. H. V. Higley to Governor Adams, December 17, 1956, Files Relating to Veterans Residing Abroad, Box 6, RG 15, NARA; Ruperto Kangleon to Elpidio Qurino, April 26, 1949, Box 17, Papers of Elpidio Qurino, Filipinas Heritage Library, Makati, Philippines.

54. John Foster Dulles, "The Nature of United States Economic Aid to the Philippines," in *American Foreign Policy: Current Documents, 1956* (Washington, DC: GPO, 1959), 857; Cornelio M. Ferrer, "Anti-US Flare-Up in Philippines," *Christian Century*, May 9, 1956, pp. 597–598; Recto, quoted in Ricardo T. Jose, "The Philippines during the Cold War: Searching for Security Guarantees and Appropriate Foreign Policies, 1946–1986," in *Cold War Southeast Asia*, ed. Malcolm H. Murfett (Singapore: Marshall Cavendish, 2012), 67; B. A. Umayam, "Irritants in Philippine American Relations," February 24, 1959, Papers of Julius Ruiz, Filipino American National Historical Society, Seattle.

55. Victor Lieberman, "Why the Hukbalahap Movement Failed," *Solidarity* 1 (October–December 1966): 25–26; Maravilla, "Postwar Huk," 240–241.

56. Max Boot, *The Road Not Taken: Edward Lansdale and the American Tragedy in Vietnam* (New York: Liveright, 2018), 141–142; Cecil B. Currey, "Edward G. Lansdale: LIC and the Ugly American," *Military Review* 68 (May 1988): 45; Jonathan Nashel, *Edward Lansdale's Cold War* (Amherst: University of Massachusetts Press, 2005), 31, 32; Joseph Burkholder Smith, *Portrait of a Cold Warrior* (New York: Putnam, 1976), 95; Thomas, *Very Best Men*, 57.

57. Marilyn C. Alquizola and Lane Ryo Hirabayashi, "Carlos Bulosan's Final Defiant Acts: Achievements during the McCarthy Era," *Amerasia Journal* 38 no. 3 (2012): 48 n. 30; Carlos Bulosan, *The Cry and the Dedication*, ed. E. San Juan Jr. (Philadelphia: Temple University Press, 1995).

58. "The President's New Conference of April 7, 1954," *PPP: Eisenhower, 1954*, p. 383.

59. Stephen J. Kinzer, *The Brothers: John Foster Dulles, Allen Dulles, and Their Secret World War* (New York: Henry Holt, 2013), 203; Richard Wright, *The Color Curtain: A Report on the Bandung Conference* (Cleveland: World, 1956).

60. Ben Cal, *FVR through the Years* (Quezon City: Philippine Academy for Continuing Education and Research, 1997), 11; Wendell W. Fertig, "Introduction," in H. von Dach Bern, *Total Resistance* (Boulder, CO: Paladin Press, 1965), n.p.

61. John J. Duffy, "Signpost: Success in the Philippines," *Army* 13 (July 1963): 60; Man, *Soldiering through Empire*, 71–72; John Prados, *Safe for Democracy: The Secret Wars of the CIA* (Chicago: Ivan R. Dee, 2006), 140; Thorpe, "Huk Hunting in the Philippines," 95, 99, 100; Harry F. Walterhouse, *A Time to Build: Military Civic Action: Medium for Economic Development and Social Reform* (Columbia: University of South Carolina Press, 1964), 88.

62. Francis J. Kelly, *U.S. Army Special Forces, 1961–1971* (Washington, DC: Department of the Army, 1973), 195; Dulles, quoted in Lansdale, *In the Midst of Wars*, 126; Man, *Soldiering through Empire*, 59, 66; Napoleon D. Valeriano, *South Vietnam Survey: March–April 1964* (n.p., 1965), 3, 5, 14, B1.

63. Arellano, quoted in Gloria Emerson, "'Doctors, Thank You!'" *The Rotarian* 89 (November 1956): 29; Diem, quoted in Arellano, "How Operation Brotherhood Got to Viet Nam," *Philippine Studies* 14 (July 1966): 402; Miguel A. Bernad, *Adventure in Viet-Nam: The Story of Operation Brotherhood, 1954–1957* (Manila: Operation Brotherhood International, 1974); Lansdale, *In the Midst of Wars*, 169–170.

64. Arellano, "How Operation Brotherhood," 407; Gloria Emerson, "Filipinos Help Laos Not with 'Handouts' but with Training," *NYT*, November 22, 1959; Lansdale, *In the Midst of Wars*, 214; Smith, *Portrait of a Cold Warrior*, 251–252.

65. Thomas J. Dodd, "Southeast Asia: The Dangers of Appeasement," in *Freedom and Foreign Policy* (New York: Bookmailer, 1962), 179–180; "Remarks of Senator Thomas J. Dodd Concerning the Crisis in Southeast Asia, Delivered on the Floor of the Senate, May 29, 1961," Box 192, Papers of Thomas J. Dodd, Thomas J. Dodd Research Center, University of Connecticut, Storrs, CT [hereafter TDRC]; Man, *Soldiering through Empire*, 68–69; Polo, "Philippine Involvement in the Korean War," 89; Smith, *Portrait of a Cold Warrior*, 252.

66. Arthur M. Schlesinger Jr., *A Thousand Days: John F. Kennedy in the White House* (Boston: Houghton Mifflin, 1965), 228–229; Karen Schwarz, *What You Can Do for Your Country: An Oral History of the Peace Corps* (New York: Morrow, 1991), 229; Theodore C. Sorensen, *Kennedy* (New York: Harper and Row, 1965), 629–633, 661; Teodoro F. Valencia, "Peace Corps Man Seized; CIA Linked," *Manila Times*, November 8, 1969, Manila Times Clippings Collection.

67. Ted Widmer, *Listening In: The Secret White House Recordings of John F. Kennedy* (New York: Hyperion, 2012), 265.

68. Thomas J. Dodd, "Remarks at Far Eastern University, April 24, 1965," Box 265, Papers of Thomas J. Dodd, TDRC.

CHAPTER EIGHT: QUAGMIRE, 1965–1977

1. Somini Sengupta, "Labor Leader Philip Vera Cruz: Reflections of a Labor Legend," in *Filipinos in America: A Journey of Faith* (South San Francisco: Filipinas Pub., 2003), 118–121; Sid A. Valledor, "Delano: Movement or Mirage (A Pilipino Perspective)," in *Diwang Pilipino: Pilipino Consciousness*, ed. Jovina Navarro (Davis: University of California Asian American Studies, 1974), 65, 69.

2. Cesar P. Pobre, *History of the Armed Forces of the Filipino People* (Quezon City, Philippines: New Day, 2000), 470–471.

3. "Remarks at the Signing of the Immigration Bill, Liberty Island, New York," October 3, 1965, *PPP: Johnson, 1965*, p. 1038.

4. "First Inaugural Address of Ferdinand E. Marcos," in *At the Helm of the Nation: Inaugural Addresses of the Presidents of the Philippine Republic and the Commonwealth*, comp. Consuelo V. Fonacier (Manila: National Media Production Center, 1973), 115, 116; Seth S. King, "Marcos, In Inaugural, Promises Clean-Up of Filipino Corruption," *NYT*, December 31, 1965.

5. "The President's News Conference," April 23, 1964, *PPP: Johnson, 1963–1964*, p. 522; Peter Grose, "Saigon Gets Aid of More Nations," *NYT*, August 14, 1964; Stanley Robert Larson and James Lawton Collins Jr., *Allied Participation in Vietnam* (Washington, DC: Department of the Army, 1975), 164.

6. Republic Act no. 4164 (July 21, 1964); State Department, quoted in Matthew Jagel, "'Showing Its Flag': The United States, the Philippines, and the Vietnam War," *Past Tense* 2 (2013): 25; Pobre, *Armed Forces of the Filipino People*, 463–474.

7. *The Statesman's Yearbook, 1964–1965* (New York: St. Martin's Press, 1964), 1326; Quintin R. de Borja, "Some Career Attributes and Professional Views of the Philippine Military Elite," *Philippine Journal of Public Administration* 13 (October 1969): 400, 403.

8. "Toasts of the President and President Macapagal," October 5, 1964, *PPP: Johnson, 1963–1964*, pp. 1211, 1212; "Joint Statement following Discussions with the President of the Philippines," October 6, 1964, ibid., 1214.

9. Marcos, quoted in William Beecher, "Philippine Force Training Hard as Vietnam Assignment Nears," *NYT*, August 2, 1966; Richard Butwell, "The Philippines: Changing of the Guard," *Asian Survey* 6 (January 1966): 48; "Filipino Marchers Protest U.S. Role in South Vietnam," *NYT*, June 19, 1965; "U.S. Vietnam Policy Hit in Manila," *LAT*, June 19, 1965.

10. William F. Buckley Jr., "Marcos and the Philippines," *National Review*, December 23, 1977, pp. 1512–1513; Richard Butwell, "The Philippines: Prelude to Elections," *Asian Survey* 5 (January 1965): 43; King, "Marcos, In Inaugural," 3; Robert Shaplen, "Letter from Manila," *New Yorker*, January 15, 1966, pp. 84–102. For Marcos's golf handicap, see Murray Gart, "Report from Manila," *Fortune* 76 (December 1967): 69. Reports at the time questioning the authenticity of Marcos's war record include "Filipino Policy Won't Change, Marcos Says," *LAT*, November 19, 1965.

11. Macapagal, quoted in "Filipino Policy Won't Change"; Marcos, quoted in Seymour Topping, "Philippines Seeks New Identity," *NYT*, November 21, 1965; "Rusk, Harriman Confer with Marcos on War," *LAT*, January 17, 1966.

12. Benigno S. Aquino Jr., "What's Wrong with the Philippines?" *Foreign Affairs* 46 (July 1968): 776; "Asks Marcos Viet Nam Help," *CT*, December 31, 1965; Almendras, quoted in Jagel, "Showing Its Flag," 30; Marcos, quoted in Dapen Liang, *Philippine Parties and Politics: A Historical Study of National Experience in Democracy*, rev. enlarged ed. (San Francisco: Gladstone, 1970), 438 n. 215; "Special Session Called on Filipino Troop Plan," *WP*, May 21, 1966.

13. Republic Act no. 4664 (June 18, 1966); Beecher, "Philippine Force Training Hard"; "Philippine Force Heads for Saigon," *NYT*, September 12, 1966; Marcos, quoted in "Philippines Is Fourth Nation to Commit Force to Vietnam," *NYT*, July 15, 1966; "Will Ink Viet Bill Today; Philcag Set," *Manila Daily Bulletin*, July 14, 1966.

14. Beecher, "Philippine Force Training Hard"; "Filipinos Encamp for Construction Duty in Vietnam," *NYT*, September 17, 1966; Pobre, *Armed Forces of the Filipino People*, 470–471, 484.

15. Valenti, quoted in Gary R. Hess, "With Friends Like These: Waging War and Seeking 'More Flags,'" in *The War that Never Ends: New Perspectives on the Vietnam War*, ed. David L. Anderson and John Ernst (Lexington: University Press of Kentucky, 2007), 63; Ward Just, "Our Affair with the Philippines," *WP*, November 30, 1969.

16. Liang, *Philippine Parties and Politics*, 397; "Marcos Makes Profitable Visit," *NYT*, September 18, 1966.

17. Settlement of Veterans Claims, TIAS 6295 (June 29, 1967).

18. Hess, "With Friends Like These," 64–66, 69–70.

19. James M. Carter, *Inventing Vietnam: The United States and State Building, 1954–1968* (New York: Cambridge University Press, 2008), 184–185; Clark Clifford, with Richard Holbrooke, *Counsel to the President: A Memoir* (New York: Random House, 1991), 451; F. Sionil José, "The Meaning of Vietnam," *Solidarity* 3 (February 1968): 1.

20. Military Bases in the Philippines, TIAS 6084 (September 16, 1966); Military Bases in the Philippines: Employment of Philippine Nationals, TIAS 6542 (May 27, 1968); Hess, "With Friends Like These," 64; Colleen Woods, "Building Empire's Archipelago: The Imperial Politics of Filipino Labor in the Pacific," *Labor* 13 nos. 3–4 (2016): 144.

21. Aquino, "What's Wrong with the Philippines?" 773; "Old Friend Turning from U.S.," *USNWR*, January 27, 1969, p. 63; "Reform or Revolution—Hard Choice in Philippines," *USNWR*, October 16, 1972, p. 35; Robert O. Tilman, "Student Unrest in the Philippines: The View from the South," *Asian Survey* 10 (October 1970): 906.

22. Latus, quoted in Yen Le Espiritu, *Filipino American Lives* (Philadelphia: Temple University Press, 1995), 84.

23. Ruben R. Alcantara, "The Filipino Wedding in Waialua, Hawaii: Ritual Retention and Ethnic Subculture in a New Setting," *Amerasia Journal* 1 (February 1972): 4, 12 n. 1; Fred Cordova, "The Filipino-American: There's Always an Identity Crisis," in *Asian-Americans: Psychological Perspectives*, ed. Stanley Sue and Nathaniel N. Wagner (Palo Alto: Science & Behavior Books, 1973), 136; F. Landa Jocano, "Filipinos in Hawaii: Problems in the Promised Land," *Philippine Sociological Review* 18 (July–October 1970): 152; Glenna Matthews, *Silicon Valley, Women, and the California Dream: Gender, Class, and Opportunity in the Twentieth Century* (Stanford: Stanford University Press, 2003), 159.

24. Latus, quoted in Espiritu, *Filipino American Lives*, 87; United Filipino Council statement, n.d. [1969], Filipino Cultural and Trade Center, San Francisco Ephemera Collection, San Francisco History Center, San Francisco Public Library, San Francisco [hereafter SFHC]. On South of Market associations, see Anselmo C. Revelo, "San Franciscan Filipinos in Focus," typescript (January 1972), Box 8, Papers of Joseph Alioto, SFHC, and "Filipino Education Center," Box 45, San Francisco Unified School District Records, SFHC.

25. Cordova, "Filipino-American," 137; Dawn Bohulano Mabalon, *Little Manila Is in the Heart: The Making of the Filipino/a American Community in Stockton, California* (Durham, NC: Duke University Press, 2013), 260–265; Roberta Peterson, *The Elder Pilipino* (San Diego: San Diego State University Center on Aging, 1978), 31.

26. Catherine Ceniza Choy, *Empire of Care: Nursing and Migration in Filipino American History* (Durham, NC: Duke University Press, 2003), 61–93; "New Strains on an Old Alliance," *USNWR*, June 5, 1972, p. 72.

27. David G. Ilumin, "Housing Problems in South of Market, San Francisco," in US Commission on Civil Rights, *Civil Rights Issues of Asian and Pacific Americans: Myths and Realities* (Washington, DC: US Commission on Civil Rights, 1980), 625–628.

28. "Amado David," in *Voices for Justice: Asian Pacific American Organizers and the New Labor Movement*, ed. Kent Wong (Los Angeles: UCLA Center for Labor Research and Education, 2001), 45–54; Revelo, "San Franciscan Filipinos in Focus," Box 8, Papers of Joseph Alioto, SFHC; Sengupta, "Labor Leader Philip Vera Cruz," 120.

29. Lorenzo "Larry" Silvestre, in *A Different Battle: Stories of Asian Pacific American Veterans*, ed. Carina A. del Rosario (Seattle: Wing Luke Asian Museum, 1999), 103–104.

30. Carillo, quoted in "Chinatown Anti-War Night," *Getting Together* 3 (August 5–19, 1972): 2; and "Nationwide Commemoration of Hiroshima and Nagasaki," *Getting Together* 3 (August 20–September 3, 1972): 2; Chalsa M. Loo et al., "Race-Related Stress among Asian American Veterans: A Model to Enhance Diagnosis and Treatment," *Cultural Diversity and Mental Health* 4 no. 2 (1998): 75–90.

31. Jeffrey D. Acosta, "Filipinos in the US Armed Forces," typescript (2014), 14; Jack Foisie, "Filipinos Glad to Be U.S. Navy Stewards," *LAT*, May 20, 1968; US Navy, Bureau of Naval Personnel, "Filipinos in the United States Navy," October 1976, "Filipinos" file, Vertical File Collection, Navy Department Library, Washington, DC.

32. 82 Stat. 1343 (October 24, 1968); Donald F. Duff and Ransom J. Arthur, "Between Two Worlds: Filipinos in the U.S. Navy," *American Journal of Psychiatry* 123 (January 1967): 837; "Filipino Stewards Still Used by Navy, But Number Drops," *NYT*, October 25, 1970; Dana Adams Schmidt, "Polishing the Top Brass—Demeaning for Aides?" *CSM*, April 24, 1973.

33. Ray L. Burdeos, *Filipinos in the U.S. Navy and Coast Guard during the Vietnam War* (Bloomington, IN: AuthorHouse, 2008), 26, 74–75, 96, 171.

34. Carlos A. Faustino, "Filipinos in the U.S.," *LAT*, May 24, 1968; "Filipino Stewards Still Used by Navy."

35. Trias, quoted in *A Different Battle*, ed. del Rosario, 111; "Filipino Stewards Still Used by Navy"; Foisie, "Filipinos Glad."

36. Amy Alipio, "All the Presidents' Manongs," in *Filipinos in America*, 78–81; H. R. Haldeman, *The Haldeman Diaries* (New York: Berkley Books, 1994), 611–612.

37. R. W. Apple Jr., "Lagging Pace of Racial Integration in the Navy Is Manifest on Aircraft Carrier off North Vietnam," *NYT*, February 26, 1967; Burdeos, *Filipinos in the U.S. Navy*, 46; Duff and Arthur, "Between Two Worlds," 837; "Navy Integration Record Is Rapped," *Chicago Defender*, March 4, 1967.

38. Navy recruiter, quoted in Earl Caldwell, "Navy Determined to Recruit Blacks," *NYT*, March 12, 1973; Duff and Arthur, "Between Two Worlds," 837; Michael Getler, "'Z-Gram 57': New Look for the Navy," *WP*, November 13, 1970; "The New Navy," *WP*, November 18, 1970; Zumwalt, quoted in Paul B. Ryan, "USS Constellation Flare-Up: Was It Mutiny?" *US Naval Institute Proceedings* 102 (January 1976): 48; Dana Adams Schmidt, "Navy Opens a Recruiting Drive to Increase Black Enrollments," *NYT*, April 1, 1971; Schmidt, "Polishing the Top Brass."

39. "Filipino Stewards Still Used by Navy"; Timothy H. Ingram, "How the U.S. Navy Solves the 'Servant Problem,'" *WP*, October 25, 1970; Ethel L. Payne, "Navy Gives Data on Its Racial Personnel," *Chicago Defender*, July 14, 1973; US Navy, Bureau of Naval Personnel, "Filipinos in the United States Navy."

40. Rudy Abramson, "Zumwalt Working to Update Navy," *BG*, November 12, 1972; "GI Butler Role Hit on Hill," *WP*, November 23, 1972; Seymour M. Hersh, "Some Very Unhappy Ships," *NYT*, November 12, 1972; "Military Urged: Drop 'Servants,'" *CSM*, July 24, 1975; Schmidt, "Polishing the Top Brass."

41. "Congress Warned on Vietnam," *NYT*, January 24, 1967; "LBJ Is Burned in Effigy at War Protest in Manila," *WP*, January 24, 1968; "Manila

to Pull Out Troops in Vietnam," *NYT*, March 21, 1969; Robert B. Semple Jr., "Nixon, in Manila, Bids Asians Widen Role in Security," *NYT*, July 27, 1969.

42. "Filipino Troops to Leave Vietnam after November," *NYT*, October 5, 1969; Osmeña, quoted in Jose Veloso Abueva, "The Philippines: Tradition and Change," *Asian Survey* 10 (January 1970): 62; "Philippines Set Plans for Vietnam Recall," unidentified clipping, October 5, 1969, Texas Tech Virtual Vietnam Archive; Robert B. Semple Jr., "U.S. Paid 39-Million to the Philippines for a Vietnam Unit," *NYT*, November 19, 1969; "Victory for Marcos," *Time*, November 21, 1969, pp. 45–46.

43. "Filipino Aide Says Saigon, Not U.S., Asked for Soldiers," *NYT*, November 29, 1969; John W. Finney, "Misuse of Funds in Manila Hinted," *NYT*, March 16, 1970; "Fulbright to Hold New Viet Hearings," *BG*, October 5, 1969; "Philippines Denies U.S. Pay for Sending Force to S. Viet," *CT*, November 20, 1969; Robert O. Tilman, "The Philippines in 1970: A Difficult Decade Begins," *Asian Survey* 11 (February 1971): 147.

44. Robert F. Emery, *The Financial Institutions of Southeast Asia: A Country-by-Country Study* (New York: Praeger, 1970), 391–394; Diosdado Macapagal, *A Stone for the Edifice: Memoirs of a President* (Quezon City, Philippines: Mac Pub. House, 1968), 213.

45. Emery, *Financial Institutions*, 391–394; Amador C. Fonacier, "The Philippine Veterans Bank: Pride of the Filipino Veteran," *Philippine Economy and Industrial Review* 15 (May–June 1968): 16–21; Mark L. Suluen, "A Study of the Living Conditions of Filipino Veterans: Their Status, Benefits, and Future" (M.N.S.A. thesis, National Defense College of the Philippines, 1991), 64–69, NDCP Library, Camp Aguinaldo, Quezon City, Philippines.

46. "All Filipinos Now Gone," *NYT*, December 21, 1969; Francis J. Kelly, *U.S. Army Special Forces, 1961–1971* (Washington, DC: Department of the Army, 1973), 195; Pobre, *Armed Forces of the Filipino People*, 479.

47. Marcos, quoted in Gart, "Report from Manila," 70.

48. Angel D. Baking, "Revolution as a Career," *Journal of Contemporary Asia* 1 (Winter 1970): 63; Barros, quoted in Delia Aguilar-San Juan, "Feminism and the National Liberation Struggle in the Philippines," *Women's Studies International Forum* 5 nos. 3–4 (1982): 256; Alfred W. McCoy, *Policing America's Empire: The United States, the Philippines, and the Rise of the Surveillance State* (Madison: University of Wisconsin Press, 2009), 502–506; Ramon E. Montaño, "The Republican Years," in Margarita R. Cojuangco et al., *Konstable: The Story of the Philippine Constabulary, 1901–1991* (Manila: ABoCan, 1991), 144, 151.

49. James M. Naughton, "Agnew Terms Manila Protest Just a 'Tactic of Modern Life,'" *NYT*, December 31, 1969.

50. Raymond Bonner, *Waltzing with a Dictator: The Marcoses and the Making of American Policy* (New York: Times Books, 1987), 101–107; Shaplen, "Letter from Manila."

51. John H. Adkins, "Philippines 1972: We'll Wait and See," *Asian Survey* 13 (February 1973): 143; Henry Kamm, "Manila's Left Jeers as Congress Opens," *NYT*, January 26, 1971; *Lansang v. Garcia*, 42 Phil. 448 (1971); Bruce Nussbaum, "Defending Malacanang," *FEER*, May 13, 1972, pp. 26–27; Santos, quoted in "Political Repression in the Philippines," *Journal of Contemporary Asia* 1 no. 4 (1971): 87.

52. Bonner, *Waltzing with a Dictator*, 96, 98–99; "Defense Chief Unharmed," *NYT*, September 23, 1972; Joven G. Maranan, "Countdown to Martial Law: The U.S.-Philippine Relationship, 1969–1972" (M.A. thesis, University of Massachusetts-Boston, 2016); Richard Nixon, *In the Arena: A Memoir of Victory, Defeat, and Renewal* (New York: Pocket Books, 1990), 303–305; State Department, quoted in Tad Szulc, "A High Marcos Aide Says in Washington that Martial Law May Last 2 Years," *NYT*, September 26, 1972.

53. Bonner, *Waltzing with a Dictator*, 100; "Defense Chief Unharmed"; "Marcos Tells Why He Chose Martial Law," *USNWR*, October 16, 1972, p. 36; "Mass Arrests and Curfew Announced in Philippines," *NYT*, September 24, 1972.

54. Rolando V. del Carmen, "Constitutionalism and the Supreme Court in a Changing Philippine Polity," *Asian Survey* 13 (November 1973): 1056–1057; Tillman Durdin, "Opposition Chief Seized by Manila," *NYT*, September 26, 1972; T.J.S. George, "Marcos Says an Uprising Is Planned," *FEER*, June 24, 1972, p. 12.

55. Moorer, quoted in Bonner, *Waltzing with a Dictator*, 108; Jack Foisie, "Why Did Marcos Act? A Question of Motives in the Philippines," *LAT*, October 15, 1972; "How Crackdown by Marcos Affects U.S.," *USNWR*, October 9, 1972, p. 82; "Marcos Tells Why," 36; "Reform or Revolution—Hard Choice in Philippines," *USNWR*, October 16, 1972, pp. 34, 35.

56. "Marcos Tells Why," 38; Fidel V. Ramos, "Peace and Order in the New Society," *Philippine Economy and Industrial Journal* 20 nos. 11–12 (1973): 82.

57. Robert O. Tilman, "The Philippines under Martial Law," *Current History* 71 (December 1976): 203.

58. Fox Butterfield, "Manila Inner Circle Gains under Marcos," *NYT*, January 15, 1978; Fox Butterfield, "U.S. Ties Still Bind Politics in the Philippines," *NYT*, April 16, 1978; George Hamilton and William Stadiem, *Don't Mind If I Do* (New York: Touchstone, 2008), 265–269; Roy Rowan, "The High-Flying First Lady of the Philippines," *Fortune*, July 2, 1979, p. 94; Daniel B. Schirmer, "Marcos—Sophisticated Dictator," *Commonweal* 102 (April 11, 1975): 44–46.

59. Bonner, *Waltzing with a Dictator*, 71; "Business around the World," *USNWR*, November 29, 1976, pp. 41–42; Fox Butterfield, "5-Year-Old Philippine Martial Law Builds Personal Power of Marcos," *NYT*, January 9, 1978; Jonathan Eig, *Ali: A Life* (Boston: Houghton Mifflin Harcourt, 2017), 420–430.

60. Butterfield, "5-Year-Old"; Butterfield, "Manila Inner Circle"; "Philippines' Fiscal Strain," *FEER*, July 16, 1973, pp. 39–41; Jack Foisie, "Ramos: Quiet, Tough Philippine 'Enforcer,'" *LAT*, October 6, 1972; David Wurfel, *Filipino Politics: Development and Decay* (Ithaca, NY: Cornell University Press, 1988), 140–153.

61. MNLF manifesto, in W. K. Che Man, *Muslim Separatism: The Moros of Southern Philippines and the Malays of Southern Thailand* (New York: Oxford University Press, 1990), 189–190.

62. "Marcos Tells Why," 37.

63. Adkins, "Philippines 1972," 146; "Filipino Regiment Hunts Unsurrendered Japanese," *NYT*, February 19, 1946; "Hiroo Onoda," *The Economist*, January 25, 2014, p. 78.

64. "Life in Philippines Returns to Normal," *LAT*, October 15, 1972; Carol Ojeda-Kimbrough, "The Chosen Road," in *Asian Americans: The Movement and the Moment*, ed. Steve Louie and Glenn K. Omatsu (Los Angeles: UCLA Asian American Studies Center Press, 2006), 65, 68.

65. Presidential Declaration no. 442 (May 1, 1974); Robyn Margalit Rodriguez, "The Labor Brokerage State and the Globalization of Filipina Care Workers," *Signs* 33 (Summer 2008): 794–800.

66. Mariano Angeles Oral History, Washington State Oral/Aural History Program (Olympia: Washington State Archives, 1974–1977), 36 [hereafter WSOAHP]; Stephen Griffiths, *Emigrants, Entrepreneurs, and Evil Spirits: Life in a Philippine Village* (Honolulu: University of Hawaii Press, 1988), 3; Zacarias Manangan Oral History, WSOAHP, 29; "Proxmire Seeks to Halt Filipino Veteran Pay Abuses," *WP*, September 1, 1977.

67. E. San Juan Jr., *Toward Filipino Self-Determination: Beyond Transnational Globalization* (Albany, NY: SUNY Press, 2009), 232.

68. BAACW, quoted in "Asians against the War," *Getting Together* 3 (May 27–June 9, 1972): 2; Gil Mangaoang, "From the 1970s to the 1990s: Perspective of a Gay Filipino American Activist," in *Asian American Sexualities: Dimensions of the Gay and Lesbian Experience*, ed. Russell Leong (New York: Routledge, 1996), 101–110.

69. Joseph Lelyveld, "A Thriving City Next Door," *NYT*, June 26, 1974; Gene Parker, "Inside Report: Filipino Prison Camps under Martial Law," Pacific News Service, n.d. [October 1972], Box 1624, American Civil Liberties

Union Records, Princeton University, Princeton, NJ; Sorenson, quoted in Nicholas von Hoffman, "A Question of Black and White in the Navy," *WP*, November 20, 1972.

70. Movement for a Free Philippines, quoted in Margarett Loke, "Asian American Communities Speak Up in 1976," *Bridge: An Asian American Perspective* 4 (November 1976): 16; Eliseo Art Arambulo Silva, *Filipinos of Greater Philadelphia* (Charleston, SC: Arcadia, 2012), 84; Mae Respicio Koerner, *Filipinos in Los Angeles* (Charleston, SC: Arcadia, 2007), 92; Lewis, quoted in "Pilipinos Protest: 'Heil Marcos!'" *Getting Together* 3 (October 22–November 4, 1972): 2.

71. Ojeda-Kimbrough, "The Chosen Road," 69, 70.

72. "The President's News Conference of April 3, 1975," *PPP: Ford, 1975*, p. 414.

73. Marcos and Romulo, quoted in Andrew J. Gawthorpe, "The Ford Administration and Security Policy in the Asia-Pacific after the Fall of Saigon," *Historical Journal* 52 (September 2009): 704.

74. "Address at the University of Hawaii," December 7, 1975, *PPP: Ford, 1975*, pp. 1951, 1954; "Banquet Given by President Marcos, Manila, December 6," *DoSB* 73 (December 29, 1975): 924; Gerald R. Ford, *A Time to Heal: The Autobiography of Gerald R. Ford* (New York: Harper & Row, 1979), 337.

75. Cordova, "Filipino-American," 13.

76. *INS v. Hibi*, 414 U.S. 5 (1973), at 8–9, 11.

77. *Filipino American Veterans and Dependents Association et al. v. United States*, 391 F. Supp. 1314 (N.D. Cal. 1974), at 1322.

78. Reporter's Transcript, pp. 8–9, 19, 32, 34, In the Matter of Petitions for Naturalization pursuant to Sections 701–702, Nationality Act of 1940, United States District Court for the Northern District of California, September 20, 1974, Case 186373, Box 13, Record Group 21: Records of District Courts of the United States, National Archives and Records Administration, San Bruno, CA.

79. *In the Matter of Petitions for Naturalization of 68 Filipino War Veterans*, 406 F. Supp. 931 (1975); *U.S. v. Mendoza*, 464 U.S. 154 (1984); "Benefits to Filipinos by V.A. Termed High," *NYT*, September 1, 1977.

CHAPTER NINE: PEOPLE POWER, 1977–2001

1. "Inaugural Address of President Jimmy Carter," January 20, 1977, *PPP: Carter, 1977*, p. 3.

2. Fox Butterfield, "U.S. Ties Still Bind Politics in the Philippines," *NYT*, April 16, 1978; Vance, quoted in Joel Rocamora, "Human Rights and

U.S.-Southeast Asia Policy: The New *Realpolitik*," *Southeast Asia Chronicle* nos. 58–59 (December 1977): 3, and Cyrus Vance, "America's Role in Consolidating a Peaceful Balance and Promoting Economic Growth in Asia," *DoSB* 77 (August 1, 1977): 141.

3. Holbrooke, quoted in Belinda A. Aquino, "The Philippines under Marcos," *Current History* 81 (April 1982): 163.

4. Transcript of Meeting, May 3, 1978, p. 10, Philippines: Meeting with President Marcos, Papers of Walter F. Mondale, Minnesota History Center, St. Paul; "U.S. and Filipinos Sign Agreement on the Use of Air and Navy Bases," *NYT*, January 8, 1979; "U.S. and Philippines Reach Accord on Aid and Use of Military Bases," *NYT*, January 1, 1979.

5. Marcos, quoted in Sheilah Ocampo, "Marcos' Cosmetic Victory," *FEER*, January 12, 1979, p. 24.

6. "Toasts of President Reagan and President Ferdinand E. Marcos of the Philippines at the State Dinner," September 16, 1982, *PPP: Reagan, 1982*, p. 1172.

7. Justin J. Green, "Why Marcos Announced the End of Martial Law," *Asian Thought and Society* 6 (April 1981): 80–82; Louis Kraar, "The Philippines Veers Toward Crisis," *Fortune*, July 27, 1981, p. 35.

8. John Brecher, "A Bouquet for Marcos," *Newsweek*, July 13, 1981, p. 39; "Bush Pledges Support for the Philippines," *NYT*, July 1, 1981; Haig, quoted in Aquino, "Philippines under Marcos," 163, and Joel Rocamora, "Marcos: Safe for Now," *Southeast Asia Chronicle* no. 83 (April 1982): 13. In his memoirs, Bush falsely described a 1985 trip to the Philippines as "my first since I flew over Manila Bay in 1944." George Bush, *All the Best, George Bush: My Life in Letters and Other Writings* (New York: Touchstone, 1999), 346.

9. B. Drummond Ayres Jr., "Annual U.S. Survey of Human Rights Finds Major Gains in Latin America," *NYT*, February 11, 1984; Barbara Crossette, "Manila's Progress on Rights Studied," *NYT*, November 19, 1981; Jeane Kirkpatrick, "Dictatorships and Double Standards," *Commentary* 68 (November 1979): 34–45.

10. William J. Crowe Jr., with David Chanoff, *The Line of Fire: From Washington to the Gulf, the Politics of the New Military* (New York: Simon and Schuster, 1993), 110.

11. *The Statesman's Year-Book, 1983–84* (New York: St. Martin's Press, 1985), 985–986; Aquino, "Philippines under Marcos," 162; K. M. Chrysler, "'Some Call It Dictatorship; I Call It Authoritarianism': Interview with Ferdinand E. Marcos, President of the Philippines," *USNWR*, August 5, 1974, p. 38; Robert A. Manning, "The Philippines in Crisis," *Foreign Affairs* 63 (Winter 1984):

403–404; Kim Rogal with Richard Vokey, "Charlie's Deadly Angels," *Newsweek*, March 15, 1982, p. 42.

12. Carolina G. Hernandez, "The Philippine Military and Civilian Control: Under Marcos and Beyond," *Third World Quarterly* 7 (October 1985): 907–923; Ramon E. Montaño, "The Republican Years," in Margarita R. Cojuangco et al., *Konstable: The Story of the Philippine Constabulary, 1901–1991* (Manila: ABoCan, 1991), 158–159; Alfred W. McCoy, *Closer than Brothers: Manhood at the Philippine Military Academy* (New Haven, CT: Yale University Press, 1999); David Wurfel, *Filipino Politics: Development and Decay* (Ithaca, NY: Cornell University Press, 1988), 140–153.

13. "Dissidence and Detente: Interview: José Maria Sison," *FEER*, November 6, 1981, p. 23; James E. Livingston, Colin D. Heaton, and Anne-Marie Lewis, *Noble Warrior: The Story of Major General James E. Livingston, USMC (Ret.), Medal of Honor* (Minneapolis: MBI Pub. and Zenith Press, 2010), 174; Manning, "Philippines in Crisis," 402.

14. Marcos, quoted in Kim Rogal, "Presidential Sweet Talk," *Newsweek*, September 13, 1982, p. 46; Robert Kaylor, "Philippines' Marcos Comes Calling for Aid," *USNWR*, September 20, 1982, p. 35; Francisco S. Tatad, "Keeping Philippine Bases," *Washington Quarterly* 7 (Winter 1984): 86; Paul D. Wolfowitz, "FY 1984 Assistance Requests for East Asia and the Pacific," *DoSB* 83 (May 1983): 33.

15. Gordon, quoted in Linda Golley, "For Sale: Girls," *Southeast Asia Chronicle* no. 89 (April 1983): 32; Paul Hutchcroft, "In the Shadow of Subic: Castaways of an Imperial Navy," *Southeast Asia Chronicle* no. 83 (April 1982): 24.

16. Diokno and Tañada, quoted in Agnes G. Bailen, *The Odyssey of Lorenzo M. Tañada* (Quezon City: University of the Philippines Press, 1998), 143, 145; Steve Lohr, "Filipinos Oppose Bases After U.S. Plan to Cut Aid," *NYT*, July 22, 1985.

17. Delia Aguilar-San Juan, "Feminism and the National Liberation Struggle in the Philippines," *Women's Studies International Forum* 5 nos. 3–4 (1982): 259; Raymond L. Garthoff, *A Journey through the Cold War: A Memoir of Containment and Coexistence* (Washington, DC: Brookings Institution Press, 2001), 297; Hutchcroft, "In the Shadow of Subic," 25; A. R. Magno, "Cornucopia or Curse: The Internal Debate on U.S. Bases in the Philippines," in *Military Basing and the U.S./Soviet Military Balance in Southeast Asia*, ed. George K. Tanham and Alvin H. Bernstein (New York: Crane Russak, 1989), 160–161; Sheilah Ocampo, "A Treaty Runs into Trouble," *FEER*, February 9, 1979, pp. 28–29; Daniel B. Schirmer, "Those Philippine Bases," *Monthly Review* 37 (March 1986): 26.

18. Tañada, quoted in Bailen, *Odyssey*, 144; Richard Gordon, "Philippine Military Bases: Economic and Social Implications," in *Military Basing*, ed. Tanham and Bernstein, 138; Paul Hutchcroft, "No Smear, No Work: Safeguarding American Interests in the Philippines," *Southeast Asia Chronicle* no. 84 (June 1982): 12–13; A. Lin Neumann, "'Hospitality Girls' in the Philippines," *Southeast Asia Chronicle* no. 66 (January–February 1979): 18–22.

19. Golley, "For Sale: Girls," 32; Leopoldo M. Moselina, "Olongapo's Rest and Recreation Industry: A Sociological Analysis of Institutionalized Prostitution," *Philippine Sociological Review* 27 (July 1979): 184. Men also pursued work in military sex and entertainment industries, as depicted in Lino Brocka's 1988 film *Macho Dancer*.

20. Richard Buttny, "Legitimation Techniques for Intermarriage: Accounts of Motives for Intermarriage from U.S. Servicemen and Philippine Women," *Communication Quarterly* 35 (Spring 1987): 125; Moselina, "Olongapo's Rest and Recreation Industry," 187; A. Lin Neumann, "Where Do You Go When the Ship Sails Home?" *Southeast Asia Chronicle* no. 66 (January–February 1979): 23.

21. Aguilar-San Juan, "Feminism and the National Liberation Struggle," 259; Audre Lorde, "Introduction," in Mila D. Aguilar, *A Comrade Is as Precious as a Rice Seedling*, 2d ed. (Latham, NY: Kitchen Table: Women of Color Press, 1987), vii.

22. Madge Bello and Vincent Reyes, "Filipino Americans and the Marcos Overthrow: The Transformation of Political Consciousness," *Amerasia Journal* 13 no. 1 (1986–87): 75–76.

23. Glenna Matthews, *Silicon Valley, Women, and the California Dream: Gender, Class, and Opportunity in the Twentieth Century* (Stanford: Stanford University Press, 2003), 160; Erin McCormick, "Filipino Guards Sue over 'Accent Discrimination,'" clipping from *San Francisco Examiner*, April 15, 1993, Box 118, American Civil Liberties Union of Northern California Records, California Historical Society, San Francisco [hereafter ACLU–NC, CHS].

24. Leonilo L. Malabed, "And Now, a Word from the Publisher," clipping from *The Filipino American*, January 22–28, 1982, "Feinstein Shows Guts," clipping from *The Filipino American*, September 30–October 6, 1982, and E. Cahill Maloney, "Philippine Friendship Library Needs Books," clipping from *San Francisco Progress*, November 17, 1982, Sister Cities: Manila Folder, San Francisco Ephemera Collection, San Francisco History Center, San Francisco Public Library, San Francisco [hereafter SFHC]; Ronald Smothers, "Jackson's 'Rainbow' May Lack Some of Spectrum," *NYT*, February 12, 1984.

25. Rita M. Cacas and Juanita Tamayo Lott, *Filipinos in Washington, D.C.* (Charleston, SC: Arcadia, 2009), 75, 104; Filipino Immigrant Services, "Progress Report," n.d. [June 1982], Box 118, ACLU–NC, CHS.

26. Stephen Engelberg, "Army Once Barred Files on Marcos," *NYT*, January 23, 1986; "Marcos's Wartime Role Discredited in U.S. Files," *NYT*, January 23, 1986.

27. Presidential Decree no. 236 (July 9, 1973); "The First Lady's Winning Ways," *FEER*, January 19, 1979, pp. 35–36; Paul D. Hutchcroft, *Booty Capitalism: The Politics of Banking in the Philippines* (Ithaca, NY: Cornell University Press, 1998), 179–180; "Philippine Bank Move," *NYT*, April 11, 1985; Lorenzo Villaflor, "A Study of the AFP Pension Fund Scheme" (M.N.S.A. thesis, National Defense College of the Philippines, 1976), NDCP Library, Camp Aguinaldo, Quezon City, Philippines.

28. Bello and Reyes, "Filipino Americans," 76, 78–80; Raymond Bonner, *Waltzing with a Dictator: The Marcoses and the Making of American Policy* (New York: Times Books, 1987), 468.

29. Benito M. Vergara Jr., *Pinoy Capital: The Filipino Nation in Daly City* (Philadelphia: Temple University Press, 2009), 80–108.

30. Aquino, quoted in Stephen J. Solarz, *Journeys to War and Peace: A Congressional Memoir* (Waltham, MA: Brandeis University Press, 2011), 113; "Manila Panel Is Told the Military Barred Aquino Backers at Airport," *NYT*, January 31, 1984; Jane Perlez, "Marcos Linked to Four Manhattan Sites," *NYT*, March 21, 1986.

31. "Manila Panel Is Told"; "Man Says Aquino Was Shot on Steps," *NYT*, February 9, 1984.

32. "Head of Aquino Panel Doubts Manila's Account," *NYT*, January 21, 1984; Solarz, *Journeys to War and Peace*, 115; "Statement by Deputy Press Secretary Speakes on the Assassination of Benigno S. Aquino, Jr.," August 21, 1983, *PPP: Reagan, 1983*, p. 1187; "Interview with Members of the Editorial Board of the New York Post in New York City," September 26, 1983, *PPP: Reagan, 1983*, p. 1359; "Mayor Drops Manila as S.F. Sister City," clipping from *San Francisco Examiner*, October 7, 1983, Sister Cities: Manila Folder, San Francisco Ephemera Collection, SFHC; "Statement by Deputy Press Secretary Speakes on the Postponement of the President's Visits to the Philippines, Indonesia, and Thailand," October 3, 1983, *PPP: Reagan, 1983*, p. 1401–1402; Joan Quigley, *What Does Joan Say? My Seven Years as White House Astrologer to Nancy and Ronald Reagan* (Secaucus, NJ: Carol, 1990), 86–87, is unreliable on this point as Quigley suggests the Reagans did travel to the Philippines.

33. Manning, "Philippines in Crisis," 394–397; Ross H. Munro, "Dateline Manila: Moscow's Next Win?" *Foreign Policy* no. 56 (Autumn 1984): 177–179.

34. Kaylor, "Philippines' Marcos Comes Calling," 36; Munro, "Dateline Manila," 183–184.

35. Executive Order no. 857 (December 13, 1982); Kaylor, "Philippines' Marcos Comes Calling," 36; Manning, "Philippines in Crisis," 397.

36. Bello and Reyes, "Filipino Americans," 76; Roxas, quoted in Michael Viola, "Toward a Filipino Critical Pedagogy: Exposure Programs to the Philippines and the Politicization of Melissa Roxas," *Journal of Asian American Studies* 17 (February 2014): 6, 8.

37. Bello and Reyes, "Filipino Americans," 80–81; "U.S. Filipinos Sending Home Published Attacks on Marcos," *NYT*, February 7, 1984.

38. Jo-Ann Q. Maglipon, "RAM Boys," in *Primed: Selected Stories, 1972–1982* (Manila: Anvil, 1993), 225–228; "A Talk with Marcos," *Newsweek*, September 20, 1982, pp. 24–26.

39. Aquino, quoted in Munro, "Dateline Manila," 173.

40. Crowe, *Line of Fire*, 111, 112; Manning, "Philippines in Crisis," 407; Lewis M. Simons, *Worth Dying For* (New York: William Morrow, 1987), 106–107; "The Transition of Power in the Philippines: An Interview with Dr. Richard J. Kessler," *Fletcher Forum* 10 (Summer 1986): 209.

41. Bello and Reyes, "Filipino Americans," 77; Crossette, "Manila's Progress on Rights Studied"; Frank H. Murkowski, "Observations on Recent Events in the Philippines," *Fletcher Forum* 10 (Summer 1986): 186; Perlez, "Marcos Linked to Four Manhattan Sites"; Solarz, *Journeys in War and Peace*, 117.

42. Crowe, *Line of Fire*, 114; Lewis E. Gleeck Jr., *On Their Own: Midwifing a Post-Colonial Philippine-American Relationship* (Parañaque City, Philippines: Loyal Printing, 1998), 17; James Mann, *The Rise of the Vulcans: The History of Bush's War Cabinet* (New York: Viking, 2004), 132; Munro, "Dateline Manila," 185; "The United States and the Philippines: An Interview with Ambassador Paul D. Wolfowitz," *Fletcher Forum* 10 (Summer 1986): 196.

43. James Clad, "Military Prize-Catch," *FEER*, October 9, 1986, p. 18; Joseph E. Persico, *Casey: From the OSS to the CIA* (New York: Penguin, 1990), 434–435.

44. Kirkpatrick, quoted in Sidney Blumenthal, "The Overthrow of Jeane Kirkpatrick," in *Our Long National Daydream: A Political Pageant of the Reagan Era* (New York: Harper and Row, 1988), 198; Armitage, quoted in Mann, *Rise of the Vulcans*, 132.

45. Crowe, *Line of Fire*, 115; Novak, quoted in *Recollections of Reagan: A Portrait of Ronald Reagan*, ed. Peter Hannaford (New York: William Morrow,

1997), 124; Reagan, quoted in Mann, *Rise of the Vulcans*, 132; Doug Rossinow, *The Reagan Era: A History of the 1980s* (New York: Columbia University Press, 2015), 262.

46. Reagan, quoted in "Election Developments in the Philippines," *DoSB* 86 (April 1986): 67; Bryan Johnson, *The Four Days of Courage: The Untold Story of the People Who Brought Marcos Down* (New York: Free Press, 1987), 99; John P. Murtha with John Plashal, *From Vietnam to 9/11: On the Front Lines of National Security*, updated ed. (University Park: Pennsylvania State University Press, 2006), 74.

47. Bonner, *Waltzing with a Dictator*, 420–421; Murtha, *From Vietnam to 9/11*, 81; Rossinow, *Reagan Era*, 262; Shultz, *Turmoil and Triumph*, 636. On Manafort's role, see Johnson, *Four Days of Courage*, 94; Kenneth P. Vogel, "Paul Manafort's Wild and Lucrative Philippine Adventure," *Politico*, June 10, 2016.

48. Fascell, quoted in Murtha, *From Vietnam to 9/11*, 81–82; Paul D. Wolfowitz, "After the Election in the Philippines," *DoSB* 86 (April 1986): 69–70.

49. Murtha, *From Vietnam to 9/11*, 82; Simons, *Worth Dying For*, 280.

50. "Election Developments in the Philippines," 68; Johnson, *Four Days of Courage*, 143; Marcos, quoted in Larry Speakes, with Robert Pack, *Speaking Out: The Reagan Presidency from Inside the White House* (New York: Charles Scribner's Sons, 1988), 206; Bosworth, quoted in ibid., 207.

51. Speakes, *Speaking Out*, 207–209, credits Habib; Mann, *Rise of the Vulcans*, 133, gives credit to Shultz, drawing heavily from Shultz's memoir.

52. Paul Laxalt, "My Conversations with Ferdinand Marcos: A Lesson in Personal Diplomacy," *Policy Review* no. 37 (Summer 1986): 5; Ronald Reagan, *An American Life* (New York: Simon and Schuster, 1990), 364–365; Shultz, *Turmoil and Triumph*, 637; Speakes, *Speaking Out*, 209–213.

53. "Interview with Philippine President Ferdinand Marcos: U.S. Under Reagan: No Longer a 'Sense of Drift,'" *USNWR*, May 17, 1982, p. 41.

54. Bello and Reyes, "Filipino Americans," 80; Tom Blanton, ed., *White House E-Mail: The Top Secret Computer Messages the Reagan/Bush White House Tried to Destroy* (New York: New Press, 1995), 28–30. Calculations of looting appear in J. C. Sharman, *The Despot's Guide to Wealth Management: On the International Campaign against Grand Corruption* (Ithaca, NY: Cornell University Press, 2017), 44; Transparency International, *Global Corruption Report* (Berlin: Transparency International, 2004), 13.

55. Henry A. Kissinger, "What Next When U.S. Intervenes?" *LAT*, March 9, 1986; Reagan, *An American Life*, 364; Bernard Weinraub, "Reagan Welcomes Change in Manila," *NYT*, February 27, 1986.

56. Blanton, *White House E-Mail*, 31; Blumenthal, "The Overthrow of Jeane Kirkpatrick," 197; "Interview with Ambassador Paul D. Wolfowitz," 201.

57. While news reports initially reported racks filled with 3,000 pairs of shoes, curators at Malacanang later counted a mere 2,400 in their inventory. Teresa Albor, "Curators Ready to Give the Boot to Imelda's Shoes," *CT*, December 29, 1989; Fox Butterfield, "In Manila Palace: Silk Dresses, 6,000 Shoes," *NYT*, March 9, 1986.

58. Aquino, quoted in Murtha, *From Vietnam to 9/11*, 87; Dole, quoted in Solarz, *Journeys in War and Peace*, 128; Pico Iyer and David Aikman, "Woman of the Year," *Time*, January 5, 1987, p. 18.

59. Gleeck, *On Their Own*, 23; Reagan, *An American Life*, 366; David A. Rosenberg, "The Philippines: Aquino's First Year," *Current History* 86 (April 1987): 162.

60. Jose Jowel Canuday, "Locating Duterte in Davao: Conversations on the Global South," *Journal of Social Transformations* 5 (2017): 121–136; Sheila S. Coronel, "The Vigilante President: How Duterte's Brutal Populism Conquered the Philippines," *Foreign Affairs*, August 12, 2019.

61. Seth Mydans, "Philippine Army and Rebels Start Cease-Fire," *NYT*, December 10, 1986.

62. Aquino, quoted in Peter Bacho, "U.S.-Philippine Relations in Transition: The Issue of the Bases," *Asian Survey* 28 (June 1988): 651, and Michael Bedford, "Mangyans Forced to Evacuate Homeland in Philippines," *Cultural Survival Quarterly* 12 (Fall 1988): 21; Isleta, quoted in Livingston, *Noble Warrior*, 173.

63. Bedford, "Mangyans Forced to Evacuate Homeland," 21; NPA, quoted in Livingston, *Noble Warrior*, 176; Daniel B. Schirmer, "Whatever Happened to Cory Aquino?" *Monthly Review* 40 (May 1988): 15; John K. Singlaub, with Malcolm McConnell, *Hazardous Duty: An American Soldier in the Twentieth Century* (New York: Summit Books, 1991), 499; Solonga, quoted in David E. Sanger, "Reliving the Longest Day, Envoy Speaks Softly," *NYT*, December 19, 1989; Martin Wright, ed., *Revolution in the Philippines?* (Harlow, UK: Longman Group, 1988), 79–80.

64. Philippine Constitution (1987), Article XVIII, Section 25; James Clad, "Basis for the Bases," *FEER*, November 19, 1987, p. 28.

65. 104 Stat. 4978 (November 29, 1990); Inouye, quoted in Marvine Howe, "Immigrant Act Aids Filipino Veterans," *NYT*, November 25, 1990; "The Fight Is Not Over Yet!," clipping from *Philippine News*, January 1991, Box 34, Office of Asian and Pacific Islander Affairs, Papers of David A. Roberti (CSLA-1), Loyola Marymount University, Los Angeles.

66. Ojeda, quoted in Bob Drogin, "Filipino Veterans Get Recognition—At Last," *LAT*, November 13, 1990; Wisner, quoted in Gleeck, *On Their Own*, 46; Solarz, quoted in Howe, "Immigrant Act Aids Filipino Veterans."

67. Graziano Battistella, "Gulf Returnees: Profile of a Crisis," *Asian Migrant* 4 (January–March 1991): 25–29; Cesar P. Pobre, *History of the Armed Forces of the Filipino People* (Quezon City, Philippines: New Day, 2000), 601–603; Patricia Santo Tomas and Jorge Tigno, "Philippine Lessons from the Gulf Crisis: Anatomy of a Contingency Plan," *Asian Migrant* 5 (April–June 1992): 49–54.

68. Hilarion Polintan, in *A Different Battle: Stories of Asian Pacific American Veterans*, ed. Carina A. del Rosario (Seattle: Wing Luke Asian Museum, 1999), 97–98.

69. Leny Mendoza Strobel, "A Personal Story: Becoming a Split Filipina Subject," *Amerasia Journal* 19 no. 3 (1993): 128.

70. Alvarez, quoted in Bailen, *Odyssey*, 153; Steven Erlanger, "Sailors Can't Paint the Town, So Sin Trade Pales," *NYT*, July 6, 1990; Seth Mydans, "Talks on Bases in Philippines Spur Defiance toward U.S.," *NYT*, June 25, 1988; Andrew Yeo, "Challenging US Military Presence in the Philippines," *South Atlantic Quarterly* 111 (Fall 2012): 861.

71. Saguisag, quoted in Bailen, *Odyssey*, 152; Fidel V. Ramos, *Developing as a Democracy: Reform and Recovery in the Philippines, 1992–98* (New York: St. Martin's Press, 1998), 120.

72. Vernadette Vicuña Gonzalez, *Securing Paradise: Tourism and Militarism in Hawai'i and the Philippines* (Durham, NC: Duke University Press, 2013), 181–214; Quinsaat, quoted in H. G. Reza, "Navy to Stop Recruiting Filipino Nationals," *LAT*, February 27, 1992.

73. Neumann, "Where Do You Go When the Ship Sails Home?" 23; Ramos, *Developing as a Democracy*, 120.

74. *Miller v. Albright*, 523 U.S. 420 (1998); Ramos, quoted Bob Drogin, "Americans Bid Farewell to Last Philippine Base," *LAT*, November 25, 1992. By the time the Court ruled, Miller had married a US citizen and obtained US permanent residency.

75. Alex B. Brillantes Jr., "The Philippines in 1991: Disasters and Decisions," *Asian Survey* 32 (February 1992): 144; Rudolph W. Giuliani, to Robin Ross, October 10, 1988, Ronald Reagan Presidential Library, Simi Valley, CA; Sharman, *Despot's Guide to Wealth Management*, 93; Emmanuel S. Tipon, "San Francisco Mayor Agnos Beats a Dead Horse," clipping from *U.S.–Philippine Times* (March 1991), Box 68, Papers of Art Agnos, SFHC.

76. Drogin, "Filipino Veterans Get Recognition"; Paul Feldman, "A Battle for Rights: Filipino Veterans of WWII Fight for Citizenship, Pensions Despite Missing Army Records," *LAT*, February 19, 1994.

77. Satoshi Nakano, "The Filipino World War II Veterans Equity Movement and the Filipino American Community," *Pacific and American Studies* 6 (March 2006): 136–137.

78. Feldman, "Battle for Rights"; Satoshi Nakano, "Nation and Citizenship in the Filipino World War II Veterans Equity Movement, 1945–2001," *JCAS Symposium Series* 18 (2002): 207, 214.

79. Bob Stump, "Filipino Vets and Fairness," *WP*, January 28, 1998.

80. Rick Rocamora, *Filipino World War II Soldiers: America's Second-Class Veterans* (San Francisco: Veterans Equity Center, 2008).

81. Feldman, "Battle for Rights"; "Filipino Veterans Press for War Benefits," *NYT*, April 20, 1998; Carina Monica Montoya, *Filipinos in Hollywood* (Charleston, SC: Arcadia, 2008), 79, 80; Jose Mozingo, "Filipino Veterans Chain Selves to Statue in Protest," *LAT*, June 17, 1997; Nakano, "Filipino World War II Veterans," 145–146.

82. US Department of Veterans Affairs, *VA Benefits for Filipino Veterans* (Washington, DC: US Department of Veterans Affairs, 2000).

83. Thomas C. Hubbard, "Issues in Philippine-American Political and Security Relations," *Bulletin of the American Historical Collection* 27 (April–June 1999): 78, 79.

84. Maceda, quoted in Brillantes, "Philippines in 1991," 142; "The President's New Conference," December 26, 1991, *PPP: Bush, 1991*, vol. 2, p. 1660; "Remarks and a Question-and-Answer Session with the Singapore Lecture Group," January 4, 1992, *PPP: Bush, 1992–93*, p. 26; Clinton, quoted in Anne Devroy, "U.S., Philippines Pledge Economic Cooperation," *WP*, November 23, 1993.

85. Meredith, quoted in Herman Tiu Laurel, ed., *The Olongapo Colonial Experience: History, Politics, and Memories* (Quezon City, Philippines: Independent Media, 2003), 92.

CHAPTER TEN: TERROR MIGRATIONS, 2001–2009

1. Kevin L. Nadal et al., *Filipinos in New York City* (Charleston, SC: Arcadia, 2015), 127; "A Nation Challenged: Portraits of Grief," *NYT*, September 30, 2001; "A Nation Challenged: Portraits of Grief," *NYT*, November 4, 2001; "A Nation Challenged: Portraits of Grief," *NYT*, November 24, 2001.

2. "Reminiscences of Jose A. Pineda," transcript, pp. 10–11, Oral History Research Office, Columbia University, New York.

3. Ma. Concepcion B. Clamor, "The Philippine Perspective," in *Terrorism in the Asia-Pacific: Threat and Response*, ed. Rohan Gunaratna (Singapore: Eastern Universities Press, 2003), 216; Cher S. Jimenez, "US Outsources War to Filipinos," *Asia Times Online*, July 15, 2006; Jana K. Lipman, *Guantánamo: A Working-Class History between Empire and Revolution* (Berkeley: University of California Press, 2009), 226; Rick Rocamora, "Made for Al-Qaeda," *Newsbreak Online*, August 4, 2002.

4. Patricio N. Abinales and Donna J. Amoroso, "The Withering of Philippine Democracy," *Current History* 105 (September 2006): 292; Jason DeParle, "A Good Provider Is One Who Leaves," *NYT*, April 22, 2007; Michael J. Montesano, "The Philippines in 2003: Troubles, None of Them New," *Asian Survey* 44 (January–February 2004): 99; Migrante International, quoted in Robyn Magalit Rodriguez, "Migration, Transnational Politics, and the State: Challenging the Limits of the Law: Filipina Migrant Workers' Transnational Struggles in the World for Protection and Social Justice," in *Globalization and Third World Women: Exploitation, Coping, and Resistance*, ed. Ligaya Lindio-McGovern and Isidor Walliman (Burlington, VT: Ashgate, 2009), 56.

5. E. San Juan Jr., "Carlos Bulosan in a Time of the Wars on Terror," *Amerasia Journal* 31 no. 3 (2005): 145.

6. Republic Act no. 8042 (June 7, 1995); R. J. May, "The Domestic in Foreign Policy: The Flor Contemplacion Case and Philippine-Singapore Relations," *Pilipinas* 29 (Fall 1997): 63–76; Rodriguez, "Migration, Transnational Politics, and the State," 49.

7. Jan M. Padios, "Call Center Agent," in *Figures of Southeast Asian Modernity*, ed. Joshua Baker et al. (Honolulu: University of Hawai'i Press, 2014), 38–40.

8. Portagana, quoted in DeParle, "Good Provider."

9. US Census Bureau, *The Asian Population: 2010* (Washington, DC: US Department of Commerce, 2012).

10. "Filipino-American Leaders Applaud Justice Department for Helping Undocumented Immigrants after September 11th," *Filipino-Asian Bulletin*, April 3, 2002, September 11 Digital Archive; Jose Antonio Vargas, "Outlaw: My Life as an Undocumented Immigrant," *NYT*, June 26, 2011.

11. Unnamed official quoted in James Kelly, "On the Sunny Side," *FEER*, August 9, 2001, p. 20.

12. Deirdre Sheehan, "A Price for Peace," *FEER*, August 30, 2001, p. 17; Deirdre Sheehan, "Swords into Plowshares," *FEER*, September 20, 2001, pp. 30–31.

13. Kit Collier, "Spoiling for a Fight: Dangerous Days in the Southern Philippines," *Asia-Pacific Defence Reporter* 28 (March–April 2002): 40; James Hookway, "Philippine Islamic Resistance Resurfaces," *WSJ*, June 22, 1999;

Mark Landler, "The Temperature's a Lot Warmer but the Mission's the Same: Hunting Down Terrorists," *NYT*, November 4, 2001; John McBeth, "The Danger Within," *FEER*, September 27, 2001, p. 22; National Commission on Terrorist Attacks upon the United States, *The 9/11 Commission Report: The Attack from Planning to Aftermath: Authorized Text* (New York: Norton, 2011), 79; Robin Wright, *In the Name of God: The Khomeini Decade* (New York: Simon and Schuster, 1989), 111.

14. "Guerrillas Attack Philippine City," *WP*, April 5, 1995; David B. Ottaway and Steve Coll, "Retracing the Steps of a Terror Suspect," *WP*, June 5, 1995; David G. Wiencek, "Mindanao and Its Impact on Security in the Philippines," in *The Unraveling of Island Asia? Governmental, Communal, and Regional Instability*, ed. Bruce Vaughn (Westport, CT: Praeger, 2002), 53.

15. Ottaway and Coll, "Retracing the Steps of a Terror Suspect."

16. Peter L. Bergen, *The Osama bin Laden I Know: An Oral History of al Qaeda's Leader*, rev. pbk. ed. (New York: Free Press, 2006), 147; Eric Lipton and Benjamin Weiser, "Qaeda Strategy Is Called Cause for New Alarm," *NYT*, August 5, 2004; National Commission, *9/11 Commission Report*, 100, 204–205, 211, 476, 574 n. 15; Lawrence Wright, *The Looming Tower: Al-Qaeda and the Road to 9/11* (New York: Knopf, 2006), 203, 267, 300.

17. Misuari, quoted in Landler, "Temperature's a Lot Warmer."

18. Steven Rogers, "Beyond the Abu Sayyaf: The Lessons of Failure in the Philippines," *Foreign Affairs* 83 (January–February 2004): 15–20.

19. Mely Caballero-Anthony, "The Winds of Change in the Philippines: Whither the Strong Republic?" *Southeast Asian Affairs* (2003): 218, 219; Deirdre Sheehan and David Plott, "A War Grows," *FEER*, October 11, 2001, p. 24.

20. Brownback, quoted in James Brooke, "Unease Grows in Philippines on U.S. Forces," *NYT*, January 19, 2002; Clamor, "Philippine Perspective," 215; "Paul Wolfowitz: Of Missiles and Terrorism," *FEER*, November 8, 2001, p. 23.

21. Landler, "Temperature's a Lot Warmer"; Jose Maria Sison, *US Terrorism and War in the Philippines* (Breda, Netherlands: Papieren Tijger, 2003), 31.

22. "Remarks Following Discussions with President Gloria Macapagal-Arroyo of the Philippines and an Exchange with Reporters," November 20, 2001, *PPP: Bush, 2001*, pp. 1430–1432; James Brooke, "Philippines Said to Have Refused Bush Offer of G.I.'s in November," *NYT*, January 18, 2002; Richard Heydarian, "Southeast Asia," in *The WikiLeaks Files: The World According to US Empire* (New York: Verso, 2015), 445; "Joint Statement between the United States of America and the Republic of the Philippines," November 20, 2001, *PPP: Bush, 2001*, pp. 1434–1436; Eric Schmitt, "U.S. and Philippines Setting up Joint Operations to Fight Terror," *NYT*, January 16, 2002.

23. Rumsfeld, quoted in Schmitt, "U.S. and Philippines Setting up Joint Operations to Fight Terror."

24. Bergen, *The Osama bin Laden I Know*, 347; Powell and Tatad, quoted in Brooke, "Philippines Said to Have Refused"; Albert del Rosario, "A Progress Report on the Philippines," Heritage Foundation Lecture, March 27, 2002; Christopher A. Parrinello, "Operation Enduring Freedom, Phase II: The Philippines, Islamic Insurgency, and Abu Sayyaf," *Military Intelligence Professional Bulletin* 28 (April–June 2002): 43.

25. Abinales and Amoroso, "Withering of Philippine Democracy," 294; Caballero-Anthony, "Winds of Change," 214, 218, 221; James Hookway, "The Business of Terrorism," *FEER*, January 16, 2003, pp. 50–52; Todd S. Purdum, "U.S. to Resume Aid to Train Indonesia's Military Forces," *NYT*, August 3, 2002.

26. Joshua Kurlantzick, "Tilting at Dominos: America and Al Qaeda in Southeast Asia," *Current History* 101 (December 2002): 423; Eric Schmitt, "U.S. Combat Force of 1,700 Is Headed to the Philippines," *NYT*, February 21, 2003; Toshi Yoshihara, "Philippines," in *Flashpoints in the War on Terrorism*, ed. Derek S. Reveron and Jeffrey Stevenson Murer (New York: Routledge, 2006), 215.

27. Unnamed official quoted in "Why Are We in Jolo?" *WP*, February 22, 2003; Heydarian, "Southeast Asia," 465; Seth Mydans, "Combat Role for the G.I.'s in Philippines Left Unclear," *NYT*, February 25, 2003; Pentagon official quoted in Rogers, "Beyond the Abu Sayyaf," 17.

28. Seth Mydans, "Filipinos Awaiting U.S. Troops with Skepticism," *NYT*, February 28, 2003.

29. Republic Act no. 9372 (February 8, 2007); Roxas, quoted in Michael Viola, "Toward a Filipino Critical Pedagogy: Exposure Programs to the Philippines and the Politicization of Melissa Roxas," *Journal of Asian American Studies* 17 (February 2014): 19; UN Committee against Torture, quoted in ibid., 29 n. 62.

30. Heydarian, "Southeast Asia," 453–454; Sison, *US Terrorism and War in the Philippines*, 38.

31. Max Boot, *The Savage Wars of Peace: Small Wars and the Rise of American Power* (New York: Basic Books, 2002), 128, 352; Jean Edward Smith, *Bush* (New York: Simon and Schuster, 2016), 176; Ron Suskind, "Faith, Certainty, and the Presidency of George W. Bush," *NYT*, October 17, 2004.

32. Charles Byler, "Pacifying the Moros: American Military Government in the Southern Philippines, 1899–1913," *Military Review* 85 (May–June 2005): 41–45; Michael V. Hayden, *Playing to the Edge: American Intelligence in the Age of Terror* (New York: Penguin, 2016), 225; Victor D. Hyder, *Decapitation*

Operations: Criteria for Targeting Enemy Leadership (Leavenworth, KS: Army Command and General Staff College School of Advanced Military Studies Monograph, 2004), 23, 24.

33. Caballero-Anthony, "Winds of Change," 224; Carijane C. Dayag-Laylo et al., "Filipino Public Opinion, Presidential Leadership and the US-Led War in Iraq," *International Journal of Public Opinion Research* 16 (Autumn 2004): 346–348, 349, 351, 352; James Hookway, "A New Front," *FEER*, March 6, 2003, p. 19; nurse quoted in Emelyn Tapaoan, "Waiting for War: Filipinos in Mideast Say U.S. War on Iraq Looms," *Filipino Express*, October 27, 2002, September 11 Digital Archive.

34. Arroyo, quoted in Dayag-Laylo et al., "Filipino Public Opinion," 353; figures from ibid., 354; Montesano, "Philippines in 2003," 100.

35. David E. Sanger, "Bush Cites Philippines as Model in Rebuilding Iraq," *NYT*, October 19, 2003.

36. Stephen A. Carney, *Allied Participation in Operation Iraqi Freedom* (Washington, DC: US Army Center of Military History, 2011), 21, 97; Congressional Research Service, *Expedited Citizenship through Military Service: Current Law, Policy, and Issues* (February 25, 2009), 7.

37. Rodel E. Rodis, "The New Filipino American War Heroes," *SF Gate*, April 30, 2003.

38. CRS, *Expedited Citizenship through Military Service*, 17–18; Iris Ho and Aaron Terrazas, "Foreign-Born Veterans of the US Armed Forces," *Migration Policy Institute Immigration Facts* no. 22 (October 2008); Rodis, "New Filipino American War Heroes"; Edward Wong, "Swift Road for U.S. Citizen Soldiers Already Fighting in Iraq," *NYT*, August 9, 2005.

39. Lipman, *Guantánamo*, 223; Bobby Tuazon, "In Harm's Way," *Bulatlat* 4 (July 18–24, 2004).

40. Rajiv Chandrasekaran, *Imperial Life in the Emerald City: Inside Iraq's Green Zone* (New York: Knopf, 2006), 292–293; Robyn Magalit Rodriguez, "The Labor Brokerage State and the Globalization of Filipina Care Workers," *Signs* 33 (Summer 2008): 798; "Second Letter to the Muslims of Iraq," in *Al Qaeda in Its Own Words*, ed. Gilles Kepel and Jean-Pierre Milelli, trans. Pascale Ghazaleh (Cambridge: Harvard University Press, 2008), 67; Somini Sengupta, "5 G.I.'s Killed in Attack; Philippines Bars Iraq Trips," *NYT*, July 9, 2004; Tuazon, "In Harm's Way."

41. Ian Fisher, "3 Americans Are Killed and 4 Are Injured in Attacks in Iraq," *NYT*, July 12, 2004; Sengupta, "5 G.I.'s Killed in Attack"; James A. Tyner, *Iraq, Terror, and the Philippines' Will to War* (Lanham, MD: Rowman and Littlefield, 2005), 103–110.

42. Lipman, *Guantánamo*, 216; Tyner, *Iraq, Terror*, 73–102.

43. Carney, *Allied Participation in Operation Iraqi Freedom*, 55, 65, 90, 93, 95, 110, 113; Anthony Spaeth, "Manila Gives In," *Time International*, July 24, 2004, p. 16.

44. CPP, quoted in Tyner, *Iraq, Terror*, 105; Ian Fisher, "3 Americans Are Killed"; Sengupta, "5 G.I.s Killed"; Paul Quintos, "Angelo de la Cruz: A Victim of an Unjust War," *Bulatlat* 4 (July 18–24, 2004).

45. Carlos H. Conde, "Manila Signals Troop Pullout," *NYT*, July 13, 2004; Carlos H. Conde, "Manila Starts Withdrawing Troops from Iraq; U.S. Criticizes Step," *NYT*, July 15, 2004.

46. Carlos H. Conde, "Philippines Viewed as Being Forced to Yield on Hostage," *NYT*, July 16, 2004.

47. Ricciardone, quoted in Conde, "Philippines Viewed as Being Forced to Yield"; James Glanz, "Hostage Is Freed after Philippine Troops Are Withdrawn from Iraq," *NYT*, July 21, 2004; San Juan, "Carlos Bulosan," 145; Tyner, *Iraq, Terror*, 108, 109.

48. Syed Ali, *Dubai: Gilded Cage* (New Haven, CT: Yale University Press, 2010), 96; Conde, "Philippines Viewed as Being Forced to Yield"; "A Filipino Retreat," *NYT*, July 19, 2004; Lipman, *Guantánamo*, 216, 224; Francis Pangilinan, "Why Manila Left Iraq Early," *FEER*, July 29, 2004, p. 24.

49. Glanz, "Hostage Is Freed"; Marc Lacey, "Filipino Returns Home," *NYT*, July 23, 2004.

50. "Where Is Ex-OFW Angelo dela Cruz Now?" ABS-CBN News, June 5, 2014.

51. "Remarks Following Discussions with President Gloria Macapagal-Arroyo of the Philippines and an Exchange with Reporters," November 20, 2001, *PPP: Bush, 2001*, pp. 1432–1433; Burr, quoted in Antonio Raimundo, "The Filipino Veterans Equity Movement: A Case Study in Reparations Theory," *California Law Review* 98 (April 2010): 608.

52. *Congressional Record*, 111 Cong., 1 Sess., February 5, 2009, pp. S1618, S1627.

53. 123 Stat. 115 (February 17, 2009); Congressional Research Service, *Overview of Filipino Veterans' Benefits* (February 20, 2009), 16. The law merely authorized the payment of one-time benefits, but did not simultaneously allocate funds for them. Thus, the widely cited figure of $787 billion stimulus did not include the $198 million authorized to be spent on Filipino veterans' payments. Most were eventually paid out in the United States, not the Philippines. Raimundo, "Filipino Veterans," 606 n. 295.

54. Audrey McAvoy, "For Filipino Veterans of WWII, the Battle Is Not Over," *LAT*, January 24, 2010; Jon Melegrito, "The Long, Hard Road to Equity," *Filipinas* 18 (April 2009): 25–27; Tony Perry and Richard Simon, "Filipino Veterans of WWII to Get Long-Overdue Funds," *LAT*, February 18, 2009; Raimundo, "Filipino Veterans," 609; Paul Watson, "End of a Long Battle Nears," *LAT*, March 7, 2009.

55. Galedo, quoted in Melegrito, "Long, Hard Road," 27; Michael Honda, "Justice for Filipino Veterans, At Long Last," *Asian American Law Journal* 16 (2009): 193.

56. Arroyo, quoted in Glanz, "Hostage Is Freed"; Annan, quoted in Tyner, *Iraq, Terror*, 105; Micki McElya, "Remembering 9/11's Pentagon Victims and Reframing History in Arlington National Cemetery," *Radical History Review* no. 111 (Fall 2011): 51–63.

CHAPTER ELEVEN: THE PIVOT AND AFTER

1. Hillary Clinton, "America's Pacific Century," *Foreign Policy* no. 189 (November 2011): 63; "Remarks to the Parliament in Canberra," November 17, 2011, *PPP: Obama, 2011*, p. 1442.

2. Clinton, "America's Pacific Century," 58; Medeiros, quoted in Renato Cruz de Castro, "Twenty-First Century Philippines' Policy toward an Emergent China: From Equi-Balancing to Strategic Balancing," *Asian Politics and Policy* 8 no. 2 (2016): 321; Jessica C. Liao, "The Filipino Fox: There's a Method to Duterte's Madness," *Foreign Affairs*, January 18, 2017; Obama, quoted in Allan Joseph F. Mesina, "Foreign Military Involvement in Filipino Relief Operations," *Peace Review* 29 (July 2017): 394.

3. "Murder in Mindanao," *The Economist*, August 4, 2018, pp. 34–35.

4. Nicole Curato, ed., *A Duterte Reader: Critical Essays on Rodrigo Duterte's Early Presidency* (Ithaca, NY: Southeast Asia Program Publications of Cornell University Press, 2017); Human Rights Watch, *World Report 2019: Events of 2018* (New York: Seven Stories Press, 2019), 468–469; Pia Ranada, "Duterte's Satisfaction Rating Bounces Back to Personal High—SWS," *The Rappler*, April 11, 2019; Felipe Villamor, "Philippine Women Fire Back after Duterte Jokes about Rape," *NYT*, September 2, 2018.

5. Paul A. Kramer, "Trump and the Legend of General Pershing," *Foreign Affairs*, September 11, 2017; Kristine Phillips, "Philippines' Duterte Keeps Lashing Out at the United States—Over Atrocities a Century Ago," *WP*, July 24, 2017.

6. Duterte, quoted in Maria Ela L. Atienza, "The Philippines in 2018: Broken Promises, Growing Impatience," *Asian Survey* 59 (January 2019): 191;

Richard C. Paddock, "Leader's Bluster Stands in Deep Contrast to Filipinos' Deep Ties to U.S.," *NYT*, October 27, 2016; Jane Perlez, "Presidents of Philippines and China Agree to Reopen Talks on a Disputed Sea," *NYT*, October 21, 2016.

7. "85% of Filipinos Love US—Survey," Pew Research Center, April 22, 2014; Daniel Llanto, "Ex-PH Navy Security Analyst Warns vs. Chinese Take-Over of Bankrupt Korean Ship Builder in Subic," *FilAm Star*, January 17–23, 2019; Corina Oliquino, "4 out of 10 Pinoys Doubt China's Good Intentions," *FilAm Star*, April 11–17 2019.

8. US Department of Defense, *Indo-Pacific Strategy Report: Preparedness, Partnerships, and Promoting a Networked Region* (Washington, DC: US Department of Defense, 2019), 3, 4, 29.

9. Mesina, "Foreign Military Involvement," 394.

10. Jim Gomez, "US Military Returns 3 Disputed Bells Taken from Philippines as Spoils of War," *Military Times*, December 11, 2018; Rodel E. Rodis, "For Whom the Bells Toll," in *Filipinos in America: A Journey of Faith* (South San Francisco: Filipinas, 2003), 73–77.

11. Gomez, "US Military Returns"; "A Peal for Friendship," *The Economist*, August 18, 2018, p. 33.

Index

Credit: Allegra Boverman

Christopher Capozzola is professor of history at MIT. Author of the award-winning *Uncle Sam Wants You*, he is also a cocurator of "The Volunteers: Americans Join World War I, 1914–1919," a traveling exhibition that originated at The National WWI Museum and Memorial to commemorate the centennial of the First World War. He lives in Boston, Massachusetts.